The Eurovision Song Contest as a Cultural Phenomenon

Drawing from the wealth of academic literature about The Eurovision Song Contest (ESC) written over the last two decades, this book consolidates and recognises the ESC's relevance in academia by analysing its contribution to different fields of study.

The book brings together leading ESC scholars from across disciplines and from across the globe to reflect on the intersection between their academic fields of study and the ESC by answering the question: what has the ESC contributed to academia? The book also draws from fields rarely associated with the ESC, such as Law, Business and Research Methodologies, to demonstrate the contest's broad utility in research, pedagogy and practice.

Given its interdisciplinary approach, this volume will be of interest to scholars and students working in cultural, media and music studies, as well as those interested in the intersections between these areas and politics, law, education, pedagogy and history.

Adam Dubin is a human rights scholar and Assistant Professor of Law at Universidad Pontificia Comillas in Madrid, Spain, as well as an Adjunct Professor of Politics at New York University, USA. He is also a Senior Research Associate at the University of Johannesburg and a Visiting Professor at Southwest University of Politics and Law in China. His research focuses on human rights in sub-Saharan Africa, as well as on the intersection between human rights and pop culture.

Dean Vuletic is a Historian of Contemporary Europe based in the Research Center for the History of Transformations at the University of Vienna, Austria. The author of *Postwar Europe and the Eurovision Song Contest* (2018), he is the world's leading academic expert on the history of the ESC and he has taught the world's first university course on this topic. He is an internationally prominent media commentator and public speaker on the ESC, and further information about his work can be found on his website www.deanvuletic.com.

Antonio Obregón was formerly Vice Rector of Academic Affairs and Dean of the Faculty of Law at Universidad Pontificia Comillas. He is a Full Professor of Criminal Law and International Relations. He holds an undergraduate degree in Law and Business Administration and a PhD in Criminal Law. He designed and taught the first seminar in a Spanish university on the ESC and is a frequent commentator on it in the Spanish media.

Routledge Research in Cultural and Media Studies

The Eurovision Song Contest as a Cultural Phenomenon

From Concert Halls to the Halls of Academia

Edited by Adam Dubin,
Dean Vuletic, and
Antonio Obregón

Routledge
Taylor & Francis Group

LONDON AND NEW YORK

First published 2023
by Routledge
4 Park Square, Milton Park, Abingdon, Oxon OX14 4RN

and by Routledge
605 Third Avenue, New York, NY 10158

Routledge is an imprint of the Taylor & Francis Group, an informa business

© 2023 selection and editorial matter, **Adam Dubin**, **Dean Vuletic** and **Antonio Obregón**; individual chapters, the contributors

The right of **Adam Dubin**, **Dean Vuletic** and **Antonio Obregón** to be identified as the authors of the editorial material, and of the authors for their individual chapters, has been asserted in accordance with sections 77 and 78 of the Copyright, Designs and Patents Act 1988.

British Library Cataloguing-in-Publication Data
A catalogue record for this book is available from the British Library

Library of Congress Cataloguing-in-Publication Data
Names: Dubin, Adam, editor. | Vuletic, Dean, editor. |
Obregón, Antonio, editor.
Title: The Eurovision Song Contest as a cultural phenomenon: from concert halls to the halls of academia/edited by Adam Dubin, Dean Vuletic, Antonio Obregón.
Description: [1.] | Abingdon, Oxon; New York: Routledge, 2022. | Series: Routledge research in cultural and media studies | Includes bibliographical references and index.
Identifiers: LCCN 2022004897 (print) | LCCN 2022004898 (ebook) | ISBN 9781032037745 (hardback) | ISBN 9781032037752 (paperback) | ISBN 9781003188933 (ebook)
Subjects: LCSH: Eurovision Song Contest--Social aspects. | Music--Competitions--Europe. | Music--Social aspects--Europe. | Music--Political aspects--Europe.
Classification: LCC ML76.E87 E85 2022 (print) | LCC ML76.E87 (ebook) | DDC 782.42164/0794--dc23
LC record available at https://lccn.loc.gov/2022004897
LC ebook record available at https://lccn.loc.gov/2022004898

ISBN: 978-1-032-03774-5 (hbk)
ISBN: 978-1-032-03775-2 (pbk)
ISBN: 978-1-003-18893-3 (ebk)

DOI: 10.4324/9781003188933

Typeset in Galliard
by MPS Limited, Dehradun

Contents

Editors

Adam Dubin is a human rights scholar and Assistant Professor of Law at Universidad Pontificia Comillas in Madrid, Spain, as well as an Adjunct Professor of Politics at New York University, USA. He is also a Senior Research Associate at the University of Johannesburg and a Visiting Professor at Southwest University of Politics and Law in China. His research focuses on human rights in Sub Saharan Africa, as well as on the intersection between human rights and pop culture.

Dean Vuletic is a Historian of Contemporary Europe based in the Research Center For the History of Transformations at the University of Vienna, Austria. The author of *Postwar Europe and the Eurovision Song Contest* (2018), he is the world's leading academic expert on the history of the ESC and he has taught the world's first university course on this topic. He is an internationally prominent media commentator and public speaker on the ESC, and further information about his work can be found on his website www.deanvuletic.com.

Antonio Obregón was formerly Vice Rector of Academic Affairs and Dean of the Faculty of Law at Universidad Pontificia Comillas. He is a Full Professor of Criminal Law and International Relations. He holds an undergraduate degree in Law and Business Administration and a PhD in Criminal Law. He designed and taught the first seminar in a Spanish university on the ESC and is a frequent commentator on it in the Spanish media.

Contributors

Jose Luis Arroyo-Barrigüete is Professor in the Quantitative Methodologies Department at Universidad Pontificia Comillas, Spain. He holds a PhD in Business Administration, a PhD in Engineering and a PhD in Philology Studies.

Catherine Baker is Reader in 20th Century History at the University of Hull, United Kingdom. Her books include *Sounds of the Borderland: Popular Music, War and Nationalism in Croatia since 1991* (2010) and *Race and the Yugoslav Region: Postsocialist, Post-Conflict, Postcolonial?* (2018). She has published on the ESC in *European Journal of International Relations, Popular Communication* and elsewhere.

Jessica Carniel is Senior Lecturer in Humanities in the School of Humanities and Communication and a researcher in the Centre for Heritage and Culture at the University of Southern Queensland, Australia. Her research focuses on cosmopolitan and transnational communities and identities in global and national popular cultures.

João Soeiro de Carvalho is Associate Full Professor at in the School of Social Sciences and Humanities at NOVA University of Lisbon, Portugal, and the President of the Ethnomusicology Institute. He obtained his doctoral and master's degrees from Columbia University, (USA). He is the principal investigator in several projects funded by the Foundation for Science and Technology and the author of various articles and book chapters.

George Cremona is Senior Lecturer and Coordinator for German and Media Literacy at the Faculty of Education of the University of Malta. He is also a radio and television producer and a presenter of educational programmes. For this work, he was awarded on three occassions the national award of the Institute of Maltese Journalists.

John Hajek is Professor of Italian Studies and Director of the Research Unit for Multilingualism and Cross-cultural Communication in the School of Languages and Linguistics at The University of Melbourne, Australia. He has a broad range of teaching and research experience, including the ESC within the broader context of European Studies.

Chris Hay is an Australian Research Council DECRA Senior Research Fellow and Senior Lecturer in Theatre History in the School of Communication and Arts at the University of Queensland, Australia. In his research, he is particularly interested in what funded and branded cultural output can tell us about national pre-occupations and anxieties.

Ariel James holds a PhD in Social Anthropology from the Universidad Autónoma de Madrid, Spain. He teaches in the Faculty of Human and Social Sciences at Universidad Pontificia de Comillas, Spain, and the Philosophy, Economics and Politics Degree Program at the University of Deusto, Spain.

Alison Lewis is Emeritus Professor of German Studies in the School of Languages and Linguistics at The University of Melbourne, Australia, where she researches among other things modern and contemporary German literature and culture, surveillance and the East German secret police as well as the ESC.

Sofia Vieira Lopes is a PhD candidate in Ethnomusicology and a researcher at in the Ethnomusicology Institute at NOVA University of Lisbon, Portugal, with a project funded by the Foundation for Science and Technology. She researches the Portuguese national selection for the ESC and is the Team Leader of the EUROVISIONS conference.

Chen Ozeri is an MA student in the Department of Sociology and Anthropology at the Hebrew University of Jerusalem, Israel. His fields of interest are political protest, the emergence of group identity, and the dynamics of social transformation through ideological thought.

Mari Pajala is Senior Lecturer in Media Studies at the University of Turku, Finland. She is co-editor, with Alice Lovejoy, of *Remapping Cold War Media: Institutions, Infrastructures, Translations* (2022). Her work has appeared in, for instance, *International Journal of Cultural Studies*, *Media History*, and *Television & New Media*.

José Luis Panea holds a PhD in Arts from the University of Castilla-La Mancha, Spain. As a post-doctoral researcher at the University of Salamanca, Spain, he leads the project 'The Social Construction of European Identity at the Eurovision Song Contest'.

Ivan Raykoff is Associate Professor of Music at The New School in New York City, USA. He co-edited *A Song for Europe: Popular Music and Politics in the Eurovision Song Contest* (2007), and his follow-up book on the contest's music is *Another Song for Europe: Music, Taste, and Values in the Eurovision Song Contest* (2021).

Lourdes Fernández Rodríguez is Professor in the Quantatiative Methodologies Department at Universidad Pontificia Comillas de Madrid, Spain. She holds a

PhD in Business Administration from the Universidad Complutense de Madrid.

Robert Deam Tobin holds the Henry J Leir Chair in Comparative Literature at Clark University, USA, where he works on German and LGBTQ Studies. With Ivan Raykoff, he is the co-editor of *A Song for Europe: Popular Music and Politics in the Eurovision Song Contest* (2007).

Irving Wolther studied Applied Language and Cultural Studies at the universities of Mainz and Geneva and Journalism at the Hanover University of Music, Drama and Media. He holds a PhD *magna cum laude* for his thesis *'Kampf der Kulturen'* – *Der Eurovision Song Contest als Mittel national-kultureller Repräsentation*. He is a lecturer and collaborator for the official ESC website of the German broadcaster NDR, www.eurovision.de.

Gad Yair is a sociologist of culture. He is an Associate Professor in the Department of Sociology and Anthropology at the Hebrew University of Jerusalem, where he has worked since 1995 – the very date of his first publication on voting blocs in the ESC, thereby gaining the nickname 'the godfather of Eurovision studies'.

Foreword

For sixty-seven years now, my colleagues around Europe have been producing one of the world's oldest and favourite television shows, the Eurovision Song Contest (ESC). It started out as a test for the emerging technology of television, to see whether the same programme could be broadcast across several countries in Europe at the same time – and live. Since then, the ESC has continued to be a trailblazer in media technologies, including with colour television and satellites and, more recently, televoting and digital stage effects. As a television production, the ESC has highlighted what can be achieved through the international cooperation that the European Broadcasting Union has been fostering since 1950. For the television professionals working behind the ESC, our view of the contest comes from how we manage, organise and make it. Every ESC is a major achievement for the national broadcasting organisation that stages it, and it has been the biggest television programme that some of them have made. That they have done so is also a testament to international cooperation, to the pooling together of enthusiasm and resources to produce this cultural mega-event. Only once, in 2020, were we unable to stage the ESC, due to the COVID-19 pandemic. That we have managed to otherwise do so every year is a technical feat that we are proud of.

We are also proud of what the ESC means to its fans and viewers in Europe and around the world. While the behind-the-scenes work that goes into making the show is not always publicly visible, through the work of the scholars represented in this book we can see how the contest is so meaningful to different audiences. This book marks an important milestone in research on the ESC by bringing together many leading scholars of the contest from around the world and from different disciplines to analyse the ESC's contribution to academia. From historical approaches that demonstrate how the contest developed into a leading cultural event uniting Europeans, to media studies chapters that explain the contest's longevity, to musicological perspectives that highlight its contribution to musical change, the contributions to this book underline the multifaceted character of the ESC that has made it such a broadly engaging cultural phenomenon.

The ESC also seeks to promote these various dimensions by embracing the values of diversity, inclusion and tolerance, which have always been marks of the contest's character and which form an intersection component in each of this book's chapters. Scholarly studies of the ESC have recently been a burgeoning phenomenon in the world of academia, and in the world of the ESC we are excited about all of these new approaches and insights that are emerging about the contest. Together, we can continue to study the specificities of what has made the ESC so attractive, challenging and special, so that we can keep on adapting the contest to ensure its longevity in a changing Europe in the years to come.

As we emerge from this pandemic and its tragic consequences, we hope that the ESC continues to be a source of pan-European spirit in the face of adversity and a reminder of the collective strength of our ESC community.

Martin Österdahl
Executive Supervisor, Eurovision Song Contest

Part I

From Lugano to the Classroom: the Eurovision Song Contest and Academia

1 The Grand Tour: the Origins of the Eurovision Song Contest as a Cultural Phenomenon

Dean Vuletic

Ciao 2020! (Vecherniy Urgant, 2020) was broadcast on 30 December 2021 on the Russian national television station and an organiser[1] of Russia's Eurovision Song Contest (ESC) entries, Channel One (Pervyy kanal). A special New Year's Eve show, *Ciao 2020!* was dedicated to Italian popular music and television variety from the 1980s. It included well-known Russian artists with their names transformed into a macaronic Italian, like the group Little Big, or 'Piccolo Grandi', which was meant to have represented Russia in the 2020 ESC that was cancelled due to the COVID-19 pandemic.[2] The producers of *Ciao 2020!* took as one of their inspirations the Sanremo Italian Song Festival, the annual national popular music competition that was the world's first such broadcasted programme. Held annually since 1951, the Sanremo Italian Song Festival was the inspiration for the ESC that was established in 1956. *Ciao 2020!* was watched by millions in Russia, but it also went viral in Italy. The major Italian media outlets reported on it: most generally viewed the show as being a smart spoof, praising its high-quality and well-financed production. Some even took the opportunity to research Italy's soft power in Russia and other parts of Central and East Europe (Castelletti 2021; Esquire, 2021; Sala, 2020). *Ciao 2020!* was an homage to the power of Italian popular culture in the Soviet Union, but it also had an element of envy: after all, Russia has never matched the global power of Italy in popular culture. When it comes to that, Russia has been a 'little big' power. Yet, in the first two decades of the twenty-first century, Moscow tried to change that, and the ESC was one of its prominent, and expensive, cultural diplomacy efforts. The record cost of the 2009 ESC in Moscow and the extravagant performances of Russian entries, usually in the English language, attested to this (Pajala, & Vuletic, 2021). That spending spree ended in February 2022, as Russia's invasion of Ukraine resulted in the former being banned from the ESC, and the Russian television stations that had participated in the contest consequently withdrew their membership from the ESC's organiser, the European Broadcasting Union (EBU).

In 2022, in the context of the war in Ukraine and Russia's consequent international isolation, *Ciao 2020!* looks like a tattered postcard from a bygone era of Russian creativity and cosmpolitanisam, with a faded love note for the ESC and for Italian popular music. Yet, at the turn of 2021, *Ciao 2020!* proved to be

DOI: 10.4324/9781003188933-2

not only popular but also prophetic, as the win of the Italian glam rock group Måneskin in the 2021 ESC again spotlighted the power of Italy in the contest and in global culture. This was especially so as the group sang its ESC entry 'Zitti e buoni' (Shut Up and Behave) in Italian. Måneskin subsequently succeeded on international music charts, including the American one, as few previous winners of the ESC have managed to. As the group made ESC history, it was a reminder of the crucial role that Italy has played in the history of the contest. Indeed, the history of the ESC can be told through the example of Italy, just as a history of Europe can be narrated through the ESC. However, the role of Italy in the invention and development of the ESC has been underestimated in the popular literature on the contest, much like Italy's soft power has, I think, been under-valued in academic studies on international relations. As a historian of con-temporary Europe, I authored the first scholarly monograph on the history of the ESC, *Postwar Europe and the Eurovision Song Contest* (2018), based on primary sources from archives of various international and national broadcasting orga-nisations, including the EBU. Understanding the cultural diplomacy, nation-branding and soft power of states has been a key area of my studies in history and international relations, with Italy being one of the examples that I have long been fascinated by. Considering that the ESC has always been about national pro-motion, few of the other states that have been represented in the contest have matched Italy in its ability to sell itself as a brand. Despite a singular Cold War-era Italian win in the 1960s, one of the most successful ESC entries ever was 'made in Italy', and other Italian entries have been politically symbolic by highlighting processes in international relations, such as Americanisation and Europeanisation. All of this also partly explains why I began teaching the world's first-ever university course on the ESC in Italy.

My work on the ESC has demonstrated not only how academic historians can use the ESC to study and teach the history of contemporary Europe. Scholarly research can also help us to better understand the history of the ESC and its attraction as one of the world's longest running and most popular television shows, as well as to redress myths that have developed around the contest which reflect historical legacies, misunderstandings and prejudices in Europe. As one of Europe's leading cultural events, the ESC can be a compass and a microphone for the uncharted, unexplained and unheard – not only in the field of history but, as this volume asserts, in other academic areas as well.

From Sanremo, Rome and Venice to Lugano...: Italy as the Inspiration for the ESC

Due to Cold War tensions between the Eastern and Western blocs, a pan-European broadcasting organisation – like the International Broadcasting Union that had existed during the interwar period – could not be maintained after the Second World War. Just as there would be the duplication of other international organi-sations for the Eastern and Western blocs in the economic ones of the Council for Mutual Economic Assistance and the European Community EC, and in the military ones of the Warsaw Pact and the North Atlantic Treaty Organisation, the EBU was established as the Western European grouping of national broadcasting organisations and the pendant to the Soviet-led International Broadcasting Organisation.[3] Despite the strength of its Communist Party and the fears that other Western powers had of the party coming to power in the late 1940s, Italy never had a communist party-led government and would remain in the Western Bloc and a member of all its organisations during the Cold War. It was one of the Western European states represented at the founding meeting of the EBU in Torquay in the United Kingdom in 1950, together with Belgium, Denmark, Finland, France, Ireland, Luxembourg, Monaco, the Netherlands, Norway, Portugal, Sweden, Switzerland, the United Kingdom and Vatican City. Yugoslavia, which had in 1948 dissented from the Eastern Bloc but maintained a communist party-led government, was represented as well, and its popular music scene would throughout the Cold War be heavily influenced by radio and television broadcasts from nearby Italy. While the membership criteria for the EBU were formulated to avoid subjective biases that would overly politicise the organisation, the International Broadcasting Organisations's membership would largely be determined by political criteria, namely that of a state having a communist party-led government. The EBU's membership criteria required only that the broadcasting organisation have a national remit and public service aim, and that it come from a state located within the European Broadcasting Area[4] and that was a member of the International Telecommunication Union, a specialised United Nations agency (Eugster, 1983, 44–46).

Membership of the EBU was initially based on national radio services, as television broadcasts had only experimentally or limitedly begun in some European states in the interwar era, including in Italy. There, regular television services were started by the national broadcasting organisation in 1954 through RAI (Radiotelevisione italiana, Italian Radio and Television); they were introduced in most European states in the 1950s, making the pursuit of the technical advancement of television broadcasting the principal aim of the EBU in that decade. As Mari Pajala and Irving Wolther highlight in their chapters in this book, the EBU and the ESC have been pioneers in various aspects of media history. The EBU reached its first milestones in transnational television broadcasting in the early 1950s with France, the Netherlands, the United Kingdom and West Germany, and these successful experiments foreshadowed the establishment of the Eurovision Network in 1954. The EBU developed the Eurovision Network for the exchange and production of common television programmes in order to cost-effectively increase the programming material for national broadcasting organisations. The network was proposed by Marcel Bezençon, the director general of the Swiss national broadcasting organisation, the Swiss Broadcasting Corporation, and a future head of the EBU. The first Eurovision Network programmes were broadcast between Belgium, Denmark, France, Italy, the Netherlands, Switzerland, the United Kingdom and West Germany in four weeks of experimental programming held in June and July 1954. Foreshadowing the importance that religious programming would have for the Eurovision Network, the first evening of the experimental programming included a speech by Pope Pius XII, who called the network 'a symbol and a promise ... of union between the nations, and in one respect, to a degree, it initiates that union' (European Broadcasting Union, 2004, 15).[5] The most-watched programmes during the experimental programming were matches from the World Cup for soccer that was then being held in Switzerland, which was the main reason why the experimental programming was scheduled for that period (Bezençon, 1954, 568, 572). Sporting events would be by far the biggest category of programmes exchanged by the Eurovision Network, due to their mass, transnational popularity and the fact that they did not face linguistic obstacles.

Italy is the centre of Catholicism and soccerism. Yet, its greatest contribution to the Eurovision Network has been the most popular and successful programme that the Eurovision Network would produce, the network's namesake and its only regular multilateral project – the ESC. While we can take the origins of the song contest phenomenon back to ancient times, as Ivan Raykoff does in his contribution to this volume, the direct inspiration for the televised ESC came from RAI (Pugliese, 1955, 1), which had been staging the Sanremo Italian Song Festival in the seaside resort town of the same name since 1951. After the Eurovision Network broadcast its first programmes in 1954, discussions ensued in the EBU as to how the offerings could be made more modern and spectacular. The Sanremo Italian Song Festival was a model for the ESC and various national song contests because it not only promoted the production of Italian popular music and television programming, but also because of its widespread popularity: it has ever since remained a cultural reference that has unified Italians.[6] Members of the EBU's Programme Committee – which became the decision-making body for the ESC – consequently attended the Sanremo Italian Song Festival in 1955, when it was also broadcast through the Eurovision Network (European Broadcasting Union, 1955b, 146b). Following suggestions put forward at the meeting of the Programme Committee in Monte Carlo in 1955, the EBU decided at the session of its General Assembly in Rome later in that year to establish the ESC; that General Assembly also received the Pope's blessing (European Broadcasting Union, 1955a, 1; European Broadcasting Union, 1956, 137–8).

Another of the discoveries that I made in my research is that the Sanremo Italian Song Festival was not the only song contest in Italy in the mid-1950s. Then, the City of Venice and RAI also organised the International Song Festival in Venice. The first edition of this contest in 1955 included entries submitted by the radio services of broadcasting organisations from Austria, Belgium, France, Italy, Monaco and the Netherlands: they each submitted six songs that were original and no longer than 3.5 minutes, with the entries being voted on by national juries and the winner being awarded the Golden Gondola prize (European Broadcasting Union, 1955c, 271c). The International Song Festival was therefore more similar in its structure to the ESC than the national Sanremo Italian Song Festival was, with the major difference between the ESC and its Venetian predecessor being that the latter was broadcast only via radio and not television. Still, the International Song Festival was the world's first ever international song contest based on the participation of national broadcasting organisations, and some of its participants would go on to compete in the ESC. The first edition of the ESC was staged in the Italian-speaking Swiss city of Lugano, when the hosting of the show was done entirely in Italian. The Italianness of the 1956 ESC epitomised a global fascination in the 1950s with Italian film and popular music, two media that produced a modern repertoire for Italian culture alongside classical genres such as literature, opera and painting. Still, the stage included a pictorial backdrop depicting a typically Swiss rural scene – the first example of host country branding through stage design in the ESC, the focus of José Luis Panea's chapter in this volume.

My research has also redressed myths that have surrounded the founding of the ESC. One is that the contest was a counter to the cultural Americanisation then taking over Western Europe. However, American popular music artists and influences were embraced in the contest from the very beginning. One of the West German entrants[7] in the 1956 ESC, the Austrian American Freddy Quinn, performed the song 'So geht das jede Nacht' (That's How It Is Every Night) in an early rock and roll style which included references to men with English-language names. Artists in the ESC have never been compelled to be citizens of the state that they represent nor to promote musical genres that are considered more typically European. There was also the phenomenon in the ESC of American artists performing, including ones who chose to emigrate to Western Europe for professional reasons. They demonstrated that it was not only the United States that was a centre of the global popular music industry, but that Western Europe could also provide career opportunities, and these American artists often figured in the ESC as symbols of cosmopolitanism, fashionability and modernity. Italy was represented in the 1975 ESC by the African American Wess, or Wesley Johnson, who performed a love song with Dori Ghezzi, which was also a social statement on the acceptance of interracial relationships. The Italian American singer Romina Power, as part of the duo with Al Bano, represented Italy in the ESC in 1976 and in 1985. Still, despite the success of some ESC entries in the United States, the EBU and its members did not make a concerted effort to expand the ESC to the United States during the Cold War. This has only happened in recent years with the creation of the American Song Contest that launched in 2022 and the inclusion of some American artists, like the Italian American Madonna in 2019, as interval acts in the ESC.

The flow of cultural exports across the Atlantic during the Cold War was never only one way, with Americans also consuming Western European popular cultural products, even though the impact of American ones on Western Europe in the postwar era was relatively greater. The emphasis on Americanisation in political debates in Western Europe was always skewed because it marginalised the influence that Western Europeans had on American popular culture. That the ESC had the potential to have an impact on the United States was demonstrated already in the first years of the contest. Italy only won the ESC once during the Cold War, in 1965 with Gigliola Cinquetti singing 'Non ho l'età' (I'm Not Old Enough) about not being old enough to have a relationship with an older man. Yet, in the 1950s Italy produced the ESC's — and the world's — biggest non-English-language hit ever. Domenico Modugno's, Nel blu, dipinto di blu' (In the Blue Painted Blue), popularly known as 'Volare' (To Fly), came third for Italy at the 1958 ESC after having won that year's Sanremo Italian Song Festival. It has been one of the most successful non-English-language songs ever in the charts of *Billboard*, the trade publication of the American music industry. It was also recognised as the 'Record of the Year' and 'Song of the Year' in the first Grammy Awards that were held in 1959. 'Volare' is the only ESC entry and non-English-language song to have ever been accorded these honours, especially as the American market has historically not been very receptive of songs that have not been in English. Modguno was also unique in being the first-ever ESC artist who embarked on a national political career. From 1987 to 1992, he was a member of the Italian parliament for the leftist Radical Party (Ternavasio, 2004, 116–117, 133–134). He had already been an advocate for social issues, including in the pro-divorce campaign in which Cinquetti's second ESC entry 'Sì' (Yes) was embroiled in 1974. The controversy over 'Sì' demonstrated how the ESC could not only be a stage for international relations, but also a battleground for national politics[8] – especially regarding gender and sexuality issues, as Catherine Baker discusses in her chapter in this book.

Another myth that has surrounded the ESC concerns the contest's relationship to European integration: that the ESC has somehow been a cultural accessory, or even an engine, for the efforts to unify European citizens through postwar economic and political processes, as well as to forge peaceful relations among European states and avoid another pan-European war. One of the justifications often cited for this myth is Toto Cutugno's winning song at the 1990 ESC in Zagreb, 'Insieme: 1992' (Together: 1992), which paid homage to the European Single Market that would transform the EC into the EU (which had been planned for 1992 but eventually happened in 1993). Cutugno is most famous for one of the most Italian of hits, 'L'Italiano' (The Italian), which came fifth in the Sanremo Italian Song Contest in 1983, but he also sang the first-ever song in the ESC that directly referred to the EU. Utopic ideas of the ESC's innate Europeanism are, however, not justified in the documental archives of the EBU: the founders of the ESC really did only conceive of it in the mid-1950s as an experiment in television. Afterwards, the EBU sought to distance itself from Western European economic and political organisations so as not to become entangled in their politics. Bezençon, for example, came from ever Eurosceptical Switzerland, where the EBU has maintained its headquarters in Geneva, originally alongside a technical centre in Brussels. In the mid-1960s, he underlined the EBU's preference for internationalism rather than supranationalism by stating that the Eurovision Network was not 'a super-State in embryo pursuing some hidden, or merely veiled, objective' (Bezençon, 1963, 6). He believed that the Eurovision Network could be used 'to build Europe' but that '[a] united Europe is not the same thing as a unified Europe' and '[t]he European game is therefore a dangerous one to play' because 'conceptions of Europe vary'

(Bezençon, 1964, 9). Cutugno's win came during a brief period of a few years when the EC sponsored some of the ESC's interval acts and postcards, at a time when the EBU was seeking new ways of financing the contest and opening it up more to commercial sponsorship. However, the EBU ended that cooperation with the EC after 1990. In the 1990s, the Eurovision Network also began to shed the circle of twelve stars in its logo, a Europeanist symbol that it had pioneered with the Council of Europe in the mid-1950s, but which had become too associated with the EU since its institutions had adopted the symbol in the mid 1980s.

To maintain its independence from political developments in post-Cold War Europe, the EBU thus symbolically distanced itself from the expansion of the EU. However, the EBU itself pioneered the expansion of Western European organisations to Central and East Europe by being the first one to include members from that region, doing so in 1993. As most of these states consequently began participating in the ESC in the course of the 1990s, Italy – a founding member of all Western European organisations, from the Council of Europe, to the EBU, the EU and NATO – withdrew from the contest from 1998 to 2010. For RAI, the withdrawal seemed an opportune idea because of what had become a small viewing audience for the ESC in Italy (Calcagno, 1996).[9] Perhaps the ESC had, ironically, lost its popularity in Italy because Italians compared it unfavourably to the original of all song contests, the Sanremo Italian Song Festival. Or maybe the growing influence of the formerly communist party-led Central and East European countries in the contest, including Russia, which gave rise to new voting blocs and patterns, had irritated Italians like it did other West European audiences (Arroyo Barrigüete, María Lourdes Fernández Rodríguez and Antonio Obregón García provide another perspective on the voting issue in their chapter in this volume). Or was it that the contest had become an event dominated by the English-language, with four Irish wins and one British one in the 1990s, which paved the way for the abrogation, from 1999, of the rule that all entries had to be performed in the national language of the state that they represented? Or maybe the ESC had lost popularity in Italy due to the new dominance of the Nordic countries, with two Swedish wins and a Norwegian one in the 1990s? Sweden had been asserting itself as a new global power in popular music since the win of ABBA in the 1974 ESC, developing the third largest export popular music industry in the world after the United States and the United Kingdom. This underlined how much the powerbases in European popular culture had changed since the 1950s, and how the ESC related to transformations in the global popular music business. Whatever the recipe of motivations for RAI's withdrawal from the ESC, it was clear that the centre of power in the ESC had since the 1950s moved from the south to the north (linguistically, for example, the French language had been the most successful in the ESC during the Cold War, but an entry in French has not won since 1988). The economic gap between northern and southern Europe similarly widened during this period – and to the north's benefit. Still, an ESC without Italy was like a stiletto without a heel. After returning to the contest in 2011,

Italy achieved a decade-long string of highly successful entries, mostly top-ten finishing, which attested to a continued power of Italian popular music world-wide. And then, in 2021, Måneskin got on stage, its male and female members all wearing high heels.

...To Florence, Vienna and Prague: Teaching the World's First University Course on the ESC

It was fortuitous that I started teaching the world's first university course in Italy. Looking back, though — and as George Cremona also considers in his chapter on the value of using the ESC in teaching high school students — the effectiveness of popular music as a tool for learning had become apparent to me when I studied Italian in high school. Italian popular music songs were then a part of our curriculum, and they tended to be songs that were socially engaged, such as ones by the *cantautori* Claudio Baglioni, Lucio Dalla and Antonello Venditti. I studied Italian as I grew up in a multicultural area in the Australian city of Perth which had a large Italian community, and the language classes reflected the multicultural policies of the Australian government in the 1980s. Having grown up in Australia, one of the reasons why I got to watch the ESC from an early age was because it had been broadcast from 1983 on the Special Broadcasting Service, which had been established to provide multilingual programming to non-English-speaking background communities, among which the Italian has been one of the largest (Cutugno and Cinquetti even directly referred to the Italian Australian viewers when they hosted the ESC in Rome in 1991). As a student of European studies at the Australian National University, I wrote my first essay on the politics of the ESC for one of my courses and I was also an organiser of ESC parties. I saw may first-ever ESC live when I was studying at the Hebrew University of Jerusalem in 1999, where popular music was also an important way for me to learn Hebrew. The ESC finally became a focus of my research when I was a doctoral student at Columbia University writing my dissertation on politics and popular music in communist party-led Yugoslavia. It was then that I had the opportunity to be part of the first academic volume on the ESC, edited by two of the authors in this book, Ivan Raykoff and Robert Deam Tobin (2007). I also participated in the first-ever academic conference on the ESC, which was held in Volos, Greece, in 2008. The conference was co-organised by Dafni Tragaki, the editor of the third academic volume to be published on the ESC (2013) which came just after that published by two other pioneers of academic research on the contest, Fricker and Gluhovic (2013).

After my doctoral studies, I taught courses in contemporary European history at Columbia University and the Cooper Union for the Advancement of Science and Art, where I also incorporated the ESC into the syllabi. I then moved to Italy for a fellowship as a post-doctoral researcher at the European University Institute, where I began developing my research project on the history of the ESC. At that time, I also taught at one of New York University's global campuses in Florence, where the academic coordinator Prof. Bruce Edelstein enthusiastically supported my idea to start teaching a course on the ESC and European history and politics. I was initially unsure as to how the course would be received by the American study abroad students at the campus, considering that the ESC had not been widely known in the United States. Yet, many of the students had already been familiar with the contest, some because of their European family backgrounds, others because they had already accessed its music via the internet. The internet now provided recordings of the entries and shows that could be shown in class and used by the students for their research papers. In the course, I also included an excursion to San Marino, so that the students could learn about the importance of the ESC in cultural diplomacy — in this case in the smallest state currently represented in the ESC, for which the contest is a rare event for it to be promoted to such a large international audience — as well as the preparations that go into organising an ESC entry. In San Marino we met with the head of the ESC delegation from San Marino Radio and Television, Alessandro Capicchioni, and the four-time San Marinese ESC entrant, Valentina Monetta.

Yet, my work became not just about researching and teaching the ESC, but also about having an impact on the contest itself. In 2013, I began a research project on the history of the ESC, funded by the Marie Sklodowska-Curie Actions of the European Commission, at the University of Vienna. I went on to teach my ESC course there, including an excursion to the headquarters of the Austrian Broadcasting Corporation (Österreichischer Rundfunk, ORF), where the students and I attended a seminar in the Public Value Centre and took a tour of the television studios. That course gained more significance in the contest of Austria's win in the 2014 ESC and ORF's subsequent hosting of the contest in Vienna, giving us the opportunity to follow the preparations for the 2015 ESC up-close. I thus began to engage more with the representatives of television stations involved in the organisation of ESC entries or, as in Vienna in 2014 and 2015, the staging of the contest itself. I also cooperated with the EBU, being one of the three keynote speakers at its London conference for the ESC's sixtieth anniversary, together with two other academics, Karen Fricker and Paul Jordan. The latter became an ESC commentator for the British Broadcasting Corporation and from 2015 to 2018 was part of the ESC's communications team. Karen Fricker and I advised the ESC's Reference Group at its meeting in 2017, and I presented the findings of my book at the EBU's headquarters in 2018. In this regard, it became apparent that academic research on the ESC could reach the contest's organisers. In this sense, we managed to turn the ESC not just into a popular and serious subject of academic research, but also to give our research results a public impact, including on the development of the ESC itself. That is also one of the motivations behind this book: to explore how research on the ESC can have a larger impact beyond the world of academia. One of the reasons for that is certainly the widespread popularity of the ESC as a cultural phenomenon, which can be used as a conduit to relay, to a wider public, ideas about and research on not just the ESC itself but also broader cultural, economic, political, social and technological issues that are highlighted through the contest.

Another way in which I sought to expand the public impact of my academic research on the ESC was to engage other actors interested in the political aspects of the contest. During the week that the ESC was held in Vienna, I organised the symposium 'Eurovision Relations: The Eurovision Song Contest and International Relations'. It had three women as keynote speakers, each of whom had participated in the ESC and had gone on to have a political career. They were Norway's Åse Kleveland, who had participated in the 1966 ESC and hosted the contest in 1986, and later became minister of culture; Ismeta Dervoz, who performed for Yugoslavia in the 1976 ESC, led the Bosnian and Herzegovinian ESC delegation in the 1990s and later became a member of the national parliament; and Claudette Buttigieg, who represented Malta in the 2000 ESC and is now deputy speaker of the Maltese parliament. Joining them were panellists from the worlds of academia, diplomacy and the media. For the same week, I also co-organised with Erste Foundation a panel discussion at the Diplomatic Academy of Vienna, which brought together former participants in the ESC who had been advocates of political and social issues, namely Radek Banga from Czechia, the Rounder Girls from Austria and Rambo Amadeus from Montenegro. These events showed that the ESC did not just command wider public interest as popular cultural entertainment, but also because it is a political phenomenon with an impact on law and international relations, as this volume's chapters by Adam Dubin, Alison Lewis and John Hayek, and Gad Yair and Chen Ozeri underline. Indeed, while the EBU remains loyal to defining the ESC as a 'non-political' event, I maintain that the contest draws such intense public interest because of its political aspects. Viewers like to watch the ESC because of its politics, defined by the relations among the states represented in it, reflected in the voting results, or articulated in the sociopolitical issues addressed in entries. As I have developed a media profile as a commentator on the ESC — being dubbed 'Professor Song Contest' by ORF — these are also the issues that I usually get asked about when journalists interview me.

I am a historian of contemporary Europe who focusses on politics and popular culture. However, as the ESC is such a huge cultural phenomenon, it can tell us much about other academic fields as well. And that is the focus of this book, to examine how the ESC, as a subject of research and teaching, can be used to discover, illuminate and question topics in a variety of areas. The idea for this volume came from Adam Dubin and Antonio Obregón García when they invited me to speak at a symposium on the ESC which they organised at Comillas Pontifical University in Madrid in 2020. That drew me into a Spanish academic circle which I had not yet had the opportunity to encounter at the several conferences and workshops on the ESC that had theretofore been held, and that circle has emergied as a new centre of research on the ESC. This is indeed a boon for research on the ESC as, like Italy, Spain's involvement in the contest highlights some special issues. One of these is the involvement of authoritarian governments in the ESC, including in its hosting, which the dictatorship of Francisco Franco first demonstrated in 1969 after Massiel won the 1968 ESC for Spain. This issue is explored in the chapter in this book by Robert Dean Tobin. Some Spanish entries in the ESC have also become global successes, such as the singer Julio Iglesias who performed in the 1970 ESC or the song 'Eres tú' (It Is You) by the group Mocedades from the 1973 ESC. Another subject that invites further research is Spain's role in expanding the global market of the ESC beyond its toponymous Europe to Latin America (where Massiel had been working before being called back to Europe to sing in the 1968 ESC), including through the first broadcast of the ESC to Latin America from Madrid in 1969 and Spain's participation in the Iberoamerican Television Organisation's Festival (Vuletic, 2019), a pendant to the ESC discussed in this volume by Ariel James. This foray into Latin America preceded the ESC's expansion to Australia — which Chris Hays and Jess Carniel offer perspectives from in their chapter — and the United States. In the geography, or even geopolitics, of this volume, we are seeking to further develop the southern European dimension of research on the ESC — as with the chapter on Portugal by Sofia Vieira Lopes' and João Soeiro de Carvalho — and also the extra-European one, especially with the inclusion of scholars from Australia, Israel and the United States.

Our Tour: Where We Take You in This Book

This first stage of our grand tour of the ESC continues with chapters by the other co-editors of this volume, who bring perspectives on the history and further potential of the ESC as a subject of scholarly study. Antonio Obregón García offers a broad overview of the ESC's development as 'An Academic Phenomenon', providing a contextual basis for the volume by examining a wide range of courses and publications to demonstrate this evolution. He argues for the recognition of the ESC as a rewarding subject for several academic fields, including economics, history, international relations, law, political science, and cultural and media studies. Adam Dubin builds on this by introducing research on the ESC into a newer field: law. He discusses human rights cases related to the ESC and how these provide a pedagogical vehicle for understanding the limits of liability when the perpetrator of violations is not a state, with his conclusions being relevant not only for legal scholars but also for the organisers of the ESC and other mega-events.

The second section, 'From Past to Present: History, Law and Politics', presents research approaches from historical, political and social perspectives. Ivan Raykoff opens the section with a creative exploration of the 'Mythology of Song Contests' and how song competitions from ancient Greece have been reimagined in historic works of European literature and music. Considering the ESC through the broader lens of these mythic scenarios, he offers a new historical approach to the aesthetic and political tensions that still resound around the song contest phenomenon. Alison Lewis and John Hayek highlight some of these political tensions as they examine the role of the ESC in international relations through the case studies of Germany and the former Soviet Union. In 'Teaching European History and Memory through the Eurovision Song Contest during the Covid-19 Pandemic', they reflect on how they have used the ESC in a course on contemporary European history at the university level, especially to teach the politics of memory and the value of historical understanding. Gad Yair and Chen

Ozeri explore further examples of the ESC as a political platform for conflict and cooperation in 'A March for Power'. They detail different forms of politics in the ESC, including those of conflict, hegemony and suspicion, and how academic studies have provided the public with theories and tools to understand these political infiltrations. Catherine Baker considers the impact of the ESC on LGBTIQ politics — one of the most controversial aspects of the contest in recent times — in 'The Molitva Factor'. She examines how pop-folk music and LGBTIQ rights in south-eastern Europe have been intertwined and become a litmus test for states' Europeanness, applying her insights on embodied performances of nationhood in the ESC to political leaders and other symbolic figures.

George Cremona continues the second section with 'A Critical Pedagogical Eurovision Euphoria', in which he explains how the ESC can serve as an effective pedagogical tool to teach curricular content and critical reflection on values propagated by the EU. He provides a first-hand perspective on how the ESC can be used in learning in primary and secondary schools, complementing the tertiary education examples discussed elsewhere in this volume. Ariel James develops the question of values in the context of the ESC and the Iberoamerican Television Organisation's pendant in 'Sharing Values in the Eurovision Song Contest and the OTI Festival'. His statistical data demonstrate that the winning songs in the two song contests offer an analytical perspective that is useful for various academic fields that deal with the understanding of how and why we become social beings. We close off the second section in the typical ESC way — with voting — as José Luis Arroyo Barrigüete, María Lourdes Fernández Rodríguez and Antonio Obregón García present a statistical analysis of how the order of entries in the ESC influences voting results. In 'Eurovision in the Boardroom', they argue that their results on the bias derived from the order of presentation can also be applied to legal trials and selection processes for personnel or suppliers.

The third section, 'From Stage to Screen: Film, Media and Music', expands on some of the historical and legal issues introduced in the first and second sections, but with more of a focus on the audiovisual and journalistic dimensions of the ESC. Robert Tobin's 'Queer Camp against Franco' connects with preceding discussions of authoritarian governments as it addresses the example of Spain under Franco. Drawing on philosophical works, Tobin exposes the interplay between politicised art and aestheticised politics in a 1969 Spanish ESC parody film, demonstrating how campy art — which the ESC is often associated with — could also be employed for political means. Jess Carniel considers the historical issue of democratisation in the ESC itself through increasing public participation in 'High, Low and Participatory'. She discusses how the history of the ESC can be useful for examining shifts in the methods and theories of cultural studies which, since its emergence at around the same time as the beginning of the ESC, has been concerned with bringing scholarly attention to popular culture. While she asserts the importance of the ESC for cultural studies, Mari Pajala does so from the perspective of media studies in 'The Eurovision Song Contest and European Television History'. For her, the ESC offers a unique perspective on the development of media events, television entertainment and public service media because it is one of the longest-running television programmes and has persisted in the changing media landscape due to its continuity, adaptation and experimentation.

The next part of the third section deals with practical applications and experiences of ESC research. In 'From Trouble to Bubble?', Irving Wolther — who wrote the first-ever doctoral dissertation on the ESC — discusses how professional journalists in the ESC have changed their approach to fan journalists, from viewing them as déclassé competitors to knowledgeable sources. Still, the unpaid work of the fan journalists affects the remuneration of professional ones, raising questions about the roles of different categories of journalism in the ESC and more widely. José Luis Panea argues in 'Domesticity, Mass Media and Moving-Image Aesthetics' that, despite the ESC's pioneering audiovisual displays, its aesthetic dimensions have been understudied by audiovisual scholars. He focusses on the stage designs for the ESC, describing the imaginaries, innovations and resources that they have been based on, as well as how they have been inspired by the idea of transnational cooperation. From the close-up perspective onstage, we go to the far-away view of 'Armchair Researchers', by Chris Hay and Jess Carniel. They explain how, for most ESC scholars, research comprises audiovisual analysis and digital ethnography rather than on-site fieldwork, and the ESC's multimodal character prompts questions regarding the definition of 'on-site' and the negotiation of public/private boundaries in research work as this is being done from private spaces. Sofia Vieira Lopes' and João Soeiro de Carvalho's 'Between Concepts and Behaviours' then takes the discussion on fieldwork to ethnomusicology, focussing on the first-ever Portuguese victory in the ESC in 2017. They view the ESC as a privileged field for understanding ethnomusicological postulates, the relationship between musical behaviours, practices and media, and how these convey meanings and values about identities and societies.

Stopping in Portugal, our grand tour of the ESC ends, hoping that this book will inspire further innovative research that will change the way we think about not only the ESC and Europe, but also cultures, ideas and issues around the world.

Notes

1 From 2007 to 2022, the organisation of Russia's ESC entries alternated between Channel One and Russia-1 (Rossiya-1).

2 The group has instead had to content itself with its ESC entry 'Uno' (One) having some 200 million YouTube views, the most of any ESC entry ever (Eurovision Song Contest, 2020).

3 The International Broadcasting Organisation was renamed the International Radio and Television Organisation in 1960 and thereafter commonly referred to by the French-language abbreviation of this name, 'OIRT'.

4 The European Broadcasting Area is a technical region that geographically encompasses Europe and the Mediterranean rim, and it was initially conceived in the late 1920s for the purpose of defining the membership of the International Broadcasting Union, as Suzanne Lommers explains in her seminal work on that organisation (2012).

5 Vatican City is the only European state whose national broadcasting organisation is a member of the EBU but which has never been represented in the ESC.

6 As Pippo Baudo, who hosted thirteen editions of the festival from 1968 to 2008, put it: 'Sanremo is a long 'Inno di Mameli' (Mameli's Hymn) [the national anthem of Italy] — whose real title, not by chance, is 'Il Canto degli Italiani' (The Song of the Italians) — that once a year, for already more than sixty years, the Italians feel obliged to sing. And it is therefore quite natural that it is closely connected to the events, situations, climate and emotions that society is experiencing, to the evolution of customs, sensibilities and tastes' (cited in Lomartire 2012, 289—90).

7 In the 1956 ESC, each of the participating national broadcasting organisations submitted two entries; after that year, the rules permitted them to send only one. The other West German entrant in the 1956 ESC was Walther Andres Schwarz who, as I discovered in my research, was a Jew and survivor of the Holocaust (Vuletic, 2018, 17). He personified how Germany's participation in the ESC has historically been appropriated to portray an image of the state as diverse, open and tolerant, as the chapter in this volume by Alison Lewis and John Hayek discusses.

8 Cinquetti came second in the 1974 ESC, which was won by ABBA singing 'Waterloo', the greatest hit to ever come out of the contest. 'Sì' was about a woman being in love with a man. It was censored by RAI as the song was perceived as advocating a position on the issue of divorce just as Italy was about to hold a referendum on this around five weeks after the 1974 ESC was held. Although it has often been interpreted that Cinquetti was calling for a 'yes' to divorce, the 'yes' on the referendum ballot actually meant being in favour of repealing the law which permitted divorce (Vuletic, 2018: 80).

9 Thirty-three per cent of the Italian audience watched the 1991 ESC that was staged in Rome, and only one per cent watched it in 1992 (European Broadcasting Union, 1991, 2; Radio Sweden Audience and Programme Research, 1992, 1; Eurodience, 1993, 1).

References

Bezençon, M. (1954). Eurovision — The pattern of the future? *E.B.U. Bulletin*, 5(2), 7.

Bezençon, M. (1963). The keys of Eurovision. *E.B.U. Review (Part B — General and Legal)*, 14(79), 6.

Bezençon, M. (1964). Eurovision, or the price of fame. *E.B.U. Review (Part B — General and Legal)*, 15(85), 9.

Calcagno, P. (1996). Italia, soltanto tu snobbi l'Eurofestival. *Corriere dell Sera* (20 May).

Castelletti, R. (2020). "Ciao, 2020!': i russi salutano l'anno della pandemia in italiano. Ecco perché". *La Repubblica* (2 January), https://www.repubblica.it/esteri/2021/01/02/news/ciao_2020_i_russi_salutano_l_anno_della_pandemia_in_italiano_ecco_perche_-280860249.

Esquire. (2021). "Ciao 2020 ci ricorda cos'è l'Italia nel mondo, quando ce n'eravamo quasi dimenticati", *Esquire* (5 January), https://www.esquire.com/it/cultura/tv/a35129062/ciao-2020-italia-video.

Eugster, E. (1983). *Television programming across national boundaries: The EBU and OIRT experience*. Artech House.

Eurodience. (1993). Highly irregular ratings for song contest. *Eurodience*, 7(67), 1.

European Broadcasting Union. (1955a). Commission des Programmes (3ème session plénière) (6 September), 1 [European Broadcasting Union Archives, Concours Eurovision de la chanson, Décisions 1].

European Broadcasting Union. (1955b). Fifth festival of Italian song. *E.B.U. Bulletin*, 6(30), 146.

European Broadcasting Union. (1955c). International song festival. *E.B.U. Bulletin*, 6(31), 271.

European Broadcasting Union. (1956). Speech by His Holiness Pope Pius XXII to EBU delegates. *E.B.U. Bulletin*, 7(35), 137–138.

European Broadcasting Union. (1991). 1991 Eurovision Song Contest: Results of audience figures (12 June), 2 [European Broadcasting Union Archives, Concours Eurovision de la chanson, 1991].

European Broadcasting Union. (2004). A First: Pope Pius XII in five languages and via Eurovision. *EBU Dossiers*, 2(1), 12–15.

Eurovision Song Contest. (2020). *Little Big—Uno—Russia—official music video—Eurovision 2020* [video], YouTube (12 March), https://www.youtube.com/watch?v=L_dWvTCdDQ4.

Fricker, K., & Gluhovic, M., eds. (2013). *Performing the "new" Europe: Identities, feelings and politics in the Eurovision song contest*. Palgrave Macmillan.

Lommers, S. (2014). *Europe — On air Interwar projects for radio broadcasting*. Amsterdam University Press.

Pajala, M., & Vuletic, D. (2021). Stagecraft in the service of statecraft? Russia in the Eurovision Song Contest. In T. Forsberg and S. Mäkinen (Eds.), *Russia's cultural statecraft*. Routledge.

Pugliese, S.R. (1955). Letter to Léo Wallenborn, EBU (Milan, 15 February 1955), 1 [European Broadcasting Union Archives, Concours Eurovision de la chanson, 1956–57].

Radio Sweden Audience and Programme Research. (1992). Ratings and viewers in thousands for the 1992 Eurovision Song Contest from Malmö, Sweden (20 May), 1 [European Broadcasting Union Archives, Concours Eurovision de la chanson, 1992].

Raykoff, I., & Tobin, R.D. (2007). *A song for Europe: Popular music and politics in the Eurovision Song Contest*. Ashgate.

Sala, C. (2020). "'Ciao, 2020!', in Russia lo show di Capodanno è tutto in italiano", *Il Messagero* (31 December), https://www.ilmessaggero.it/televisione/ciao_2020_capodanno_russia_italiano_canzoni_ivan_urgant-5675150.html.

Ternavasio, M. (2004). *La leggenda di mister Volare: Vita di Domenico Modugno*. Giunti.

Tragaki, D., ed. (2013). *Empire of song: Europe and nation in the Eurovision Song Contest*. The Scarecrow Press.

Vecherniy Urgant. (2020). *Ciao 2020! Polnaya versiya* [video], YouTube (30 December), https://www.youtube.com/watch?v=lYgu75EwuPo.

Vuletic, D. (2018). *Postwar Europe and the Eurovision Song Contest*. Bloomsbury.

Vuletic, D. (2019). Latin America and the Eurovision Song Contest. *Ibero-Online*, 13, 85–91.

2 The Eurovision Song Contest: An Academic Phenomenon

Antonio Obregón

"There is nothing quite like the Eurovision Song Contest." This hyperbolic assertion by Georgiou and Sandvoss (2008: 125) is not just a literary device designed to honour a show that has become a point of reference in the media. It is also a way of conveying some notion of the significance achieved over time by the ESC in several different fields, including the academic. Such a state of affairs certainly owes much to the prolonged and growing success of the ESC over a number of decades: its longevity and vast number of fans are particularly striking features of the ESC's current stature. But, as we will seek to show, if the ESC constitutes an unparalleled phenomenon, including in the academic world, this is not the circumstantial result of pure chance. Its very nature and characteristics, accentuated and renewed, have allowed it to become what it is today. The ESC's success emanates from what it was when it was first conceived and from what it has gradually become. It also derives from the fact that the ESC is "much more than a song contest" (Petersen & Ren, 2015). In this instance, it soon becomes clear that "the whole is greater than the sum of its parts".

Few television programmes in the world have as long a tradition or re-percussions as far-reaching as the ESC. The three words making up its name are a good reflection of its essential content: it is a musical and artistic programme (*Song*), but also a television show that is, in principle, European (*Eurovision*) and, peculiarly, a contest (in French, *concours*) which sees the participation of various countries represented by their national television broadcasting organisations. If we take into account another commonly used term, encountered above all in south-west Europe, where the ESC is known as the *Festival de Eurovision* or *Eurofestival*, it becomes possible to identify another singular trait progressively acquired over the years: that of the ESC as a cultural, festive, celebratory and commemorative display. This aspect is of particular importance in current con-ceptions of the ESC/*Eurofestival* and reveals the importance the competition has gained in its long history as "a reflection of Europe in its most fundamental aspects, its culture, its politics and its society" (Sberro, 2021: 177).

This set of elements has provided the ESC with uninterrupted success for more than sixty years running (with the sole exception of 2020, when the event was cancelled as a result of the pandemic caused by the COVID-19 virus). In addi-tion, it has given rise to a phenomenon that has become the subject of academic

DOI: 10.4324/9781003188933-3

study from multiple perspectives. As Yair (2019: 1) has pointed out, the Festival, often considered by commentators a "silly kitsch show of musical mediocrity", is today "an appealing and productive area for the serious study of European civilization and its discontents". Thus it is that Tobin (2021: vii) underlines the existence of "an exciting blossoming of research and writing on the contest from an ever-expanding network of scholars". In the words of Spaziante (2021: 185), the ESC "is a highly studied object from the point of view of academic literature", with "its paradoxical characters making it an extremely interesting case under various aspects: political, economic, media, sociological, semiotic … ". In short, the ESC has broken into the halls of academia, as can be seen from the number of academic conferences held in recent years whose exclusive or main theme is the contest, to say nothing of the very considerable number of books, book chapters and articles on various aspects of the ESC that have been published in high-impact journals.

As Lewis and Hajek (2019: 165) have suggested, the scope of the ESC as a research topic encompasses a wide range of academic disciplines. Obviously, its nature as a television programme explains its presence in the field of media studies. It is also logical, given that it is a song contest, that there are references to it in artistic studies (music, dance, the visual arts) and cultural studies (ethnographic, linguistic, educational). Its singular trajectory in the second half of the twentieth century and the first two decades of the twenty-first, as well as its international dimension, have made it an object of study in the areas of history, politics and international relations (especially with reference to issues such as European integration, national identities or international rivalries and alliances). In addition, the show's voting system generates a great deal of data which can be used in analytical studies. Last, as I have mentioned above, the ESC has become a cultural phenomenon in a wider sense, reaching the areas of economics and business as well as the socio-legal field (studies on gender, immigration, social demands, human rights). The main aim of this introduction is to provide a brief outline of the influence of the ESC in a number of different areas of knowledge, relating its reach to the show's major identifiable traits.

The ESC as a contest

A decisive part of the transformation of the ESC into an academic topic derives from its nature as a contest in which the show ends with a voting process designed to be able to declare a winner, whose victory generally leads to the victorious country becoming the host of the event the following year. From this procedure derive at least two of the most significant characteristics of the ESC when considering it as an academic phenomenon.

The first aspect to take into account has its origins in the nature of the "contest" between several countries, which vie to obtain a victory which can bring prestige, renown, media repercussion and, amongst other favourable spin-offs, considerable economic gains. All of these factors have given rise to an awakening of political interest among nations in participating in the ESC which

goes beyond the pure communicational inducement of the corporations inter-
vening to represent those nations.

Second, the competitive nature of the ESC generates a huge amount of data,
given that "it is Europe´s biggest election" (Vuletic, 2018 a: 1). The voting
process at the end of the ESC generates data which, added to other data associated with the contest (the number of participants, gender of the singers, languages used in songs, order of appearance on stage and many others, multiplied
by the large number of editions) make it possible to tackle analytically different
elements that are the object of study. This reinforces the scientific value of
conclusions reached in any of the fields in which the research has been carried
out. The analytical study of the data provided by the ESC (and especially its
votes) crosses multiple disciplines in a transversal manner. The ESC's standing as
a data-generator has likely been the main factor in the spectacular boom, both in
quantity and quality, in academic studies focused on the show. The ESC has
attracted the attention of researchers who do not just examine the show as such
(so-called "acafans", Carniel, 2018: 1), but also extrapolate their conclusions to
other aspects of their disciplines.

The political dimension attained by the ESC is undeniable, for, as Raykoff
(2016: 3) has underlined, "both blatant and subtle political aspects have been
evident throughout the contest's history". Even if the original purpose of the
show was not strictly political, it is clear that the ESC's development process has
led to its role being projected in several different ways. One of the elements most
closely examined by academics is that referring to the use of the ESC as a mechanism for reinforcing state or national identities, as well as those of regions and
localities. In line with this, many studies have pointed to the link between the
ESC and the political pretensions of participating countries seeking to affirm
their identities, display their idiosyncratic values (and on occasions, their adherence to predominant European values) and, in sum, as a way of strengthening
national branding. This angle has been developed to such an extent that, as
Vuletic (2018 a: 7) has pointed out, "the ESC has thus been a highly flexible tool
of cultural diplomacy", meaning that it "has historically been significant" (2018
b: 302). This circumstance has at the same time led to the ESC constituting a
reflection of the politics of affinity or blocs, as well as reflecting rivalries and
confrontation/conflict between the nations making up the European space
(Jackson, 2017). As Carniel (2019: 151) concludes, "the Song Contest is perceived as a safe arena for national competitiveness to play out and for international relationships to be fostered, developed, or even be performed in more
negative terms".

It is precisely this view of the ESC, as an arena in which alliances and con-
frontations between European countries can play out, that has led to an unusual
interest in the analytical study of voting patterns, seen as a mirror of relations
between nations. The path first laid out with the articles on this subject by Yair
(1995) and Yair and Maman (1996) has been followed by authors who have
perfected, through the use of various techniques, an analysis of the factors influencing Eurovision voting in their attempts to identify or sift out the weighting

of political elements from those of an artistic nature. However, although a large number of studies focus on the influence of political factors on voting, ESC results are also used to analyse other factors influencing the professional juries or televoters, such as the gender of singers or the languages used in songs. They also examine certain psychological effects which may be present in other kinds of decision-making, such as business or legal decisions. This is the case of the so-called "mere-exposure" effect (Abakoumkin, 2011; Verrier, 2012; Abakoumkin, 2018) or "order" effect (see Haan et al., 2005). ESC voting results serve to illustrate phenomena occurring outside the contest itself, and particularly interesting studies have been carried out which quarry consequences of an economic nature (for example, Felbermayr, & Toubal, 2010; Siganos & Tabner, 2020), or of a political-legal nature (as in the case of Charron, 2013), or even within the field of health sciences (Filippidis & Laverty, 2018).

The ESC as *Euro*(vision)

Linked to the ESC's political dimension, largely attained as a result of its character as a contest between nations, another aspect has become an important object of study and even the cause of considerable academic controversy. In this instance, we are referring to the possible unifying role played by the ESC in the process of European integration, as well as acting as a showpiece for the informing values of Europeanisation, possibly summarised by the very term *Eurovision*.

It is easy to find an abundance of references in the literature asserting the existence of links between the ESC, European history and the construction of a distinct identity. For example, Pyka (2019:465): "[t]he Eurovision Song Contest is intricately entangled with the history of Europe". Raykoff and Tobin also highlight in no uncertain terms the ESC's contribution to the process of European unification: "established in 1956 by the European Broadcasting Union as a live televised spectacle to unify post-war western Europe through music" (2016: xvii). Nonetheless, such enthusiastic claims should be qualified, in the authoritative opinion of Vuletic (2018a), who has written of "perpetuated clichés, exaggerations" tied to "fantasies of a unified Europe" (2018a: 8). Even so, there is no doubt, even in this author's view, that "the contest still had a meaning in Europe´s international relations" (2018a: 13).

At all events, it is indisputably the case that the ESC has become part of European history during the post-war period and, even if its initial aims were not deliberately political, its sudden significance has made it a catalyst in the processes of internationalisation in Europe and, in a very special way, in that of European integration. As Wellings and Kalman famously put it: "If Jean Monnet were to start again with culture, it is far from certain that the Eurovision Song Contest would be the cultural arm of European integration that he would choose" (2019: 16).

Bearing all this in mind, what have come to be known as the "values" of the ESC have become particularly significant (e.g., Vuletic, 2018 a; Raykoff, 2021).

Indeed, most academic research points out that the ESC not only constitutes an element which is at the least favourable towards the idea of European integration, but also represents many of the values that are identified with what has come to be known as "Europeanisation", or with an even loftier and more cosmopolitan ideal. Thus, for Tobin, "on the level of culture, Eurovision offers its own vision of European citizenship" (2016: 27) and, going even further, for Jackson (2014: 88) the ESC can be seen as "the embodiment of a rather utopian strive for universal citizenship". It is understandable, then, that so many studies deal with the influence of the ESC on the process of European integration, the definition of its principles and the structuring of the values that sustain it.

The ESC as a *Song* Contest

The ESC's standing as a political event has at times overshadowed its essence as a music festival, to such an extent that the inquiry "It´s a Song Contest?" (Vignoles, 2015: 64) has come to seem quite legitimate. But the fact is that, as Raykoff (2021) has highlighted, "with more than 1,500 songs in over 50 languages and a wide range of musical styles since it began in 1956, Eurovision features the most musically and linguistically diverse song repertoire in history".

This quote serves as a reminder that, clearly, the ESC is a musical event harbouring a large number of compositions. Its artistic value also encompasses, obviously, the lyrical facet (Van Hoey, 2016), the importance of which is increased by the variety of languages historically used in the ESC, though English is currently the most predominant. Linked to this is the fact that the ESC is an audio-visual show, in which dance and the performing arts are of special importance. The ESC thereby becomes a shopwindow for modern artistic conceptions, and this is intensified by the substantial sums invested by some of the participating countries and the variety of styles present, as well as the competitive character of the contest. The latter enables it to gain the favour not only of audiences but also the professional jury by the presentation of innovative and striking proposals (Hindrichs, 2016).

The ESC's artistic importance has earned the academic appreciation of musicologists and students of the other arts involved. Significantly, it has also attracted the interest of linguists who have dedicated particular attention to the content of the messages contained in the songs' lyrics (Ivković, 2013).

The ESC as a TV programme

According to Vuletic (2018 a), it should not be forgotten that the ESC was originally conceived as a televisual experiment made possible by technological development and the connection between different television corporations. The ESC is above all a television show, an entertainment programme (Pajala, 2013) which achieves extremely high audiences and ratings in most of the participating countries and even in others which regularly broadcast it despite not being a member of the EBU. In short, every year it is a major world media event, and one which has acquired greater dimensions over time, not just because of its continuity, but also because of the extension of its "duration", now that semi-final events and even rehearsals are also broadcast. In addition, we should not lose sight of the growing production of ESC-related news throughout the year. Countless well-followed websites produce material on the ESC which sometimes even reaches the general-interest media. Related programmes have also been created which explore the Eurovision brand and strengthen its standing (e.g., Eurovision Junior or the national pre-selection contests held in many participating countries). It is not surprising, then, that media studies should have turned attention to the ESC and that today it should be an object of study not just in journals but also in numerous doctoral or master's theses covering themes such as audience analysis, public communications systems or issues relating to elements of audio-visual production (Förster & von Rimscha, 2015).

However, the media phenomenon of the ESC is not limited to its nature as a television programme. Internet and social networks have contributed to the consolidation of the ESC since the late 1990s and this enthusiasm has been returned with interest by the ESC: it offers varied and sustained content which feeds into its digital existence to an extraordinary extent. The development of the internet and social networks has found in the ESC a frenetic area of activity, as explained by several studies examining these new forms of communication (Highfield et al., 2013).

The ESC as a festival

The ESC's stature as a cultural manifestation with an influence going far beyond its artistic value is, as has been stated above, one of the consequences of its survival over a period of more than six decades (Beckan & Uz Hançarli, 2021). The ESC's evolution has facilitated knowledge about customs and ways of life, the interests and concerns of citizens, and the degree of development of different facets of European society as a whole and of the countries comprising it in particular. As is claimed by Fricker and Gluhovic (2013: 25), "we see continuing evidence that as Europe goes, so does the ESC". We could also say that as the ESC goes, so does Europe. Thus, it is possible to conclude, like Le Guern (2000), that the ESC "becomes part of the social memory". The ESC has turned into an annual celebration, like the major *fiesta* of a locality or nation, articulating hallmarks of identity and behavioural patterns. The effects, as occurs in other commemorative events of this kind, also touch upon the social, legal and economic.

With this in mind, academic approaches to the ESC, apart from those already mentioned in the area of politics and International Relations, plus those relating to artistic and media displays, are multiplied across the social disciplines to include ethnography, anthropology, sociology, education, law, business or economics. Several of these fields have seen particularly striking developments. This is very obvious, for instance, in the field of education: many university courses have been organised on the ESC, such as the one run by Professor Dean Vuletic on the Florence campus of New York University, the University of Vienna and

Charles University in Prague, or those held at Australian universities such as Melbourne, Sydney or Monash. In this way, the ESC has come to be used as a teaching tool, as has been shown, for example, by Cremona (2018) or Yair (2019).

Yet, there can be little doubt that it is in gender studies and work on the LGBTIQ presence in the ESC that Eurovision's cultural stature can be seen most clearly from a sociological and legal viewpoint. Both the third part of Fricker and Gluhovic's book on the ESC (2013) and the writings of many other authors, led by Professor Catherine Baker, constitute a highly qualified and accurate body of work, framed within the perspective of the ties between the ESC and an effective recognition of the human rights of individuals and collectives.

The notion of the ESC as cultural expression cannot be complete without some reference to its resonance in the economic and business spheres. As was suggested earlier, many of the analytical studies concerning the ESC which have proliferated in recent years lead to conclusions of an economic or business nature. However, the ESC is itself the object of academic scrutiny on account of the economic consequences which the celebration of the event can bring about (see Fleischer & Felsenstein, 2002; Bard, 2018; Abudy et al., 2020). This serves to reinforce the thesis of a widespread political interest in taking part in and winning the ESC.

Conclusion

The ESC is a television show in which songs are presented. It might be thought that its significance is likely to be modest, or at least restricted to the spheres of the arts and media. However, there is no doubt that its value grows when one takes into account its longevity, regularity, extension and repercussions. In addition, it continues to be a contest in which television corporations represent the different countries that take part and that seek to gain victory through the voting system. As such, the ESC has come to acquire a political dimension which has been magnified to a greater or lesser extent by its ties to the values surrounding the processes of European integration, or "Europeanisation", as well as supplying a vast base of data deserving of scientific analysis. These multiple facets of the ESC have also turned it into a cultural agent in the broadest sense, making it a representative and significant symbol of a social grouping throughout its historical evolution.

Clearly, the academic community could not remain aloof to a phenomenon that encompasses so many varied aspects, extended over time and deeply rooted in society. The numerous bibliographical references provided thematically below are not exhaustive. Still, they do allow us to confirm that, although it took some time to occur, the ESC has not only knocked at the doors of academia, but has come to occupy a preferential and welcoming place within it: in the same way that every year families and groups of friends gather together in the best place they can find to celebrate a *festival* which will form a part of their lives forever.

References

Media and cultural studies

Akin, A. (2013). The Reality is Not as It Seems From Turkey": Imaginations About the Eurovision Song Contest From Its Production Fields. *International Journal of Communication*, *7*, 2303–2321.

Aston E. (2013). Competing Femininities: A 'Girl' for Eurovision. In: K. Fricker & M. Gluhovic (eds.), *Performing the 'New' Europe: Identities, Feelings and Politics in the Eurovision Song Contest*, Palgrave Macmillan, London. 10.1057/97811373 67983_9

Baker, C. (2015). Gender and Geopolitics in the Eurovision Song Contest. *Contemporary Southeastern Europe*, *2*(1), 74–93.

Baker, C. (2017). The 'gay Olympics'? The Eurovision Song Contest and the politics of LGBT/European belonging. *European Journal of International Relations*, *23*(1), 97–121. 10.1177/1354066116633278

Baker C. (2019). If Love Was a Crime, We Would Be Criminals: The Eurovision Song Contest and the Queer International Politics of Flags. In: J. Kalman, B. Wellings, K. Jacotine (eds.), *Eurovisions: Identity and the International Politics of the Eurovision Song Contest since 1956*. Palgrave Macmillan, Singapore. 10.1007/978-981-13-9427-0_9

Baker, C. (2019). I am the voice of the past that will always be: the Eurovision Song Contest as historical fiction. *Journal of Historical Fictions*, *2*(2), 102–125.

Bard, K. (2018). Does Winning Eurovision Impact a Country's Economy?. *University of Tennessee*. Honors Thesis Projects. https://trace.tennessee.edu/utk_chanhonoproj/2160

Björnberg, A. (2016). Return to ethnicity: The cultural significance of musical change in the Eurovision Song Contest. In: Raykoff, I. & Tobin, R.D. (eds.), *A Song for Europe. Popular Music and Politics in the Eurovision Song Contest*, Routledge, London and New York.

Carniel, J. (2015). Skirting the issue: finding queer and geopolitical belonging at the Eurovision Song Contest. *Contemporary Southeastern Europe*, *2*(1), 136–154.

Cervi, L., Marín Lladó, C., & Sanandrés, C. (2021) Prosumers y la profesionalización del periodismo ciudadano: El caso www.eurovision-spain.com. *Ámbitos, Revista Internacional de Comunicación*, *52*, 8–25. 10.12795/Ambitos.2021.i52.0

Coleman, S. (2008). Why is the Eurovision Song Contest Ridiculous? Exploring a Spectacle of Embarrassment, Irony and Identity, *Popular Communication*, *6*(3), 127–140, DOI: 10.1080/15405700802197727

Cremona, G. (2018). The Eurovision Song Contest Within Formal Learning Contexts: A Critical Multimodal Interpretation of Possible Inter-Disciplinary Connections. *Symposia Melitensia*, *14*, 151–160.

Fleischer, A., & Felsenstein, D. (2002). Cost-Benefit Analysis Using Economic Surpluses: A Case Study of a Televised Event. *Journal of Cultural Economics*, *26*, 139–156. 10.1023/A:1014447018099

Fraile Prieto, T. (2019). 1, 2, 3 … ¡Al escondite inglés! Eurovisión, psicodelia y cine en la España ye-yé. *EU-topias*, *18*, 87–101.

Gluhovic M. (2013). Sing for Democracy: Human Rights and Sexuality Discourse in the Eurovision Song Contest. In: K. Fricker & M. Gluhovic (eds.), *Performing the*

'New' Europe: Identities, Feelings and Politics in the Eurovision Song Contest, Palgrave Macmillan, London. 10.1057/9781137367983_11

Gripsrud, J. (2007). Television and the European Public Sphere. *European Journal of Communication, 22*(4), 479–492. 10.1177/0267323107083064

Halliwell, J. (2018). All Kinds of Everything'? Queer Visibility in Online and Offline Eurovision Fandom. *Westminster Papers in Communication and Culture, 13*(2), 113–120. DOI: https://doi.org/10.16997/wpcc.289

Heller. D. (2016). "Russian body and soul": t.A.T.u performs at Eurovision 2003. In: I. Raykoff & R.D. Tobin (eds.), *A Song for Europe. Popular Music and Politics in the Eurovision Song Contest*, Routledge, London and New York.

Highfield, T., Harrington, S., & Bruns, A. (2013). Twitter as a Technology for Audiencing and Fandom. *Information, Communication & Society, 16*(3), 315–339. DOI: 10.1080/1369118X.2012.756053

Hindrichs, T. (2016). Chasing the "magic formula" for success: Ralph Siegel and the Grand Prix Eurovision de la Chanson. In: I. Raykoff & R.D. Tobin (eds.), *A Song for Europe. Popular Music and Politics in the Eurovision Song Contest*, Routledge, London and New York.

Ibrus, I., Rohn, U., & Nani, A. (2019). Searching for public value in innovation coordination: How the Eurovision Song Contest was used to innovate the public service media model in Estonia. *International Journal of Cultural Studies, 22*(3), 367–382. 10.1177/1367877918757513

Ivković, D. (2013). The Eurovision Song Contest on YouTube: A Corpus-based Analysis of Language Attitudes. *Language@Internet, 10*(1), www.languageatinternet. org, urn:nbn:de:0009-7-34803

Kazakov, V., & Hutchings, S. (2019). Challenging the 'Information War' Paradigm: Russophones and Russophobes in Online Eurovision Communities. In: M. Wijermars & K. Lehtisaari (eds.), *Freedom of Expression in Russia's New Mediasphere*, (pp. 137–158). Routledge, Abingdon.

Kürti, L. (2012). Twenty Years After: Rock Music and National Rock in Hungary. *Region: Regional Studies of Russia, Eastern Europe, and Central Asia, 1*(1), 93–130. doi:10.1353/reg.2012.0000

Kyriakidou, M., Skey, M., Uldam J., & McCurdy, P. (2018). Media events and cosmopolitan fandom: 'Playful nationalism' in the Eurovision Song Contest. *International Journal of Cultural Studies, 21*(6), 603–618.

Lemish, D. (2016). Gay brotherhood. Israeli gay men and the Eurovision Song Contest. In: I. Raykoff & R.D. Tobin (eds.), *A Song for Europe. Popular Music and Politics in the Eurovision Song Contest*, Routledge, London and New York.

Lewis A., & Hajek J. (2019). Lessons Learned: Teaching European Studies in Full Eurovision. In: C. Hay, & J. Carniel (eds), *Eurovision and Australia* (pp. 165–187) Palgrave Macmillan, Cham. 10.1007/978-3-030-20058-9_9

Linden, H., & Linden, S. (2018). There were only friendly people and love in the air: fans, tourism and the Eurovision Song Contest. In: C. Lundberg and V. Ziakas (eds.). *Handbook of Popular Culture and Tourism*. Routledge, London.

Lopes, S. (2015-1). O Festival RTP da Canção: definição de um objecto de *estudo. Revista do Fórum Internacional de Estudos em Música e Dança, 3*, 257–265.

Lopes, S. (2015-2). From Sunset Winter to Caetano's Spring: The Importance of a Song Contest in the Portuguese Music Scene of the 1960's and 1970's. *Journal of*

Literature and Art Studies, 5(6), 461–470. doi: 10.17265/2159-5836/2015. 06.011

Mayer (2020). Der Eurovision Song Contest als Mittler europäischer Integration? Sprachenbegeisterung im romanischen Fremdsprachenunterricht. In: R. Issler & U. Küchler (eds.), *Impulse zur Fremdsprachendidaktik – Issues in Foreign Language Education*, V&R unipress, Göttingen.

Ortiz Montero, L. (2017). El Festival de Eurovisión: más allá de la canción. *Fonseca, Journal of Communication*, 15, 145–162. DOI: 10.14201/fjc201715153170

Pajala M. (2013). Europe, with Feeling: The Eurovision Song Contest as Entertainment. In: Fricker K., Gluhovic M. (eds) *Performing the 'New' Europe. Studies in International Performance* (pp. 77–93). Palgrave Macmillan, London. 1 0.1057/9781137367983_4

Panea, J.L. (2017). El Festival de Eurovisión como convocatoria para la fijación de imaginarios: hospitalidad, contención, pronunciación y serialidad. *Revista de Estética y Teoría de las Artes*, 17, 80–111.

Panea, J.L. (2020). Las escenografías del Festival de Eurovisión: Estética, tecnología e identidad cultural al albor de la reconstrucción europea (1956-1993). *Ámbitos. Revista de estudios de Ciencias Sociales y Humanidades*, n° 44(2020), 23–40.

Pérez-Rufí, J.P. & Valverde-Maestre, A.M. (2020). The spatial-temporal fragmentation of live television video clips: analysis of the television production of the Eurovision Song Contest. *Communication & Society*, 33(2). 10.15581/003.33. 2.17-31

Petersen, M., & Ren, C. (2015). "Much more than a song contest": Exploring Eurovision 2014 as Potlatch, *Valuation Studies*, 3(2), 97–118. DOI: 10.3384/ VS.2001-5992.153297

Rehberg P. (2013). Taken by a Stranger: How Queerness Haunts Germany at Eurovision. In: K. Fricker & M. Gluhovic (eds.), *Performing the 'New' Europe: Identities, Feelings and Politics in the Eurovision Song Contest*, Palgrave Macmillan, London. 10.1057/9781137367983_10

Sandvoss, C. (2015). Popular culture, fans, and globalization. In B.S. Turner, & R.J. Holton (Eds.), *The Routledge International Handbook of Globalization Studies* (2 ed., pp. 395–411). (Routledge International Handbooks). Taylor and Francis Inc.

Singleton, B., Fricker, K., & Moreo, E. (2007). Performing the queer network. Fans and families at the Eurovision Song Contest, 12–24. *SQS – Suomen Queer-Tutkimuksen Seuran Lehti*, 2(2). Noudettu osoitteesta https://journal.fi/sqs/ article/view/53665

Sieg K. (2013). Conundrums of Post-Socialist Belonging at the Eurovision Song Contest. In: K. Fricker & M. Gluhovic (eds.), *Performing the 'New' Europe: Identities, Feelings and Politics in the Eurovision Song Contest*, Palgrave Macmillan, London. 10.1057/9781137367983_12

Şivgin, Z.M. (2015). Rethinking Eurovision Song Contest As A Clash Of Cultures. *Gazi Akademik Bakış*, 17, 193–213.

Stiernstedt, F., & Golovko, I. (2019). Volunteering as Media Work: The Case of the Eurovision Song Contest. *Culture Unbound*, 11(2), 231–251. DOI: 10.3384/ cu.2000.1525.19112231

Thorne, S., & Ivković, D. (2015). Multilingual *Eurovision* meets plurilingual *YouTube*. Linguascaping discursive ontologies. In: D. Koike & C. Blyth (eds).

Dialogue in Multilingual and Multimodal Communities, 167–192. DOI: 10.1 075/ds.27. John Benjamins Publishing Company.

Van Hoey, T. (2016). Love love peace peace': a corpus study of the Eurovision Song Contest. *Graduate Institute of Linguistics*, National Taiwan University. Paper accessible at http://www.academia.edu/26868613.

Verschik, A., & Hlavac, J. (2009). *Eto leto svet*: Estonia's 2008 Eurovision song as a source of folk-linguistic controversy. *Monash University Linguistics Papers*, 6(2), 47–64.

Vignoles, J. (2015). *Inside the Eurovision Song Contest: Glamour, Music and Myth*. Liffey Press, Dublin.

Yair, G. (2019). The Eurovision as a key educational experience: Teaching European politics and identities with impact. *New Zealand Journal for Research on Europe*, 13, 87–100.

Politics and Euro(vision)

Allatson, P. (2007). Antes cursi que sencilla': Eurovision Song Contests and the Kitsch-Drive to Euro-Unity. *Culture, Theory and Critique*, 48(1), 87–98. 10.1 080/14735780701293540

Baker, C. (2008). Wild Dances and Dying Wolves: Simulation, Essentialization, and National Identity at the Eurovision Song Contest. *Popular Communication*, 6(3), 173–189. DOI: 10.1080/15405700802198113

Baumgartner, M. (2016). Chanson, canzone, Schlager, and song: Switzerland's identity struggle in the Eurovision Song Contest. In: I. Raykoff & R.D. Tobin (eds.), *A Song for Europe. Popular Music and Politics in the Eurovision Song Contest*, Routledge, London and New York.

Bekcan, U., & Uz Hançarli, P. (2021). Evaluation of Eurovision Song Contest as a Cultural Impact Tool. *Journal of History Culture and Art Research*, 10(1), 84–97. doi: 10.7596/taksad.v10i1.3009

Bolin, G., & Stählber, P. (2015). Mediating the Nation-State: Agency and the Media in Nation-Branding Campaigns. *International Journal of Communication*, 9(2015), 3065–3083.

Brunt, S.D. (2016). Changing Japan, unchanging Japan: Shifting visions of the Red and White Song Contest. In: I. Raykoff & R.D. Tobin (eds.), *A Song for Europe. Popular Music and Politics in the Eurovision Song Contest*, Routledge, London and New York.

Carniel, J. (2017). Welcome to Eurostralia: the strategic diversity of Australia at the Eurovision Song Contest. *Continuum*, 31(1), 13–23, DOI: 10.1080/10304312 .2016.1262089

Carniel, J. (2018). *Understanding the Eurovision Song Contest in Mutilcultural Australia. We got Love*, Palgrave Macmillan, Cham. 10.1007/978-3-030-02315-7

Carniel, J. (2019). Nation Branding, Cultural Relations and Cultural Diplomacy at Eurovision: Between Australia and Europe. In: J. Kalman, B. Wellings, & K. Jacotine (eds.), *Eurovisions: Identity and the International Politics of the Eurovision Song Contest since 1956* (pp. 151–173). Palgrave Macmillan, Singapore. 10.1007/ 978-981-13-9427-0_8

Coupe, T., & Chaban, N. (2020). Creating Europe through culture? The impact of the European Song Contest on European identity. *Empirica*, *47*, 885–908. 10.1 007/s10663-019-09461-6

Förster, K., & von Rimscha, M.B. (2015). *Transnational television: The Eurovision Song Contest in the light of research*. Österreichischer Rundfunk, ORF, Wien.

Fricker, K., & Gluhovic, M. (2013). Introduction: Eurovision and the 'New' Europe. In: K. Fricker & M. Gluhovic (eds.), *Performing the 'New' Europe: Identities, Feelings and Politics in the Eurovision Song Contest* (pp. 1–28). Palgrave Macmillan, London.

Fricker, K., & Gluhovic M. (2013). The Song Contest Is a Battlefield: Panel Discussion with Eurovision Song Contest Broadcasters, 18 February 2011. In: K. Fricker & M. Gluhovic (eds.), *Performing the 'New' Europe: Identities, Feelings and Politics in the Eurovision Song Contest*, Palgrave Macmillan, London. 10.1057/ 9781137367983_5

Fricker, K. (2013). It's Just Not Funny Any More: Terry Wogan, Melancholy Britain, and the Eurovision Song Contest. In:K. Fricker & M. Gluhovic (eds.), *Performing the 'New' Europe: Identities, Feelings and Politics in the Eurovision Song Contest*, Palgrave Macmillan, London. 10.1057/9781137367983_3

Gauja, A. (2019). Europe: Start Voting Now! Democracy, Participation and Diversity in the Eurovision Song Contest. In: J. Kalman, B. Wellings, & K. Jacotine (eds), *Eurovisions: Identity and the International Politics of the Eurovision Song Contest since 1956* (pp. 201–219). Palgrave Macmillan, Singapore. 10.1007/978-981-13-9427-0_10

Georgiou, M., & Sandvoss, C. (2008). Editors' Introduction, *Popular Communication*, *6*(3), 125–126, 10.1080/15405700802198279

Georgiou, M. (2008) In the End, Germany will Always Resort to Hot Pants: Watching Europe Singing, Constructing the Stereotype, *Popular Communication*, *6*(3), 141–154, DOI: 10.1080/15405700802198188

Gluhovic, M. (2013). Sing for Democracy: Human Rights and Sexuality Discourse in the Eurovision Song Contest. In: K. Fricker & M. Gluhovic (eds.), *Performing the 'New' Europe: Identities, Feelings and Politics in the Eurovision Song Contest* (pp. 194–217). Palgrave Macmillan, London, .

Gumpert, M. (2016). Everyway that I can": Auto-Orientalism at Eurovision 2003. In: I. Raykoff & R.D. Tobin (eds.), *A Song for Europe. Popular Music and Politics in the Eurovision Song Contest*, Routledge, London and New York.

Ingvoldstad, B. (2016). Lithuanian contest and European dreams. In: I. Raykoff & R.D. Tobin (eds.), *A Song for Europe. Popular Music and Politics in the Eurovision Song Contest*, Routledge, London and New York.

Isaacs, R., & Polese, A. (eds.) (2016). *Nation-Building and Identity in the Post-Soviet Space. New tools and approaches*, Routledge, London. 10.4324/9781315597386

Ismayilov, M. (2012). State, identity, and the politics of music: Eurovision and nation-building in Azerbaijan. *Nationalities Papers*, *40*(6), 833–851. doi: 10.1 080/00905992.2012.742990

Jackson, P. (2014). 'Welcome Europe!' The Eurovision Song Contest as a Continuum for Cosmopolitanism, in A. Yilmaz, R. Trandufoiu & A. Mousoutzania (eds.), *Media and Cosmopolitanism* (pp. 71–92). Peter Lang AG, Bern.

Jackson, P. (2017). Wenn Politik die Eruovisions-Blase piekst. .... *Religion & Gesellschaft in OST und West*, *45*(7–8), 16–17.

Jones, S., & Subotic, J. (2011). Fantasies of power: Performing Europeanization on the European periphery. *European Journal of Cultural Studies, 14*(5), 542–557. 10.1177/1367549411412199

Jordan, P. (2011). The Eurovision Song Contest: nation branding and nation building in Estonia and Ukraine. PhD thesis, University of Glasgow.

Jordan, P. (2014). *The Modern Fairy Tale. Nation Branding, National Identity and the Eurovision Song Contest in Estonia*. University of Tartu Press. DOI: 10.26530/ OAPEN_474310

Jordan, P. (2015). From Ruslana to Gaitana: Performing "Ukrainianness" in the Eurovision Song Contest. *Contemporary Southeastern Europe, 2*(1), 110–135.

Kalman J., Wellings B., & Jacotine K., (eds.) (2019). *Eurovisions: Identity and the International Politics of the Eurovision Song Contest since 1956*. Palgrave Macmillan, Singapore.

Kalman, J. (2019). Which Belgium Won Eurovision? European Unity and Belgian Disunity. In: J. Kalman, B. Wellings, K. Jacotine (eds.), *Eurovisions: Identity and the International Politics of the Eurovision Song Contest since 1956*. Palgrave Macmillan, Singapore. 10.1007/978-981-13-9427-0_4

Kiel, C. (2020). Chicken dance (off): competing cultural diplomacy in the 2019 Eurovision Song Contest. *International Journal of Cultural Policy, 26*(7), 973–987. DOI: 10.1080/10286632.2020.1776269

Le Guern, P. (2000). From National Pride to Global Kitsch: The Eurovision Song Contest. *The Web Journal of French Media Studies, 3*(1). Available online: http:// wjfms.ncl.ac.uk/leguWJ.htm

Lewis, A. (2019). Germany as Good European: National Atonement and Performing Europeanness in the Eurovision Song Contest. In: J. Kalman, B. Wellings, & K. Jacotine (eds.), *Eurovisions: Identity and the International Politics of the Eurovision Song Contest since 1956*. Palgrave Macmillan, Singapore. 10.1007/978-981-13-9427-0_2

Markovic, K.N. (2019). Negotiating Post-war Nationhood: Serbia, Croatia, Bosnia-Herzegovina and the Eurovision Song Contest. In: J. Kalman, B. Wellings, & K. Jacotine (eds.), *Eurovisions: Identity and the International Politics of the Eurovision Song Contest since 1956*. Palgrave Macmillan, Singapore. 10.1007/978-981-13-9427-0_5

Meerzon Y., & Priven D. (2013). Back to the Future: Imagining a New Russia at the Eurovision Song Contest. In: K. Fricker & M. Gluhovic (eds.), *Performing the 'New' Europe: Identities, Feelings and Politics in the Eurovision Song Contest*, Palgrave Macmillan, London. 10.1057/9781137367983_6

Miazhevich, G. (2012). Ukrainian Nation Branding Off-line and Online: Verka Serduchka at the Eurovision Song Contest, *Europe-Asia Studies, 64*(8), 1505–1523, DOI: 10.1080/09668136.2012.712274

Militz, E. (2016). Public events and Nation-Buliding in Azerbaijan. In: R. Isaacs & A. Polese (eds.), *Nation-Building and Identity in the Post-Soviet Space. New tools and approaches* (pp. 174–192). Routledge, London.

Mitrović, M. (2010). New face of Serbia at the Eurovision Song Contest: international media spectacle and national identity. *European Review of History: Revue européenne d'histoire, 17*(2), 171–185. DOI: 10.1080/13507481003660829

Motschenbacher, H. (2016). *Language, Normativity and Europeanisation. Discursive Evidence from the Eurovision Song Contest*, Palgrave Macmillan, Basingstoke. DOI: 10.1057/978-1-137-56301-9

Mutsaerts, L. (2016). Fernando, Filippo and Milly: Bringing blackness to the Eurovision stage. In: I. Raykoff & R.D. Tobin (eds.), *A Song for Europe. Popular Music and Politics in the Eurovision Song Contest*, Routledge, London and New York.

Pajala, M. (2016). Finland: zero points. Nationality, failure, and shame in the Finnish media. In: I. Raykoff & R.D. Tobin (eds.), *A Song for Europe. Popular Music and Politics in the Eurovision Song Contest*, Routledge, London and New York.

Pavlyshyn, M. (2019). Ruslana, Serduchka, Jamala: National Self-Imaging in Ukraine's Eurovision Entries. In: J. Kalman, B. Wellings, & K. Jacotine (eds.), *Eurovisions: Identity and the International Politics of the Eurovision Song Contest since 1956*. Palgrave Macmillan, Singapore. 10.1007/978-981-13-9427-0_7

Piotrowska, A.G. (2020). The Eurovision Song Contest: A Continent (still) Divided? *Journal of Historical Sociology, 33* (3), 371–388. 10.1111/johs.12285

Pollock, D.K., & Woods, D.L. (1959). A study in international communication: Eurovision, *Journal of Broadcasting, 3*(2), 101–117, DOI: 10.1080/08838155 909385866

Pot, F. (2021). Mapping favouritism at the Eurovision Song Contest: doesd it impact the results?. *RUG – Faculty of Spatial Sciences*, 1–9.

Press-Barnathan, G., & Lutz, N. (2020). The multilevel identity politics of the 2019 Eurovision Song Contest. International Affairs, *96*(3), 729–748. 10.1093/ia/iiaa004

Pyka, M. (2019). The Power of Violins and Rose Petals: The Eurovision Song Contest as an Arena of European Crisis. *Journal of European Studies, 49*(3–4), 448–469. 10.1177/0047244119859178

Raykoff, I. (2014). Empire of Song: Europe and Nation in the Eurovision Song Contest. D. Tragaki (ed.), *Music and Letters, 95*(2), 316–318. 10.1093/ml/gcu032

Raykoff, I. (2016). Camping of the borders of Europe. In: I. Raykoff & R.D. Tobin (eds.), *A Song for Europe. Popular Music and Politics in the Eurovision Song Contest* (pp. 1–12). Routledge, London and New York.

Raykoff, I., & Tobin, R.D. (2016), Introduction. In: I. Raykoff & R.D. Tobin (eds.), *A Song for Europe. Popular Music and Politics in the Eurovision Song Contest* (pp. xvii–xxi). Routledge, London and New York.

Raykoff, I., & Tobin, R.D. (eds.) (2016). *A Song for Europe. Popular Music and Politics in the Eurovision Song Contest*, Routledge, London and New York. 10.4324/9781315097732

Raykoff, I. (2021). *Another Song for Europe. Music, Taste, and Values in the Eurovision Song Contest*, Routledge, London and New York. 10.4324/97804292 81532

Sandvoss, C. (2008). On the Couch with Europe: The Eurovision Song Contest, the European Broadcast Union and Belonging on the Old Continent, *Popular Communication, 6*(3), 190–207. 10.1080/15405700802198238

Sberro, S. (2021). Eurovision 2020, retrato de una Europa golpeada, pero resiliente en pie. *Strategy, Technology and Society, 11*, 177–204.

Singleton B. (2013). From Dana to Dustin: The Reputation of Old/New Ireland and the Eurovision Song Contest. In: K. Fricker & M. Gluhovic (eds.), *Performing the 'New' Europe: Identities, Feelings and Politics in the Eurovision Song Contest*, Palgrave Macmillan, London. 10.1057/9781137367983_8

Solomon, T. (2016). Articulating the historical moment: turkey, Europe, and Eurovision 2003. In: I. Raykoff & R.D. Tobin (eds.), *A Song for Europe. Popular Music and Politics in the Eurovision Song Contest*, Routledge, London and New York.

Spaziante, L. (2021). So Disarmingly European. Eurovision Song Contest and the European Identity. In: F. Mangiapane & T. Migliore (eds.), *Images of Europe. The Union between Federation and Separation*, Springer, Cham, Swtizerland.

Ståhlberg, P., & Bolin. G. (2016). Having a soul or choosing a face? Nation branding, identity and cosmopolitan imagination. *Social Identities, 22*(3), 274–290, DOI: 10.1080/13504630.2015.1128812

Stychin, C. (2011). Unity in Diversity: European Citizenship Through the Lens of Popular Culture. *Windsor Yearbook of Access to Justice, 29*(1), 1–25.

Szeman I. (2013). Playing with Fire' and Playing It Safe: With(out) Roma at the Eurovision Song Contest In: K. Fricker & M. Gluhovic (eds.), *Performing the 'New' Europe: Identities, Feelings and Politics in the Eurovision Song Contest*, Palgrave Macmillan, London. 10.1057/9781137367983_7

Tobin, R.D. (2016). Eurovision at 50: Post-Wall and Post-Stonewall. In: I. Raykoff & R.D. Tobin (eds.), *A Song for Europe. Popular Music and Politics in the Eurovision Song Contest* (pp. 25–35). Routledge, London and New York.

Ural, H. (2019). Turkishness on the stage: Affective nationalism in the Eurovision Song Contest. *International Journal of Cultural Studies, 22*(4), 519–535. 10. 1177/1367877918820335

Vuletic, D. (2016). The socialist star: Yugoslavia, Cold War politics and the Eurovision Song Contest. In: I. Raykoff & R.D. Tobin (eds.), *A Song for Europe. Popular Music and Politics in the Eurovision Song Contest*, Routledge, London and New York.

Vuletic, D. (2018a). *Postwar Europe and the Eurovision Song Contest*. Bloomsbury Academic, London, New York.

Vuletic, D. (2018b). Public Diplomacy and Decision-Making in the Eurovision Song Contest. In: M. Dunkel & S.A. Nitzsche, *Popular Music and Public Diplomacy. Transnational and Transdisciplinary Perspectives*, transcriptVerlag, Bielefeld (pp. 301–314).

Vuletic, D. (2018c). The Eurovision Song Contest in the Musical Diplomacy of Authoritarian States. In: F. Ramel, & C. Prévost-Thomas (eds), *International Relations, Music and Diplomacy* (pp. 213–234). The Sciences Po Series in International Relations and Political Economy. Palgrave Macmillan, Cham. 10.1007/ 978-3-319-63163-9_10

Vuletic, D. (2019). The Intervision Song Contest: A Commercial and Pan-European Alternative to the Eurovision Song Contest. In: E. Mazierska, & Z. Győri (eds), *Eastern European Popular Music in a Transnational Context* (pp. 173–190). Palgrave European Film and Media Studies. Palgrave Macmillan, Cham. 10.1007/ 978-3-030-17034-9_9

Vuletic, D. (2019). Recognising Kosovo in the World of Televised International Song Contests. In: J. Kalman, B. Wellings, & K. Jacotine (eds.), *Eurovisions: Identity and the International Politics of the Eurovision Song Contest since 1956*. Palgrave Macmillan, Singapore. 10.1007/978-981-13-9427-0_6

Wellings, B., & Kalman, J. (2019). Entangled Histories: Identity, Eurovision and European Integration. In: J. Kalman, B. Wellings, & K. Jacotine (eds.), *Eurovisions: Identity and the International Politics of the Eurovision Song Contest since 1956* (pp. 1–20). Palgrave Macmillan, Singapore. 10.1007/978-981-13-942 7-0_1

Wellings B., Jay Z., & Strong C. (2019). Making Your Mind Up': Britain, Europe and Eurovision-Scepticism. In: J. Kalman, B. Wellings, & K. Jacotine (eds.), *Eurovisions: Identity and the International Politics of the Eurovision Song Contest since 1956*. Palgrave Macmillan, Singapore. 10.1007/978-981-13-942 7-0_3

West, C. (2017). *Eurovision! A History of Modern Europe through the World's Greatest Song Contest*. Melville House UK, London.

Wolther, I. (2008). Mehr als Musik: die sieben Dimensionen des "Eurovision Song Contests". In K.-S. Rehberg (Hrsg.), *Die Natur der Gesellschaft: Verhandlungen des 33. Kongresses der Deutschen Gesellschaft für Soziologie in Kassel 2006*. Teilbd. 1 u. 2 (S. 4896-4905). Frankfurt am Main: Campus Verl. https://nbn-resolving. org/urn:nbn:de:0168- ssoar-154477

Woods, D. (2020). From *Eurovision* to *Asiavision*: the *Eurovision Asia Song Contest* and negotiation of Australia's cultural identities. *Media International Australia, 175* (I), 36–49. 10.1177/1329878X20906535

Yair, G. (1995). 'Unite Unite Europe' The political and cultural structures of Europe as reflected in the Eurovision Song Contest". *Social Networks, 17*(2), 147–161. 10.1016/0378-8733(95)00253-K

Yair, G., & Maman, D. (1996). The Persistent Structure of Hegemony in the Eurovision Song Contest, *Acta Sociologica, 39*(3), 309–325. 10.1177/00016993 9603900303

Yair, G. (2019). Douze point: Eurovisions and Euro-Divisions in the Eurovision Song Contest – Review of two decades of research, *European Journal of Cultural Studies, 22*(5–6), 1013–1029, 10.1177/1367549418776562

Yekelchyk, S. (2010). What Is Ukrainian about Ukraine's Pop Culture?: The Strange Case of Verka Serduchka, *Canadian-American Slavic Studies, 44*(1–2), 217–232. doi: 10.1163/221023910X512877

Zaroulia, M. (2013). Sharing the moment': Europe, affect and utopian performatives in the Eurovision Song Contest. In: K. Fricker & M. Gluhovic (eds.), *Performing the 'New' Europe: Identities, Feelings and Politics in the Eurovision Song Contest* (pp. 31–52). Palgrave Macmillan, London. 10.1057/9781137367983_2

EurovisionAnalytics

Abakoumkin, G. (2011). Forming Choice Preferences the Easy Way: Order and Familiarity Effects in Elections 1. *Journal of Applied Social Psychology, 41*(11), 2689–2707. 10.1111/j.1559-1816.2011.00845.x

Abakoumkin, G. (2018). Mere Exposure Effects in the Real World: Utilizing Natural Experiment Features from the Eurovision Song Contest. *Basic and Applied Social Psychology, 40*(4), 236–247. 10.1080/01973533.2018.1474742

Abudy, M., Mugerman, Y., & Shust, E. (2020). The Winner Takes It All: Investor Sentiment and the Eurovision Song Contest. Available online www.researchgate.net

Antipov, E.A., & Pokryshevskaya, E.B. (2017). Order effects in the results of song contests: Evidence from the Eurovision and the New Wave. *Judgment and Decision Making, 12*(4), 415–419.

Blangiardo, M., & Baio, G. (2014) Evidence of bias in the Eurovision song contest: modelling the votes using Bayesian hierarchical models. *Journal of Applied Statistics*, *41*(10), 2312–2322. 10.1080/02664763.2014.909792

Bruine de Bruin, W., & Keren, G. (2003). Order effects in sequentially judged options due to the direction of comparison. *Organizational Behavior and Human Decision Processes*, *92*(1–2), 91–101. 10.1016/S0749-5978(03)00080-3

Bruine de Bruin, W. (2005). Save the last dance for me: Unwanted serial position effects in jury evaluations. *Acta Psychologica*, *118*(3), 245–260. 10.1016/j.actpsy.2004.08.005

Bruine de Bruin, W. (2006). Save the last dance II: Unwanted serial position effects in figure skating judgments. *Acta Psychologica*, *123*(3), 299–311. 10.1016/j.actpsy.2006.01.009

Budzinski, O., & Pannicke, J. (2017). Culturally biased voting in the Eurovision Song Contest: Do national contests differ? *Journal of Cultural Economics*, *41*(4), 343–378. 10.1007/s10824-016-9277-6

Charron, N. (2013). Impartiality, friendship-networks and voting behavior: Evidence from voting patterns in the Eurovision Song Contest. *Social Networks*, *35*(3), 484–497. 10.1016/j.socnet.2013.05.005

Clerides, S., & Stengos, T. (2012). Love thy neighbour, love thy kin: Strategy and bias in the Eurovision Song Contest. *Ekonomia*, *15*(1), 22–44.

D'Angelo, S., Murphy, T.B., & Alfò, M. (2019). Latent space modelling of multi-dimensional networks with application to the exchange of votes in Eurovision song contest. *The Annals of Applied Statistics*, *13*(2), 900–930. 10.1214/18-AOAS1221

Dekker, A. (2007). The Eurovision Song Contest as a 'friendship'network. *Connections*, *27*(3), 53–60.

Dogru, B. (2012). Modeling Voting Behavior in the Eurovision Song Contest. *Journal of Research in Economics and International Finance*, *1*(6), 166–168.

Felbermayr, G., & Toubal, F. (2010). Cultural Proximity and Trade. *European Economic Review*, *54*, 279–293. ff10.1016/j.euroecorev.2009.06.009ff. ffhalshs-00641280

Fenn, D., Suleman, O., Efstathiou, J., & Johnson, N.F. (2006). How does Europe make its mind up? Connections, cliques, and compatibility between countries in the Eurovision Song Contest. *Physica A: Statistical Mechanics and its Applications*, *360*(2), 576–598. 10.1016/j.physa.2005.06.051

Filippidis, F.T., & Laverty, A.A. (2018). *Euphoria*" or "*Only Teardrops*? Eurovision Song Contest performance, life satisfaction and suicide. *BMC Public Health*, *18*, 582. 10.1186/s12889-018-5497-3

García, D., & Tanase, D. (2013). Measuring cultural dynamics through the eurovision song contest. *Advances in Complex Systems*, *16*(8), 1350037. 10.1142/S0219525913500379

Gatherer, D. (2006). Comparison of Eurovision Song Contest simulation with actual results reveals shifting patterns of collusive voting alliances. *Journal of Artificial Societies and Social Simulation*, *9*(2).

Ginsburgh, V., & Noury, A.G. (2008). The Eurovision song contest. Is voting political or cultural?. *European Journal of Political Economy*, *24*(1), 41–52. 10.1016/j.ejpoleco.2007.05.004

Haan, M.A., Dijkstra, S.G., & Dijkstra, P.T. (2005). Expert judgment versus public opinion–evidence from the Eurovision song contest. *Journal of Cultural Economics, 29*(1), 59–78. 10.1007/s10824-005-6830-0

Kokko, A., & Tingvall, P.G. (2012). The Eurovision Song Contest, Preferences and European Trade. *Ratio Working Papers, 183*, 1–30.

Kumpulainen, I., Praks, E., Korhonen, T., Ni, A., Rissanen, V., & Vankka J. (2020). Predicting Eurovision Song Contest Results Using Sentiment Analysis. In: A. Filchenkov, J. Kauttonen, & L. Pivovarova (eds), *Artificial Intelligence and Natural Language. AINL 2020. Communications in Computer and Information Science*, 1292. Springer, Cham. 10.1007/978-3-030-59082-6_7

Mantzaris, A.V., Rein, S.R., & Hopkins, A.D. (2017). Examining collusion and voting biases between countries during the Eurovision song contest since 1957. *arXiv preprint arXiv, 1705*, 06721.

Mantzaris, A.V., Rein, S.R., & Hopkins, A.D. (2018). Preference and neglect amongst countries in the Eurovision Song Contest. *Journal of Computational Social Science, 1*(2), 377–390. 10.1007/s42001-018-0020-2

Millner, R., Stoetzer, M.W., Fritze, C., & Günther, S. (2015). Fair oder Foul? Punktevergabe und Platzierung beim Eurovision Song Contest. *Jenaer Beiträge zur Wirtschaftsforschung, 2015/2*, Ernst-Abbe-Hochschule, Fachbereich Betriebswirtschaft, Jena.

Ochoa, A., Muñoz-Zavala, A., & Hernández-Aguirre, A. (2009). A Hybrid System Approach to Determine the Ranking of a Debutant Country in Eurovision, *Journal of Computers, 4*(8), 713–720.

Page, L., & Page, K. (2010). Last shall be first: A field study of biases in sequential performance evaluation on the Idol series. *Journal of Economic Behavior & Organization, 73*(2), 186–198. 10.1016/j.jebo.2009.08.012

Saavedra, S., Efstathiou, J., & Reed-Tsochas, F. (2007). Identifying the underlying structure and dynamic interactions in a voting network. *Physica A: Statistical Mechanics and its Applications, 377*(2), 672–688. 10.1016/j.physa.2006.11.038

Schweiger, W., & Brosius, H.-B. (2003). Eurovision Song Contest – beeinflussen Nachrich-tenfaktoren die Punktvergabe durch das Publikum? *M&K Medien & Kommunikationswissenschaft, 51*(2), 271–294. 10.5771/1615-634x-2003-2-271

Siganos, A., & Tabner, I.T. (2020). Capturing the role of societal affinity in cross-border mergers with the Eurovision Song Contest. *Journal of International Business Studies, 51*(2), 263–273, 10.1057/s41267-019-00271-3

Spierdijk, L., & Vellekoop, M. (2009). The structure of bias in peer voting systems: lessons from the Eurovision Song Contest. *Empirical Economics, 36*(2), 403–425. 10.1007/s00181-008-0202-5

Stockemer, D., Blais, A., Kostelka, F., & Chhim, C. (2018). Voting in the Eurovision Song Contest. *Politics, 38*(4), 428–442. 10.1177/0263395717737887

Verrier, D. (2012). Evidence for the influence of the mere-exposure effect on voting in the Eurovision Song Contest. *Judgement and Decision Making, 7*(5), 639–643.

3 A Human Rights-Based Analysis of the Eurovision Song Contest and the European Broadcasting Union

Adam Dubin

In the lead-up to the 2012 ESC in Baku, Azerbaijan, international news agencies and human rights non-governmental organisations (NGO), from the British Broadcasting Corporation (BBC) to Human Rights Watch, rang with headlines about human rights abuses in the country. Amnesty International proclaimed in the days prior to the contest "Azerbaijan: Eurovision is Deaf to Human Rights Abuses" (Amnesty International, 2021), and the BBC noted that "Eurovision Puts Spotlight on Azerbaijan Human Rights" (BBC, 2021). It should be no surprise that the ESC, like other mega-events, is linked in some way to human rights issues. Mega-events have historically been intertwined with human rights abuses, though not necessarily always in the form of grave violations. These abuses are usually the result of government policies in preparation for the mega-event, such as when New Delhi evicted people from informal settlements to make way for the Jawaharlal Nehru Stadium, where the 2010 Commonwealth Games were held. Or when the Spanish Government, under General Franco, refused to allow Joan Manuel Serrat from performing in Catalan, leading him to withdraw from the 1968 ESC, arguably a violation of cultural rights under the International Covenant on Economic, Social and Cultural Rights (1966). In other instances, human rights activists use the attention surrounding the ESC and other mega-events to highlight the host country´s alleged human rights record, as was the case during the 2019 ESC in Israel, when activists called for the contest to be held elsewhere because of Israel´s human rights record towards Palestinians.

The chapters in this book so far have highlighted a broad swath of the ESC´s intersection with different academic disciplines, from mythology to stage scenery to business. Antonio Obregón´s chapter provides a broad panorama that sets the stage for how the ESC has seeped into many different academic disciplines, both in terms of scholarship and pedagogy. However, seldom does the academic literature on the ESC engage with law and the legal implications surrounding the ESC. Human rights are often discussed within the context of the ESC by news organisations, blogs and NGOs, and by academics in non-Law disciplines discussing the contest´s intersectionality with, for example, sexual orientation and gender identity. While grave human rights violations related to the ESC do not

DOI: 10.4324/9781003188933-4

occur as commonly as with other mega-events, such as the World Cup or the Olympics, what happened in Azerbaijan shed light on a certain reality: that the ESC now joins a list of mega-events associated with serious violations of human rights. The reoccurrence of such violations is possible in states where the rule of law and democracy are limited, which include a number of European Broadcasting Union (EBU) countries, particularly in the east of Europe. Furthermore, the EBU, which hosts the ESC, ostensibly stands as a beacon for freedom of expression and press and, as such, is in an inherently strong position to speak out against violations of human rights committed by host states.

No scholar has written extensively from a human rights point of view of the value of the ESC, both as a scholarly question and also as a pedagogical tool. This chapter "Dare[s] to Dream", to draw on Eurovision terminology, by describing how studying human rights violations in relation to the EBU and ESC are useful in law school. It argues that such a study contributes to an analysis of the formal and informal human rights accountability mechanisms for violations occurring in the context of mega-events. The chapter is divided into three parts. The first analyses the response by international human rights mechanisms to state evictions by Azerbaijan in preparation for the ESC. From this analysis, certain conclusions can be extrapolated that confirm the challenges faced by these international mechanisms towards the protection of human rights. The second part explores how the EBU and ESC can be leveraged to achieve a more impactful approach to preventing human rights violations. The chapter ends by offering a conclusion about the importance of human rights scholars in expanding research to focus more on less conventional methods of achieving human rights protection, such as through popular culture.

A Human Rights Response to State Violations Linked to the ESC: Urban Transformation and Forced Evictions in Azerbaijan

There is no singular definition of what constitutes a mega-event, but Martin Miller (Müller, 2015: 634) defines it as "an ambulatory event of a fixed duration that attracts a large number of visitors, has a large mediated reach, is accompanied by large costs, and has large impacts on the environment or population". The ESC is a smaller-sised mega-event, with other mega-events of a larger magnitude being the Olympic Games, Superbowl, World Cup and World Expo. Mega-events often have a transformative impact on urban landscapes through infrastructure upgrades, new auditoriums and entertainment zones, parks, hotels and transport lines. Copenhagen, for instance, invested in the redevelopment of the B&W Hallerne, an industrial shipyard turned into "Eurovision Island", now an entertainment complex for public use. The cost of the ESC to host cities runs well upwards of millions of dollars: 29 million euros in Tel Aviv and 20 million euros in Lisbon, for example (ESCXtra 2018), often leading to cost overruns and putting smaller cities in complicated financial positions. (This was comically highlighted in the movie *Eurovision Song Contest: The Story of Fire Saga*, in which

Iceland's finance minister is adamant against not hosting the ESC, going so far as to kill contestants to avoid any possibility of winning.) The impact of preparations for mega-events often leads to human rights abuses when the government acts outside of the rule of law. This is often true in lower income countries, where corruption and a lack of democracy, transparency and accountability create a perfect storm for human rights violations during mega-events. Matheson and Baade (2004: 13) point out that "the experience of developing nations hosting a mega-event may differ widely from that of a developed nation". The former United Nations (UN) Special Rapporteur for Adequate Housing, Raquel Rolnick, in a report to the United Nations Special Rapporteur for Adequate Housing (2009:6), argues that while these events have historically served as a catalyst for development, at the same time they bring about "economic, social and demographic changes that have long term negative consequences", often resulting in human rights abuses.

A case in point was the 2012 ESC in Baku, in which the city council accelerated the rate of evictions from the center of Baku to clear space for the building of the Baku Crystal Hall in which the ESC would be staged, as well as for surrounding redevelopment plans. Reports showed that hundreds of people were forcibly evicted from their homes. Residents' homes were destroyed, along with their belongings, and evictees were not given due process to contest the evictions and demolition in a court of law. A report by Human Rights Watch noted that:

> the authorities have forcibly evicted remaining residents with little or no notice and then immediately demolished their houses or apartment buildings. Large numbers of police and other government officials surrounded the buildings and filled the stairwells in some instances, then forcibly entered apartments and removed residents. In at least three cases police detained residents in police stations while workers demolished the buildings. The homeowners returned to find their possessions buried in a pile of rubble.

The Azerbaijani government, however, insisted that such evictions were lawful, while it silenced journalists who were reporting on these and other human rights abuses committed by the state. Not stopping there, the Azerbaijani government used the ESC as an opportunity to showcase its image as a modern, advanced country, open for tourism and investment. Although this is a common appropriation of mega-events, it was nevertheless an afront to human rights activists and victims. Wolfe et al notes that "[o]ne of the key aspects of this process is the production and distribution of a sanitized image of the host city, manufactured for consumption by a global tourist and broadcast audience". The EBU, for its part, sought to distance itself from the human rights abuses, noting that the ESC is an apolitical event and essentially washing it hands of what it seemed to consider a domestic political matter. Unfortunately, the EBU missed an opportunity to directly speak out and admonish the host country, and potentially pursue some other remedy that would have set an important example that human rights cannot take a backseat to mega-events. Nevertheless, the EBU did engage the Azerbaijani government in a soft power approach through a joint conference on freedom of expression and media freedom, held in Baku days before the ESC. The conference included members of the Council of Europe, NGOs and members of the Azerbaijani government to discuss the balancing of economic and political interests in relation to the protection of human rights, namely freedom of expression and the media. However, the issue of the forced evictions was not a topic of the conference despite the grave nature of the violations. EBU Director General Deltenre (2012) stated that "the discussions took place in a very constructive and open atmosphere of mutual respect. All participants agreed that free and independent media, together with technological infrastructures and legislative frameworks that allow unrestricted, uncensored distribution of media content, are cornerstones of any democracy". Arguably, the conference was little more than window dressing in response to accusations that the EBU was failing to respond to grave violations of human rights. After 2012, Azerbaijan has still been one of the worst countries in the world for media and journalist freedom, with Reports without Borders and other NGOS continuing to document cases of intimidation and jailing of journalists.

The violations of the Right to Adequate Housing under the International Covenant on Economic, Social and Cultural Rights presents an interesting case study on the response by the international community to human rights abuses perpetrated in the name of urban redevelopment. The issue of forced evictions has become a common point of discussion by human rights advocates. However, what makes this situation particularly interesting from pedagogical and academic points of view is analysing the response by international and regional governments and human rights bodies to violations related to mega-events and, ultimately, the inconsequential outcomes of these responses. One of the first responses of a serious character came in 2012, when the European Parliament took up the issue of illegal evictions committed during the lead up to the ESC in Baku. The EP passed a resolution just days before the event, stating that "the 2012 Eurovision Song Contest taking place on 26 May in Baku should be an opportunity for Azerbaijan to show its commitment to democracy and human rights" and calling on it to end violations "linked to the upcoming Eurovision Song Contest" (European Parliament Resolution 2012). It calls out the Right to Adequate Housing violation, stating that:

> hundreds of properties have been expropriated in a non-transparent and nonaccountable way and thousands of homeowners in Baku forcibly evicted in the name of development projects, including in the neighbourhood adjacent to the National Flag Square, which is the location of the Baku Crystal Palace, the venue hosting the 2012 Eurovision Song Contest among other future events
>
> (European Parliament Resolution 2012).

Not surprisingly, these words fell on deaf ears and Azerbaijan offered no response to the European Parliament or its resolution. The issue emerged soon again, however, in the year after the 2012 ESC, but this time in UN human rights treaty monitoring bodies, which confronted the Azerbaijani government on what appeared to be well-documented violations of human rights. In the formal *List of Issues* submitted to the Azerbaijani government in preparation for its Treaty Monitoring Review by the UN Committee on Economic, Social and Cultural Rights, the Committee specifically made reference to the preparations for the ESC, asking the Azerbaijani government to respond to the following question:

> Please indicate, in the context of the general housing situation in the State party, the number of persons and families evicted within the last five years, and in particular, in relation to the renovation of Baku and the construction of the Eurovision venue. Please also provide information on the legal provisions regulating these evictions as well as on the measures taken to ensure that evictions are carried out with due process safeguards and that effective remedies are available to those affected. (2013:3)

The Azerbaijani government, in its response to the committee's questions, made no direct refence to the ESC, but various NGOs, in the civil society reports they contributed to the monitoring process, explicitly call out the government for "compulsory resettlements with the purpose of expanding Flag Square to accommodate the venue for the Eurovision Song Contest (Human Rights Council, 2013: 3)". The evidence provided by NGOs led the Committee, composed of independent human rights experts, to conclude that in fact there were such violations, and it imposed soft law liability on Azerbaijan by calling on it to "provide effective legal remedies, adequate compensation and guarantees of adequate alternative housing" and to ensure that any relocation of homes necessary for city renewal is carried out with prior consultation amongst affected households" (United Nations Committee on Economic, Social and Cultural Rights, 2013:6).

These allegations resurfaced again during the UN Human Rights Council's Universal Periodic Review (UPR) of Azerbaijan in 2013. Multiple civil society reports cited human rights violations by the Azerbaijani authorities in the run-up to the ESC, but no report specifically mentioned housing violations and illegal evictions. Instead, the stakeholder reports focused primarily on civil and political rights, namely infringements on freedom of speech and press "before, during and after the Eurovision Song Contest" (Human Rights Council 2013: 8). What makes this UPR session interesting, and perhaps speaks to the often politicised and weak nature of the process, as discussed by Pilar Elizalde (2019) and many other human rights scholars, is that in the concluding observations no government openly mentions the ESC, a sensitive topic for the Azerbaijani government, despite the prominent references to the contest in civil society reports. In fact, no participating government in their anemic observations mentions forced evictions, nor do the observations call attention to issues involving housing, beyond calling on the Azerbaijani government to "ensure a non-discriminatory approach" to the issue (Human Rights Council 2013: 18).

A question for law students on this case is what other legal options victims have to hold the state accountable for these actions. Interestingly, and for reasons unbeknownst to this author, neither NGOs nor direct victims sought to use the European Court of Human Rights to seek interim measures or file a complaint against Azerbaijan. At the time the evictions started, individuals affected could have submitted a petition to the European Court of Human Rights under Article 39 on Interim Measures of the European Convention on Human Rights, in an attempt to prevent the evictions from moving forward. The EBU, as well, could have supported the complaint through a third-party intervention, which will be discussed further in the next section. The hypothetical petitioners from Azerbaijan could have relied on the unanimous judgement handed down just a month before the ESC took place, in the case of *Yordanova and others v. Bulgaria*, in which the Court found Bulgaria in violation of Article 8 Right to Private and Family life due to the forced eviction of vulnerable populations and the lack of procedural safeguards in place. The Court's decision had relevance for the victims of the forced evictions in Baku, even though the case itself did not concern a mega-event. On one hand, the European Court has recognised in its jurisprudence a wide of margin of appreciation for states pursuing urban renewal, but this judgement narrows the margin when "the right at stake is crucial to the individuals' effective enjoyment of intimate or key rights (2012: para 118(ii))". As such, this judgment could have been used to hold Azerbaijan accountable for the evictions that took place outside of the scope of international law and in violation of Article 8 of the European Convention on Human Rights. Adelaide Remiche notes that "[t]he ECtHR's case law on forced evictions in general, and in *Yordanova* in particular, reveals the central role that can be played by judges in the concrete and effective protection of rights, including rights having implications of [a] social or economic nature" (2012: 800).

Nevertheless, this case study on the response by international institutions to hold the Azerbaijani state accountable demonstrates to students the underlying challenges of state accountability within the broader international framework, and more so in the context of mega-events such as the ESC, which often have significant direct and indirect economic benefits for the host city and country. It ultimately confirms what former Columbia Law School professor Louis Henkin referred to as the "S-Word", sovereignty, and the ensuing limited effectiveness that often results when states operate in isolation from each other (Henkin 1999). He argues, however, that we need to understand sovereignty "not as a pretext for indifference, for isolationism, but for responsibility and opportunity to secure human values (1999:14)". To date, there is no evidence that the pressures that were exerted, whether by the European Parliament or the UN, led to any form of remedy for the victims of these human rights violations or the promulgation by the state of procedural safeguards or changes to prevent further violations of the Right to Adequate Housing. The failure of the EBU to respond more proactively to the human rights violations in Baku also raises the question of what options are open to the EBU, a non-government actor, for influencing human rights protection. To what extent can the transnational nature of broadcasting mitigate the tendency of states to cling to sovereignty in defense of non-interference by foreign actors, overcoming the belief, in the words of Poet Laureate Robert Frost, that "good fences make good neighbors" (1914)? The next section uses the example of public service media to explore possible policy approaches by the EBU as a soft power towards influencing human rights protection within the context of the ESC.

The EBU as a Soft Power Regional Mechanism: Leveraging Public Service Media (PSM) for Human Rights Protection

I PSM As a Human Right

The EBU plays an integral role in supporting PSM around Europe and extra-European EBU members, with PSM being protected under both international human rights instruments and the European Convention on Human Rights. In 2012, the Director General of the EBU (2012), recognised this role of the EBU in protecting human rights by saying that "well-functioning public service media can be decisive in the protection of human rights, particularly freedom of expression. The EBU is steadfastly committed to supporting its members in fostering an informed society where all voices are heard, and we will continue to pursue action to strengthen management structures and cultivate journalism". The ESC Grand Finale and the shows prior are broadcast on PSM through the EBU´s alliance of national PSM stations across Europe and through commercial broadcasters internationally in countries such as the United States and China. The EBU therefore plays an essential role in supporting the broadcast infrastructure in pursuance of permitting artistic participation and expression — protected human rights — and does so by ensuring that the processes for participation in the ESC are open, free and fair across EBU member countries. Without the EBU framework, the legitimacy of the ESC would potentially be threatened.

The EBU can be understood as acting as a soft power complement to international institutions towards the protection of freedom of expression and media across EBU member states. In fact, the EBU has historically had a fairly close relationship with the Council of Europe (Vuletic, 2018), which has played an important role post-World War II in advancing human rights amongst member states. The role of the EBU in advancing PSM through a soft power approach provides a useful case study in law school for thinking about ways in which the EBU (or other non-state actors) could more affirmatively influence the protection of human rights during mega-events such as the ESC, to leverage more meaningful change. According to the Council of Europe, PSM provides "unbiased information and diverse political opinions". PSM is an essential component of government accountability and fosters ideological pluralism and the free exchange of ideas. In addition, as mentioned above, it is part of fulfilling the Right to Receive and Impart information under the International Covenant on Civil and Political Rights (Article 19), which in itself is intersectional with other rights, especially those involving women and children, refugees, and people with disabilities. Recognising its importance, some national constitutions in Europe, such as in Greece, have codified the constitutional right to an independent PSM. It would, however, be naïve to call PSM in any country, including Greece, fully independent and insulated from interference, since governments often maintain some form of control, for example, through the directors appointed to manage the PSM or through budgetary approvals. In fact, as will be discussed later, in 2013 the government of Greece closed down the PSM broadcaster due to supposed financial difficulties and despite opposition from the EBU.

Alternatively, there are countries whose PSM (and media generally) can be classified as most obviously not independent. In some countries, such as Bulgaria, Moldova, Russia and Ukraine, there have been attacks on journalists, budget cuts and substantial political influence on PSM programming and free and fair debate. In some instances, these have led to judicial proceedings against the state at the European Court of Human Rights or through communications to UN human rights treaty bodies. Many of these countries, too, have had scandals related to the ESC involving corruption and political interference, perhaps itself a sign of a larger problem concerning not free and fair PSM (Vuletic, 2018). The Council of Europe notes that

> ensuring media independence remains one of the main challenges to freedom of expression in Europe. Licensing restrictions, arbitrary interference in the work of media professionals and different forms of censorship and self-censorship are examples of how the independence of the media, whether public or privately owned, is restricted and how undue influence is exerted on their editorial freedom"
>
> (Report of the Secretary General of the Council of Europe RSGCE, 2017: 46).

States have an obligation under international law to not interfere with media, including PSM. The U.N. General Comment to Article 19 of the International Covenant on Civil and Political Rights obligates states "to prevent such control of the media as would interfere with the right of everyone to freedom of expression" (1983). The EBU has also sought to help states put international law into practice and advance a free and fair public service media through its co-organisation of the 2016 Prague Conference on Public Service Media and Democracy, in which best practices were exchanged towards fostering and protecting independent PSM.

However, despite laws and regulations protecting PSM and journalism from state interference, many people living in EBU member countries do not hold favorable opinions of PSM in their home countries and suspect the media to not be independent, free or fair. This includes states such as France and Spain, which generally register quite high on democracy indexes, most of which consider journalistic independence and media freedom in their equations. A 2016 report by the European Commission titled *Media Pluralism and Democracy* found that 60 per cent of Europeans believe that the PSM in their countries are not free from political pressure, and 28 per cent believe that media is less free than five years ago (2016). Often, however, these perceptions are not correct, like in Spain and France, where media is generally ranked by objective sources such as the World Press Freedom Index as free and independent. Yet, these negative public perceptions have problematic implications for the perceived legitimacy of public broadcasting and its ability to create an informed citizenry based on a free and pluralistic exchange of ideas. It also limits PSM's effectiveness to hold governments and political parties accountable when they fail to act in accordance with international and regional human rights standards. To some extent, though not surprisingly, the growth of populism across Europe has likely cast doubt on the credibility of PSM. Populist parties have worked to discredit news sources and media that oppose populist agenda as "the enemy of the people" and "illegitimate".

Although anecdotal, a possible predictive indicator of a country's PSM legitimacy is whether that country had a previous ESC corruption scandal. Two of the states that are represented in the EBU that come lowest on The Economist's Democracy Index, which considers civil liberties as factors, are Azerbaijan and Russia. Both countries have suffered multiple accusations of corruption during national selections for ESC entries. Just this year, in response to allegations of irregularities in voting in the national selection, one respected Russian journalist reflected (WiWI Bloggs 2021):

> In the middle of the night, the whole country unexpectedly came to know that a national final for Eurovision would start a few days after. Such a thing doesn't happen in any other country that takes part in the contest. '...' We don't have anything besides an advertisement, unexpectedly emerging from Channel One, that says that we are suddenly going to choose a participant for Eurovision. From whom we are going to choose, who these participants are, from where they appeared, how they were chosen ... everything is completely unknown.

Both Azerbaijan and Russia score extremely low on the democracy index, as well as on other indices focused specifically on world press freedom (World Press Freedom Index 2020). Although in need of further research, ESC scandals are potentially indicative of broader legitimacy problems with PSM in a country and a human rights situation involving infringements on civil and political rights, which are underlying components of free and fair media.

II *The EBU's Soft Power to Leverage Human Rights Protection*

Recognising the importance of access to PSM as a human right, what can the EBU do to protect it from state interference and what lessons can be extrapolated that might be useful for dealing with human rights abuses related to the ESC? It is important to mention that the EBU is not a supranational organisation, yet its statutes permit a certain level of intervention to attempt to influence human rights compliance. To understand the EBU's position relative to the international and regional organisations discussed in the previous section, this chapter categorises the EBU approaches to state intervention into soft, medium and hard approaches. Each of these involves a different level of interference by the EBU into state affairs and demonstrates the role of certain non-government organisations in influencing human rights compliance. Each of these approaches has policy lessons that can be extrapolated and applied in relation to human rights abuses occurring in the context of Eurovision.

The "soft" approach to promoting PSM has traditionally focused on capacity building through the development of good practices towards public service media by providing technical assistance, legal support and values' promotion towards a free and fair media in states, at the invitation of the state itself. The EBU has been active in the Western Balkan states, where it has launched the EBU Pilot Partnership to promote common principle adoption on funding and governance structures. It also provides capacity building in areas integral to supporting PSM within the current PSM structures, in order to "deliver urgent assistance they need to undertake an audacious reform agenda and adapt to a rapidly changing media environment (Jiandi, 2017)". Similarly, in the South Caucus states, the EBU has worked with the Organization for Security and Cooperation in Europe to organise conferences on media freedom, bringing together regional human rights organisations, academics and government officials to engage in dialogue on ways to support PSM without arbitrary government interference. Another example of a soft approach is the work of the EBU to promote programs amongst youth in order to encourage the dissemination of ideas, dialogue and discussion appealing to younger generations via PSM, in furtherance of, for example, the Right of the Child to be Heard, under Article 12 of the Convention on the Rights of the Child (CRC).

Linking this capacity building of the EBU to human rights abuses, a number of potential policy approaches could be applied to tne ESC. Under a 2011 Memorandum of Understanding signed between the Council of Europe and the EBU, both parties agree to engage in standard–setting activities (EoC – EBU 2011). The EBU should look to recent actions taken by the International Olympic Committee (IOC) as an example of actions that could be taken, in conjunction with the Council of Europe, in order to undertake more consequential efforts related to human rights protection. In 2019, the IOC adopted a strategy that provides a blueprint for meeting human rights responsibilities (Raad AL Hussein & Davis 2020). Importantly, it recognises that even where the IOC cannot directly control the behavior of external entities, it nevertheless can influence or leverage them through actions such as direct capacity building on human rights norms, quiet political pressure, sanctions written into agreements and memoranda of understanding with the host city on issues such as supply chain labor standards, gender equality and the protection of human rights locally.

Importantly, as of 2026, the IOC will integrate a human rights requirement into the host city contract based on the UN Guiding Principles on Business and Human Rights. The EBU, working through the memorandum of understanding signed with the Council of Europe, could adopt and advance a more human rights based approach in which it draws on these recent lessons learned from the IOC to prepare a comprehensive framework to human rights protection during the ESC (and PSM, generally).

A second category of EBU intervention in the protection of PSM can be referred to as the "medium" interventionist approach and is slightly more stick than carrot. This approach can be traced to 2014, when the EBU intervened through third party intervention status under Article 44(3) of the Rules of the European Court of Human Rights in a case titled *Kalfagiannis and Pospert v. Greece* (2020). The EBU submitted a third-party intervention pleading, which is similar to what other courts call an *amicus curiae*.

Importantly, this case and the intervention by the EBU seeking to protect Greek PSM came off the heals of a previous case at the European Court of Human Rights involving Moldova, *Hyde Park and Others v. Moldova*. In this instance, the Court heard the case on the merits and ruled against Moldova for violating Article 11 Freedom of Assembly and Association, finding that restrictions on protests, which were organised in response to a lack of transparency around the national selection for the ESC in Moldova, were "disproportionate and thus not necessary in a democratic society".

The *Kalfagiannins* case represents an important moment in terms of EBU intervention beyond the soft interventionist approach. The trade union representing employees of the Greek public broadcaster (ERT) alleged against Greece a violation of Article 10 of the European Convention on Human Rights for closing down ERT based on a ministerial order in the midst of a financial crisis. According to the Greek government´s arguments, "ERT was a burden on the State budget and that it was imperative to establish a new organisation which would serve the democratic, social and cultural needs of society, as well as the need to ensure pluralism in the media. All television, radio and Internet activities would immediately stop and all contracts would be terminated with immediate effect". The case was ultimately dismissed as being incompatible *ratione personae* for failure by the petitioners to be "directly affected" by the closure of the ERT — an arguably narrow interpretation of victim status under the Convention. However, even though the Court dismissed the case based on jurisdictional grounds, it nevertheless left open the possibility that further cases of a similar nature could be heard on the merits. In particular, it noted regarding the petitioner trade union that "…the impact of the closure of ERT on the second applicant might have raised issues under Article 11 of the Convention, an article that has never been pleaded by the second applicant, neither before the domestic court nor before this Court". Though a disappointing outcome, the fact that the case had been taken up by the Court and not dismissed outright on a jurisdictional basis likely meant that the Court was interested in examining it on the merits, even if it ultimately decided that the case was incompatible *ratione personae*. In an analysis commissioned by the EBU in support of this case, professors Berka and Tretter (2013) argue that "the closure of an existing public service broadcaster is a definite interference with freedom of expression". Although the analysis does not dispute that some level of interference into PSM by the state may be permitted during economic downturns, actions taken by the state must ultimately be proportionate to the aims pursued.

The precedent set by the EBU through its third-party intervention in this case demonstrates the organisation's willingness to intervene — to an extent — in more direct ways in human rights cases and opens the door to potential future litigation. The precedent set within the EBU by its intervention could be used to justify supporting subsequent litigation should cases arise involving human rights abuses during the ESC. The EBU could use third party intervention status — whether through amicus curiae in domestic courts (if available), through Article 44(3) status in the European Court of Human Rights or through the rule of procedures of the individual UN treaty bodies — to support victims of human rights abuses. Ultimately, an intervention of this nature would test the EBU's resolve at supporting human rights with more concrete action. As one rule of law specialist has noted, "it is high time for the EBU to go beyond the mantra of being non-political and explore how it can complement, rather than contradict, the effort to build a democratic Europe founded on respect for human rights (Williams, 2012)".

Nevertheless, despite the potential importance of the Greek case, in 2015 another case more directly involving the ESC was filed before the European Court of Human Rights and is currently pending. The case, *Lili Minasyin and Others vs. Armenia* (2015), also known as the "Conchita Wurst Case", deals with an alleged Right to Private and Family Life (Article 8) violation by Armenia. In 2014, representatives of ESC stated that they awarded the fewest points to the Austrian bearded drag queen Conchita Wurst because they were revolted by her sexual identity. Many of those in attendance challenged these comments openly as discriminatory, hateful and offensive to sexual minorities. In retaliation, Hayk Babukhanyan the editor of Iravnuk, an Armenia newspaper, who was also a sitting member of parliament, released an article that included a "blacklist" of Armenians involved with a supposed "gay lobby" which harassed the jury members who made those comments. The article included links to the so-called "gay lobbies'" Facebook pages. There were other disparaging articles and comments made against the LGBTQIA+ community by this newspaper editor, but the domestic courts dismissed the case on grounds for lack of meritorious claims made by the petitioner. The EBU does not seem to have commented publicly on this case. The fact that the EBU has maintained such distance from this case involving the intimidation of Armenian journalists and others who support LGBTQIA+ rights speaks to its desire to remain apolitical and distance itself from domestic human rights issues, unless PSM is directly threatened, like in the Greek case. Similar to when Azerbaijan committed grave violations through its forced evictions, the EBU seems to prefer an approach that largely avoids the issue or engages in a soft interventionist approach on broader themes of journalistic freedom, like it did at the joint conference in Baku. The EBU's non-intervention in this case is particularly ironic considering the large LGBTQIA+ fan base that follows the ESC. In fact, when an official from Turkish Radio and Television Corporation said publicly it would not broadcast acts like Conchita Wurst, the response by the EBU was anything but confrontational. It simply confirmed the EBU's values of inclusivity and diversity, and welcomed Turkey to one day participate in the ESC again, noting its "huge contribution" to the ESC.

The last and final form of intervention can be characterised as "high level" and is significantly more stick than carrot. This approach involves the sanctioning and suspension of EBU members. Similar to the powers held by the UN Security Council under the UN Charter, or the IOC under its By-Laws, the EBU has available to it under Article 5 of its Statutes (December 2020) a number of options to address infractions by members that fail to meet obligations under these regulations. Interestingly, the language of this statute draws on terminology typically associated with the human rights lexicon, such as "fulfillment" and "respect" to denote both the positive and negative obligations of members. The UN defines the obligation to fulfill as meaning that states "must take positive action to facilitate the enjoyment of basic human rights". "Respect" refers to the obligation of states to "refrain from interfering with or curtailing the enjoyment of human rights", generally understood as a negative action by the state. When members fail to fulfill or respect their obligations under the statutes, the EBU has a number of remedies available in order to either force compliance or penalise for failure to comply. Under Article 5 (2) of its statutes, EBU members failing to respect and fulfill obligations under the statutes' Sections 3.2, 3.3, 3.4, 3.5 and 3.6 may have their membership revoked by the Executive Council, subject to a ratifying decision by the EBU General Assembly. Section 5.6 permits the EBU to sanction or expel a member from the EBU, based on the seriousness of the infraction committed. The powers granted to the EBU under Article 5 have been used on multiple occasions to sanction members which are out of compliance with the EBU statutes. In some instances, this has led national public broadcasters from being prevented from accessing and participating in the EBU's services, including the broadcasting of popular programmes, such as the ESC and sporting ones. When this happens, headlines on national news and Eurovision blogs have splashed across screens with announcements such as "Romania Expelled from Eurovision 2016" — unwelcome news for a country's citizens, public broadcaster and government. The major reason why the EBU has suspended members has been related to outstanding debts. In 2016, Romanian public broadcaster (TVR) failed to make payments on EBU debt, which led the EBU to revoke membership and privileges. As a result, Romania was unable to participate in the 2016 ESC. Similarly, in 2017, Macedonia's (now North Macedonia) public broadcaster was threatened with sanctions by the EBU for its mounting debts. However, unlike Romania, Macedonia paid down these debts just prior to the release of the final list of participating countries in the ESC, on which Macedonia was included.

To date, the only suspension from the EBU related to human rights has been that of the Belarusian national broadcaster (BTRC) in 2021. It had initially been excluded from participating in the 2021 ESC due to the political nature of the two songs it submitted, both of which were rejected by the ESC's Reference Group. The first song submitted by Belarus titled "I'll Teach You" reads like a dictator talking to his populous, especially when understood in the backdrop of the ongoing protests. The lyrics of the song, sung by a pro-Lukashenko band, tell listeners to "look ahead, forget the past, put yesterday out to pasture, break your walls, make me trust you … I'll teach you to walk on a string. You will be happy and glad about everything … I will teach you toe the line". After rejecting this song, BTRC was given the opportunity to choose another song, which it did with "Song about a Bunny". This song, however, was also rejected on political grounds. In the context of the protests already taking place in the country over the sham election of its authoritarian president, Aleksandr Lukashenko, the EBU arguably sought to subtly contribute to these protests by blocking Belarus' participation. The EBU released a public statement that placed blame squarely on the government-run BTRC, noting that "[a]s BTRC have failed to submit an eligible entry within the extended deadline, regrettably, Belarus will not be participating in the 65th Eurovision Song Contest in May (Eurovision 2021)". In the weeks after this incident, the EBU went a step further and, under Article 5 of its statutes, voted to suspend BTRC altogether, for what it referred to as "exceptional developments" and a failure to "to uphold our core values of freedom of expression, independence and accountability". This suspension of BTRC was based on its incompliance under Article 5.6 for failing to meet membership obligations under Article 3.7.1 to "further the purposes of the EBU as set out in Article 1.2", which makes reference to states acting in accordance with the core values of public service, safeguarding freedom of expression and information and enhancing freedom and pluralism of the media (Articles 1.2.1, 1.2.2., 1.2.3). Similar to the EBU's third party intervention in the Greek case, this represents a potential turning point for the EBU in taking a more direct stance against governments that perpetrate human rights violations related to PSM. It remains to be seen whether the EBU is prepared to take such a direct approach against states not in the midst of political turmoil against a dictatorship, but it sets a precedent about its ability to take more decisive action than it had ever done so before.

A next step in strengthening the EBU's capacity to confront countries is through a modification of its statutes under Article 3.7 on Membership Obligations. Namely, the EBU should include a reference to member obligations to uphold human rights in accordance with recognised standards, not only through media, but also through actions linked in some form to the broadcast of an EBU event. Since countries themselves are not members of the EBU, language of this type in the statute could include the possibility of enacting sanctions and revoking membership when actions by the state towards promoting an EBU-broadcasted event in some way violate international or regional human rights. The statutes should also make reference to the UN Guiding Principles on

Business and Human Rights. Doing so would allow for an indirect form of pressure to hold states accountable. Analysing the response by the EBU in comparison to that in the previous section by the UN and European Parliament, the EBU arguably has the potential to impact human rights in a more direct way. This is not to say that the EBU or ESC are by any means the panacea for human rights compliance — Belarus still has a dictator in office and the opposition is still under attack. However, the options available through informal channels such as the EBU or by leveraging the ESC are more direct and impactful than those available to the Human Rights Council and the UN treaty bodies. On the other hand, by suspending states from participating in the ESC or blocking access to EBU broadcasts — adopting a more high interventionist approach — that may offer some promise towards galvanising change, especially if other non-state actors, such as the IOC, World Cup, and FIFA, also advance similar agendas of human rights protection, which appears to be the direction in which the IOC is headed.

Pop Culture as a Medium for Studying Human Rights

This analysis represents a case study that the author has conducted in class in which students were asked to analyse different forms of human rights liability and potential responses by the international community to violations related to mega-events. This, however, is just the starting point for discovering human rights through the ESC. The contest presents a broad swath of topics that law professors and students could work through to understand how informal instruments and channels, such as the EBU, can impact on human rights — both positively and negatively — and how policies can be advanced that prevent mega-events like the ESC from leading to human rights violations. It also raises prospects about potential synergies between international governmental organisations, such as the EU and UN, and non-governmental actors such as the EBU. This study also highlights the importance of conceptualising human rights outside of more traditional notions, in search of more effective and impactful policy responses to human rights issues. It represents a term that this author hesitates to use: a "think outside the box" moment in which students are challenged to put down their human rights textbooks and set aside the doctrinal knowledge acquired, and instead think creatively about how to hold states and non-state actors accountable for human rights violations through more unconventional means. Pop culture, music and cinema and the institutions behind them can and must play an important role in advancing a human rights agenda. From the increasing attention to gender equality in Bollywood films and music, to songs such as "Ghetto", by Ugandan musician-turned-politician, Bobi Wine, that demands respect for human rights, human rights studies should increasingly expose students to alternative ways of addressing complicated rights issues and developing advocacy programs that lie outside of traditional approaches.

Note

This chapter was finished and submitted before Russia was banned from participating in the 2022 Eurovision Song Contest due to its invasion of Ukraine.

Bibliography

Amnesty International, *Azerbaijan: Eurovision is deaf to human rights abuses*, accessed 8 July 2021, available at: https://www.amnesty.org/en/latest/news/2012/05/azerbaijan-eurovision-deaf-human-rights-abuses/

BBC, *Eurovision Puts Spotlight on Azerbaijan Human Rights*, accessed July 8th, 2021, available at: https://www.bbc.com/news/world-europe-17479011

Berka, W., & Tretter, H. (December 2013). *Public service media under Article 10 of the European Convention on Human Rights*, Study on European Broadcasting Union

Christou, C. *Details of the budget for Eurovision 2019 have been released*, ESCXTRA, accessed July 10th, 2021, available at: https://escxtra.com/2018/12/02/details-of-the-budget-for-eurovision-2019-have-been-released/

Committee on Economic, Social and Cultural Rights, General Comment No. 10: Freedom of expression (Art. 19): 29/06/1983.

Council of Europe, *Public Service Media*, accessed September 1, 2021, available at: https://www.coe.int/en/web/freedom-expression/public-service-media

Decision in *Hyde Park and Others v. Moldova*, no. 33482/06, ECHR, 31 March 2009.

Decision in *Kalfagiannis and Pospert v. Greece*, no 74435/14, ECHR, 9 July 2020.

EBU (2012). EBU and Council of Europe See Eye to Eye on Good Public Service Media Governance (16 February 2012), accessed August 18th, 2021, available at: https://www.ebu.ch/news/2012/02/ebu-and-council-of-europe-see-ey

EBU (2012). *EBU Conference: Pledge for Independent Media and Free Access to Media of Choice*, accessed on: August 8th, 2021, available at: https://www.ebu.ch/fr/news/2012/04/ebu-conference-pledge-for-indepe.

EBU (2014). *Public Service Broadcasters: Vital Role in Advancing Media Freedom in the South Caucus Region*, accessed on: July 28th 2021, available at: https://www.ebu.ch/news/2014/11/public-service-broadcasters-vita

EBU, *EBU Executive Board Agrees to Suspension of Belarus Member BTRC*, 28 May 2021, available at: https://www.ebu.ch/news/2021/05/ebu-executive-board-agrees-to-suspension-of-belarus-member-btrc

EBU, *Statement on Belarusian Participation*, 26 March 2021, available at: https://eurovision.tv/story/ebu-statement-on-belarusian-entry-2021

EBU, *Western Balkan Members Positively Assess EC-Funded Project*, 3 July 2020, accessed on: September 1st, 2021, available at: https://www.ebu.ch/news/2020/07/western-balkan-members-positively-assess-ec-funded-project

Elizalde, P. (2019) A horizontal pathway to impact? An assessment of the Universal Periodic Review at 10. In: A. Brysk & M. Stohl, (eds.), *Contesting Human Rights: Norms, Institutions and Practice. Elgar Studies in Human Rights* (pp. 83–106). Edward Elgar Publishing Ltd, Cheltenham, UK. ISBN 9781788972857

Erickson, A. *Mass evictions in Baku as Eurovision Nears*, Bloomberg, accessed on August 5th 2021, available at: https://www.bloomberg.com/news/articles/2012-02-29/mass-evictions-in-baku-as-eurovision-nears.

European Commission (2016). *Media Pluralism and Democracy* (Summary), Special Eurobarometer 452 – Wave EB86.1.

European Parliament, Azerbaijan European Parliament Resolution of 24 May 2012 on the human rights situation in Azerbaijan(2012/2654(RSP)). https://eur-lex.europa.eu/legal-content/EN/TXT/?uri=CELEX%3A52012IP0228

for Human Rights in accordance with paragraph 5 of the annex to Human Rights Council resolution 16/21, A/HRC/24/13.

Frost, R. (1917). Mending wall. In Amy Lowell (Ed.), *Tendencies in modern American poetry* (pp. 92–93). Macmillan.

Henkin, L. (1999). *That "S" Word: Sovereignty, and globalization, and human rights, et cetera,* 68 Fordham L. Rev. 1. https://crossworks.holycross.edu/econ_working_papers/102

Human Rights Club, *Submission for the 50th Session of the Committee on Economic, Social and Cultural Rights in relation to the Third Periodic Report of AZERBAI-JAN* (E/C.12/AZE/3).

Human Rights Council (2013). *Report of the Working Group on the Universal Periodic Review – Azerbaijan,* A/HRC/24/13.

Human Rights Council (2013). *Summary prepared by the Office of the High Commissioner*

Jiandi, S. (2 November 2017). *EBU secures EU funding to help broadcasters in the Balkans,* ESC Today, available at: http://esctoday.com/151811/ebu-secures-eu-funding-help-broadcasters-balkans/

Judgement on the Merits (2012). *Yordanova and Others v. Bulgaria,* no. 25446/06, ECHR.

Lili Minasyan and Others vs. Armenia, Application no. 59180/15, ECHR, 24 November 2015 (Pending).

Matheson, V., & Baade, R. (2004). Mega-Sporting events in developing nations: Playing the way to prosperity? *Economics Department Working Papers.* Paper 102.

Memorandum of Understanding Between the Council of Europe and the European Broadcasting Union, (2011), available at: https://www.ebu.ch/files/live/sites/ebu/files/News/2011/MoUEBU_CoE_tcm6–72236%255B1%255D.pdf

Müller, M. (2015). What makes an event a mega-event? Definitions and sizes. *Leisure Studies,* 34(6), 634.

Raád Al Hussein, Z., & Davis, R. (March 2020). *Recommendations for an IOC Human Rights Strategy,* International Olympic Committee.

Remiche, A. (2012). Yordanova and Others v. Bulgaria: The Influence of the social right to adequate housing on the interpretation of the civil right to respect for one's home (December 22, 2012). *Human Rights Law Review,* 12 (4), 787–800.

Report of the Secretary General of the Council of Europe (RSGCE) (2017). *State of Democracy, Human Rights and Rule of Law: Populism-How Strong are Europe's Checks and Balances?* 127th Session of the Committee of Ministers, Nicosia, 19 May 2017.

Reporters without Borders, (2021). World Press Freedom Index, accessed on September 10th, 2021, available at: https://rsf.org/en/ranking/2021.

Wolfe, S.D., Gogishvili, D., Chappelet, J.-L., & Müller, M. (2021). *The urban and economic impacts of mega-events: mechanisms of change in global games.* Sport in Society.

Wolfe, S.D., Gogishvili, D., Chappelet, J.-L., & Müller, M. United Nations Committee on Economic, Social and Cultural Rights (2013), *List of issues in connection with the consideration of the third periodic report of Azerbaijan con-cerning articles 1 to 15 of the International Covenant on Economic, Social and Cultural Rights (E/C.12/AZE/3).*

United Nations Committee on Economic, Social and Cultural Rights (2013), *Concluding observations on the third periodic report of Azerbaijan, adopted by the Committee at its fiftieth session* (29 April–17 May 2013).

United Nations Special Rapporteur for Adequate Housing, (18 December 2009). *Report of the Special Rapporteur on adequate housing as a component of the right to an adequate standard of living, and on the right to non-discrimination in this context*, Raquel Rolnik, UN Doc A/HRC/13/20.

Vuletic, D. (2018). *Postwar Europe and the Eurovision Song Contest*, Bloomsbury.

Williams, R. (March 19, 2012). *Eurovision in Baku: Should the European Broadcasting Union care about human rights?* TerraNullius Blog.

WiWi Bloggs (3 March 2021). *Russia: Eurovision 2021 national final criticised by entertainment professionals over secrecy*, accessed on: July 22nd 2021, available at: https://wiwibloggs.com/2021/03/03/russia-eurovision-2021-national-final-criticised-by-entertainment-professionals-over-secrecy/262779/

Part II

From Past to Present: History, Politics and Society

4   The Mythology of Song Contests

Ivan Raykoff

What does it mean to sing a song for a prize in a contest? This performance ritual is familiar to audiences today, considering the numerous televised singing competitions such as *Pop Idol* and *The Voice* and the ESC, the world's largest and longest-running international song contest. More than just a music competition and a popular form of entertainment, though, the song contest is an age-old ritual and a foundational mythic structure evident across various cultures and eras since Antiquity, whether in national institutions such as the Welsh *eisteddfod*, an annual competitive festival of poetry and song, or musical works based on historical traditions, such as Richard Wagner's famous operas *Tannhäuser* (1843), depicting the medieval *Sängerkrieg* (a contest of the *Minnesänger*), and *Die Meistersinger von Nürnberg* (1868). What are the stakes and struggles in song contests, what are the criteria by which singers and their skills are judged, and what broader perspectives do the mythic tales of Antiquity offer that could apply to a modern media event like the ESC?

Competition is intrinsic to social interactions and ritualized in cultural practices, whether the impulse might be expressed through the athletic prowess of sports games or the stylized aesthetics of a beauty pageant. We are familiar with the classical Greek concept of *agōn* (ἀγών) — meaning a conflict, struggle, or contest — as enacted in the competitive quadrennial ritual and festival of the Olympic Games (Wang, 2010). We might also recognize this concept in religious traditions that conceptualize a struggle within the soul to attain transcendence or salvation, as in the New Testament exhortation to "fight (*agōnízomai*) the good fight (*agṓn*) of the faith" (I Tim. 6:12). This concept of *agōn* is enacted in theater, where a drama or tragedy presents the *agōn*ies of a prot*agon*ist against an ant*agon*ist. It is also demonstrated in the musicking rivalries of singers competing in front of an audience for a prize awarded by judges.

In the ancient Greek perspective, the song contest offers a stage for performing more than beautiful melodies with exceptional musical skill; it also represents cultural, political and ethical principles that determine the relationships between mortals and the gods, between communities and among individuals. "The competitive aspect of musical performance," notes Andrew Barker, "was a well-established element of Greek practice from very ancient times" (1984, p. 22 n9). John Herington (1985) writes about the centrality of performance in the "song

DOI: 10.4324/9781003188933-6

culture" of ancient Greece from at least the eighth century BCE until the rise of "book culture" in the late fourth century, asserting that "poetry, recited or sung, was for the early Greeks the prime medium for the dissemination of political, moral, and social ideas," especially in the public religious festivals that included *agōnes mousikoi*, contests of poetic and musical performances (pp. 3–10). H. Alan Shapiro (1992) discusses of the place of music contests in the Panathenaic festivals over several centuries primarily based on evidence from surviving texts and inscriptions and the visual art of vase-painting, since "the music of the ancient Greeks is almost entirely lost to us and can never be recovered acoustically" (p. 53). Derek Attridge (2019) summarizes the broader aims of these ancient festivals and their musical contests: "at once celebrating the gods by the presentation of splendid examples of human creativity, reasserting the old values enshrined in noble deeds of the past, cementing panhellenic unity, and winning glory and economic gain for both the city-state sponsoring the event and for the successful competitors themselves" (p. 35).

Herington categorizes three genres of poetic performance in the ancient festivals: the art of rhapsody (an unaccompanied recitation, usually of epic verse), *kitharody* (solo singing to the accompaniment of the *kithara*, a string instrument akin to the lyre or harp) and accompanied choral singing. Rhapsodic verse had a declamatory or incantatory delivery balancing between speaking and singing. The *kithara* (from which we get the modern word "guitar") was associated with Apollo, whose epithet "Apollo Citharoedus" is represented by statues of the god holding this instrument and crowned with a laurel wreath. The *citharode* was a professional musician who accompanied his singing on this instrument, as in the case of Terpander, called "the father of Greek music," whose playing and singing won contests at the Pythian and Carnean festivals (Barker, 1984, pp. 209, 214; Power, 2010).

Andrea Rotstein (2012) discusses the details of musical contests in three major festivals from the fourth century BCE: the Great Panathenian festival at Athens, the Amphiaraia festival at Oropos and the festival to Artemis at Eretria. In addition to rhapsodic recitations and singing to accompaniment of the *kithara*, these contests also featured solo performances of the *kithara* and the *aulos* (a double-reed instrument akin to the shawm or oboe). These various genres were not equally privileged. "From the number of prizes awarded to specific categories and from the value of prizes a hierarchy can be inferred: singing scores higher than playing without singing, the *kithara* higher than the *aulos*, men higher than boys, and serious performances higher than comic ones," Rotstein writes. Furthermore, she notes "the rather disdainful attitude towards the world of professional entertainment found in ancient elite sources, an attitude that pervades to some extent ancient literary criticism as well. Perhaps such disdain can explain why the role of musical contests within the literary system has remained largely overlooked, even though they were one of the most ubiquitous ancient Greek institutions for public performance of poetry and song" (pp. 116, 93).

Who would have judged these ancient contests, and by what criteria? For the Athenian in Plato's *Laws*, hierarchies of social class determine how a singer's performance will be evaluated, considering "music should be judged by the criterion of pleasure, but not just anyone's pleasure". The best musician will be "the one who gives us the most delight and enjoyment," since "the best music is probably that which delights the best people," specifically those who are "outstanding in excellence and education". Music is best evaluated by the elites who understand the established rules and cultural traditions, and not by "the whistling or the uneducated shouts of the mob, as it is now, or clappings that signal applause". The competitions should inspire a vicarious pleasure for the established older men of moral character and wisdom who will adjudicate them: "For our nimbleness has now left us, and it is our nostalgic longing for it that makes us set up contests for those who can best arouse us, in our memory, into youthfulness". Recitations of the established classics seem to be preferred, because "old men would listen with most pleasure to a *rhapsōdos* giving a good performance of the *Iliad* or the *Odyssey*, or of one of Hesiod's works, and would say that he had won by a long way" (*Laws*, 657d–659c, 700c; Barker, 1984, pp. 145–147, 156).

In his *Politics*, Aristotle classifies melodies and musical modes (*harmoniai*) according to their uses and social effects: "the most moral ones" for educating and forming the character of the good man, and "the most invigorating and inspirational ones" for "harmless delight" and for "amusement for the sake of relaxation and relief from tension," uses especially applicable to "the contestants who perform the music of the theater". This latter type of music is more suitable for carefree leisure and entertainment, not for intellectual edification or for imparting deeper truths or values (Ford, 2004). Aristotle categorizes two types of spectators for the contests, "one a free and educated man, the other vulgar (this group consists of artisans and hired menials and others of that kind)," but he recognizes that these events should offer invigorating and inspiring music for the lower-class listeners as well. "Each man is given pleasure by what fits his nature, and this is why contestants should be given license to use this category of music when dealing with that sort of spectator" (*Politics*, 1342a; Barker, 1984, p. 180).

In his fifth Idyll, the Greek poet Theocritus (third century BCE) depicts a high-art poetic contest disguised as a rustic singing match, a bucolic *agōn*, between a boisterous and quarrelsome pair of herdsmen, the older goat-keeper Comatas and his former student and lover, the shepherd Lacon. The scene begins with an argument about whether Lacon had stolen the goat-skin of Comatas, or whether the latter stole Lacon's *syrinx* (an end-blown flute known as the Pan flute or pan pipes). They decide to have a singing battle to compare their skills of poetic persuasion, asking Morson, a nearby woodsman, to adjudicate their contest impartially. The two herdsmen engage in a rapid-fire capping of cleverly improvised stanzas, an ancient Greek version of a rap battle, with insults and innuendo about their former relationship as well as their current amorous interests and skills. The younger Lacon might seem a bit too self-assured, taunting Comatas to "match song for song, till you give in," and prompting his older partner to "come here and start your song — your last". After fourteen couplets, however, the judge Morson declares Comatas to be the winner, perhaps because Lacon answers an unexpectedly self-deprecating prompt from Comatas ("I gave her the ring-dove, but I didn't get kissed by the ears in return") with a self-congratulatory boast ("I gave him the pipe, and he gave me a marvelous kiss in return"), or perhaps because Lacon admits that his pipe had not actually been stolen by Comatas after all!

Kathryn Gutzwiller (1991) interprets the stakes of this singing match to be manhood and male honor, noting that "much of the dramatic tension of the poem arises from the need for each to distinguish a weak response, signaling shame or exhaustion, from a deception ploy, a pretense at nonaggression" (p. 138). This depiction of a contest of poetic wits and wiles conveys some of the entertainment appeal of the ancient artform, especially with the touches of clever banter and amusing innuendo to balance its literary and elite associations. On the other hand, many mythic tales about song contests between the mortals and the gods do not reveal a good-natured rivalry, but rather a disturbing streak of violent aggression. What are the power plays underlying these matches?

* * *

As the Greek god of *mousike* — the "arts of the Muses" encompassing music, poetry, songs and dance — Apollo plays a central but complicated role in the mythic musical contests of Antiquity. The Hymn to Apollo, the third of the anonymous Homeric Hymns, praises the island of Delos, where the Ionians "please you whenever they hold their festivals (*agōn*), remembering you with boxing, dancing, and singing" (Attridge, 2019, p. 36). The contest at the Pythian Games at the sanctuary of Apollo at Delphi, Pausanias writes, was "the oldest contest and the one for which they first offered prizes" for singing a hymn to the god. Apollo's own son Philammon won one contest, and then his son, Apollo's grandson, Thamyris, won another. Feeling boastful about his musical talents, as the story is told in *The Iliad*, Thamyris challenged the Muses themselves to a contest, but their punishment for his presumptuousness was to take away his ability to sing and to play the lyre (*Iliad*, 2.595). The punishment is more severe in other accounts. Since Thamyris had demanded that if he won the contest he would have intercourse with them all, the goddesses first silenced and then blinded the singer too. Apollo may well have caused this cruel fate, since he and Thamyris were rivals for the love of the beautiful youth Hyacinth (Woods, 1998, p. 17).

In another set of stories, Marsyas is a satyr who dares to challenge Apollo to a contest of musical skills judged by the Muses. Marsys plays the *aulos*, which the goddess Athena had cast aside because it distorted her beautiful face whenever she blew into it. Apollo plays the *kithara*, so he is able to sing along to his own accompaniment, demonstrating his mastery of song as the union of music and word. Raising the stakes even higher, Apollo even plays his instrument held upside down in a further display of musical virtuosity. Marsyas can imitate neither of these feats with his rudimentary pipe, so Apollo wins the contest and takes his infamously violent reward (or perhaps revenge) by hanging Marsyas upside down from a tree and stripping off all his skin (Ovid, *Metamorphoses*, 6.382–387). Debate continues over the meanings of this allegorical tale. Does it convey a lesson about the hierarchy of the gods over the mortals, or the perils of hubris, or the symbolic value of stringed instruments (representing the mind and cosmic music in their proportions) over wind instruments (representing the physical body), or civilization over nature, Apollonian over Dionysian impulses, "high art" over "low," or some other fraught dichotomy? (Maniates, 2000; Van Keer, 2004; Leppert, 2011)

Another classic tale of a singing match highlights both the technique of the performance and the reception and evaluation of the message of the songs by both audience and adjudicator. In a mythic contest between Homer and Hesiod from the seventh century BCE (Koning, 2010), Hesiod challenges Homer to "sing not to me of things that are, or that shall be, or that were of old; but think of another song". Homer completes Hesiod's prompts ("But for you your father and lady mother lay in love —" ... "When they begot you by the aid of golden Aphrodite") and answers his riddles ("What do men mean by happiness?" ... "Death after a life of least pain and greatest pleasure"), after which they recite the best lines of their own poems. Hesiod describes how the Pleiades stars guide the work of ploughing, planting and harvesting crops (*Works and Days*, 383–392); Homer describes the threatening array of sharp spears and gleaming shields in a battle of the Trojan wars (*Iliad* 13.126–133, 339–344). The audience applauds Homer and wants him to be crowned the winner, but the king chooses Hesiod instead, explaining that a poet "who called upon men to follow peace and husbandry should have the prize rather than one who dwelt on war and slaughter" (Hesiod, 565–597).

The nineteenth-century German philosopher and critic Friedrich Nietzsche offers one interpretation of this tale and similar agonistic myths in his un-published essay "Homer's Contest," written soon after his 1872 book *The Birth of Tragedy*. Reflecting on Hesiod's observations about the two sides of Eris, the Greek goddess of strife and rivalry, Nietzsche discusses how "evil" Eris inspires acts of cruelty, warfare and destruction, but "good" Eris motivates people to honorable achievement through creative and productive ambition and envy: "not to the action of fights of annihilation, but rather to the action of *contests*". This difference does not apply to "envy of the heavenly," as in the contests between hubristic mortals and gods — Thamyris *vs.* the Muses, or Marsyas *vs.* Apollo — which Nietzsche considers "the horrible opposition of two powers who must never fight with each other". Instead, the contests of the ancient agonistic fes-tivals present "a struggle between rivals worthy of each other," and they de-monstrate a quality of "contesting ambition" in how they harness the urge of competitive rivalry towards the pursuit of excellence and noble victory in the service of the civic and social good. For Nietzsche this is the foundation for education, ethics and the preservation of the state. As he explains, "the youth thought of the well-being of his native city when he sang or threw or ran in contests; he wished to increase the city's share of glory by increasing his own glory; to his city's gods he dedicated the wreaths that the judges placed upon his head in honor". Each contestant was motivated by ambition, but also by "the burning wish to be an instrument of the well-being of his city in the contest of the cities: with this his selfishness was enflamed, with this it was bridled and restrained" (pp. ii–iii, 3–7).

Christa Davis Acampora's reflections on Nietzsche's essay includes a relevant summary of the motivating principles behind the mythic contests of Antiquity. "Nietzsche was fascinated by the formal function of the ancient Greek *agon* and how it seemed to underwrite so many cultural institutions—education, politics, art, and even philosophy," she writes. The contest was not just an opportunity to display an individual's talent, but even more importantly it was an opportunity for the "creation of a community," whether the city or a nation-state. Nietzsche "had an interest in how *eris*, a powerful drive in competition, could also be re-lated to *eros* in the form of drawing together those who might otherwise have very diverse interests, values, and aspirations" (2013, p. 5–6). How does this notion of the agonistic contest as a unifying force for community, a catalyst for cooperation through competition, compare with the violence that marks some of these myths, as with the blinding of Thamyris or the flaying of Marsyas?

A century after Nietzsche, and drawing on Theodor W. Adorno and René Girard (Collins, 1985), the French theorist Jacques Attali discusses the dualism of music's productive/destructive power in his 1977 book *Noise: The Political Economy of Music*. Attali views music as a creative "channelization" of an un-controllable and destructive "noise" through ritual practices that serve to do-mesticate and sublimate its effects in order to maintain social and political order. Nietzsche views the ancient contests as agonistic rituals for encouraging but channeling ambition towards the greater good. Attali considers the musical concert, perhaps like the ancient contest, to be "a simulacrum of the sacrifice," another form of ritual for containing and directing the destructive capacity of noise towards more constructive ends. "Listening to music is listening to all noise, realizing that its appropriation and control is a reflection of power," Attali writes. "Music, the quintessential mass activity, like the crowd, is simultaneously a threat and a necessary source of legitimacy; trying to channel it is a risk that every system of power must run". In this light we can reinterpret the stories about the violent outcomes of contests between Apollo or the Muses with mortal musicians, what Attali calls the primal "magic-music-sacrifice-rite," to under-stand how the musician serves as "a channeler of violence" in these mythic rituals (pp. 6, 12, 14, 26).

In Attali's historical overview of noise and/or music as a "tool of power," the ancient era of "sacrifice" gives way to the era of "representation," a transition from music's use as a form of "ritual power, when it is a question of making people forget the fear of violence," to music as an enactment of "representative power, when it is a question of making them believe in order and harmony". In the era of representation, starting in the early eighteenth century, music becomes a form of spectacle and a "simulacrum" of order through the the conventions of tonal harmony and the formal structures of Baroque and Classical music. Indeed, Attali asserts, the works of Johann Sebastian Bach and Wolfgang Amadeus Mozart "reflect the bourgeoisie's dream of harmony better than and prior to the whole of nineteenth-century political theory". The social and political usefulness of this music is its capacity "to replace the lost ritualization of the channelization of violence with the spectacle of the absence of violence, ... to stamp upon the spectators the faith that there is a harmony in order". If Nietzsche values the potential for the creation of community through the rituals of "contesting ambition," Attali seems warier of an "ultimate social cohesion" achieved through music as a sublimation of an underlying originating violence (pp. 5–6, 19, 46).

* * *

To apply Attali's notion of the representation of the sacrificial ritual, consider an eighteenth-century musical representation of another mythic contest, the duel between Apollo (Phoebus) and Pan, the god of nature and shepherds, which re-imagines the violent punishment of flaying with a more humorous conclusion. As related in Ovid's *Metamorphoses*, Pan, playing the *syrinx*, foolishly boasts to the nymphs that his music is better than Apollo's playing on the lyre, offering to challenge Apollo to a contest of musical skill. The mountain god Tmolus adjudicates the duel, but King Midas, Pan's friend, is also present to offer his opinion. Pan's "uncouth" rustic melody on the pipes pleases Midas, but Apollo's "artful touch" on the lyre creates a "charming melody," so Tmolus awards the prize to the god. When the foolish Midas protests this decision, preferring the rough piping over the sweet strings and song, Tmolus rewarded his stupidity by changing his ears into those of an ass (11.146).

Johann Sebastian Bach's secular cantata *Geschwinde, ihr wirbelnden Winde* (Hurry, you Whirling Winds) BWV 201, written around 1729, is a musical setting of Ovid's story about the contest between Phoebus and Pan that resulted in Midas' donkey ears. The libretto by Picander (Christian Friedrich Henrici) includes the four characters plus Mercurius, the god of commerce, and Momus, the god of ridicule and sarcasm. This cantata features six *da capo* arias preceded by recitatives, one for each character, and the cantata opens and closes with a chorus sung by all six characters together. Slow and lyrically expressive arias sung by Phoebus, Tmolus and Mercurius alternate with livelier and more light-hearted arias for Momus, Pan and Midas. The juxtaposition of these two broad categories suggests an underlying distinction between music of refinement and sophistication compared to songs of more mundane inspirations and general popular appeal.

The conflict in this "drama with music" is introduced with a boastful argument between Phoebus and Pan about whose singing is more beautiful and appealing, especially in relation to their intended audiences. Pan declares that the entire forest admires his music: the nymphs dance to his piping, and even the birds want to learn how to sing from him. Phoebus counters that Pan's flute is far too lowly for the gods to appreciate. Momus concludes this first recitative by mocking Pan as "the great master singer" (*Meistersänger*), then sings about how Pan's braggadocio is just a lot of hot air ("*das macht der Wind*"). In the next recitative, Mercurius interrupts this quarrel to suggest that each singer should select someone to adjudicate their songs in a proper contest. Pan chooses his friend Midas, and Pheobus chooses Tmolus.

Phoebus begins with an aria in B minor, marked *largo*, describing his intense longing for his beautiful young lover Hyacinth and the pleasure he feels in stroking Hyacinth's soft cheek or kissing his eyes. The opening words "*Mit Verlangen*" (with longing) are sung to the expressively rising interval of a minor sixth, and then a minor seventh, to convey this sense of yearning. Bach also engages in some musical word-play with the middle syllable of *Verlangen* ("*lang*" is "long" in German) when he sets it to long melismas — five measures long twice, and then six measures.

In the middle section of the aria too, the long sustained melismas on the final "*der Seele Sonne*" (the sun of my soul) has *Seele* stretched out across four measures, and *Sonne* over ten measures! The upward reach and extended length of notes in the melodic line of this aria are compositional devices to represent the sentiment of heartfelt longing in musical terms, an embodiment of these physical and emotional feelings that sets a high bar for the artistry of the next contestant.

Pan takes his turn with his playful aria in the key of A major and a prancing triple meter marked *Allegretto scherzando*, like a musical joke. Bach does not score this aria with any winds, as one might expect for the god associated with the flute or pan pipes. However, the fun-loving nature of that faun-like character is evident in the first part of this aria, which consists of one repeated sentence about dancing and leaping around: "*Zu Tanze, zu Sprunge, so wackelt das Herz*". The word *Herz* translates as "heart," but the verb *wackeln* is usually associated with the hips or the buttocks, as in "to wiggle" or to shake your booty. Bach has some fun with the first syllable of this word, repeating it on the same note over two measures ("wack-ack-ack") like the quacks of a waddling duck. Bach later used this same music, but with different lyrics, as the aria "*Dein Wachstum sei feste und lache vor Lust!*" (Let your growth be strong and laugh with joy!) in his "Peasant Cantata," BWV 212, where the word *lache* is sung on those repeated notes like laughter, another touch of humorous word-painting.

If the first part of Pan's aria celebrates the physical delights of the dance in the accessible *galant* style, the second part is about the detriments of music that is too serious for its own good, parodying the more "learned" compositional styles with some awkward harmonic complexities (Aspden, 2010, p. 20). Pan laments "*Wenn der Ton zu mühsam klingt*" (When the music sounds too labored) as the strings play high chromatic sighs, poking fun at the heightened expressivity of Phoebus' song — "*so erweckt es keinen Scherz*" (thus it arouses no fun). The resolution for this heaviness is a return to the first part of Pan's aria and its preference for light music, dancing and pleasurable feeling. As Julian Mincham interprets this aesthetic distinction, Pan's aria prioritizes the joys of "rustic and countrified, pleasant, but undemanding" music (like a simple dance song) over the seriousness and sentimentality of the second part of the aria (like a heartfelt ballad), in which "the chromatic wailings of the violin obligato lines are exaggerated almost to the point of becoming mock heroic" (Mincham, 2010).

After the two contestants have performed their songs, it is time for the two judges to offer their decisions. Pan may have charmed the nymphs of the forest, Tmolus proclaims, but Phoebus takes the prize for his most beautiful song, since those who understand the way music works will admire Phoebus' song. Midas counters this argument with his preference for Pan's song because it is more accessible and enjoyable — indeed Midas was able to learn it easily and immediately — while Phoebus' song is just "too colorful" (*gar zu bunt*). Bach offers a musical commentary on Midas' humiliation by writing donkey-like braying into the accompaniment when Midas sings "*Denn nach meinen beiden Ohren singt er unvergleichlich schön*" (since according to both my ears he sings incomparably well). These "hee-haws" are downward leaps of an octave and tritone (E to A#) played each time Midas mentions his ears. In giving him the donkey's ears, Phoebus teases Midas by reminding him of the terrible punishment he once meted out on poor Marsyas: "*Soll ich dich schinden oder schaben?*" (Should I flail or even flay you?).

With the closing aria by Mercurius we hear the moral of the story, though Bach sets it in somewhat ironic musical terms. Whoever has "*Aufgeblasne Hitze, aber wenig Grütze*" (literally: puffed-up heat, but not enough grits) will be judged the fool, but this aria is accompanied by two puffing flutes, a musical representation of the argumentative "hot air" Momus complained about at the beginning of the cantata. Momus gets the final word in the last recitative, telling Midas to go back to the forest where he belongs, and to take some comfort in the realization that so many people confuse ignorance and irrationality with wisdom. The closing chorus, "*Labt das Herz, ihr holden Saiten*" (Refresh our hearts, lovely strings) confirms Apollo's victory in this competition of musical aesthetics and cultural values.

* * *

The ESC, founded in the mid-twentieth century and still going strong today, would seem to be relatively distant in its inspirations and motivations from the mythic song contests of Antiquity. However, some common themes arise when we consider it as a modern-day manifestation of the agonistic ritual of a competitive musical performance for a prize of honor and achievement. This song contest pits singers representing nation-states (or more specifically, national broadcasting agencies) against each other in a ritual of creative rivalry reflecting shared cultural values. The quality of "contesting ambition" is evident in the contest, but there is never a sense that one singer is competing directly against another singer; instead there is a feeling of communal cooperation even if, by the end of the voting tally, there is often a very tense moment when the top finalists await the announcement of the winning total of points.

The ancient festival contests enacted political, cultural, economic, ethical and aesthetic agendas. The stated ideals of the twenty-first century ESC reflect many of these same agendas, from the political and economic benefits of participation to the cultural and ethical values the song contest strives to represent through its established rules and rituals. The founding of the Eurovision television network in 1954 was commemorated by an address from Pope Pius XII that extolled the sense of community, peaceful cooperation, international understanding and aesthetic edification this new medium of television could promote. The ESC, established two years later in 1956, intended to demonstrate a kind of competition rooted in cosmopolitanism (Raykoff, 2021, pp. 6–8). The mission statement for the 2015 ESC hosted in Vienna, Austria, published by the Austrian national broadcaster ORF (Österreichischer Rundfunk), articulates some of these same ideals. The country would strive to be "a charming, liberal, and generous host for all participants" offering "a cosmopolitan party of tolerance, acceptance and variety," and the contest itself would showcase "artistic quality and originality" through a competition "characterized by respect, fairness and transparency" (Böhm, 2015, p. 52).

Age-old debates over the appropriate weight of elite professional evaluation compared to more general popular appeal surfaces in the modern ESC as well, where "expert" national juries comprised of music industry leaders, critics and former contestants ranked the songs before the implementation of public televoting in 1998 (Haan et al, 2005); since 2009 there is now a 50/50 balance between the jury vote and public vote to determine the winners. Rotstein's observations about a tendency towards elitist critical disdain of the ancient festival singing contests could still apply to the ESC today, which has been a popular media event for over six decades but has only become a widely accepted topic and field of critical and scholarly attention since the early 2000s.

In the ESC there is no place for the violence that befell Marsyas when he lost to Apollo, of course. Yet there is still the appeal of the tensions between heroism and hubris, or glory and shame, when we witness the downfall of those who imagined they would win, or the elation of the longshot who eventually and unexpectedly takes the prize. The aesthetic channelization of agonistic rivalry in pursuit of a shared sense of community still applies today to the gatherings of the ESC, an annual musicking ritual, festival and celebration that may well have ancient origins.

Bibliography

Acampora, C.D. (2013). *Contesting Nietzsche*. University of Chicago Press.

Aspden, S. (2010). Bach and the feminised galant. *Understanding Bach*, 5. https://www.bachnetwork.org/ub5/aspden.pdf

Attali, J. (1977). *Noise: The political economy of music*, trans. B. Massumi (1985). University of Minnesota Press.

Attridge, D. (2019). *The experience of poetry: From Homer's listeners to Shakespeare's readers*. Oxford University Press.

Barker, A. ed. (1984). *Greek musical writings, Vol. I: The Musician and his art*. Cambridge University Press.

Böhm, E. (2015). Mission statement ESC 2015. *Texte 14: Public Service Media in Europe* (p. 52). http://zukunft.orf.at/rte/upload/download/15i0002.pdf

Collins, D. (1985). Ritual sacrifice and the political economy of music. *Perspectives of New Music*, 24/1, 14–23.

Ford, A. (2004). Catharsis: The power of music in Aristotle's *Politics*. In P. Murray & P. Wilson (Eds.), *Music and the Muses: The culture of Mousike in the classical Athenian city* (pp. 309–336). Oxford University Press.

Gutzwiller, K.J. (1991). *Theocritus' pastoral analogies: The formation of a genre.* University of Wisconsin Press.

Haan, M.A., Dijkstra, S.G., & Dijkstra, P.T. (2005). Expert judgment versus public opinion — Evidence from the Eurovision Song Contest. *Journal of Cultural Economics, 29/1,* 59–78.

Herington, J. (1985). *Poetry into drama: Early tragedy and the Greek Poetic tradition.* University of California Press.

Hesiod. (1914). On the origin of Homer and Hesiod, and of their contest. In *Hesiod, the Homeric Hymns and Homerica,* trans. H. G. Evelyn-White. Putnam.

Homer. (2011). *The Iliad,* trans. A. Verity. Oxford University Press.

Koning, H. (2010). *Hesiod: the other poet — ancient reception of a cultural icon.* Brill.

Leppert, R. (2011). Music, violence, and the stakes of listening. In J.F. Fulcher (Ed.), *The Oxford Handbook of the new cultural history of music* (pp. 39–67). Oxford University Press.

Maniates, M.R. (2000). Marsyas Agonistes. *Current Musicology, 69,* 118–162.

Mincham, J. (2010). Chapter 103: BWV 201 "Geschwinde, ihr wirbelnden Winde." http://www.jsbachcantatas.com/documents/chapter-103-bwv-201/

Nietzsche, F. (1996). Homer's contest, trans. C.D. Acampora, *Nietzscheana, 5.*

Ovid. (1922). *The metamorphoses,* trans. B. More, Cornhill Publishing.

Power, T. (2010). *The culture of Kitharôidia.* Center for Hellenic Studies.

Rotstein, A. (2012). *Mousikoi Agones* and the conceptualization of genre in ancient Greece. *Classical Antiquity, 31/1,* 92–127.

Shapiro, H.A. (1992). *Mousikoi Agones:* Music and poetry at the panathenaia. In J. Neils (Ed.), *Goddess and Polis: The Panathenaic festival in ancient Athens* (pp. 53–75). Princeton University Press.

Theocritus. (2002). *Idylls,* trans. A. Verity. Oxford University Press.

Van Keer, E. (2004). The myth of Marsyas in Ancient Greek Art: Musical and mythological iconography. *Music in Art, 29/1-2,* 20–37.

Wang, D. (2010). On the ancient Greek αγων. *Procedia Social and Behavioral Sciences, 2,* 6805–6812.

Woods, G. (1998). *A history of gay literature: The male tradition.* Yale University Press.

5 Teaching European History and Memory through the Eurovision Song Contest during the COVID-19 Pandemic

Alison Lewis and John Hajek

Introduction

The annual Eurovision Song Contest (ESC), which was founded a little over a decade after the cessation of hostilities at the end of the Second World War, offers a unique snapshot of Europe each year. The moment in time that the contest captures through song and spectacle is inextricably tied to Europe's traditions and history. Each year, Europe invents itself anew with new artists and new songs. The participating national broadcasters create a new 'usable past' for the present, or as historian Jeffrey K. Olick puts it, they create 'a retrospective reconstruction to serve the needs of the present' (Olick, 2007, 19). They 'recall' a version of their past that the present wants to hear. In other words, the performance of identity we see in the contest — whether it be national, sub-national, ethnic, or related to gender or sexual identity — changes constantly, and each iteration of the contest allows competing nations to re-invent themselves and their traditions anew. The image of the present is dynamic, as is the image of the past that is recalled in the present. The present is therefore always contingent on history, tradition and memory. How actors such as national broadcasters choose to shape the national entry and fashion the past is a matter of politics or of the politics of memory. As Olick, in formulating a presentist viewpoint, reminds us, 'behind every version of the past there must be a set of interests in the present' (Olick, 2007, 20).

Contemporary Europe cannot be properly understood without acknowledging its diverse set of entangled national and regional histories. Something similar could be claimed for Eurovision. Through the medium of popular culture, the ESC plays an important part in the 'presentist' construction of contemporary Europe (Wellings & Kalman, 2019, 2), whether this be in highlighting geopolitical realities or in forging an 'idealised, imagined space' of belonging to a European community (Wellings & Kalman, 2019, 11). In the imagining of Europe that occurs in the ESC (and its referencing of the past), presentist interests, as defined by Olick, are in evidence everywhere — from the lyrics of songs, the choice of performers and language to the use of cultural symbolism in the staging. Indeed, the very format of Eurovision, in which national broadcasters select a new performer each year with an original song, enables

DOI: 10.4324/9781003188933-7

participants to respond agilely to current sensibilities. That means that the past can be invoked, recalled and invented afresh with each iteration of the contest. As such, the contest has infinite ability to refresh, reboot and reinvent itself and the fortunes of its participating countries.

In this chapter, we outline how, as teachers of European studies at the University of Melbourne, we designed and implemented a syllabus to address questions of history and memory in Europe, among other things, through the lens of the ESC. We discuss, first, some of the ways in which national and transnational history impinges on the contest and, second, the strategies we use to foster a curiosity in national, regional and transnational histories and cultures. By way of illustration of the first of our aims, we examine Germany as one of the case studies treated in the course. In the second part of this chapter, we explore the pragmatics and pedagogy of teaching history and memory in Eurovision through the case study of countries previously part of the Union of Soviet Socialist Republics. The second example in particular serves to illustrate how we attempt to further students' comprehension of how the politics of memory plays out in the contest. Since the syllabus was created prior to the COVID-19 crisis, we will discuss our pedagogical approach prior to the pandemic and then evaluate how we pivoted to a totally digital course during the pandemic itself.

Teaching History and Memory Pre-Pandemic

The subject 'Eurovisions,' designed as a first-year European studies subject, appeals to language students as well as to other cohorts from across the university. It usually attracts diehard fans of the contest, second and third generation migrants to Australia who were raised on Eurovision at home, as well as arts, humanities and music students more generally. The subject takes a case study approach that deals with several regional and national examples as well as additional topics such as gender and sexuality, nation branding, fans and audiences. We have outlined the rationale for the subject elsewhere (Lewis & Hajek, 2019). All the national and regional case studies in our subject touch on the entangled histories of Europe. Dominant themes amongst these involve histories of empire, two world wars, the Cold War and more recently the post-Cold War period and its wars of independence. What is important in the context of Eurovision is how and when these histories are invoked, by whom and for what purpose. This leads us to the question of what presentist concerns are behind historical or traditional inflections in a national song that explicitly references the past. Is nostalgia at play, or does the past serve current political concerns, or both (see Johnson, 2014)? And can the past even be present when it does not appear to be, that is, can it be present through its conspicuous absence?

The past is frequently experienced in ESC through acts of collective memory, although this does not exclude the explicit expression of personal memories (as we saw in Germany's 2018 entry 'You Let Me Walk Alone', performed by Michael Schulte). In his seminal study of collective memory, Maurice Halbwachs takes an instrumental view that argues that collective memories are 'remembered' in such ways as to serve the interests of particular groups in society. In other words, the 'past is a social construction mainly, if not wholly, shaped by the concerns of the present' (Halbwachs, 1992, 29). These concerns can vary widely and encompass political statements or gestures as well as a homage or nod to traditions. The mode in which the past is conjured up may also vary. It may occur in earnest in high cultural rituals, such as commemorations of war or liberation, or in popular culture, where the past may be conjured up ironically, critically or simply in jest.

We can see the impact of cultural history on the contest most overtly through the citing of national and regional traditions at the level of the song. The contest offers immense scope for putting national or regional musical traditions on display and for asserting diverse forms of identity (of singers and musicians) through connecting these to different national and cultural traditions. Cultural references are an important way in which artists can underscore their uniqueness and set themselves apart from others (Wolther, 2012, 169). Cultural or folk traditions may be invoked in earnest such as in nostalgic or even historicist performances or through irony or playful citations. Folk music traditions may dominate the style of a song (as in Portugal's winning song 'Amar Pelos Dois' [To love for the both of us] in 2017) or be limited to short inserts or riffs in the bridges or the choruses (such as in Cyprus's song from 2018 'Fuego'). Nostalgic songs have always been popular at Eurovision, and these have ranged in more recent times from songs such as Russia's 2009 song 'Mamo', sung by Anastasia, the Russian ethno-pop band Buranovskiye Babushki and their 2012 song 'Party for Everyone', and France's 2021 entry 'Voilà'. Entries such as these represent the more traditional end of the nostalgic spectrum, while Azerbaijan's 2020 and 2021 entries and Ukraine's 2021 entry by Go_A sit at the more modern contemporary end of the spectrum.

Eurovision entries are multimodal social-semiotic acts of communication that incorporate aural, visual, technological, linguistic, textual and performative facets (Lewis & Hajek, 2019, 173). Visually the contest provides for a vast array of expressions of cultural traditions, whether it be through the style of costumes, dance moves or the inclusion of traditional musical instruments on stage such as violins. Aurally, ethnic diversity can be expressed through both language (such as languages other than English and the use of dialects) as well as musical style and idiom. More recently, we see these folkloristic elements being used as ethnic segments or inflections in otherwise generic pop songs. Some entries have shown a preference for hybrid pop songs, which represent an intriguing blend or montage of styles. As indicated above, the ethnic idioms are often introduced through musical licks or hooks featuring traditional instruments or ethnic musical styles of singing, such as Sami joiking in Norway's 2019 entry performed by the group KEiiNO.

A presentist approach provides an apt starting point for examining history and memory in the ESC. On the one hand, historical references to the past can be invoked consciously, that is as a result of deliberate decisions taken on the part of broadcasters and singers. On the other hand, we find that not every aspect of a

Eurovision entry can be controlled by the broadcasters and their delegation teams. There is substantial scope within the contest for spontaneous political gestures or statements, some of which allude to suppressed national memories. This includes, for example, the display of sub-national flags in the green room or the flying of the Palestinian flag in protest at the politics of Israel.[1] We argue, therefore, that both scripted and unscripted references to the past in the contest, in particular to past conflicts and wars, are indebted to this presentist instrumental view.

In the subject as taught, we deal with six case studies in total, each of which begins with an overview of the most salient events in the country or region's history, including the country's relationship to the European Union. The teaching is normally organised around 1.5-hour formal lectures and one-hour small group tutorials (of under twenty students in size). In 2020, the lectures were presented exclusively and directly online for the first time, moving from the traditional lecture theatre presentation and recording for subsequent upload and viewing. We did a combination of pre-recorded chunks and live delivery through online tools, such as Zoom. When we used pre-recorded chunks, at least one lecturer was present to introduce the recordings and to conduct online quizzes. This ensured students remained engaged in the live performance of the lecture. Lecture attendance was very good throughout the whole semester. The quizzes were interposed throughout the lecture and positioned after students had watched a video clip of a song.

The first case study in the course that explicitly addresses the themes of history and memory centres on Germany. Of all our cases, Germany presents the best example of a country in which a nation's historical record is paramount to understanding its participation in Eurovision. Until 1990, only West Germany (the Federal Republic of Germany, FRG) was permitted to participate in the ESC, while its communist party-led twin, East Germany (the German Democratic Republic, GDR), was a participant in the Eastern Bloc's version of the contest, Intervision, which served the Soviet sphere intermittently from 1965 to 1980 (Vuletic, 2019, 175–178). After reunification in 1990, both the eastern and western parts of Germany participated as one. When we speak about Germany in this chapter, we are referring both to the pre-1990 West German public broadcasters which were members of the EBU, and the post-1990 network of nine public broadcasters, into which the East German national broadcaster *Fernsehen der DDR* (GDR Television) was integrated upon reunification (Steinmetz, 2016, 148).

We have discussed elsewhere Germany's peculiar 'habitus' in the contest and how, even when it loses, it is keen to be seen as a good competitor and a good sport (Lewis & Hajek, 2019, 21–45). By the same token, when Germany wins, it is determined to be viewed as an unassuming, non-threatening victor. Germany has only won the contest twice, first in 1982 with Nicole's 'A Little Peace', and then for a second time in 2010 with Lena's 'Satellite.' In the lecture and tutorials, we ask students to bear in mind Germany's troubled past when analysing its entries and to think about why a winning strategy for Germany has thus far focused on using female performers (see Lewis & Hajek, 2019, 33).

Germany's National Socialist (Nazi) past has been referred to as the 'past that will not pass' (see Nolte in Stackelberg & Winkle, 2002, 414), and we argue that this also holds true for Eurovision. Key to understanding Germany's long-term approach to Eurovision are its strategies in public diplomacy in Europe, and its genuine efforts to mitigate the long-term effects of its criminal past. Public diplomacy is often a crucial channel of contact between regions or countries when diplomatic routes are closed off or re-opened after conflict. As Óscar J. Martín García and Rósa Magnúsdóttir argue, public diplomacy can be particularly effective as an 'instrument of rehabilitation, projection and international acceptance of compromising regimes' (García & Magnúsdóttir, 2019, 4). From the start of the postwar era German diplomatic efforts were deeply committed to improving Germany's international image by promoting it as a chastened European power dedicated to healing the wounds of Second World War. Like many middle powers, Germany relies far more on soft power than on hard power. As Max Otte (2000) points out, West Germany had limited sovereignty, and its foreign policy was heavily focused on the security partnership with the United States and with European stability and integration. Even as a rising middle power toward the end of the Cold War period, West Germany was never, and in many ways still is not, a 'normal' power (Otte, 2000).

As traditional diplomacy became hamstrung by the escalating Cold War, both East and West Germany turned to foreign cultural policy. Surprisingly, it was East Germany that led the way with West Germany to follow (Hillaker, 2020 373). Dedicated state-run media outlets pursued the work of promoting favourable self-images of each Germany to outsiders (Hillaker, 2020, 375–78). Around the time that the European Broadcasting Union (EBU) launched its idea for a song contest in 1956, the West German foreign office was increasingly concerned that its communist rivals in East Germany were winning many propaganda battles in the cultural realm (Hillaker, 2020, 378). The East Germans were shamelessly promoting themselves as the better, anti-fascist Germany, spreading suspicions that West Germany was still dominated by Nazis (Hillaker, 2020, 379). East Germany quickly hit on a suitable formula for crafting its image abroad while the West German foreign office struggled, both in terms of finding funding for initiatives and in formulating a coherent persuasive image. The East Germans' campaign focused on the role of gender equity in communist society, thus supporting a cause with universal appeal (Hillaker, 2020, 382). In the 1950s, West Germany emphasised its economic success and an image of itself as 'nonthreatening, democratic, and cosmopolitan' (Hillaker, 2020, 382) in its promotion materials.

Eurovision became an integral part of the self-promotion that West Germany invested in because of its broad value for international relations and public diplomacy (Dunkel & Nitzsche, 2018, 10). Rather like the project of the European Steel and Coal Community (ESCC), established in 1951, and the European Economic Community (EEC), set up in 1957, Eurovision, as the flagship event of the EBU, focused on rebuilding relations between countries that were previously at war through sharing telecommunications technology thereby encouraging peace and stability in the region (Vuletic, 2018, 19). While historians and political scientists have long placed the ESCC and the EEC under the gaze of European political diplomacy, Eurovision has only recently attracted scholarly attention as an 'arena for cultural diplomacy' in which 'ideas, norms, and values can be communicated as particularly European to audiences from around Europe' (Wilken, 2019, 171). Cultural practices such as music events have, as Dunkel and Nitzsche argue, significant capacity to acquire cultural capital for governments (2018, 10) and become effective political instruments. The opposite is also true, that the 'diplomatic politicization of music also reverberates in the cultural sphere' (10).

The interesting thing to consider about German cultural diplomacy in the ESC is how it deals with Germany's Nazi past. The question we ask students to contemplate is how a country with such a recent criminal record presents itself in the ESC and how it is perceived by its neighbours, many of whom were invaded and occupied during the war. How do German public broadcasters navigate the parameters of a pan-European televised entertainment show and the medium of popular song in ways that can contribute favourably to its post-conflict self-image and reputation. All countries need to manage reputation risk around the selection of entries and often do so via internal selection processes overseen by the national broadcaster (Wolther, 2012, 166). Indeed, as Wolther points out, national broadcasters may not even be concerned with choosing the song with the highest commercial potential if reputation is of greater concern to them (166). Many countries keep tight controls on the kind of song chosen and the artist they send. Germany's blemished history in the twentieth century means that it has better reasons than most to want to control the selection process than, for instance, countries like Sweden, where entries are chosen through a public vote. In light of this, it seems pertinent to ask to what extent artists selected by Germany serve as a form of atonement for its bellicose and aggressive history. We therefore ask students to think about whether there are certain themes that lend themselves to performing memory work.

We have written elsewhere about the importance for Germany of choosing non-national artists, singers from Scandinavia or with English-sounding names, and even an Australian, Jane Comerford, as part of the band Texas Lightning in 2006. In the lecture, we examine Germany's image at the ESC of a good European, as well as a good sport when it loses (see Lewis & Hajek, 2019, 28), and how this correlates with artist and song selection. A key part of Germany's image-making at ESC is its use of language. It was a keen adopter of the free language rule in 1999 and, unlike France and Italy, it almost always sends entries in English (see Lewis & Hajek, 2019, 28). Germany's music market, indeed, the German-language music market of the region, is large enough for it to safely sing in German, yet it chooses not to. We argue that singing in English is a marker of Germany's wish to promote itself as cosmopolitan and non-nationalistic, given that the lingua franca of global pop music is English.

Germany's self-promotion as a peace-loving, reformed European power can also be elicited from its choice of song topics. The themes of peace, love and friendship often feature in German entries and are one of the means by which Germany attempts to present itself as a 'chastened, tamed, peaceful power' (Lewis & Hajek, 2019, 42). In the 1950s, ESC songs sought to display West Germany as an open, tolerant and cosmopolitan country (see Lewis & Hajek, 2019, 28–29). The most striking example of this cosmopolitanism occurred already in the first year of the context in 1956 when the German national broadcaster ARD sent singer Walther Andreas Schwarz, a Jew and Holocaust survivor, and the Austrian-American performer Freddy Quinn, who sang an American-style rockabilly song (Vuletic, 2018, 17). This ethos of openness extended notably to the Allied occupying forces, which can be seen in 1959 when the ARD sent the popular twins, Alice and Ellen Kessler and the song 'Heute Abend wollen wir tanzen gehen' [Tonight We Want to Go Dancing]. The song was a swing number, popularised by the American troops and big bands of the era, and, while sung in German, had a modern, almost American feel to it reinforced by the opening line of the verse 'Hallo boy'. In 1962, West Germany sent the popular German artist Conny Froboess, who sang a song titled 'Zwei kleine Italiener' [Two Little Italians] about two Italian guestworkers in Germany who are homesick for their girlfriends back home in Napoli. Their longing stands in positive contrast to the more superficial 'chic' love of German tourists for holidaying in Italy. In the song Italy, once an ally in war, is both fashionable tourist attraction for Germans (as it was for many West Europeans) and the scene of Italian longing. 1963s entry sung by Heidi Brühl with the title 'Marcel' also references a romance with the eponymous Marcel, who could possibly be a foreigner.

Although German entries went on to deal with an array of other topics such as theatre and disability (Hindrichs, 2007, 55, 57), the most persuasive theme Germany has chosen to sing about at ESC is peace. There was a particular poignancy to the West Germany entry singing about peace in the year of 1982. It came at a critical juncture in the Cold War, when the Soviet Union had deployed nuclear missiles close to West Germany's borders and NATO troops were threatening to face them off by deploying cruise missiles along the inner-German border. Ralph Siegel, who wrote the song, captured brilliantly the anxieties of the Cold War era against the backdrop of Ronald Reagan's calls to the Soviet Union to tear down the Berlin Wall. West Germans understandably felt as if they had been thrust out of the frying pan of the Second World War into the fire of a nuclear war. While peace songs in the ESC go back to the 1960s, Nicole's song about peace came at a time when a new grassroots peace movement was gathering momentum across Europe (see Lewis & Hajek, 2019, 34). West Germany's fortunes were entangled in Europe's fortunes and vice-versa, for if West Germany was to be targeted in a nuclear war, then Europe too would no doubt suffer.

As Hindrichs points out, Siegel's magic formula involved a clever 'synthesis of musical and visual signs' and a subject that captured the '*contemporary zeitgeist*' (Hindrichs, 2007, 57). A pacified West Germany, as presented by a peace-loving innocent young woman, was precisely the image of Germany that Europeans welcomed at that historical point. European juries responded by voting West Germany the winning entry for 1982. As Nicole's win demonstrates, by the early nineteen-eighties West Germany seemed utterly transformed from its former Nazi self. Coming after a string of key diplomatic events such as the Munich Olympics in 1972, in which a new, modern and non-authoritarian West Germany was on public display, West Germany presented itself convincingly at Eurovision in 1982 as a modest, almost feminised power. While Nicole's act made no explicit references to Nazi Germany — it is not in the spirit of the contest to point out one's own crimes for the world to see — Nicole's audiences certainly would have had strong collective memories of the Second World War and Germany's less than illustrious role in it. This is supported by the fact that some of West Germany's closest neighbours did not award high points to West Germany. In Austria, Luxembourg and the Netherlands, memories of Germany as an aggressor stifled sympathies for West Germany as a victim in a nuclear war (see Lewis & Hajek, 2019, 35). Nicole's act thus functioned in many ways as a kind of counter-memory of an entirely different Germany, serving possibly as an idealised national self that was more of a collective European construction than a German invention.

Overall, throughout the history of the ESC, German public broadcasters have strived to choose artists who would not cause offense or upset Germany's neighbours, and taken the risk of reputational damage very seriously. This is born out recently by the poor choice of Xavier Naidoo by internal selection processes in 2016. Naidoo, a soul and RnB singer-songwriter born in Germany to South African parents of Indian, German and Irish descent, had connections to extreme right-wing groups and some of his songs were read as racist and homophobic in content. Despite attempts to defend their choice of artist, the NDR (one of the nine broadcasters tasked with organising Eurovision, and the hosting one since 1996) quickly removed Naidoo as its representative. It replaced him with Jamie-Lee, a former children's choir singer and winner of *The Voice of Germany* — and a much more wholesome choice.

Teaching History and Memory Online

As outlined above, the main teaching tools used in 2020 in the teaching of Eurovisions were formal interactive Zoom lectures and small group tutorials, also conducted on Zoom. Assessment items were class presentations, a mid-semester online test and a final essay. In tutorials, students would normally give an oral PowerPoint presentation on specified topics related to the lecture theme from the previous week. In 2020, we were reluctant to take up valuable online classroom time with live class presentations and decided to devote all the face-to-face time on Zoom to discussions. This required students to pre-record their presentations in digital form and upload them prior to the class onto the canvas class website. This proved to be a key decision in pivoting to online, allowing far more discussion time and more group interaction, and hence encouraging greater student engagement.

In each online class, students were assigned randomly to a breakout group for a task, and each one-hour class (in practice fifty minutes for timetabling reasons) consisted of three breakout group tasks, which were followed up by a general classroom roundup and discussion. To record the outcomes of each of the discussions in the groups, we set up Padlet worksheets which students could write to and which all students could see. This enabled each group to work on a different aspect of topics and facilitated reporting on their answers back to the whole group. It saved valuable time since oral feedback was not needed for all tasks, and allowed for flexibility in time management. The teacher could slip in and out of breakout groups, highlighting the salient points discussed and prompting a scribe to record that point onto the Padlet.

Case Study: The Soviet Union and Russia

History and memory are crucial to understanding the participation of former republics from the Soviet Union in the post-Cold War period. In the lecture in 2020, we explored how the ESC became an essential part of the public diplomacy of many countries, in particular the Baltic states, which harnessed the ESC to fashion radically new images of themselves in the 1990s and consciously developed nation-branding strategies that included the ESC (Jordan, 2014). Because of the extreme diversity of the Soviet Union, the tutorials focus on how some countries evoke a past history — often a troubled and traumatic one — for presentist political concerns. We are also interested in how the politics of some of these countries mean that they are equally interested in whitewashing a troublesome past and present in the persecution of minorities or the discrimination of LGBTIQ+ communities.

The focus in the tutorials about this topic is 'Becoming European, Performing Europeanness' in the ESC. As Russia provides a fertile case for analysis in the week on gender and sexuality, Russia is not chosen for in-depth analysis in this week. However, students have by this stage already seen how Russian politics can play into its approach to gender and sexuality in the contest. During that week, students are allocated a topic on Russia's win with Dima Bilan in 2008, Moscow's consequent hosting of the ESC in 2009 and the question of Russia's homophobia and pinkwashing. Suffice it to say that the issue of a selective performance of progressive attitudes to non-normative sexuality and gender has been well covered by the time we address Russia's self-presentation in the ESC in more depth and the self-presentation of former Soviet republics.

In the tutorials, we focus on the intriguing cases of Azerbaijan, Armenia and Ukraine because they allow us to highlight a different aspect of the symbolism of performing in the ESC: each spotlights a different historical conundrum. In 2020, two topics were set for class presentations. The first topic was to discuss the pros and cons of Azerbaijan's participation in the ESC and its hosting in 2012 in terms of national promotion and human rights. Topic two aimed to look at the question of whether the ESC is useful for working through historical grievances. Despite the prohibition on political songs, students were asked to think about how the ESC has been a forum for airing historical grievances. They were instructed to discuss this issue with reference to Armenia's 2015 ESC entry 'Face the Shadow' and the Armenian genocide of 1915.

In a further exercise for this week, the class focused on another instance of airing historical grievances in the ESC by examining Jamala's winning entry, '1944', for Ukraine in 2016. Crimean Tatar singer Jamala (Susana Jamaladinova) was the televoters' and the expert juries' choice to represent Ukraine in 2016, a choice that was enthusiastically endorsed after her victory by both the president Petro Poroshenko and the former prime minister Arseniy Yatsenyuk, who stressed the Ukrainianness of the Crimea (Pavlyshyn 2019, 139). The Ukrainian national broadcaster PBC was only too happy to have a member of an ethnic minority represent the country because of the annexation of Crimea by Russia in 2014 and the subsequent harassment of Crimean Tartars (Pavlyshyn, 2019, 141). While ostensibly about the historical acts of aggression by Stalinist Russia in 1944, the song evoked, at least implicitly, far more recent violations of Ukrainian territory by Russia in 2014.

To tease out the ways in which history and politics converge in this song, students were given the lyrics on an online Padlet page and the class was divided into three random breakout groups. Padlet enables members of the class to work on a document at the same time, and for breakout groups to document the results of their conversations on the Padlet in note form for the entire class to see (see Figures 5.1 and 5.2). The first group discussed the question of whether the song was political. The second looked at the question of whether the lyrics were historical and how so. The third group looked at the music and the staging and was asked what elements of ethno-nationalism it could perceive.

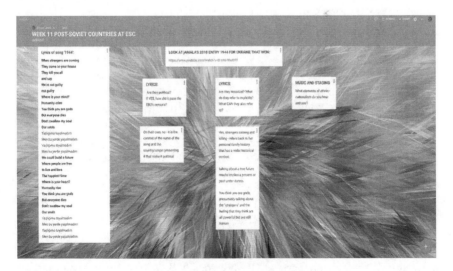

Figure 5.1 Padlet exercise on history and politics in Ukraine's 2016 entry: group 1.

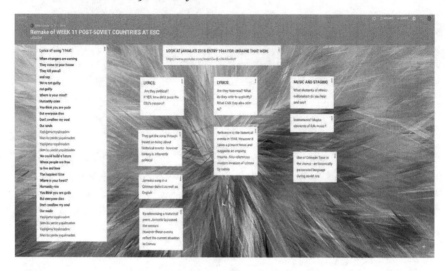

Figure 5.2 Padlet exercise on history and politics in Ukraine's 2016 entry: group 2.

In response to the question whether the lyrics were political, and hence in contravention of the EBU's ban on political statements, the first group had this to say: 'On their own, no [the lyrics are not political] — it is the context of the name of the song and the country/singer presenting it that make it political'. Their answer highlighted the fact that there is no reference to explicit perpetrators of this violence, with the song referring to them simply as 'strangers' and 'they'. Yet the reference to the year 1944 in the title and the widely known context of Jamala's Crimean family heritage make this song clearly about the Stalinist deportations during the Second World War, when suspected Nazi collaborators among the Crimeans were persecuted. Furthermore, the use of the pronoun 'you' in later lines implies a powerful overreaching group of perpetrators who think they are gods. Who the perpetrator 'you' refers to is open; it can be a you in the present or a you in the past, namely the Soviet persecutors in 1944 or the Russian invaders in 2014.

Yet, crucially, the song makes no reference to any political leader, past or present, by name. Nor does it 'allude to particular nations or national minorities,' as Marko Pavlyshyn observes (2019, 143). It is, as he points out, universalist in its construction (142). To read into it a message about the Crimean Tartars we have to know something about the biographical context of Jamala's family, that is, to know that her grandparents were the victims of the Stalinist terror. The song thus becomes both 'a reflection of the tribulations of her family and the modern history of the Crimean Tartars' (Pavlyshyn, 2019, 140). Of course, family history is a sub-set of national and sub-national histories and Jamala's story of her grandmother's expulsion from Crimea to Uzbekistan was 'symptomatic of the fate of the Crimean Tartars' (Pavlyshyn, 2019, 140). On this account, the song is historical and personal rather than anything else, a view that Jamala has been keen to uphold in interviews (Pavlyshyn, 2019, 141).

The second tutorial group addressed the question of how the song managed to bypass the EBU's censors and wrote this summarising their discussion: 'They got the song through based on [it] being about historical events — however history is inherently political' (see Figure 5.2). Another answer provided was: 'By referencing a historical event, Jamala bypassed the censors. However, these events reflect the current situation in Crimea'. Here the students were referring to Russia's 2014 annexation of Crimea. Hence, students made a distinction between an overtly political song and a historical one with personal meaning that had political resonances. They realised that it was the present political climate in Ukraine and the context of the recent invasion of Crimea that had ruffled Russian feathers when the song won. Students agreed that it was fair that the song had not been banned.

The second group replied in answer to the question to what extent it was historical and what the lyrics referred to: 'Yes, strangers coming and killing — refers back to her personal family history that has a wider historical context — talking about a free future maybe implies a present or past under duress. You think you are gods, presumably talking about the "strangers" and the feeling that they think are all powerful but are still human'. The second verse of the song, sung in a higher register, has lines about building a future of freedom. The introduction of a further reference group in the lyrics, as indicated by the 'we', suggests a suppressed minority and their utopian ideals of liberation from oppression, presumably from the 'you' who think they have god-like powers. The conditional tense expressed in the 'could' seems to point to the present moment rather than to 1944 as it posits the possibility of a better future for Crimean Tartars.

The second tutorial group had this to say about the history question: 'Reference to the historical events in 1944. However, it takes a present tense and suggests an ongoing trauma. Also references modern invasion of Crimea by Russia.' This group's answer focused on the use of tenses in the song to create ambiguity around whether it was talking about the past or the present. The third group addressed the style of music, perhaps less well than the other questions, mainly because most did not have a deep enough knowledge of musical traditions of the region to recognise what elements of Ukrainian folk music were being incorporated. However, they did refer to the fact that the Crimean Tartar language was used in the song, which may have added to the controversy surrounding it: 'Use of Crimean Tatar in the chorus — an historically persecuted language during Soviet era.'

Conclusion

The ESC provides a unique vehicle for teaching tertiary students European history and memory and the impact of the past on the present. The COVID-19 pandemic forced us to take the teaching of the tertiary subject 'Eurovisions' online and to explore new ways of encouraging student engagement with questions of history, tradition and memory in the ESC. History, especially a recent transnational history of conflict or war in the region, is a powerful driver behind multiple aspects of the contest, from the choice of singer, language and musical style to the topic of the song. The most obvious means by which history is expressed in the contest is through cultural and musical traditions as well as language use. Less obvious are the national strategies entries deploy to reflect on and work through past conflict and suffering. Some reformed, former perpetrator nations such as Germany attempt to atone for their criminal past by fore-grounding certain universal, cosmopolitan themes and by presenting themselves as a peaceful, often feminised power. The countries from the former Soviet Union offer a further rich example of how past memories of violence in the Second World War can be explicitly evoked in the contest to serve presentist national concerns, such as when the Ukrainian song in 2016 protested the Russian invasion of Crimea in 2014. In both case studies, the ESC, in its capacity as a persuasive tool of public diplomacy, offers a means of engaging with a troublesome past: by allaying collective memories and fears of war and conflict or protesting current acts of violence by new aggressors such as post-Soviet Russia. The above examples demonstrate that, while presentist concerns invariably drive a national broadcaster's approach to history, the ESC permits a wide array of possibilities to give expression to these interests without violating the non-political spirit of the contest.

Note

1 See Catherine Baker on the importance of other kinds of flags such as the rainbow flag (Baker, 2019, 177).

References

Baker, C. (2019). If Love Was a Crime, We Would Be Criminals: The Eurovision Song Context and the Queer International Politics of Flags. In J. Kalman, B. Wellings & K. Jacotine (Eds.), *Eurovisions, Identity and the International Politics of the Eurovision Song Contest Since 1956* (pp. 175–200). Palgrave Macmillan.

Baker, C. (2010). *Sounds of the Borderland: Popular Music, War and Nationalism in Croatia since 1991*. Ashgate.

Čvoro, U. (2016). *Turbo-folk Music and Cultural Representations of National Identity in Former Yugoslavia*. Routledge.

Dunkel, M., & Nitzsche, S. A. (2018). Popular Music and Public Diplomacy: An Introduction. In M. Dunkel, & S. A. Nitzsche (Eds.), *Popular Music and Public Diplomacy: Transnational and Transdisciplinary Perspectives* (pp. 9–26). Transcript.

García, Ó. J. M., & Magnúsdóttir, R. (2019). Machineries of Persuasion: European Soft Power and Public Diplomacy during the Cold War. In Ó. J. M. García & R. Magnúsdóttir (Eds.), *Machineries of Persuasion: European Soft Power and Public Diplomacy during the Cold War* (pp. 1–15). De Gruyter Oldenbourg. 10.1515/ 9783110560510-009

Halbwachs, M. (1992). *On Collective Memory*. Ed, trans. and with an introduction by L. A. Coser. University of Chicago Press.

Hillaker, L. (2020). Representing a "Better Germany": Competing Images of State and Society in the Early Cultural Diplomacy of the FRG and GDR. *Central European History, 53*, 372–392.

Hindrichs, T. (2007). Chasing the 'magic formula' for success: Ralph Siegel and the Grand Prix Eurovision de la Chanson. In Raykoff, I. & Tobin, R.D. (Eds.), A Song For Europe: Popular Music and Politics in the Eurovision Song Contest, 49–59. Ashgate.

Johnson, E. (2014). A New Song for a New Motherland: Eurovision and the Rhetoric of Post-Soviet National Identity. *The Russian Review, 73*, 24–46.

Jordan, P. (2014). *The Modern Fairy Tale: Nation Branding, National Identity and the Eurovision Song Contest*. University of Tartu Press.

Judah, T. (2006). Eurovision Hits a Serious Note. *BBC News*. 16th April. http://news.bbc.co.uk/2/hi/programmes/crossing_continents/4904234.stm

Karamanić, S., & Unverdorben, M. (2019). Balkan High, Balkan Low: Pop-Music Production Between Hybridity and Class Struggle. In E. Mazierska & Z. Györi (Eds.), *Eastern European Popular Music in a Transnational Context: Beyond the Borders* (pp. 155–170). Palgrave Macmillan.

Lewis, A., & Hajek, J. (2019). Lessons Learned: Teaching European Studies in Full Eurovision. In C. Hay & J. Carniel (Eds.), *Eurovision and Australia: Interdisciplinary Perspectives From Down Under* (pp. 165–187). Palgrave Macmillan.

Marshall, A. (2016). When Eurovision was a Matter of Life and Death. BBC 13 May. https://www.bbc.com/culture/article/20160513-when-eurovision-was-a-matter-of-life-and-death

Olick, J. K. (2007). From Usable Pasts to the Return of the Repressed. *The Hedgehog Review, 9*(2), 19–31.

Otte, M. (2000). *A Rising Middle Power? German Foreign Policy in Transformation, 1989-1999*. St. Martin's Press.

Pavlyshyn, M. (2019). Ruslana, Serduchka, Jamala: National Self-Imaging in Ukraine's Eurovision Entries. In J. Kalman, B. Wellings & K. Jacotine (Eds.), *Eurovisions, Identity and the International Politics of the Eurovision Song Contest Since 1956* (pp. 129–150). Palgrave Macmillan.

Steinmetz, R. (2016). Television History in Germany: Media Political and Media-Ethical Aspects. In L. Powell & R. Shandley (Eds.), *German Television: Historical and Theoretical Approaches* (pp. 133–154). Berghahn.

Scott, D. B. (2013). Imagining the Balkans, Imagining Europe: Balkan Entries in the Eurovision Song Contest. In R. P. Pennanen, P. C. Poulos & A. Theodosiou (Eds.), *Ottoman Intimacies, Balkan Musical Realities* (pp. 157–169). Foundation of the Finnish Institute at Athens.

Stackelberg, R., & Winkle, S. A., eds. (2002). *The Nazi Germany Sourcebook: An Anthology of Texts*. Routledge.

Vuletic, D. (2012). Sounds Like America: Yugoslavia's Soft Power in Eastern Europe. In P. Romijn, G. Scott-Smith & J. Segal (Eds.), *Divided Dreamworlds? The Cultural Cold War in East and West* (pp. 115–131). Amsterdam University Press.

Vuletic, D. (2018). *Postwar Europe and the Eurovision Song Contest*. Bloomsbury Academic.

Vuletic, D. (2019). The Intervision Song Contest: A Commercial and Pan-European Alternative to the Eurovision Song Contest. In E. Mazierska & Z. Győri (Eds.), *Eastern Popular Music in a Transnational Context: Beyond the Borders* (pp. 173–190). Palgrave Macmillan.

Wellings, B., & Kalman, J. (2019). Entangled Histories: Identity, Eurovision and European Integration. In J. K., Ben Wellings & K. Jacotine (Eds.), *Eurovisions, Identity and the International Politics of the Eurovision Song Contest Since 1956* (pp. 1–20). Palgrave Macmillan.

Wolther, I. (2012). More Than Just Music: The Seven Dimensions of the Eurovision Song Contest. *Popular Music, 31*(1), 165–171.

Wilken, L. (2019). The Eurovision Song Contest as Cultural Diplomacy During the Cold War: Transmitting Western Attractiveness. In Ó. J. Martín García & R. Magnúsdóttir (Eds.), *Machineries of Persuasion: European Soft Power and Public Diplomacy during the Cold War* (pp. 171–190). De Gruyter Oldenbourg. 10.1515/9783110560510-009

6 A March for Power: The Variety of Political Programmes on the Eurovision Song Contest Stage

Gad Yair and Chen Ozeri

Backstage

It was 1987, and I was a master's student, living in dorms in Jerusalem. One afternoon – hours before the live broadcast of the Eurovision Song Contest (ESC), the students in the dorms debated: what countries would exchange votes this evening? Are there political loyalties and biases in the contest? At that point, no one really had robust academic answers for such questions. There was no data, no one made formal analyses of the results. Academic research and the Eurovision were still far apart and consequently – the idea that the ESC is impregnated with political elements was but an idea, an anecdote, an opinion.

But at that night, as the results came in, I analysed the voting matrix for the first time – and actually observed the map of loyalties underlying the voting. The computer screen made apparent the hidden political and cultural map of Europe. Happy to report the results, I asked my mentors at the university how to proceed. 'One year of data is not enough,' advised my department's statistical expert. Consequently, I asked the archive of the Israel Broadcasting Authority (IBA) to allow me to observe the voting stage of the contest in prior years. Alas, the recordings only retained the songs. I then ventured to get the data from elsewhere, sent notes and published requests. After months, an adolescent sent a note that he got the data from the EBU. He then sent me the matrices on paper. Now, with advanced PCs and newly developed software for social networks analyses (STRUCTURE by Ron Burt), I could put the debate to rest. With data about voting in the ESC from 1973 until 1992 I could finally provide an answer: Yes, the Eurovision is rife with political loyalties and cultural biases. This effort allowed the publication of the first ever studies of the ESC.

In two decades, this modest academic effort to expose hidden political loyalties and cultural biases in the ESC was followed by a floodgate of studies of the Eurovision. Today, dozens of papers and books are published annually, academic conferences are held, and universities provide advanced courses on the Eurovision and European politics. The anecdote and opinion were now replaced with data, advanced statistical modelling, and the best of interpretive studies. There is now a science of the Eurovision. Now, more than two decades after I published the first two papers – most everybody knows that the Eurovision is

DOI: 10.4324/9781003188933-8

politicised. Experts know about politics and bloc voting, commentators and news media focus public attention on political references, and even lay publics engage in political prediction games. The academic effort to shed light on the Eurovision enlightened the general public and transformed the consciousness of millions.

The present paper reviews recent studies of politics and political events on the Eurovision stage. We advance beyond the now accepted truism, namely that the Eurovision is political, by detailing several different forms of politics that creep into the supposedly apolitical stage of the ESC. This apolitical stance of the organisers sets the stage for our analyses of the variety of political strategies and events that recur in the Eurovision year after year.

The Apolitical Stance of the EBU

On the eve of the 2021 ESC in Rotterdam, the Reference Group of the European Broadcasting Union (EBU) decided to disqualify Belarus from participation in the event. The Belarusian band Galasy ZMesta (Voices from Places) was supposed to perform a song titled "'Ja nauchu tebya" (I'll Teach You), which seemingly had a political subtext, intimating support for the Belarusian dictator Alexander Lukashenka. The EBU claimed that the song "puts the non-political nature of the Contest in question", and demanded the Belarusian national broadcasting organisation Belteleradiokampanya (Belteleradiocompany, BTRC) send an alternative, non-political, song. However, the new submission had political connotations, too, eventuating with the organisers concluding "that the new submission was also in breach of the rules of the competition that ensure the Contest is not instrumentalized or brought into disrepute".[1] This exchange concluded another policing incident that reflected the EBU's policy, namely: the ESC is not a political platform.

A similar situation occurred with China's growing alliance with Europe and the ESC — until the tie broke down in 2018. Beginning in 2013, Chinese television stations began broadcasting the ESC and considered participating in the contest. However, during the contest in 2018, the Chinese authorities censored performers who exhibited values that Europe embraces but China abhors: gay relationships (Ireland's entry), body tattoos (Albania), and LGBT flags (during the performance of Switzerland). The Chinese censorship of those performances collided with EBU's embrace of gay rights, which it presents as a hallmark of European identity. In that sense, China clearly misaligned with the avowed politics or ideology of the EBU. As a result of China's censorship, the EBU declared that Europe's values are not for sale. In a critical political statement, it made clear what the ESC stands for:

> On the 9th of May, Chinese broadcaster Mango TV broadcast the first Semi-Final of the 2018 Eurovision Song Contest live but two performances were censored. This is not in line with the EBU's values of universality and inclusivity and our proud tradition of celebrating diversity through music. It is with regret that we will therefore immediately be terminating our

partnership with the broadcaster and they will not be permitted to broadcast the second Semi-Final or the Grand Final.

This statement made it clear that the ESC has clear political visions of inclusivity and universality, of diversity, peace and global integration. However, the EBU also made it clear that the ESC is an apolitical event.

But is it really? In this chapter, we review repeating political incidents that seem to encroach on the non-political policy of the EBU. We review three cases in which politics loomed large over the ESC stage. We also mention a few other cases that had political undertones. We thereby provide testimony to the ubiquity of nationalistic sentiments and ideological, political, historical, and even military tensions that pulsate underneath the agenda of European integration and European peace-abiding values.

We should note that, while the ESC has clear political intrusions, the contest is indeed mostly about music. While some broadcasting agencies and artists use the ESC stage to advance political interests, most do not do so every year. And while we can discern political elements in the ESC almost every year, those are far from the central facets of the contest. Music, performance, appearances, sexuality, style, teamwork and stage architecture — all those elements play a decisive role. So, while we do emphasise a variety of political element in the ESC, for most people the contest is about entertainment. As a *Time* correspondent wrote in 2012, the Eurovision "allows countries to duke it out through songs rather than bombs".[2] Songs, in this sense, are centre stage. Politics is a backstage intruder.

The ESC as a Cultural Seismograph

Knowing that Europe experienced perpetual war, Immanuel Kant suggested in 1795 that it should create an infrastructure for 'perpetual peace' (Kant, 1983). More than a century after he proposed a philosophical framework for advancing the integration of European nations, the continent had demonstrated that some countries were still engaging in perpetual war. After two World Wars, and as the Cold War was clamping on European freedoms, the EBU – though focused on TV broadcasting technicalities – unintentionally offered a modest means for advancing Kant's ideas of cosmopolitanism, peace, integration, and solidarity (Vuletic, 2018). It first launched the ESC with seven Western European participants. But new countries have since joined in, creating an ever expanding, extravagant, entertaining "show" with a competitive element, a tournament of nations of sorts. Like the Olympic Games, the ESC has served as a kind of sublimation — replacing national conflicts with competitive arenas — of sports and music. Yet, politics has remained a silent participant.

So, while the EBU created a unique musical festival with no political intents, it practically advanced political purposes of peace, diversity, reconciliation and cultural integration. And while the ESC is often conceived as a non-serious pop festival, we argue that it is full of political undertones of various forms. While the EBU presents a non-political agenda of peace and love, with common European ideals and values embracing diversity and cosmopolitan unification, we show that nationalistic undertones often send alternative messages (Yair, 1995). In a recent review of more than two decades of Eurovision studies, I offered that the contest can serve as a political or cultural seismograph for Europe's deep political and cultural tensions (Vuletic, 2018; Yair, 2018). The ESC, after all, is one more form of cultural diplomacy.

The ubiquity of politics in the ESC has historical precedents. Notwithstanding claims about the autonomy of art, sociologists and historians have shown that art and artists were often recruited to serve political agendas. Rulers used artistic means for political purposes. Painters were recruited to portray victories and kingly fame, musicians were composing to celebrate aristocratic benefactors. Indeed, art was used as a kind of "soft power" (Bourdieu, 1996; Adler, 2004), a means of cultural diplomacy that countries used to justify political positions. They used art to convince audiences about the appropriate order of things, or present them with clear "we and them" themes that justified military invasions or steadfast resistance.

For example, rulers used operas and operettas as political shields. For centuries, composers and performers were sent to other countries as "political delegations". Regimes generously funded those delegations and sent them to perform in European capitals. "Enlightened tyrants", be it an emperor or empress, a tsar or tsarina, or a king or a queen, generously funded artists and performers who delivered these rulers with prestige and influence across borders. It is legitimate to argue, therefore, that Richard Wagner was a German agent, and Pyotr Ilyich Tchaikovsky was a Russian one. Theatrical plays enjoyed the same dynamics. Molière was a French agent of the pre-French Revolution, Victor Hugo of the aftermath. And Federico García Lorca was a Spanish agent of the Republican camp.

True, some artists volunteered to serve political agendas out of patriotism and ideology, without institutional support. For example, the playwright Bertolt Brecht launched his communist bravura alone, only later becoming a mouthpiece of the socialist regime. Either way, whether serving the Church, the monarchy, or the state, art and artists were rarely a political. Even in postmodern times, art is often used as a weapon of soft power. In this sense, the ESC is merely one more tool that countries use to advance their particularistic visions and — at times — contrarian political agendas. And, since Europe has continued to experience national animosities and repeated wars even in recent decades — it is no surprise that performers are still recruited — or volunteer — for advancing nationalistic sentiments and interests.

Indeed, performances, lyrics and voting strategies in the ESC expose hidden political and cultural layers that betray the contest's political visions of peace and unification (Vuletic, 2018). Analysed through the lens of 'bloc voting,' for example, the ESC exposes latent political and cultural divisions across Europe — west and east, north and south, Soviet and post-Soviet (Gatherer, 2006; Charron, 2013; Dekker, 2007; Kalman et al., 2019). According to Dekker, for example, the "Contest results provide a window into European politics"

(Dekker, 2007, p. 53). And, as Pot proposed, "The Eurovision appears to be not only an entertaining event for many, but also an annual poll of how relations are developing on the European continent" (Pot, 2021, p.1).

It is no surprise, therefore, that through various manners and means, the ESC gives presence to deep cultural traumas and national animosities. Azerbaijan and Armenia, Turkey and Greece, Russia and the Ukraine, Russia and Georgia, Turkey and Armenia, Croatia-Bosnia and Serbia — these are some examples of the rifts that disrupt the expectation for the cultural brotherhood of European nations. Therefore, close attention to songs, lyrics, media interpretations, and voting patterns provide a useful seismograph for exposing deep divisions that lie under the ESC stage. As a colleague claimed with respect to the Israeli participation in the contest, the Eurovision is part of the wider dialogue between Europeans and Israelis, and often echoes the state of their relations. And, as Philip V. Bohlman suggess, (Bohlman, 2007, p. 66), "[t]he Eurovision Song Contest, however camp and jouissance, minority and majority politics compete for and on the mainstage, allows us to chart the roads that diverge and intersect on the landscapes of a Europe that has the potential to collapse into fragments or cohere with a new wholeness. As a site of power, pleasure, and prayer, the Eurovision Song Contest also becomes the site of politics, utopian and dystopian".

The following analyses expose repeating nationalistic sentiments and national animosities on the ESC stage. They expand on prior studies of politics in the ESC by exposing a variety of political agendas. Specifically, we do so by using three in-depth case studies: Sweden, Israel, and the cultural battle between Russia and the Ukraine. We focus attention on the past two decades, namely from 2000 to 2020, having scanned through all the semi-finals and the grand finals in those twenty years. We find that each of the three case studies had a distinct political motive or narrative. Furthermore, we pay special attention to the years in which the countries won and hosted the competition: Kyiv in 2005, Moscow in 2009, Malmö in 2013 and Stockholm in 2016, and Kyiv again in 2017. Our analyses rely on official and other indirect sources: delegation press conferences, media appearances, social media, and interviews with producers and performers.

The Politics of Hegemonic Control

We begin with Sweden. Seemingly the least political of the three case studies — Sweden won the ESC time and again and currently runs the contest even in other countries. It has won the ESC six times, with another twenty-four entries finishing top five in the contest. However, Sweden's power in the ESC goes well beyond the stage. While the format of the ESC initially took on Italy's Sanremo festival, it is now based on Sweden's *Melodifestivalen* (Melody Festival). Leaders in the music industry acknowledge that Sweden is behind the scenes of many elements of the ESC. In 2004, the Swedish television executive Svante Stockselius became the executive supervisor of the ESC on behalf of the EBU. Martin Österdahl, another Swedish television executive, was appointed as the latest executive supervisor of the ESC from 2020.[3] The influence goes deeper.

Current voting procedures at the ESC emulate the procedures of the Swedish *Melodifestivalen*. Moreover, Swedish teams help winning countries in designing the event with local experts. Some also allege that Swedish officials unofficially hold power over decision-making in the EBU (personal communication). And if that is not all, given its centrality in European pop culture, many ESC entries have a Swedish element to them: the Swedish composer Thomas G:son, for example, has produced sixty-nine songs for the national finals of twelve different countries.[4]

Sweden cements its hegemonic moral position while relying on unique national sentiments — with Swedish statesmen seeing themselves as a cornerstone of enlightenment and peace, at least since the Cold War and EU integration (Johansson, 2017). This sentiment spills onto the ESC stage. In the edition in Stockholm in 2000, the Swedish producers celebrated the EU's new political slogan of "United in Diversity" by staging an ethnic song by a native Lapland-born singer. They also presented a video on the dangers of climate change, well ahead of global awareness of forthcoming environmental risks. At the 2013 competition in Malmö, which has a large immigrant population, the Swedish team created a smiling and self-conscious parody about politics in the event, with presenter Petra Mede joking: "We all shout contempt at Moldova-Romania or Greece-Cyprus, and God forbid, for the Nordic countries only taste determines the outcome". During this event, the Swedish organisers added the first national 'flags parade' that now traditionally opens the grand final of the ESC. And when Stockholm hosted the contest once again in 2016, the organisers arranged a tremendous spectacle of self-confidence with self-referential jokes at the expense of the host country. Måns Zelmerlöw and Petra Mede also presented an unforgettable parody of how to win the ESC with the song "Love and Peace". Overall, Swedish presenters and performers mocked disguised politics but made sure that everyone knew that the ESC is political through and through. But while it presented itself as a-political, Sweden sealed its central position in the ESC.

Israel and Europe: The Politics of Suspicion

Israel provides another interesting — and yet altogether different — case for the centrality of political elements in the ESC and its manipulation for national branding. The Israeli case reveals its entangled relations with the EU – which expects a final settlement for the Israeli-Palestinian conflict. In countering the EU's pressures and suspecting a deep European animosity against it, Israel uses the ESC to send alternative messages to sooth critiques. However, the politics of suspicion is mostly apparent during the voting stages, with spectators and commentators suspecting some countries to ban Israeli performers.

But the Israeli-European altercation goes beyond the ESC, of course. In recent years, Israeli diplomats have attempted to shift the European focus on the Israeli-Palestinian conflict to other areas of Israeli life. This has followed the branding of Israel as a high-tech "startup nation", celebrating global demand for Israeli innovative technologies (Senor & Singer, 2009; Beyar et al., 2017).

Notwithstanding political critiques from conservative circles, Israeli decision-makers have also shifted focus to Israel's progressive LGBT rights. The municipality of Tel Aviv sponsored the preparations for the 2019 ESC while branding its role as an international hub for the LGBT scene. Indeed, it was Israel's Dana International who exposed the close association of LGBT communities with ESC fandom. The early study of Israeli gay participants in Eurovision parties (Lemish, 2004) directed future academic studies in this area (Cassiday, 2014; Heller, 2007; Singleton et al., 2007) but thereby provided a unique lens to appreciate the appropriation of LGBT issues as a political tool.

The Israeli government has never shied from using media campaigns for branding itself in a light that Europe often ignores. It adopts a kind of "upright defiance" *vis-à-vis* Europe to claim that Israel should not be seen singly through the prism of the Palestinian cause. For example, in 2009 the Minister for Public Diplomacy and Diaspora, Yuli Edelstein, has asked Israeli tourists to serve as mini-ambassadors. The government printed a leaflet and distributed it at Ben Gurion Airport, providing Israeli passengers abroad with short messages on how to present Israel in a positive light. Emphasising Israel's success in various areas, the pamphlet listed the first Israeli Nobel Prize in 1966, the invention of the USB flash drive in 2000, and, of course, Dana International's Eurovision victory in 1998. Similarly, in 2016, the Israeli foreign affairs and tourism ministries invited all artists participating in the ESC that year to tour Israel and perform a mini preview concert. Such national efforts at branding Israel through a non-conflictual lens was a clear exercise in public diplomacy. Indeed, recent presentations of Israel's postcards in the shows follows a clear tourist-oriented branding strategy, promoting Israel as a modern country and a worthy tourist destination. With parties in Tel Aviv, Israel has branded itself as a destination for young travellers, with white beaches and dance parties. Palestine is simply ignored.

Israeli artists, however, have pushed the political button. One of the most famous Israeli entries had a distinct political message against dictators and atomic weapons. In 2007, the Israeli Broadcasting Authority selected the Israeli pop-rock band Teapacks with the song "Push the Button", which provoked criticism in Europe. The lyrics warned against "crazy rulers" with "demonic, technologic willingness to harm". Kobi Oz, the lead singer of the group, warned that those dictators are "gonna push the button". Commentators argued that Teapacks and Kobi Oz were referring to the attempts by the Iranian government to develop nuclear weapons and that, consequently, the submission should be banned as a political entry. Indeed, the EBU considered disqualifying the band. However, Kobi Oz denied any reference to actual rulers. "It turns out that the BBC thinks that [Iranian president Mahmud] Ahmadinejad is crazy", he told the daily *Maariv.* (The Evening), "[w]e didn't mention names". After deliberations, the band was allowed to perform, but eventually did not pass the semi-finals.

"Push the Button" followed another Israeli pop band that took politics to the hilt – directly onto the stage. The pop quartet Ping Pong represented Israel in Stockholm in 2000. The lyrics of the entry, "Sameakh" ("Happy"), referenced an Israeli kibbutz member longing for her Syrian lover, thereby referencing the peace talks that the Israeli government was having with Syria (Seale, 2000). This overt political reference joined more latent allusions to cross-national sexual relations — which provoked critical discussion over the band and its submission. Public critiques were heated when Ping Pong released a video in which they waved the Israeli flag alongside a Syrian one. Similar concerns were raised about its use of a cucumber to symbolise male genitalia. The IBA threatened to withdraw the entry, and politicians criticised the whole debacle, arguing that Ping Pong could not represent the Jewish State. Notwithstanding those pressures, Ping Pong continued to follow their plan. When onstage in Stockholm, the band waved a Syrian flag, thereby stretching the patience of Israeli ESC fans. For Israel, this was too much politics.

Wars of Song: Politics of Conflict

Another form of cultural battles fought on the ESC stage was offered by Russia and Ukraine. Actually, the ESC cultural seismograph long exposed latent tensions between the two countries, even well before the Russian invasion of Crimea in 2014. This was made evident by Ukraine's 2004 ESC winner, Ruslana, who declared that "Russia is our past, Europe must be our future".[5] Indeed, Ruslana criticised the Russia-oriented Ukrainian president Viktor Yanukovych for years, calling for Ukraine to align itself with Western Europe, liberalism and democracy. Years later, in 2014, Ruslana visited Washington to receive the State Department's Women of Courage award — reflecting her clear political voice in support of democracy and against war. As she made clear during that event, "[d]on't do something, do everything – to keep peace [in Ukraine] … before Putin will kill us".

Notwithstanding the centrality of recent military clashes between Russia and Ukraine, the ESC sent signs of their rift during the 2005 Orange Revolution and following the eruption of the 2014 conflict. For example, the Ukrainian struggle with its Soviet past, while facing new threats by Russia, made an early appearance in 2007, with Vera Serduchka's "Lasha Tumbai". For many commentators, the song stood to declare — Russia, goodbye! Several critiques argued that the lyrics were politically motivated. In response, the lead singer, Andriy Danylko claimed that the phrase means 'whipped cream' in Mongolian, thereby mocking again the apolitical stance of the EBU. As Galina Miazhevich suggested, "[t]he Ukrainian entry by Verka Serduchka in 2007, as well as the online responses to the show, aimed to articulate a vision of European nationhood, which simultaneously staked a position among other states of the former Soviet Union and reconfigured relationships with the shared Soviet past" (Miazhevich, 2012, p. 1505). Clearly, Vera Serduchka's performance opted to present Ukraine in the guise of 'progressive modernity' while distancing itself from its Soviet past.

Furthermore, a paper by Emily Johnson focused on the tension which erupted between Russia and Ukraine around the 2009 Russian entry "Mamo" – performed by the Ukrainian singer Anastasia Prikhodko, echoing prior latent critiques of Russia by Ukraine. If one listened to the debates around the event, suggested Emily Johnson, one could get a premonition for the current crisis between the former members of the Soviet Union. According to Johnson (Johnson, 2014),

> Given the controversy that erupted over Prikhod'ko's nomination and the tensions that divided Russia, Ukraine, and Georgia in spring 2009, less than a year after the Russo-Georgian War over South Ossetia and Abkhazia, the presence of these nostalgic elements in "Mamo" inevitably seemed politically freighted: the song effectively juxtaposed Soviet-style "ethnic harmony" to the quarrels of the present and hence, depending on one's point of view, either read as a touching appeal for peace and tolerance or as a veiled threat that hinted at the possible renewal of Russia's cultural dominance over the other former Soviet republics…The fact that "Mamo" evoked both Soviet rhetoric and the USSR's old borders might reasonably be read as a veiled threat — in the context of post-Soviet politics it can be difficult to tell a desire for unity and closer cooperation from aggressive expansionism (p. 43).

The spat with Russian aggression was not over for the ESC. Ukraine made it all the more apparent after the Russian invasion of Crimea. The victory by Jamala in 2016 — with the intimated anti-Russian song '1944' — is perhaps one of the clearest examples of the penetration of political rivalries onto the ESC stage. In spite of early predictions for a Russian victory by the singer Sergey Lazarev, with "You Are the Only One", Lazarev and Russia were "punished" by European voters who elected Ukraine's Jamala as the winner. Her song focused on the Soviet deportation of the Tatars from the Ukraine during the Second World War, a fear that Ruslana made clear during her stint in Washington in 2014: "Today I had a call from Crimean Tatars who told me, 'We know that we will be the first to be killed" if new fighting breaks out in Crimea".[6] As Peter Dickinson stated recently to the Atlantic Council, Jamala's entry "was to prove a major soft power triumph for Ukraine. The song drew renewed international attention to the plight of Crimean Tatars living under Russian occupation in Crimea. It also raised awareness about Soviet crimes against humanity, while undermining Moscow's attempts to falsely claim that Crimea had "always been Russian".[7] The response by Russian officials was prompt. As Frances Robinson wrote in *Politico*, "Kremlin officials and lawmakers slammed the voting system and claimed there was an "information war" against the country. Alexey Pushkov, head of the State Duma foreign affairs committee, said on Twitter that the ESC had "turned into a field for political battles".[8]

The Russian-Ukrainian conflict was reignited by a recent Ukrainian boycott of a Russian entry to the 2017 ESC event in Kyiv. The wheelchair-bound singer Yulia Samoylova, was then sent set to represent Russia, but was barred from entering Ukraine for three years because she had entered Crimea "illegally", namely directly from Russia, not via Ukraine. The EBU was disconcerted. In a statement about the Ukrainian boycott of Samoylova, it said "[we] have to re-spect the local laws of the host country; however, we are deeply disappointed in this decision as we feel it goes against both the spirit of the contest and the notion of inclusivity that lies at the heart of its values".[9] Nevertheless, the Ukrainian government did not accede. In response, Russian politicians called other countries to boycott the event in Kyiv, but none did. Either way, by the absence of Samoylova from the ESC, the Russian-Ukrainian conflict again loomed large over the ESC.

Discussion

Three decades ago people might have suspected that the ESC is not an impartial competition. Today – after hundreds of studies, this has become a popular truism across Europe: The ESC is political in various guises. The present chapter added to the academic discussion of political intrusions onto the stage and pointed to different political strategies: Hegemonic, suspicion and conflict. We have joined prior studies which suggested that the ESC is a cultural seismograph for detecting persistent national and cultural rifts that divide Europe (Vuletic, 2018). Though only in rare cases, this popular contest exposes grim inter-regional struggles (Watts, 2007; Tanase & García, 2013; Gatherer, 2006). Should we indeed seek better testimonies than the Russia-Ukraine conflict for the persistence of national and cultural rivalries? And should we be surprised when such cultural animosities on the ESC stage turn into geopolitical conflicts or reflect them? And as the present chapter made apparent, the ESC reveals various forms of doing politics – some more apparent, some less so. And part of the fun in the contest is to detect the surprising infiltrations of political elements into this seemingly a-political competition.

Those political elements explain international relations that are practically unrelated to the ESC. For example, studies of bloc voting in the ESC have found that voting patterns — which sometimes reflect political positions — also help explain international trade relations. One study suggested "that cultural proximity is a more important determinant of bilateral trade than researchers usually allow with the sort of cultural variables they include" (Felbermayr & Toubal, 2010, p. 280). They also pointed out that "ESC scores indeed reflect cultural proximity" and that "proximity is a major determinant of bilateral trade volumes" (op cit, p. 291). In a paper published by business professors from the University of Copenhagen, Kokko and Tingvall, (2014) argued that "[t]he choice of export destinations and locations for foreign direct investment is not determined by objective economic data alone but also by how familiar the exporter or investor is with the target market". To capture the effects of international "familiarity" on trade patterns they used the idea of "psychic distance" or cultural homology, and added them to traditional economic variables like distance, preferences and price. Since cultural affinities can be a predictor for ESC voting patterns, they argue that the "results of the European Song Contest are a robust predictor of bilateral trade" (Kokko & Tingvall, 2014). This implies, they suggest, that "[a] stronger preference for country i in country j's ESC votes suggests that country j will also import more goods from country i, controlling for other determinants of trade". They also suggest that ESC data became better predictors with the move to popular televoting, as publics are more relevant to economic consumption than expert juries. As Tanase and Garcia have added, ESC results are indeed sensitive to economic conditions (Tanase & García, 2013). They argue that the monetary crisis in Europe has widened the gap between countries and blocs. As they consider it, "[t]he polarization in the Eurovision would be an early indicator for a social and cultural phenomenon, which is followed by states of distrust in the economy of the involved countries" (Tanase & García, 2013, p. 28). Recent Greek performances, for example, provided clear testimonies of German-Greek tensions — either self-critique of the Greek character or its economic conditions, or against external monetary control of Greece by Germany. Overall, it seems that economic crises affect cultural distances between countries, and this growing distance can be observed through voting patterns.

However, politics in the ESC is not just about the money, of course. A new study by Felix Pot — which used a unique technique to assess the political "over-evaluation" of songs — provided an interesting observation on the post-Soviet bloc: Russia remains loyal to its former satellites, but with the years the latter are less and less supportive of Russian songs. As Pot writes: "It is striking that the former Eastern Bloc countries that are now part of the European Union do receive any overvaluations from Russia. These countries themselves have also given less and less overvaluations to Russia, and since 2014 they have on average not even given overvaluations to Russia anymore" (Pot, 2021, p. 3). The bloc — once a politically cemented Soviet stronghold — gives way to song, pop, and parade. Still, ESC voting patterns — as with the lyrics and performances — are indeed a political and cultural seismograph.

Viewed from this perspective, one could argue that the EBU's a-political stance is often betrayed by deeper national and cultural schisms. After unification, the EU's intent of reconciling the nations of the continent that had recently been torn apart by the atrocities of the Second World War – well, that intent is often mocked by artists. We may suggest that those political intrusions actually drive the popularity of the event with broadcast ratings consistently on the rise. It is now believed that the competition draws as much as 200 million viewers worldwide, which makes it the biggest contest of its sort, and one of the biggest television shows in terms of rating figures. It may be also the largest political event – at least in Europe.

Furthermore, while critics often view the ESC as a frivolous, superficial event, it occasionally does serve as a platform for progressive messages that go far beyond sheer "musical entertainment". Notwithstanding the EBU's decree against political statements in the ESC, countries still find ways (e.g., the postcards or the interval act) to include sharp, though disguised political messages, and raise awareness of social and political issues — all during a song of no longer than three minutes. This should not surprise anyone. After all, the original mechanism of the ESC was the de-facto creation of a multicultural space for all sorts of artistic expression. That political conflicts and agendas pop up from the backstage should be seen as one of the fascinating elements of the ESC.

Notes

1 https://eurovision.tv/story/ebu-statement-on-belarusian-entry-2021
2 https://world.time.com/2012/03/05/ukraines-eurovision-selection-marred-by-right-wing-racism/
3 https://eurovision.tv/story/martin-osterdahl-new-eurovision-song-contest-executive-supervisor
4 https://www.politico.eu/article/13-times-eurovision-song-contest-got-political/
5 Reported by Reuters, December 12 2013.
6 https://www.atlanticcouncil.org/commentary/event-recap/singer-activist-ruslana-do-everything-to-avert-war-in-ukraine/
7 https://www.atlanticcouncil.org/blogs/ukrainealert/why-eurovision-is-ukraines-soft-power-secret-weapon/
8 https://www.politico.eu/article/13-times-eurovision-song-contest-got-political/
9 https://www.bbc.com/news/world-europe-39354775

References

Adler, D. (2004). Painterly politics: Wölfflin, formalism and German academic culture, 1885–1915. *Art History, 27*(3), 431–456.

Beyar, R., Zeevi, B., & Rechavi, G. (2017). Israel: a start-up life science nation. *The Lancet, 389*(10088), 2563–2569.

Bohlman, P.V. (2007). The politics of power, pleasure, and prayer in the Eurovision Song Contest. *Musicology, 7,* 39–67.

Bourdieu, P. (1996). *The Rules of Art: Genesis and Structure of the Literary Field,* Cambridge, UK: Polity Press.

Cassiday, J.A. (2014). Post-Soviet Pop Goes Gay: Russia's Trajectory to Eurovision Victory. *Russian Review, 73*(1), 1–23.

Charron, N. (2013). Impartiality, friendship-networks and voting behavior: Evidence from voting patterns in the Eurovision Song Contest. *Social Networks, 35*(3), 484–497.

Dekker, A. (2007). The Eurovision Song Contest as a "Friendship" Network. *Connections, 27*(3), 53–58.

Felbermayr, G.J., & Toubal, F. (2010). Cultural proximity and trade. *European Economic Review, 54*(2), 279–293.

Gatherer, D. (2006). Comparison of Eurovision Song Contest Simulation with Actual Results Reveals Shifting Patterns of Collusive Voting Alliances. *Journal of Artificial Societies and Social Simulation, 9*(2), 1–13.

Heller, D. (2007). t.A.T.u. You! Russia, the global politics of Eurovision, and lesbian pop. *Popular Music, 26*(2), 195–210.

Johansson, K.M. (2017). Sweden and the european union. In *Oxford research encyclopedia of politics.* Oxford University Press.

Johnson, E. (2014). A New Song for a New Motherland: Eurovision and the Rhetoric of Post-Soviet National Identity. *The Russian Review, 73*(1), 24–46.

Kalman, J., Wellings, B., & Jacotine, K. eds. (2019). *Eurovisions: Identity and the International Politics of the Eurovision Song Contest since 1956.* Springer Singapore.

Kant, I. (1983). *Perpetual Peace and Other Essays.* Hackett Publishing Company.

Kokko, A., & Tingvall, P.G. (2014). Distance, transaction costs, and preferences in european trade. *The International Trade Journal, 28*(2), 87–120.

Lemish, D. (2004). my kind of campfire": the eurovision song contest and israeli gay men. *Popular Communication, 2*(1), 41–63.

Miazhevich, G. (2012). Ukrainian Nation Branding Off-line and Online: Verka Serduchka at the Eurovision Song Contest. *Europe-Asia studies, 64*(8), 1505–1523.

Pot, F. (2021). *Mapping favouritism at the Eurovision Song Contest: does it impact the results?* Master thesis.

Seale, P. (2000). The Syria-Israel Negotiations: Who Is Telling the Truth? *Journal of Palestine studies, 29*(2), 65–77.

Senor, D., & Singer, S. (2009). *Start-up Nation: The Story of Israel's Economic Miracle*. A Council on Foreign Relations Book.

Singleton, B., Fricker, K., & Moreo, E. (2007). Performing the queer network. Fans and families at the Eurovision Song Contest. *SQS, 2*(2), 12–24.

Tanase, D., & García, D. (2013). Measuring Cultural Dynamics Through the Eurovision Song Contest. *Advances in Complex Systems, 16*(8), 1350037.

Vuletic, D. (2018). *Postwar Europe and the Eurovision Song Contest*. Bloomsbury.

Watts, D.J. (2007). The Politics of Eurovision. *The New York Times*, Op-Ed Section (May 22).

Yair, G. (2018). Douze point: Eurovisions and Euro-Divisions in the Eurovision Song Contest – Review of two decades of research. *European Journal of Cultural Studies, 22*(5–6), 1013–1029.

Yair, G. (1995). Unite Unite Europe: The Political and Cultural Structure of Europe as Reflected in the Eurovision Song Contest. *Social Networks, 17*, 147–161.

7   The Molitva Factor: The Eurovision Song Contest and 'Performing' National Identity in World Politics

Catherine Baker

'Sooner or later Eurovision explains everything,' my Twitter bio says, and world politics keep agreeing. Repercussions of Russian president Vladimir Putin's annexation of Crimea from Ukraine marked almost every Eurovision Song Contest (ESC) between 2014 and 2019. They might only have waned in 2021 because Russia's hastily-reselected representative vocally championed multiethnic Russian nationhood and LGBTQ rights, so Russian disinformation channels ignored the contest instead. The ESC's historic associations between queerness and nationhood, forged first through fandom then also by iconic openly-LGBTQ performances, have made it a site of struggle over transnational LGBTQ visibility. And while it might be facetious to say the state of Serbia and Montenegro broke up in 2006 because its two components could not agree a joint ESC entry, the impasse still revealed the union's fragility. A year later, Marija Šerifović won the ESC for Serbia on its first solo appearance with the intimate sapphic ballad 'Molitva' ('Prayer').

The ESC also uniquely illustrates the idea of contestants, and even leaders, as symbolic representatives of the nation, whose bodies and embodied practices 'perform' national identity. The idea of 'performing' national identity implies that certain bodily ways of appearing, dressing, speaking and moving are interpreted, both in ritual and everyday life, as signs of belonging (or not) to a nation, which are further inflected by other social identities including gender, race and class. It stems from Judith Butler's notion of gender itself as 'performative', that is, continually being reconstituted through the repeated impression of individuals' bodily appearance and practices (Butler, 1988: 519). The performance scholar Diana Taylor (1997) applied this to nationhood in researching conformist and non-conformist public spectacle during Argentina's 1976–83 dictatorship. Indeed, for Taylor, gender and nationhood 'are the product of each other's performance and therefore difficult to imagine separately' (1997: 92). This manifests visibly in gender-segregated international sport. For instance, in figure skating – where Ellyn Kestnbaum (2003) used performance studies to understand how skaters performed gender and nation (and the often-unspoken layer of race) together – competitors must not only master technique but also synchronise costume, movement and music. That assemblage, live singing aside, approaches the elements of meaning involved in designing entries for the ESC stage.[1]

DOI: 10.4324/9781003188933-9

The idea of 'performing' national identity informs how I study nationalism and nationhood, alongside the idea of 'narratives' of national identity, which often clash underneath struggles over whether performances of national identity are authentic or appropriate. In post-Yugoslav popular music, my first specialism, these struggles frequently concern 'European' belonging. First in contemporary south-east European cultural history, then in International Relations, the ESC has helped me research these issues in two domains that might initially seem disconnected – pop-folk music and LGBTQ rights. Both, since the 1990s, have become what Bojan Bilić (2016: 118) calls a 'litmus test' of nations' Europeanness itself. Embodied performances of nationhood such as those made at the ESC – but also those made by political leaders and other symbolic figures – can sway or attempt to sway the litmus test in particular ways. The 'Molitva factor', as this chapter terms it, denotes what happens when they are made.

Performing National Identity at the ESC

Besides occasional entries that present themselves as performances of national identity immediately by incorporating national names or flags into what viewers see on stage, the ESC's structure as an international competitive event and the perpetual reinforcement of that fact through practices structured into its broadcasts frame *all* entries as representing their nation – or rather the state associated with it, which funds or licences the public service broadcasters who belong to the ESC through membership of the European Broadcasting Union (EBU). Entries have long appeared under national denominations and flags, and the permanent ESC logo introduced in 2004 accommodates any host's or participant's national flag within its heart shape, assimilating any potential nation into the ESC's institutional branding. All these techniques frame the ESC and its performances as making nationhood structurally salient (Bolin, 2006), just as the structure of international sport normalises a 'banal nationalism' of territorially-bounded nations as the natural order of things (Billig, 1995).

An even deeper level on which performing at the ESC performs embodiment of the nation arises from the hallowed place of shared national culture in the idea of nationalism. Narratives of every nation's cultural identity encode certain musical practices, singing styles, dance traditions, dress customs, instruments, and of course languages, as authentic expressions of nationhood. These, in John Armstrong's words, are 'symbolic "border guards"' of national identity, delineating boundaries between 'us' and 'them' (Yuval-Davis, 1993: 627). Other sets of practices connote belonging to transnational musical, entertainment and consumption cultures (especially but not only the Anglophone West). Other sets again connote regional rather than narrowly national cultural identities, with origins that predate a territory's division into bounded nation-states. The ESC's ritual structure conditions us to observe such meaning-making at work, but more everyday modes of 'performing' the nation operate all the time.

Postsocialist south-east European cultural politics continually set practices marked 'as 'western' and therefore 'European', and practices marked as 'eastern' therefore 'Balkan', against each other. Thanks to intercultural exchange and diffusion during the Ottoman period, within the so-called 'Ottoman ecumene' national folk music cultures from south-east Europe to the Caucasus, Anatolia and the Middle East exhibit interwoven similarities (Buchanan, 2007: xviii). The ESC makes them internationally visible and audible as 'ethnopop'. In 1990s world music, and then in the ESC, 'Balkan' musical practices were well-suited for capitalising on audiences' thirst for exoticism, but also carried high cultural risks lest they frame nations as 'backward' rather than as knowing, cosmopolitan purveyors of tradition. Every performance of national identity at the ESC, but especially those navigating the Europeanness 'litmus test' in peripheralised regions, can thus be seen as taking a position in the continual struggles to define and fix the substance of national identity which, to constructivist scholars, constitute 'nationalism' as we recognise it in the world.

Although nationalism emphases shared history and culture, narratives of national identity in every nation are actually multiple, and are often in competition during socio-political struggles (Bellamy, 2003). Assertions of national identity thus also represent acts in an ongoing contestation about which version of national identity should prevail. Which individuals, groups and institutions are most able to define and communicate their preferred version, or to mobilise others around it, is a matter of power relations but sometimes also prefigures changes in them; at the ESC, we may sometimes even observe this taking place. Such processual views of national identity also recognise that outside observers contribute to making assertions and performances of national identity meaningful, by interpreting them and completing their meaning. Individuals' experiences of national belonging differ greatly depending on how far others accept them as members, with powerful social, material and emotional consequences if acceptance is denied or made conditional – as frequently happens to those who exhibit linguistic, ethnic, racial, religious and/or sexual Otherness (Yuval-Davis, 1993). Throughout peripheralised regions of Europe, and indeed peripheralised regions of the world, the afterlife of coloniality makes the judging gaze of the West another all but inescapable reference point.

The ESC and the Litmus Test of 'Europeanness'

The stakes of being evaluated as modern and progressive rather than ethnocentric and backward overshadow cultural production, but also the politics of European Union (EU) accession. To be accepted as EU member states, postsocialist candidates had to demonstrate they had 'caught up' with the EU in implementing the package of obligations known as the "acquis communautaire". These covered everything from the rule of law to safety standards, border security regimes and social rights. After the EU added protection from homophobic discrimination to the 1997 Treaty of Amsterdam, demonstrable progress on LGBTQ rights became another requirement for accession (Stychin, 2004: 962–3). As right-wing nationalisms mobilised against LGBTQ activism, holding Pride parades and successfully securing them against far-right attacks thus became seen, within the EU and on its eastern periphery, as another benchmark of accession-readiness (Slootmaeckers, 2017). The ESC too came under this scrutinising lens, even though the EBU and EU are institutionally completely separate. In 2002, when Slovenia selected the drag trio Sestre and they faced a campaign of homophobic and transphobic abuse, a Dutch liberal member of the European Parliament, Lousewies van der Laan, famously stated 'perhaps, Slovenia is not yet ready for EU membership' if society was still questioning 'the issue of gay rights' (BBC, 2002). Such articulations of a European 'Pink Agenda', Francesca Ammaturo (2015: 1152) argues, have drawn 'lines of fracture' between a queer-friendly interior of Europe and a subordinate queerphobic outside, excluded from full European citizenship even when it is part of Europe geographically.

In the early 2000s when I began researching the ESC as part of researching the cultural politics of post-Yugoslav popular music, Croatia's and Serbia's greatest cultural 'litmus test' concerned pop-folk music drawing on traditions from the Ottoman ecumene. Symbolic boundaries around it were even more charged in the post-Yugoslav region than elsewhere, since Slovenian and Croatian governments and media in the 1990s had aggressively sought to distance national identity from anything 'Balkan', 'Yugoslav', 'Serbian' or 'eastern', while pop-folk's detractors in Serbia associated it with the corrupt values of Slobodan Milošević's regime. An opposite pole of new musical production based on traditional music, in post-Yugoslav taste cultures, was 'etno'. 'Etno' implied authenticity, research, discernment, professional training, and engagement with the world music market before domestic commercial pop – elements testifying to a musician's skill and intellect, which were seen as suited to a Western gaze (Čolović, 2006).

Since 1993, when post-Yugoslav broadcasters began competing in the ESC independently and many other postsocialist broadcasters sought to debut, these countries' very presence in ESC appeared to be enacting their region's so-called 'return to Europe' (Jordan, 2015). This then-common discourse maintained communism had kept each country back from being modern European economies, societies and cultures – though arguably at the expense of their former anti-colonial solidarities with the Global South (Mark et al., 2020: 18–19). In the late 1990s the ESC's staging and voting practices were also in transition, encouraging delegations to experiment with non-orchestral music genres, larger-scale props and choreography (while the first openly gay ESC contestant, Páll Óskar, appeared in 1997, and the first openly trans ESC participant plus first LGBTQ winner, Dana International, appeared in 1998). Moreover, these efforts paid off: all 2001–9 contests had first-time winners, most were from central and eastern Europe, and the rest were also on European peripheries (Finland, Turkey and Greece). Estonia's 2001 victory, deftly incorporated into a new governmental nation-branding strategy to reframe Western perceptions of Estonia when Tallinn hosted the ESC in 2002, made national promotion through the ESC appeal to other broadcasters too (Jordan, 2015).

Winning Eurovision in these years demonstrated nations could stage European-standard productions and create memorable concepts which would play to viewers' preconceptions but perhaps also update them. The winning entries in 2001–2 could both be taken as performing a comfort with (ethnic or sexual) difference, as well as global musical style, which Western viewers might not have associated with the Baltic States (Aston, 2013: 168–9). The 2003–4 winners enshrined a mode of self-exoticism in ESC performance that postsocialist creative entrepreneurs negotiating Western-dominated world music and cinema markets had already developed (see Buchanan, 1997). Sertab Erener, Turkey's 2003 winner, played on orientalist harem fantasies and the beginning of Western pop's fashion for 'oriental R&B' to stage a seductive spectacle around 'Every Way That I Can' (Solomon, 2007). The concept of Ruslana's 'Wild dances', which she had already been developing in Ukraine before being selected for the 2004 ESC, remained iconic enough in 2014 to provide the opening note of the ESC interval act 'Love, love, peace, peace', a remarkably faithful satire of twenty-first-century ESC performance ('Step 1: Get everyone's attention. A powerful, majestic start. Maybe a battle horn of some kind?').

Ruslana's mobilisation of 'wildness' and the sexualised Amazon was ostensibly grounded in her ethnomusicological research with Carpathian Hutsuls, though also mediated for many viewers via *Xena: Warrior Princess*. Maria Sonevytsky (2020: 43) summarises it as 'a dedicated endeavor to appease Europe by perfecting the Eurovision aesthetic that blends catchy global pop with essentialised national self-presentation' – indeed, defining it for a wave of subsequent entries. Yet within Ukraine her performing body carried 'the weight of internal national discourses of Ukrainian sexuality and femininity', with many Hutsul villagers unimpressed by her eroticisation of Hutsul femininity and what they felt as 'the shame of being called "wild"' (Sonevytsky, 2020: 42, 44). Ensuing debates in Ukraine about whether a nation representing itself 'as a cradle of ancient, primitive expressive culture' could also be 'taken seriously as a "European" state' (Sonevytsky, 2020: 49) anticipated similar debates around post-Yugoslav entries.

The same year Ruslana won by creatively packaging essentialised folklore, Serbia-Montenegro came second on its debut with another version of the same approach, Željko Joksimović's 'Lane moje' (My Darling). Joksimović's perfor-mance, expressing a soft pastoral masculinity, has been read as seeking to reframe Western perceptions of Serbia from the Yugoslav wars (Mitrović, 2010). In Serbia, its traditional instruments (the saz and kaval) and neotraditional costume elements also coded its use of folklore as 'etno', not 'turbo folk' – conveying suitable mastery and erudition for a Serbia performing readiness to join or return to 'Europe'. Joksimović's model inspired several other post-Yugoslav entries aspiring to bring home what the ESC had brought Tallinn and Kyiv. Bosnia-Herzegovina Radio-Television (BHRT) even recruited Joksimović as composer for Hari Mata Hari's 'Lejla' in 2006. In Croatia – the post-Yugoslav state with strongest ESC results in the 1990s – Boris Novković repackaged folk tradition for the ESC twice, with his own entry in 2005 and another for Severina in 2006.

Having dealt with both entries extensively elsewhere (Baker, 2008a, 2008b), it suffices to say here that Novković's performance ruffled no cultural feathers but Severina's became Croatia's most scandalous ESC entry to date. For numerous reasons, including the ex-Yugoslav world music entrepreneur Goran Bregović's role as arranger and a needless rumour that the lyrics were actually in Serbian, 'Moja štikla' provoked a perfect discursive storm of claims that the song was not authentically Croatian enough for 'Europe', and counter-claims by the song's team pointing to features that justified the song's Croatian identity. This case unfolded in the middle of my PhD on narratives of identity in Croatian popular music, and my theorisation of the ESC's gazes of meaning-making and pleasure towards such performances of essentialised folklore became my first contribution to ESC research (Baker, 2008b). Here, the 'litmus test' had turned on 'Balkan' folk elements. A year after 'Moja štikla', Marija Šerifović became the first post-Yugoslav ESC winner with 'Molitva' – bringing the test sharply towards Serbia just as the ESC was becoming a site in the European and world politics of LGBTQ rights.

'Molitva' and the Politics of LGBTQ Visibility in Europe

'Molitva' was not only an LGBTQ landmark for the ESC but also another episode in cosmopolitan Serbian identity-making, especially since Serbia then hosted the 2008 ESC – having won on its standalone debut, now Serbia-Montenegro was no more. (Serbia-Montenegro's last preselection for the ESC in 2006, two months before Montenegro's independence referendum, had ended too acrimoniously to send an entry.) 'Molitva' stood out from previous 2000s winners as a ballad in national language, and as a lyric which (unusually for the ESC) blended sacred and secular love (Bohlman, 2007). Neither did it adopt the glittery form of camp then most associated with the ESC, which viewers familiar with that cultural code projected on to the cross-gender performance of Verka Serduchka, Ukraine's runner-up (Miazhevich, 2012). The butch/femme impression of Šerifović's gender-non-conforming, casually-rumpled appearance beside her backing vocalists' high-femme style and intimate movements nevertheless gave the performance legibility as 'lesbian camp' (Vänskä, 2007).

Since Šerifović was not yet openly discussing her sexuality in 2007 (she came out in 2013), it was primarily performance design, overseen by Radio-Television Serbia (RTS), that queered 'Molitva' on stage (Vuletic, 2018: 191). As an embodied performance of national identity, Šerifović and her backing vocalists could be read as symbolising a Serbia which was comfortable sending a potentially queer ESC entry: even viewers for whom it did not register as sapphic camp would have noticed the hand-holding and Šerifović's gender variance. Such a Serbia would simultaneously be proud enough of national linguistic tradition to deploy it in the global-English-dominated medium of pop, and open to personal faith more inclusively than the national institutionalised Church. This was perhaps a more amenable balance between sexual difference and nationhood than the 'globalised gay' identity articulated through coverage of Belgrade's first Pride in 2001 (Slootmaeckers, 2017: 525). As well as confirming the ESC as somewhere where, in Peter Rehberg's now much-cited words, '*both* queerness *and* national identity' could be celebrated at once (Rehberg, 2007: 60, emphasis original), the conjunction perhaps even allowed for simultaneously celebrating queerness, national identity *and* faith.

As with Tallinn, Riga and Kyiv, Belgrade's ESC gave its organisers an opportunity to reframe international perceptions of the host city and country even more widely by demonstrating they could hold successful mega-events. RTS's director, Aleksandar Tijanić, famously promised to present 'the new face of Serbia' to the world, and also directly stated '[h]osting Eurosong will help Serbia improve its image in the European Union' (Mitrović, 2010: 176). He told the Serbian tabloid *Blic* after hosting the contest that 'we have managed to change the stereotypical image of Serbia', and the Serbian president Boris Tadić's congratulations to Tijanić's team stated 'Serbia and its capital have again proved to be a part of Europe'. While these remarks addressed Serbian audiences, Marijana Mitrović (2010: 176–7) found CNN, Deutsche Welle, Itar-Tass, the BBC, Czech and Polish media hailing Serbia's friendly face similarly. Yet this was still tempered by the EBU having had to take security soundings about whether to relocate the contest after riots in Belgrade followed Kosovo's unilateral independence declaration in February 2008 (Mitrović, 2010: 175–6). Furthermore, a briefing for foreign journalists and fan media signed by the ESC's executive supervisor and RTS's executive producer for the contest had to advise them 'to avoid political discussions, public same gender sexual expressions and jaywalking', as reported by Vänskä (2007: 60).

In cities where strategic official LGBTQ-friendliness coexists with high anti-LGBTQ militancy, hosting the ESC still manifests these tensions between the ideal and symbolic space of performance and material city space. In 2017, for instance, Kyiv Pride published a map of LGBTQ-friendly venues in order to reassure queer foreign tourists they would be welcome there (and avoid them visiting riskier places). The city council began redecorating the People's Friendship Arch, built under Soviet rule in 1982, as a rainbow 'Arch of Diversity'. However, the works were interrupted halfway by militant members of Right Sector – leaving Kyiv's celebration in an unfinished stalemate that Kyiv Pride's Zoryan Kis described as 'a good metaphor' for contemporary Ukraine, consisting of 'only changes on the outside', and incomplete at that (Miller, 2017).

Between 2007–8 and 2017, much had changed for the visibility of LGBTQ rights in world politics, and as a political issue at the ESC. In later research, I have explained how LGBTQ rights rose up the international agenda following the 2007 Yogyakarta Principles, and how activists campaigning to raise awareness of host countries' violations of LGBTQ rights and other human rights during international mega-events started targeting the ESC as well as the Olympic Games (Baker, 2017). This feedback loop encompassed the 2008 Beijing Summer Olympic Games, the 2009 ESC in Moscow (where Pride had been banned since 2006), the 2012 ESC in Baku (see Gluhovic, 2013), and the London Summer Olympic Games' performance of diversity including LGBTQ inclusion. The 2013 ESC in Malmö exhibited echoes of the same. One month later, Russia's parliament passed its 'gay propaganda' law. Then followed the catalysing events of 2014 – when Russia hosted the Winter Olympic Games in Sochi, Western campaigners called for a boycott over Russia's anti-LGBTQ law, Putin's regime began annexing Crimea as the Games concluded, and the bearded Austrian drag queen Conchita Wurst, a character created by Tom Neuwirth, won Eurovision. Wurst's victory was widely taken as confirmation that sexual and gender diversity were part of 'Europeanness' today, especially once she dedicated her reprise to 'everyone who believes in a future of peace and freedom. You know who you are. We are unity, and we are unstoppable!' (Weber, 2016: 162). Commentators gladly swept her up into their visions of a 'new Cold War' between Europe and Russia.

These developing politics of also caught up Pride marches in Belgrade, and other post-Yugoslav cities, as apparent evidence of countries' whole records on LGBTQ equality, thus symbols of how 'European' the nation was (Kahlina, 2015). This 'litmus test', as Bilić (2016: 118) describes the politics around Belgrade Pride, is the same test that has charged ESC performance and hosting with symbolic significance. Within Serbia, Belgrade Pride exists in tension between asserting LGBTQ residents' 'right to the city' in coalition with other social movements (Bilić and Stubbs, 2015) and recognition that Belgrade-centric activism one day per year does not fully represent economically-disadvantaged LGBTQ people across Serbia (Radoman, 2016: 182). Belgrade's first Pride, in 2001, had been broken up by far-right militants in attacks that still emotionally affected some participants a decade later (Kajinić, 2019: 69–74). A second Pride in 2004 was called off for fear of further far-right violence given the security situation in Kosovo (Radoman, 2016: 174). When 'Molitva' won the ESC and Belgrade hosted it, therefore, Pride had not been held in Belgrade or anywhere else in Serbia since 2001.

Plans for Belgrade Pride were however revived in September 2009, six months after Serbia passed an Anti-Discrimination Law, until far-right threats led police to move the march from central Belgrade to the city's periphery; organisers cancelled it rather than abandon its visibility in symbolic urban space. In October 2010, Belgrade finally held its second Pride, under heavy armed police guard, who clashed with violent far-right counter-demonstrators all night. Permission for Pride was again denied in 2011–13, but given in 2014, under a new prime minister, Aleksandar Vučić – with LGBTQ rights higher on the international political agenda after the Russian 'homopropaganda' law and the Sochi boycott campaign. This pride march proceeded without violence for the first time on 28 September – five months after Wurst had won the ESC and the Serbian Orthodox Church's patriarch had blamed her and the LGBTQ community for inviting divine punishment via that summer's devastating floods. It was now clear that whether Pride could be held peacefully, or at all, depended on state whim, the authorities' willingness to leverage their ambiguous relationships with groups that threatened Pride, and how far the government desired to be seen as performing Serbia's readiness for Europeanisation (Ejdus & Božović, 2019).

Amid the 'litmus test' around Pride, Koen Slootmaeckers argues, 'the government (particularly Vučić)' had most to gain from enabling it:

> Playing on the organisers' desperation to exercise their freedom of assembly, Vučić used Pride as a move to align with EU's expectations, a tool to bolster his (inter)national image as a reforming Pro-EU force and to highlight his capacity to enforce Serbia's constitution (2017: 529).

In Serbian LGBTQ politics, this made the heavily-policed Belgrade Pride into a ritualistic 'transparent closet' (Slootmaeckers, 2017: 529) – one where LGBTQ people were visible to foreign news cameras but not in everyday city life, and where police showed off their power to enforce EU expectations of Serbia. Vučić's opportunistic stance towards LGBTQ visibility was equally apparent after he won Serbia's presidential elections in 2017 and appointed Ana Brnabić as replacement prime minister. The wide literature on Belgrade Pride, and an emerging literature on Brnabić, thus deals with the very litmus test we observe through the ESC – symbolic politics of readiness for 'Europe'; contestations between cosmopolitan and traditionalist society; ideas for alternative forms of expression and organising that can bridge them. Yet neither 'Molitva', nor Belgrade's hosting the ESC and needing to secure city space for thousands of LGBTQ tourists, have been widely acknowledged as context for Belgrade Pride's reinstatement, or for that matter Brnabić's political persona.

Europeanisation, LGBTQ Visibility and Embodied Performances of National Identity: the Molitva Factor

Brnabić, formerly Serbia's non-party-political minister for public administration and local government, is not only Serbia's first female prime minister, but also the first openly LGBTQ prime minister in postsocialist Europe, the second openly lesbian prime minister anywhere (following Iceland's Jóhanna Sigurðardóttir in 2009–13), Serbia's only openly LGBTQ politician, and the first serving prime minister to have a same-gender partner give birth – all 'firsts' she has been hailed for by international media (and even my own university, where Brnabić took an MBA in 2000–1). Her gender expression is also visibly masculine-of-centre: unlike most female world leaders, Brnabić typically wears blazers, dark trousers, open-necked shirts and brown or black lace-up shoes, and is rarely if ever photographed in skirts or dresses. Her choice not to wear make-up stands out perhaps even more from the conventions of femininity expected of female leaders. Together, these practices make her style 'legible' (Lewis, 1997: 104) as lesbian or queer. Though Brnabić distanced herself from LGBTQ rights reforms as a priority and stated she did 'not want to be branded "Serbia's gay PM"' (Wintour, 2017), she did attend Belgrade Pride in 2017–19 – to some resistance from campaigners who believed she had not done enough for LGBTQ rights, even though Pride organisers themselves still welcomed her (Maričić & Živić, 2018).

The critical queer and feminist scholar Bojan Bilić acknowledges both these dimensions of Brnabić's impact on Serbian gender and sexual politics. On one hand, her masculine-of-centre gender expression as a female, lesbian political/ diplomatic figure 'has the potential to destabilise gender dichotomies and widen the spectrum of ways in which women can be represented' (Bilić, 2020: 380). In practice, however, she disappointed feminists by refusing to connect her personal sexual difference and gender non-conformity to wider critiques of gender and class relations; she shows disinterest in legal recognition for same-gender marriage and parenting even though it would protect her household; her own success within the managerial class insulates her family from most same-gender couples' marginality; and in May 2019 she called Kosovar politicians who had belonged to the Kosovo Liberation Army 'people who have literally just come out of the woods', a statement that 'quickly activated racist discourses about Albanians which are in the marrow of Serbian nationalism' (Bilić, 2020: 386). In 2018 she directly refused to call the Army of Republika Srpska's actions at Srebrenica a genocide in a Deutsche Welle interview (Deutsche Welle, 2018), and she continues to give Srebrenica the minimising description of a 'terrible crime' (Husarić et al., 2021). Her acceptance of the Order of Republika Srpska from Bosnia-Herzegovina's Serb entity during its self-proclaimed national day celebrations in 2019 was criticised for legitimising separatist policies there (Banjac, 2019).

The contentions in Serbia that manifested first through Belgrade Pride, then through Brnabić's appointment, were national-level expressions of global struggles over LGBTQ visibility and rights that International Relations scholars were starting to address within a new field of 'Queer IR' (Richter-Montpetit & Weber, 2018: 222), dealing with problems such as homonationalism and ex-clusionary liberal definitions of sexual citizenship. Its landmark monograph, Cynthia Weber's *Queer International Relations*, demonstrated how queer analytics could inform IR's understandings of sovereignty and the 'will to knowledge' that states exercise over sexuality, producing sexual categories like 'the homosexual' and giving them political meaning. Weber sought to expose the limitations of constructing all such figures as either 'normal' or 'perverse' in the way that conventional liberal logics establish opposing 'good' and 'bad' gay figures. Weber uses the figure of 'Neuwirth/Conchita', who had just won the ESC when Weber was writing, to show their assemblage could not be framed solely as either 'normal' or 'perverse'.[2]

Debates about Neuwirth/Wurst in 2014 had attempted to fix them as either the 'normal' homosexual, representing LGBTQ-friendiy European integration and a homophobia-free Europe, or the 'perverse' homosexual, transgressing gender boundaries and embodying the corrupting influence of 'Gayropa' on national morals. Yet in queer theory's terms, Neuwirth/Conchita could not 'signify monolithically' on either side of the border, not least because of their beard, which on Conchita's body simultaneously evoked bearded drag queens, bearded female saints, and a cross-gender Christ (Weber, 2016: 158, 161). Weber thus writes, citing blog posts I wrote before and after the 2014 ESC:

> Neuwirth/Wurst's Eurovision victory mattered for 'Europe itself', then, because – in Catherine Baker's terms – Neuwirth/Wurst's victory made her/him/them 'available as a symbol for denoting … ideological and geopolitical clashes' as well as agreements around what it means to be a unified and/or fractured 'Europe' and what it means to be identified as/with this 'Europe'
> (Weber, 2016: 153)

This imagined modern, progressive and tolerant 'Europe', critical scholarship in postcolonial queer studies was pointing out, is commonly played off against Islam, the Global South and its diasporas to stigmatise them as 'behind' Europe, creating racialised symbolic boundaries around 'Europe' and even within European city space (El-Tayeb, 2011). Postsocialist queer studies had argued that central and eastern Europe was subjected to an analogous, though often not connected, temporality (Kułpa and Mizielińska (ed.) 2011). In these debates, the ESC illuminates the fact that the relationship between 'Europeanisation' and LGBTQ rights claims is not solely produced by states and activist NGOs, but also by popular culture and the individuals and institutions creating it (Baker, 2017). It also reveals the complex entanglement of nationhood and sexual difference in an international competition with strong LGBTQ associations. Indeed, while nationalist opponents of Europeanisation often point to LGBTQ movements, supposedly driven by 'Europe', as separating people from national traditions of masculinity and femininity, one precondition for a transnationally emancipatory queer politics is to be able to imagine ways of being queer that are simultaneously national, that is, not confined to so-called 'globalised gay' identities from the commercial West.

The ESC even contains potential for these hinges to be forged, whether through Šerifović's interweaving sapphic camp with personal faith and native-language expression, or the response of Montenegro's Slavko Kalezić in 2017 when Montenegrin internet users attacked the homoeroticism of the video for his entry 'Space'. With lyrics crammed with allusions to ejaculation, orgasm and switching gender roles (including 'Wet dreams, wild nightmares, I surrender/ Come into me from within/We can be as one in the sin', and 'I've got my suit on, no need to worry' – gay fans readily took this as a condom, not just a spacesuit), a video directed by Dejan Milićević, and visual nods to Byzantine iconography and even perhaps Sufi tradition, Kalezić's entry was more conscious of, and adapted to, gay spectatorial pleasures than any other that year.[3] Moreover, it cast him as enjoying sexual receptiveness – a riskier, queerer and more compromising position in many binaries of male sexuality compared to the active role. Reacting to comments including the remark that 'Njegoš would be turning in his grave', Kalezić told one Montenegrin webportal that 'if Njegoš were alive, he'd actually support me', because he had been '[f]ull of symbolic energy and the energy of life' (CDM, 2017) – not even just queering the ESC or queering the nation, but queering Montenegro's national hero.[4] Unfortunately for Kalezić, his entry's sparse stage presentation did not excite viewers enough to make the grand final. His participation still represents the same aspiration to embody queerness without having to sever oneself from national tradition that organisers of Montenegro's first Prides channelled into the language and symbols describing their 'processions' in 2013–14, including a traditional Montenegrin moustache (Kalezić & Brković, 2016: 173).

The quite distinct embodied performances of Šerifović, Brnabić and Kalezić all express the 'Molitva factor' at work – that is, the signifying power of embodied performances of national identity where an individual is understood to symbolise the nation and where the litmus test of progress on LGBTQ rights as a proxy for European belonging is active. Indeed, Vučić's very appointment of Brnabić can be read as instrumentalising that litmus test. This is not to suggest Šerifović's win alone made Brnabić a more thinkable prime minister, and Šerifović herself has been lukewarm about Brnabić's social significance (in 2018, she told one web-portal 'I think she was chosen because someone in authority estimated she was familiar with what needed to be done. As far as a more free society goes, I still don't think we're very close to one' (Espreso.rs, 2018)). Nevertheless, under-standing how 'Molitva' enabled RTS to reframe Serbia for a European gaze in 2007–8 helps to explain what Vučić stood to gain from appointing a lesbian, gender-non-conforming prime minister in 2017, while there is still more to explore about how hosting the ESC and welcoming many foreign LGBTQ visitors in 2008 might have influenced activity in 2009 around the Anti-Discrimination Law and Belgrade Pride.

Fresh aspects of LGBTQ politics continue to enact themselves at the ESC, including alliances between queer activism and Palestinian solidarity which were tested when the Boycott, Divestment, Sanctions (BDS) movement mobilised against the 2019 ESC; the 2021 contest's open alignment with trans equality via co-presenter Nikkie de Jager, the trans YouTuber whose on-screen outfits all incorporated trans pride colours; and Jeangu Macrooy's articulation of a Black, queer and explicitly anticolonial stance as the 2021 Dutch host entry. The contest's LGBTQ associations expose it to reaction from institutions captured by state homophobia, which has been alleged to account for the withdrawals of Turkey and Hungary even though other financial and commercial reasons may have been more decisive. Questions of LGBTQ visibility might not have charged the ESC with such international political significance if policymakers and activists had not already made LGBTQ rights a 'litmus test' of Europeanness. Yet the litmus test of performing Europeanness in south-east Europe existed long before it turned towards LGBTQ rights. The ESC makes such sensitivities visible and audible – and calls attention to the roles that embodied performances of national identity also play in other political domains.

Notes

1 One skater has even appeared in the ESC: Evgeni Plushenko, with Dima Bilan in 2008.
2 Neuwirth uses he/him and Conchita uses she/her; 'they' here means them both.
3 Milićević's sexualised male bodies have created a local homoerotic aesthetic in contemporary post-Yugoslav pop-folk (Dumančić & Krolo, 2017: 175).
4 Njegoš, the poet and Prince-Bishop of Montenegro in 1830–51, wrote the epic 'Gorski vijenac' ('The mountain wreath'). This has codified heroic masculinity in Montenegrin nationalism – and also fuelled Islamophobic imaginations in Montenegro and Serbia with its vehement antagonism towards Turks and Muslim Slavs (Longinović, 2011: 72).

References

Ammaturo, F.R. (2015). The "Pink Agenda": Questioning and challenging European homonationalist sexual citizenship. *Sociology*, *49*(6), 1151–1166.

Aston, E. (2013). Competing femininities: Q "girl" for Eurovision. In K. Fricker & M. Gluhovic ed., *Performing the 'New' Europe: Identities, Feelings and Politics in the Eurovision Song Contest* (pp. 163–177). Palgrave Macmillan.

Baker, C. (2008a). When Seve met Bregović: folklore, turbofolk and the boundaries of Croatian musical identity. *Nationalities Papers*, *36*(4), 741–764.

Baker, C. (2008b). Wild dances and dying wolves: simulation, essentialization, and national identity at the Eurovision Song Contest. *Popular Communication*, *6*(3), 173–189.

Baker, C. (2017). The "gay Olympics"?: the Eurovision Song Contest and the politics of LGBT/European belonging. *European Journal of International Relations*, *23*(1), 97–121.

Banjac, D. (2019). Srbiji i Ani Brnabić glavne uloge na derneku u Banjoj Luci. *Al-Jazeera Balkans*, 9 January. https://balkans.aljazeera.net/opinions/2019/1/9/srbiji-i-ani-brnabic-glavne-uloge-na-derneku-u-banjoj-luci (accessed 25 August 2021).

BBC, (2002). Transvestite Sisters stir Eurovision storm. *BBC News Online*, 5 March. http://news.bbc.co.uk/1/hi/world/monitoring/media_reports/1855726.stm (accessed 9 August 2021).

Bellamy, A.J. (2003). *The Formation of Croatian National Identity: a Centuries-Old Dream?* Manchester: Manchester University Press.

Bilić, B. (2016). Europe [heart] gays?: Europeanisation and Pride parades in Serbia. In B. Bilić ed., *LGBT Activism and Europeanisation in the Post-Yugoslav Space: On the Rainbow Way to Europe* (pp. 117–154). London: Palgrave Macmillan.

Bilić, B. (2020). Ana je tu: figure zazora, klasne privilegije i premijerka Ana Brnabić. *Sociologija*, *62*(3), 378–396.

Bilić, B., & Stubbs, P. (2015). Unsettling "the urban" in post-Yugoslav activisms: "right to the city" and Pride marches in Serbia and Croatia. In K. Jacobsson ed., *Urban Grassroots Movements in Central and Eastern Europe* (pp. 119–138). London and New York: Routledge.

Billig, M. (1995). *Banal Nationalism*. London: Sage.

Bohlman, P.V. (2007). The politics of power, pleasure, and prayer in the Eurovision Song Contest. *Muzikologija*, *7*, 39–67.

Bolin, G. (2006). Visions of Europe: cultural technologies of nation-states. *International Journal of Cultural Studies*, *9*(2), 189–206.

Buchanan, D.A. (1997). Bulgaria's magical Mystère tour: postmodernism, world music marketing, and political change in eastern Europe. *Ethnomusicology*, *41*(1), 131–157.

Buchanan, D.A. (2007). Preface and acknowledgements. In D.A. Buchanan ed., *Balkan Popular Culture and the Ottoman Ecumene: Music, Image, and Regional Political Discourse* (pp. xvii–xxviii). Lanham, MD: Scarecrow Press.

Butler, J. (1988). Performative acts and gender constitution: an essay in phenomenology and feminist theory. *Theatre Journal*, *40*(4), 519–531.

CDM, (2017). Slavko Kalezić: Njegoš bi mi podržao. *CDM*, 15 March. https://www.cdm.me/zabava/muzika-film-tv/kalezic-ne-podilazim-primitivnoj-rulji-vec-sam-mnogo-dobio-njegos-bi-podrzao/(accessed 16 August 2021).

Čolović, I. (2006). *Etno: priče o muzici sveta na internetu*. Belgrade: XX vek.

Deutsche Welle (2018). Serbian PM Ana Brnabić: Srebrenica "a terrible crime", not genocide. 15 November. https://www.dw.com/en/serbian-pm-ana-brnabic-srebrenica-a-terrible-crime-not-genocide/a-46307925 (accessed 25 August 2021).

Dumančić, M., & Krolo, K. (2017). Dehexing postwar West Balkan masculinities: the case of Bosnia, Croatia, and Serbia, 1998 to 2015. *Men and Masculinities*, *20*(2), 154–180.

Ejdus, F., & Božović, M. (2019). Europeanisation and indirect resistance: Serbian police and Pride parades. *International Journal of Human Rights*, *23*(4), 493–511.

El-Tayeb, F. (2011). *European Others: Queering Ethnicity in Postnational Europe*. Minneapolis, MN: University of Minnesota Press.

Espreso.rs. (2018). Marija Šerifović nikada otvorenije o gej premijerki Ani Brnabić, usvajanju deteta i emotivnoj partnerki!. *Espreso*, 2 January. https://www.espreso.co.rs/showbiz/zvezde/212199/marija-serifovic-nikad-otvorenije-o-gej-premijerki-ani-brnabic-usvajanju-deteta-i-emotivnoj-partnerki (accessed 16 August 2021).

Gluhovic, M. (2013). Sing for democracy: human rights and sexuality discourse in the Eurovision Song Contest. In K. Fricker & M. Gluhovic ed., *Performing the 'New' Europe: Identities, Feelings and Politics in the Eurovision Song Contest* (pp. 194–217). Basingstoke: Palgrave Macmillan.

Husarić, A., Kuloglija, N. & Stojanović, M. (2021). Genocide denial condemned as Srebrenica anniversary commemorated. *Balkan Transitional Justice*, 11 July. https://balkaninsight.com/2021/07/11/genocide-denial-condemned-as-srebrenica-anniversary-commemorated/ (accessed 15 August 2021).

Jordan, P. (2015). Walking in singing: Brand Estonia, the Eurovision Song Contest, and Estonia's self-proclaimed return to Europe, 2001–2002. In L. Clerc, N. Glover & P. Jordan ed., *Histories of Public Diplomacy and Nation Branding in the Nordic and Baltic Countries* (pp. 217–236). Leiden: Brill.

Kahlina, K. (2015). Local histories, European LGBT designs: sexual citizenship, nationalism, and "Europeanisation" in post-Yugoslav Croatia and Serbia. *Women's Studies International Forum*, *49*, 73–83.

Kajinić, S. (2019). Cartographies of fear and freedom: lesbian activists in the first Belgrade and Zagreb Pride parades. In B. Bilić & M. Radoman ed., *Lesbian Activism in the (Post-)Yugoslav Space: Sisterhood and Unity* (pp. 61–86). London: Palgrave Macmillan.

Kalezić, D., & Brković, Č. (2016). Queering as Europeanisation, Europeanisation as queering: challenging homophobia in everyday life in Montenegro. In B. Bilić ed., *LGBT Activism and Europeanisation in the Post-Yugoslav Space: On the Rainbow Way to Europe* (pp. 155–177). London: Palgrave Macmillan.

Kestnbaum, E. (2003). *Culture on Ice: Figure Skating and Cultural Meaning*. Middletown, CT: Wesleyan University Press.

Kułpa, R., & Mizielińska, J. (ed.). (2011). *De-Centring Western Sexualities: Central and Eastern European Perspectives*. Farnham: Ashgate.

Lewis, R. (1997). Looking good: the lesbian gaze and fashion imagery. *Feminist Review*, *55*, 92–109.

Longinović, T.Z. (2011). *Vampire Nation: Violence as Cultural Imaginary*. Durham, NC: Duke University Press.

Maričić, S., & Živić, P. (2018). Serbia Pride: gay PM Brnabić "not wanted" at parade. *BBC News Online*, 16 September. https://www.bbc.co.uk/news/world-europe-45524385 (accessed 14 August 2021).

Mark, J., Iacob, B.C., Rupprecht, T., & Spaskovska, L. (2020). *1989: a Global History of Eastern Europe*. Cambridge: Cambridge University Press.

Miazhevich, G. (2012). Ukrainian nation-branding off-line and online: Verka Serduchka at the Eurovision Song Contest. *Europe–Asia Studies*, *64*(8), 1505–1523.

Miller, C. (2017). Ukraine "celebrates diversity" with Eurovision, but critics complain it's all "a show"'. *RFE/RL*, 7 May. https://www.rferl.org/a/ukraine-eurovision-diversity-critics-complain/28472671.html (accessed 25 August 2021).

Mitrović, M. (2010). '"New face of Serbia" at the Eurovision Song Contest: international media spectacle and national identity'. *European Review of History*, *17*(2), 171–185.

Radoman, M. (2016). Towards a more inclusive Pride?: representing multiple discriminations in the Belgrade Pride parade. In B. Bilić & S. Kajinić ed., *Intersectionality and LGBT Activist Politics: Multiple Others in Croatia and Serbia* (pp. 171–190). London: Palgrave Macmillan.

Rehberg, P. (2007). Winning failure: queer nationality at the Eurovision Song Contest. *SQS: Journal of Queer Studies in Finland*, *2*(2), 60–65. https://journal.fi/sqs/article/view/53668 (accessed 25 August 2021).

Richter-Montpetit, M., & Weber, C. (2018). Everything you always wanted to know about sex (in IR) but were afraid to ask: the "queer turn" in International Relations. *Millennium*, *46*(2), 220–240.

Slootmaeckers, K. (2017). The litmus test of Pride: analysing the emergence of the Belgrade "ghost" Pride in the context of EU accession. *East European Politics*, *33*(4), 517–535.

Solomon, T. (2007). Articulating the historical moment: Turkey, Europe, and Eurovision 2003. In R.D. Tobin & I. Raykoff ed., *A Song for Europe: Popular Music and Politics in the Eurovision Song Contest* (pp. 135–145). London: Routledge.

Sonevytsky, M. (2020). *Wild Music: Sound and Sovereignty in Ukraine*. Middletown, CT: Wesleyan University Press.

Stychin, C. (2004). Same-sex sexualities and the globalization of human rights. *McGill Law Journal*, *49*(4), 951–968.

Taylor, D. (1997). *Disappearing Acts: Spectacles of Gender and Nationalism in Argentina's 'Dirty War'*. Durham, NC: Duke University Press.

Vänskä, A. (2007). Bespectacular and over the top: on the genealogy of lesbian camp. *SQS: Journal of Queer Studies in Finland*, *2*(2). https://journal.fi/sqs/article/view/53669 (accessed 25 August 2021).

Vuletic, D. (2018). *Postwar Europe and the Eurovision Song Contest*. London: Bloomsbury Academic.

Weber, C. (2016). *Queer International Relations: Sovereignty, Sexuality, and the Will to Knowledge*. Oxford: Oxford University Press.

Wintour, P. (2017). Ana Brnabić: "I do not want to be branded Serbia's gay PM"'. *The Guardian*, 28 July. https://www.theguardian.com/world/2017/jul/28/ana-brnabic-serbia-prime-minister-interview (accessed 14 August 2021).

Yuval-Davis, N. (1993). Gender and nation. *Ethnic and Racial Studies*, *16*(4), 621–632.

8 A Critical Pedagogical Eurovision Euphoria: The Potential of the Eurovision Song Contest to Promote Values Propagated by the European Union within Formal Learning Contexts

George Cremona

Introduction

While the term 'popular culture' holds different meanings (Storey, 2019) depending on who is defining it and the context in which it is being used (Delaney, 2007), nowadays it generally refers to 'the beliefs and practices and the objects through which they are organized that are widely shared among a population' (Mukerji and Shudson in Grindstaff, 2008, 207–208). Alvermann et al. (1999) suggest that currently we are living in an age of popular culture dominated by products of a capitalistic mass culture. These products include shopping malls, tabloid newspapers, talk shows, Music Television (MTV) and the World Wide Web. Consumers of all ages and backgrounds, particularly children and adolescents, are often criticised for mindlessly buying into these cultural artifacts, which in turn lead to different reactions and responses from different consumers.

When back in 2004 I started teaching German and Maltese in a secondary school in Malta, I could observe that the eleven to fifteen-year-old adolescent students sitting in my classes were not an exception to this trend. As a novice teacher, for me it was logical that in order to motivate them through student-centred lessons, I needed to use texts referring to elements of the popular culture, such as sports, music, fashion and food, that they were keen on.

The definition of texts which I will be using includes both textbooks (De Vincenti, 2017), as well as the wider variety of authentic texts (Konyukhova & Abramova, 2020) which Morrow defined as authentic and containing 'a stretch of real language, produced by a real speaker or writer for a real audience and designed to convey a real message of some sort'(cited in Gilmore, 2007, 98). These include daily used resources such as those mentioned by Hadley (2001):

> use of real or simulated travel documents, hotel registration forms, biographical data sheets, train and plane schedules, authentic restaurant

DOI: 10.4324/9781003188933-10

menus, labels, signs, newspapers, and magazines will acquaint students more directly with real language than will any set of contrived classroom materials used alone (97).

With these texts, I felt I could build bridges between the above-mentioned popular culture driven out-of-class reality and my lessons. I started realising that without these texts during my lessons, I would end up creating learning contexts which Buckingham (2003) defines as characterised by an 'extraordinary contrast between the high levels of activity that characterise children's consumer cultures and the passivity that increasingly suffuses their schooling' (313).

In order to opt for adequate texts which could help me start making a connection between out-of-class and in-class realities, I continuously observed which texts were constantly featured and readily available in Malta. Amongst the most popular texts were ESC related audio-visual texts, which include songs with music and lyrics, music videos, promotional material and interviews. These texts were particularly relevant because about 180 million people around the world annually follow this major global media event — some loving it while others ridicule it (Kyriakidou et al., 2017, p. 604). Furthermore, year after year, younger audiences, such as the age groups sitting in my classrooms, are increasingly following the show (European Broadcasting Union, 2019). Falling within this age group are students growing up and living in Malta, often referred to as 'the Eurovision island', with over 95 per cent of the population following the ESC annually (Public Broadcasting Services, 2017). They therefore tend to naturally be exposed to a strong frequent dose of Eurovision-related material. This material includes elements from popular culture and at the same time itself influences popular culture both in Malta and around the globe.

In the context of the ESC's popularity on Malta, at the beginning of my teaching career I regularly used to include ESC-related texts as part of my lessons. Identifying the grammar or language related skill (i.e., writing, reading, listening or speaking) that I was going to teach, I would choose ESC-related texts, particularly songs, music videos and interviews referring to singers participating in the festival of that particular year. The texts were then used as instruments through which adolescents enthusiastically immersed themselves in popular culture and were swiftly able to master new technologies and fields, in this case learning a language and improving their language skills (Marsh, 2008).

In response, some colleagues and parents initially reacted by telling me they felt that these ESC-related texts, compared to other official texts created specifically for pedagogical contexts, presented a shallow image of culture which was viewed as having less educational value (Marsh & Millard, 2000). On the other hand, from the way the lessons proceeded, the feedback I received from students and lesson evaluations, I realised that these texts were helping students feel 'that what is taught and learnt in the classroom is actually of real use' (Pachler et al., 2009, 280–281). The texts served as factors to creating a friendlier learning environment, through which students felt more comfortable and faced less language anxiety while learning (Horwitz, 2016).

From the Initial to the Critical Use of ESC-Related Texts

Once this congenial learning environment was created, I started feeling that, while students were willing to participate, somehow I was not maximising the potential of these ESC-related resources. Therefore, I started challenging my own use of these ESC-related resources to somehow only 'decorate' the lesson. Instead, I looked for ways through which these ESC-related texts could help students not only grasp a language aspect, but also to reflect about popular tastes and concerns and to start rejecting those ideas fostered by mass culture.

While as a teacher my priority was to teach a language, I still wanted to investigate whether as a by-product of these texts I could start seeking for ways of gradually moving students away from assuming roles of uncritical mass audience consumers. Instead, through my lessons, I was willing to see how students could start understanding that popular culture develops because the audience is aware of what is being presented. This could initiate a process in which students could look at the texts through a critical lens (Fiske, 2010).

I felt that I could not do this through lessons built on the concept of education based on rote memorisation and which intended to preserve and only pass down linguistic skills and knowledge from the adult generation to the younger generation. Instead, I began searching for ways through which these ESC-related texts, while strengthening their language skills, could possibly initiate more analytical thinking. This also meant helping students to be ready to create solutions to problems which they might encounter along the way (Bass & Good, 2004).

The first step in this direction was inspired by O'Regan (2006), who advocates treating texts as critical objects rather than as merely linguistic entities or vehicles of information, as is common in a good deal of foreign language pedagogy. This shifted my perspective from treating these ESC-related texts as mere instruments through which I might motivate students to improve their language skills, to a perspective which also incorporated a focus on deeper reflective levels and issues.

I was also influenced by Kress (2010), who suggests that similar situations in which one aims to move from linguistic to deeper critical levels could be helped by a social-semiotic approach. This approach asks quesions which include:

> 'Whose *interest* and *agency* is at work here in the making of meaning?', 'What *meaning* is being made here?', '*How* is meaning being made?', 'With *what resources*, in *what social environment?*' and 'What are the *meaning potentials* of the resources that have been used?', 'How can *past tense* be an indicator of *power?*', 'How is it that a form that signals distance in time can signal social distance, a 'distance' produced by difference in social power?'. There is an orientation to the *interests of the sign-maker;* to the *environment* in which *meaning* is made; to *meaning* and to the *semiotic/cultural resources* which are available for the *realization/materialization of meaning* as a *motivated sign.*
>
> (Kress, 2010, 57)

Fit for Purpose and Tailor-Made ESC Roots

The idea of shifting to this social-semiotic approach was also encouraged by the very own nature of the ESC. Since its beginning in 1956, the ESC never intended to focus only on the aesthetics of the music show. In fact, when Bezencon started working on the idea of initiating the contest (In a Nutshell, 2021) it was intended to serve as an entertaining non-military tool (Sasson in Oliver, 2008) through which the EBU could start a technical project to experiment with the nascent technology of television. This was a move which eventually came to reflect political and social changes in Europe, especially as it developed parallel to Western European integration during the Cold War.

Today, the contemporary ESC format retains the same nature. While the European Union (EU) has managed to achieve relative unity and create dialogue and cooperation between European nations, more than sixty-four years since its first broadcast, the ESC seems to have served as an effective tool to help the EU to reach its goals (Lawson, 2014)[1]. Through the on-stage performances of each year's ESC, the behind-the-scenes lobbying and related events, as well as through what happens during the build-up events weeks and even months before the actual week of the ESC, the contest manages to spark discussion and debate about EU goals and targets which are common to EU countries, such as inclusion, tolerance, justice, solidarity and non-discrimination (European Commission, 2021). These goals and targets are continually enhanced through the promotion by the ESC of six main EU values: human dignity, freedom, democracy, equality, rule of law and human rights (European Union, 2007; European Union, 2012).

According to Ifversen (2002), thanks to the ESC, the concept of Europe is contested since, as Vuletic (2019) suggests, the hosting of Eurovision each year becomes a contest of international relations played to a soundtrack of Europop. Therefore, while being an international contest, in the view of Fricker and Gluhovic (2013) the ESC also serves as a vehicle that, while promoting the values propagated by the EU, also reminds viewers about transnational European identity and solidarity. Therefore, the ESC does not just serve as a mirror but potentially as a driver for changing conceptions and realities of Europe and Europeanness since the fall of the Berlin Wall. The ESC serves to examine:

> 'weaknesses and failures of Europe as an inclusive and functional public sphere', as well as 'the ways in which individual contest acts, and the spectacle and gesture of the contest as a whole, stimulate feelings and different levels of identification (with the nation, with the region, with Europe itself, and with subaltern groupings, such as gay/queer or immigrant').
>
> (Fricker & Gluhovic 2013, 11–12)

Discussions and debates about such important and fundamental factors and issues, in Dayan and Katz's words, is able to happen more peacefully and cordially between nations during and through the ESC, due to three qualities the contest posseses:

> They argue that media events can be defined on syntactic, semantic and pragmatic levels. Syntactic because it is something which interrupts the routine of daily life, it monopolises the media coverage at the time that the event is taking place. It can be seen as a media event on a semantic level given that it represents an occasion or a "historic" ceremony with reverence. Finally, Dayan and Katz argue that the ESC is a media event on a pragmatic level in that it enthrals large scale audiences who view them in a festive style.
>
> (Dayan and Katz 1992, 9–14 in Jordan, 2011 19)

Therefore, this comfortable and safe space where people feel free to express themselves, discuss important and fundamental values and issues, converts what seems to be just a music show into:

> the fabric of European (and wider) popular culture and identity. It is more than a television programme, it really is a way of life […] providing ample avenues for research".
>
> (Eurovision.tv, 2016)

Intrigued by these elements of the roots of the ESC, initially as a secondary school teacher of languages and later as a resident lecturer and teacher educator within the Faculty of Education at the University of Malta, I embarked on a research project called *Learning through the Eurovision*, focusing on one pertinent question:

> *Can the festive ESC serve as a pedagogical tool for enhancing values propagated by the European Union?*

Since the start of the project, *Learning through the Eurovision* has had over one hundred invitations and requests by teachers working in different schools. These included primary, secondary and tertiary education institutions in Malta. The project seeks to work with language teachers who themselves are willing to participate. Upon receiving a formal request, I meet the teachers and during the initial phase, together we identify both the curricular content area the lesson(s) will be about, as well as the European value(s) we intend to focus on during the lesson(s). Together, we then design each lesson plan based on the most relevant contemporary language methodologies at hand. Throughout, we adapt the lessons according to the needs of the students within the particular language learning context. The research project adopts qualitative data collection tasks that provide fieldnotes which include the designed lesson plan, the observation of the conducted lesson and an evaluation both from the teachers' point of view as well as that of students who participate in the lessons.

To ensure that deeper social-semiotic levels are reached and that the ESC-related texts are viewed as critical objects, a theoretical framework called the MIRROR framework (Cremona, 2017) is utilised from the initial lesson designing stage when the most relevant ESC-related texts for the particular lesson are selected. Later, while preparing and conducting the lesson in class, through the framework, teachers can identify the most adequate modes to use to present student-centred activites during the lesson. The framework also supports teachers and students before, during and after the lesson while identifying the social aspects presented in the ESC-related texts and evaluating their reactions towards the EU-propagated value.

Later, the collected data — which includes lesson plans, fieldnotes, resources used in class and other material collected during and after the lesson — are analysed using a thematic approach (Creswell, 2014).

Data Collected From the *Learning through the Eurovision* Research Project

I am selecting one of the hundred experiences I had as part of the *Learning through the Eurovision* research project to give an example of how the lessons proceeded. This will also give an idea of how the designed lesson plan amalgamated the linguistic aims of the lesson with an aspect of the selected values propagated by the EU.

The selected lesson was intended to teach a group of twenty fourteen-year-old second year students of German how to describe people around them. Each lesson follows an introduction-reinforcement-conclusion pattern. This lesson also gave students the opportunity to learn how to describe people, while revising the vocabulary and grammar content they had covered in previous lessons. The lesson, which consisted of activities aimed at addressing all the four language skills (i.e., writing, reading, speaking and listening), was conducted on Tuesday the 10th of March 2020. This came a couple of days after Destiny Chukunyere, whose father is Nigerian, won the right to represent Malta in Eurovision 2020. This Eurovision edition was later cancelled because of the Covid-19 pandemic.

Among the six values propagated by the EU, we selected the value of human rights for this lesson. The EU advances the right of individuals to be free from discrimination on the basis of sex, racial or ethnic origin, religion or belief, disability, age or sexual orientation, the right to the protection of personal data and the right to have access to justice (European Union, 2012). For this lesson, we examined one of these foci with students: human rights linked to racial and ethnic origins.

This is a step-by-step outline of the particular lesson:

Lesson introduction: The lesson started with a speaking activity. Students began by guessing two mysterious singers by seeing only an image of their lips, their forehead and their eyes. The two singers were Destiny Chukunyere and Ira Losco (ESC singer for Malta, 2002 and 2016).

[5 minutes]

After guessing the two singers, students were shown thirty-second clips, first of Ira Losco's "Walk on Water" music video, and then of Destiny's "All of My Love" music video. Students were then given ten descriptive phrases on small pieces of paper and were asked to use the phrases to describe each singer according to what they observed in the video.

These were the phrases describing Destiny:	These were the phrases describing Ira:
The singer can reach high notes.	The singer has a particular husky voice.
The singer is still a teenager.	The singer is in her mid-thirties.
The singer wears dark clothes.	The singer wears colourful clothes.
The singer's brother is seen in the video.	The singer is pregnant, expecting her first child.
The singer appears focused.	The singer appears more relaxed.

Through this reading activity (i.e., by reading the phrases on the Silps of paper) students were gradually guided into forming the initial description of the two singers.

After this, as a whole-class activity, the ten phrases and the descriptions students had written were checked and students discussed their choices further.

[5 minutes]

Reinforcement Activity 1

Students were now asked to focus specifically on the physical appearance of the two singers. To help them do this, a black-and-white photo of each singer was projected on the interactive whiteboard.

Students were asked to jot down as a writing activity a number of sentences which included descriptive adjectives — a minimum of five — which they associated with each singer's physical appearance.

Once this list was compiled, this served as a task through which students:

- used the adjectives in a context and described the singers' physical appearance;
- came to the front of the class to add colour on the whiteboard according to the mentioned adjective;
- also practised ways they could describe the singers without discriminating when referring to features linked to the appearance of their skin (i.e., fair and dark). The teacher guided students not only through the choice of the right adjectives, but also through how these adjectives are used without discriminating against a particular racial background.

[6 minutes]

Reinforcement Activity 2

The next step involved students in a speaking activity in which they conducted a role-play in groups. Students formed groups of four. Each group was given either a photo of Ira and her family or a photo of Destiny and her family. The photo was in pieces, similar to a jigsaw puzzle. Students needed to initially arrange the different parts of the photo correctly.

Once people in the photo were identified, students were asked to take the role of one of the members of the family seen in the photo and then move to meet members from the other family by joining another group in class. This ended up with an imaginary encounter between members from Ira and Destiny's families. Once the different families met, they were asked to introduce and describe themselves in five to six sentences. Those listening were asked to react to the descriptions they heard.

Through this role-play, the teacher helped students to:

- use the adjectives in a context and build grammatically correct sentences in German;
- become aware of how to behave when participating in similar conversations in which Maltese come into contact with people from other cultures or countries;
- use appropriate non-discriminatory words and phrases, especially when someone with dark skin introduces himself/herself as Maltese.

[6 minutes]

Reinforcement Activity 3

The next excercise was a listening activity. The students heard a short interview with Lena Mayer-Landrut (ESC 2010 winner, ESC 2011 participant, for Germany) in which she describes her appearance and character in German.

Students were asked to listen to the way Lena describes herself and the adjectives used, and then fill in the missing gaps left on a provided handout. This handout, which consisted of a short description of a person (i.e., the aim of the lesson), was primarily intended to serve as a written note which students could refer to later when studying outside of school.

[7 minutes]

Homework Assignment

Students were asked to react to Lena's description. They were asked to think of the qualities they often attributed to people living in Germany (such as blond, tall, eat sausages and drink beer, Protestant) and to compare them to the description of the 'actual' German singer, Lena (i.e., short, dark hair, mentions Turkish food as her favorite food).

This exercise was intended to give students the opportunity to:

- study how descriptions are written;
- react against their own stereotypes and shift away from discriminatory thoughts, words and ideas.

[3 minutes]

Lesson Conclusion

As a conclusion to the lesson, students were asked to imagine that they were newscasters producing a one-minute report about different ESC singers. Students were given the opportunity to practise descriptions using German, while also remembering the importance of avoiding discriminatory comments linked to race and ethnicity.

Student watched a one-minute video of each of the ESC singers below:

- Aminata, the dark-skinned ESC 2015 singer for Latvia whose father was from Burkina Faso;
- Dami Im, the ESC 2016 singer for Australia who is Korean-born and has Asian facial features;
- Jamala, the 2016 ESC winner whose country suffered because of ethnic conflict and whose song was about ethnic cleansing;
- Michela, the ESC 2019 singer for Malta, whose fair features were for many in Malta quite 'untypically' Maltese;
- Jessika, the Maltese ESC 2019 singer for San Marino who had the right to participate for a third country.

The students first had five minutes to prepare a short, one-minute description of one of the singers they had selected. Later, with a microphone in hand and wearing headphones, they imagined they were on-air sharing a report with millions of spectators watching ESC-related news. After this activity, they received feedback from their friends and the teacher. The feedback received was both about the way they used German, as well as about the way they commented on the singer and her racial or ethnic features.

[Total: 10 minutes]

It should also be noted that, with the same class, the teacher and I planned seven more lessons throughout the particular school year (September 2019 – March 2020) which focused on other aspects included by the EU in the definition of human rights. While the lesson above focused on the right of individuals to be free from discrimination on the basis of ethnic or racial origin, each of the other seven lessons focused on different aspects of human rights. The teacher and I planned the term in such a way as to covering different linguistic aspects, but also tackle an aspect of EU human rights priorities at least once throughout the term. Table 8.1 below illustrates how this was done.

Insights Obtained From the Research Venture

Feedback received from teachers and students participating in the *Learning through the Eurovision* research project sheds light on a number of challenges which those participating frequently encounter.

Table 8.1 Lessons teaching linguistic aspects while focusing on the EU propagated value of human rights

Date and linguistic aspect covered during the particular German as a foreign language lesson	Aspect of human rights	ESC singers and ESC related material included in the particular lesson
9th October 2019 Gender – masculine and feminine	right of individuals to be free from discrimination on the basis of sex and sexual orientation	1 Conchita Wurst (ESC winner 2014), who is gay and a drag queen; 2 Duncan Laurence (ESC winner 2019) and his messages about bisexuality; 3 Dana International (ESC winner 1999 and ESC contestant 2016), who is transsexual; 4 Maria Šerifović (ESC winner 2007), who identifies herself as lesbian; 5 Emmelie de Forrest (ESC winner 2013) and Alexander Rybak (ESC winner 2009 and ESC contestant 2018), who identify themselves as straight.
24th October 2019 Names of countries	right of individuals to be free from discrimination on the basis of nationality	1 The ESC scoreboard of 2017, 2018 and 2019; 2 Comments about neighbour countries voting for each other.
20th November 2019 Daily routine	right of individuals to be free from discrimination on the basis of age	Comparing the daily routine of young ESC singers to that of older singers. Younger singers: 1 twenty-six-year-old 2018 ESC winner Netta, 2 Sandra Kim (youngest ESC winner 1986) winning the ESC at thirteen. Older singers: 1 Johnny Logan (ESC winner 1980 and 1987), 2 Buranovskiye Babushki (Russian Grannies) (Russian Eurovision contestants, 2012)

(Continued)

Table 8.1 (Continued)

Date and linguistic aspect covered during the particular German as a foreign language lesson	Aspect of human rights	ESC singers and ESC related material included in the particular lesson
21st November 2019	right of individuals to be free from discrimination on the basis of religion	1 Lena Mayer-Landrut (ESC winner 2010 and ESC contestant 2011) studying theology and wearing a tau cross on the ESC stage; 2 Francesco Gabbani (ESC singer 2016) with "Occidentalis Karma", the song with lyrics and an music video including references to Buddha and Nirvana and the controversial aspect of the evolution from the ape; 3 Alexander Rybak (ESC winner 2009 and ESC contestant 2018) who is Christian Orthodox.
4th December 2019 Question words	right of individuals to be free from discrimination on the basis of disability	1 Yulia Samoilova (ESC Russia 2018) who has the neuromuscular condition spinal muscular Atrophy; 2 Agnete (ESC Norway 2016 singer) who at the time of the festival struggled daily with depression and bipolarity; 3 The punk rock band Pertti Kurikan Nimipaivat whose members have Down's syndrome and autism (ESC singers for Finnland 2015); 4 Monika Kuszynska (ESC singer Poland 2015) who uses a wheelchair after a car accident left her paralysed in 2009; 5 Corinna May who is blind (ESC singer for Germany 2002) and Diana Gurtskaya who is also blind (ESC singer for Georgia 2008).
14th January 2020 Writing and speaking about an opinion (1)	right of individuals to be free from discrimination on the basis of protection of personal data	Different episodes from ESC 2017, 2018 and 2019 about aspects from contestants' private and personal life and how sometimes these featured in the media. The main question discussed and debated in class was whether such news should be made public or should remain private.

(Continued)

Table 8.1 (Continued)

Date and linguistic aspect covered during the particular German as a foreign language lesson	Aspect of human rights	ESC singers and ESC related material included in the particular lesson
21st February 2020 Writing and speaking about an opinion (2)	right of individuals to be free from discrimination on the basis of getting access to justice	In this lesson we focused on how the relationships between certain countries in the ESC lead to uneasy and unjust situations in which contestants are treated unfairly by their competitors. During the lesson we used ESC-related texts such as interviews and news items referring to relations between Russia and Ukraine, Azerbaijan and Armenia, and Israel and Palestine, as well as the relations among the Balkan states and among the nordic states, We also discussed how Malta and Georgia both had a song called "Warrior" in the 2015 ESC and how this issue was tackled.
10th March 2020 Desriptions of people	right of individuals to be free from discrimination on the basis of ethnic or racial origins	1 Destiny Chukunyere 2 Ira Losco 3 Lena Mayer-Landrut 4 Aminata 5 Dami Im 6 Jamalla 7 Maltese Michela and Jessika. A detailed description of this lesson is given above

The majority of teachers felt that to prepare such lessons one needs more time (similar to Nagro et al., 2019) and knowledge about the particular popular culture ESC topic (similar to Cremona, 2018). A further hurdle all the teachers and students encountered was the need to constantly keep up to date with the ESC material at hand. As one teacher explained:

> the fact that each year there are around forty new songs and forty new singers requires constantly that one is up to date, otherwise you won't be certain that you are using the right text at the right moment.
>
> (Secondary school teacher, Lesson 77 conducted in 2018)

Another common point which several students and teachers mentioned, was the need to follow up on certain aspects raised during these lessons. They mentioned sensitive issues in which students and the teachers themselves required guidance. One teacher stated:

> To start with, I am not always sure about whether my perspective of the particular value is valid and whether I should teach my views. Furthermore, I am not a psychologist. I am not a counsellor. For example, students talk about their sexual orientation, which of course they are discovering and establishing during their adolescence. There were cases where I felt I lacked the expert ability to help them. In moments like these I suggest to them that we should follow-up the matter with a guidance teacher who can help them further about this matter. Students appreciate this, yet for me this is extra work and a bigger responsibility.
>
> (Secondary school teacher, Lesson 45 conducted in 2015)

Nonetheless, these realistic challenges which frequently featured as early as the lesson planning stages, and continued into the lesson evaluation stages, were outnumbered by the positive outcomes teachers and students believed they obtained through the project.

The teachers mentioned positive effects they felt had helped students improve their language competencies. These (similar to Azri & Rashid, 2014) included the advantage of teaching the language through texts based on popular culture:

> which create in class an authentic context with fresh examples based on what is happening in the real outside contexts which students are very familiar to.
>
> (Secondary school teacher, Lesson 43 conducted in 2015)

Furthermore, the majority of teachers and students highlighted the fact that ESC songs are only three minutes-long, and that this increased song variety in the classroom.

Another positive factor which all teachers mentioned was that these ESC-related texts facilitated language teaching based on the most common language teaching methodologies (similar to Petriciuc, 2019). The communicative approach and task-based learning are some examples. Therefore, instead of being viewed by the teachers as an extra task, in the frequently short time they had with large unfavourable-in-size classes (similar to Richards, 2015) in which students frequently lacked advanced linguistic skills, the use of these texts was viewed as: ... nothing extra. Instead, these ESC-related texts serve as a tool through which material set in the syllabus can be brought in class and delivered in ways which appeal more to the students.

(Secondary school teacher, Lesson 40 conducted in 2015)

Together with these positive factors which facilitate the teaching and learning of the target language, the majority of teachers and students also mentioned that through their participation in the project (similar to Mansour, 2013) they:

embarked on a life-changing process. A process through which I could talk, reflect and evaluate my beliefs. Through the preparation and delivery of lessons, I started trying to assimilate new ideas, at times changing my beliefs and also constructing new views.

(Secondary school teacher, Lesson 29 conducted in 2012)

All the teachers suggested that this process happened gradually and at times was very slow. However, they felt that even the slightest advance needed to be celebrated because it implied personal growth and led to holistic education.

The majority of teachers also suggested that, before the project, they refrained from using particular texts for fear that these could create misinterpretations, misinformation or disruptions in class. Moreover, their participation in the project directed them to view a very clear positive shift in their perspective. They felt that from a perspective based on fear and ignorance (i.e., not knowing), they moved to more informed tolerant perspectives. One teacher explained that in this way:

Before participating in the project, I was afraid to use Conchita's example during my lessons. I feared I would end up with nine-year-old female students asking me whether they will get a beard when they grow up. Before I was afraid. Today, I feel comfortable using Conchita's song during my lesson. She visited Malta, and before that, all my students had seen her on TV during Eurovision and on the next day they were talking about her before the lesson. So why not use my classroom as a source of education to help the students learn through informed contexts about different realities around them? And a couple of months later, at school, we found out that a ten-year-old student was manifesting transgender feelings. Therefore, today through the project I am aware that my classroom, through Conchita, serves to educate students preparing them for life.

(Primary school teacher, Lesson 61 conducted in 2017)

Similarly, a teacher working in a Catholic church school had the same view:

I asked my head of school whether I could use Conchita's song during the lesson. My head of school, a nun, replied clearly that our view as a Catholic school is and has always been very open to promote Catholic values which above all include love to all without distinction.

(Secondary school teacher, Lesson 55 conducted in 2016)

Conclusion

The insights obtained from the qualitative data analysis indicate that texts based on elements of popular culture can serve this purpose effectively. The answer to this research question however should also suggest that these ESC-related texts can only be effective if used in learning environments with teachers and students who:

1   understand that holistic learning requires time, is gradual, slow and step by step;
2   create a learning context which embraces variety through the inclusion of both ESC- related texts as well as other texts which present elements from popular culture other than the ESC. These include texts related to sports, food, fashion, other types of music, and other mundane elements which students are very familiar with.

This creation of learning contexts which welcome a variety of texts from popular culture also leads to the conjecture that these give equal space to different voices and opinions in class. These include the voices of avid ESC followers, the voices of those who have never heard of the ESC, as well as the voices of those who disparage the ESC and never follow it.

I hope that the insights from this chapter serve as a way forward to help contemporary educators create learning environments through which the younger generations they are teaching are helped to open their minds in favor of change and diversity (Moecharam & Kartika, 2014) and gradually transform Europe into a freer, democratic, more egalitarian place, while also promoting human rights and dignity.

Note

1   It is also worth noting that this applies to similar values promoted by the United Nations and the Council of Europe. However, due to space, I will only focus on values promoted by the EU.

References

Alvermann, D. E., Moon, J., & Hagood, M. C. (1999). *Popular culture in the classroom: Teaching and researching critical media literacy.* International Reading Association.

Azri, A. R. & Rashid, H. M. (2014). The effect of using authentic materials in teaching. *International Journal of Scientific & Technology Research, 3*(10), 249–254.

Bass, R. V., & Good, J. W. (2004). Educare and educere: Is a balance possible in the educational system? *The Educational Forum, 68,* 161–168.

Buckingham, D. (2003). Media education and the end of the critical consumer. *Harvard Educational Review, 73*(3), 309–327.

Cremona, G. (2018). The Eurovision Song Contest within formal educational learning contexts: A critical multimodal interpretation of possible inter-disciplinary connections. *Symposia Melitensia, 14,* 151–160.

Cremona, G. (2017). The Mirror Framework: A critical text analysis pedagogical tool for the foreign language (FL) learning context. *International Journal for 21st Century Education, 4*(1), 43–56.

Creswell, J. (2014). *Research design: Qualitative, quantitative, and mixed methods approaches* (4th ed.). Sage.

Dayan, D., & Katz, E. (1992). Media events: The live broadcasting of history. Harvard University Press.

Delaney, T. (2007). Pop culture: An overview. *Philosophy Now* Volume 64, November/December 2007 Popular Culture and Philosophy, 6–7.

De Vincenti, G. (2017). Fostering 'knowledge' through representations of eating habits in Italian foreign language textbooks: An intercultural challenge. *Forum Italicum, 51*(3), 761–774.

European Broadcasting Union, (2019). 182 Million tune in to 64th Eurovision Song Contest as young audience numbers surge. Retrieved March 30, 2021, from https://www.ebu.ch/news/2019/05/182-million-tune-in-to-64th-eurovision-song-contest-as-young-audience-numbers-surge

European Commission, (2021). The EU values – About – ECL v2. Retrieved 31 March 2021, from https://ec.europa.eu/component-library/eu/about/eu-values/

European Union, (13 December 2007). *Treaty of Lisbon Amending the Treaty on European Union and the Treaty Establishing the European Community,* 2007/C 306/01, Retrieved 31 March 2021: https://www.refworld.org/docid/476258d32.html

European Union, (26 October 2012). *Charter of Fundamental Rights of the European Union,* 2012/C 326/02, Retrieved 31 March 2021: https://www.refworld.org/docid/3ae6b3b70.html

Eurovision.tv. (2016). Education, education and … Eurovision!. Eurovision.tv. Retrieved 31 March 2021, from https://eurovision.tv/story/education-education-and-eurovision

Fiske, J. (2010). *Understanding Popular Culture,* 2nd ed. Routledge.

Fricker, K., & Gluhovic, M., eds., (2013). *Performing the 'New' Europe identities, feelings and politics in the Eurovision Song Contest.* Palgrave Macmillan.

Gilmore, A. (2007). Authentic materials and authenticity in foreign language learning. *Language Teaching, 40*(2), 97–118.

Grindstaff, L. (2008). Culture and popular culture: A case for sociology. *The Annals of the American Academy of Political and Social Science, 619,* 206–222. Retrieved March 30, 2021, from http://www.jstor.org/stable/40375803.

Hadley, A. (2001). *Teaching language in context* (3rd ed.). Thomson Heinle.

Horwitz, E. K. (2016). Factor structure of the foreign language classroom anxiety scale: Comment on park (2014). *Psychological Reports, 119,* 71–76.

Ifversen, J. (2002). Europe and European culture - a conceptual analysis. *European Societies, 4*(1), 1–26.

In a Nutshell. (2021). Retrieved 31 March 2021, from https://eurovision.tv/history/in-a-nutshell

Jordan, P. (2011). *The Eurovision Song Contest: nation branding and nation building in Estonia and Ukraine.* Thesis (Ph.D.), University of Glasgow.

Konyukhova, E. S., & Abramova, G. S. (2020). Methods of teaching adapted and authentic texts based on Tolstoy's Novel 'Anna Karenina' to Foreign Audiences. *Russian Linguistic Bulletin,* 2020, *4*(24), 53–58.

Kress, G. (2010). Multimodality: *A Social-Semiotic approach to contemporary communication.* Routledge.

Kyriakidou, M., Skey, M., Uldam, J., & McCurdy, P. (2017). Media events and cosmopolitan fandom: 'Playful nationalism' in the Eurovision Song Contest. *International Journal of Cultural Studies* 2018, *21*(6), 603–618.

Last Update Thursday 17th June 2021 12.12 pm + references.

Lawson, M. (2014). Putin and Cameron, take note: Eurovision has a fine record of predicting geopolitical tensions. *New Statesman, 2014,* 55–56.

Mansour, N. (2013). Consistencies and inconsistencies between science teachers: Beliefs and practices. *International Journal of Science Education, 35*(7), 1230–1275.

Marsh, J. (2008). Popular culture in the language arts classroom. In J. Flood, S. B. Heath, & D. Lapp (Eds.), *Handbook of research on teaching literacy through the communicative and visual arts* (Vol. 2, pp. 529–536). Erlbaum.

Marsh, J., & Millard, E. (2000). *Literacy and popular culture: Using children's culture in the classroom.* London: Paul Chapman.

Moecharam, N. Y., & Kartika S. A. (2014). Let's talk and tolerate strengthening students' cultural awareness through literature circles. *Indonesian Journal of Applied Linguistics, 3*(2), 117–127.

Nagro, S. A., Fraser, D. W., & Hooks, S. D. (2019). Lesson planning with engagement in mind: Proactive classroom management strategies for curriculum instruction. *Intervention in School and Clinic, 54*(3), 131–140.

Oliver, S. (2008). *The Secret History of the Eurovision Song Contest* [Video]. Brook Lapping Productions and Electric Pictures.

O'Regan, J. P. (2006). The text as a critical object: on theorising exegetic procedure in classroom based critical discourse analysis. *Critical Discourse Studies, 3*(2), 179–209.

Pachler, N., Barnes, A., & Field, K. (2009). *Learning to teach modern foreign languages in the secondary school.* (3rd/Ed.). Routledge.

PBS, Għandi xi ngħid, Radju Malta, 4 February 2017, Retrieved May 6, 2020 http://www.tvm.com.mt/mt/radio-programme/ghandi-xi-nghid-3/

Petriciuc, L. (2019). Constrastive-comparative study on students' perceptions of using literary texts as authentic language learning resources. *Revista De Pedagogie, LXVII(1), Revista de pedagogie, 2019-07-01, LXVII*(1).

Richards, J. C. (2015). The changing face of language learning: Learning beyond the classroom. *RELC Journal, 46*(1), 5–22.

Storey, J. (2019) *Cultural Theory and Popular Culture*, 8th ed. Routledge.

Vuletic, D. (2019). Eurovision Is Political This Year. As It Is Every Year. *The Washington Post (Online)*. The Washington Post (Online), 2019-05-13. Web.

9 Sharing Values in the Eurovision Song Contest and the OTI Festival: The Moral Fourth Person in the Lyrics of the Winning Songs

Ariel James

Introduction

Guy Debord used to talk about how the proletariat could exercise an anti-aesthetic dictatorship. It would be possible to ask today, when the proletariat no longer exists, because it has become omnipresent, what is the type of aesthetics of the spectacle that governs our cultural consumption. It is possible to ask whether what is usually understood by aesthetics and anti-aesthetics has any connection with what is typically understood by ethics and anti-ethics. To put it bluntly: Is it possible to separate so sharply the aesthetic dimension from the ethical dimension of human thought and feeling?

Following this initial concern, in this work I shall propose a leap from ethnomusicology to ethics. From the ethnomusicological point of view, I will analyse the semantic role played by the cross-cultural concept of a "musical person" expressed in the winning songs of the Eurovision Song Contest (ESC). The musical person is the ideal personage, being singular or plural, who serves as the semantic axis of the song's lyrics, either because it is the subject of the enunciation (*I, we*), the object or the reference of action (*you, them*), or because it is a summary of all the different voices (*all of us*).

Thus, for example, if a song is about two lovers, the musical person is dual, since it includes both personages, even if one of them represents the action and the other the passion. If, on the contrary, the song refers to a definite or indefinite community of individuals, the musical person is diluted into a collective subject that can be represented by any of the three grammatical persons of the plural (the speakers, the addressees, the others), including an abstract "fourth person" that stands for every possible individual.

Even in cases where the main personage or character is the first person singular, the musical person or "persona" is not limited to the rhetorical figure of the speaker(s). The listeners, once they receive the song, usually build their own idiosyncratic notion of the "musical person". It is a symbolic and conceptual construction, but also an emotional, sentimental, intuitive, and passionate intersubjective act of *personification*.

DOI: 10.4324/9781003188933-11

In this study I start from the assumption that each song proposes its own musical person(s). In the first place I will describe the model of the "musical person" that emerges from the winning songs of the ESC. Then, I analyse the meaningful content that this musical person transmits, focusing on the main topics that emerge from the lyrics. Finally, I show that the musical person in the lyrics of the winning songs of the ESC undergoes a transformation from a merely *aesthetic* voice/character, based upon the three traditional grammatical persons, to the configuration of a *moral* voice/character, based on the semantic concept of a fourth person. The "fourth" person represents not *one* or *some* persons, but rather *universal quantification* ($\forall$): each-and-every one of the members of the set *homo sapiens* is included.

In the second part, I compare the model of the musical person that emerges from the lyrics of the ESC songs with the model of the musical person that can be inferred from the winning lyrics of the OTI Festival of the Song. I then explore whether both musical contests share the same figure of the *moral* fourth person, in other words, whether the transcultural notion of an ethical person can be described using generic attributes. If so, then the lyrics of the winning songs from the ESC and OTI festival are a very rich window into the process of building basic ethical agreements that seems to be cross-cultural and to some extent global.

The ESC

The ESC can be construed as a visual and sound spectacle that provides a symbolic space for building inter-cultural agreements between different musical performances, each of them representing a specific country. As Antonio Obregón pointed out,

> *The intention of Eurovision is precisely to propose a way of relating to citizens and peoples in society, through an artistic and festive manifestation, seeking to promote values of coexistence and respect.*
>
> (Obregón García, 2019)

Thus, ESC is based upon a cultural process of building an imagined community with its own characteristics, assuming the traits of the "global village" that had been foreshadowed by McLuhan,

> *The ESC is one of the clearest examples of a staging of [Benedict Anderson's concept of] an imagined community.. Song and music give the event a special quality of oneness—both in the general assumption of what music can do as an assumed universal language and in relation to the oneness created by the ability of television to address a massive audience to a shared event. McLuhan's "global village" is a suitable metaphor for the 'togetherness' of the final competition which presently draws around one hundred and fifty million viewers.*
>
> (Kirkegaard, 2013, 81)

As a complement to this comment by Kirkegaard, it is worth noting that the sense of universality is not an exclusive feature of verbal language, but also of musical language, and specifically, of the lyrics of songs. One of the ways of expressing universality is through the meaningful game that is established between the implicit content and the explicit content of the songs.

Explicit versus Implicit Message

The content of the songs moves between two semantic planes: the explicit message (i. e. grammatical) and the implicit message (i. e. pragmatic). If we focus on purely grammatical analysis, in principle it would be possible to compare a wide corpus of pop songs with specific ESC using different matrices, and from there infer, by repetition of words, the typical features ("uniqueness") of the ESC songs (c.f., Van Hoey, 2016). In this case, the research would be focused on content analysis. This would consist of filling a matrix with a large set of word data, with the expectation that the matrix would be able to establish the *correct* correlations between these words, from which certain inferences could be made. Although this method of analysis could be productive in the sense of a numerical accumulation of concepts, it leaves *implicit* and *contextual* meaning, the most important aspect of the lyrics of songs, virtually untouched.

The use of formal matrices to investigate the meaning of songs is easy prey to the problem of the *underdeterminacy of grammar*, namely, the fact that the explicit coded messages cannot expose the deep meaning of the texts (Carston, 2002; Levinson, 2000). The grammatical text, by itself, does not tell us anything relevant beyond the mere accumulation of singular data or tokens of information. It seems that, for the case of the lyrics of songs, social and cultural discourse is the most important factor in shaping grammatical texts. Therefore, if we want to understand the content of the songs, the solution is to understand the function of the speech (c.f., Givón, 2002).

The Role of Discourse Functions

When deciphering the content of the songs, two crucial factors must be considered, namely:

a   the cognitive concept behind the words, or implicated by the text,
b   the discourse role played by the specific grammatical categories (Hopper & Thompson, 1984).

In short, concepts must be supplemented by discourse functions, in other words, by the intentions and motivations of the musical person. A literary text such as a song is a complete unit of intentions plus the concepts that convey those intentions (see Du Bois, 2003). The main problem with the quantitative interpretation of songs is that meaning is not explicitly given in the literal discourse; therefore, we must look for it elsewhere. An interesting way to approach the implicit content is to try to figure out what kind of "person" is constructed in the narrative of the songs.

A "person" is a set of mental properties, emotional attributes, and character traits that we consider to be pertinent, following some criteria of relevance, to define an individual. If the lyrics of the songs are rich enough in the semantic sense to convey a notion of person, then it is possible to explore the concept of the human condition expressed there going beyond the collection of mere numerical data. A person is no longer defined by an alphanumeric symbol, but by a meaning. Meanings, as de Saussure pointed out, are mental contents. Hence, a song could be a privileged space for expressing the meanings of the soul, most of which are non-explicit.

The Concept of a Musical Person

I shall focus this reflection on the concept of the "musical person", used to represent the ideal personage proposed by any concrete musical action, in this case a song. Here the musical person is understood as the representation of the ideal character(s) in the song's lyrics.

The musical person could be the first person singular or plural, that is, the subject or subjects who state their own point of view, but it could also stand for the addressee of the song (the second person), or the other referents of the song (third person both singular and plural). In this article, I will show that, studying the content of the winning songs of the ESC and OTI Festival, we can infer the presence of an abstract "fourth" person, that is usually dedicated to express moral principles that are common to *all* individuals.

It is important to distinguish between three different variants of the category "person", applied to the field of musical production and interpretation, namely:

1   the "person" understood as the musical/cultural identity of players, interpreters, and of the public, with the song being a means by which people formulate and express their "individual identities" (MacDonald et al., 2017),

2   the "person" understood as the role or character that some artists assume when they perform a musical work: the actor's specific personage (Graver, 2003; Auslander, 2006),

3   and the category of "musical person" (Cf. Nahajec, 2019), understood as the abstract subject(s) of the musical enunciation.

The crucial point regarding the musical person is not that the listener should feel the *same* feelings as the performer (e. g. the singer, dancer, or percussionist, for example). Two different individuals can share the model of the musical person without feeling the same sensations. What people share is not the same feeling, but the same *type* of feeling.

My concept of certain feeling expresses certain mental associations that are so private that they are hardly shared with another individual. My sentiment is not a copy: it is rather a completely new and subjective feeling. However, all these different feelings can be represented using the same ideal model of the "persona": the musical person.

Exploring the Nature of the Musical Person

Accordingly, this article seeks to answer the following questions:

a   What are those ideal aspects (sentiments, beliefs, values, virtues) that are part of the musical person that emerges from the lyrics of the songs in the ESC, also in comparison with the OTI Festival?
b   Whether/do those ideal values point in one specific direction, that is, can they translate into an intersubjective and interpersonal model of being a moral person?

Step One: semantic and Pragmatic Types

The present study is concentrated on a reduced corpus of song lyrics, considering only those songs that have obtained first place in the ESC — to date, sixty-eight winning songs, from 1956 to 2021. On this occasion, I have refrained from proposing an a priori typology of the semantic content of the songs. Instead, I have divided the corpus studied according to the central themes that the musical person wants to convey, specifically, grouping these themes into the following two large classes:

1   Content that expresses an ideal model of existential values, such as *ideal* emotions, feelings, intuitions, attitudes, intentions, and expectations,
2   Content that expresses character traits (virtues and vices) and different models of behavior (positive versus negative ones).

Therefore, the songs are not classified according to their musical genre, but according to the type of intentionality (desire, belief, goal) that the musical person transmits through the song. Let us mention the core categories within class number one (i. e., the model of existential values), which emerge from the lyrics of the winning ESC songs:

•   Category I. LOVE. Between 1957 and 2019, the songs dedicated to transmitting an ideal model of "love", embodied in and through an ideal model of person, tend to be the winning songs in the contest. See Figure 9.1.

Following closely the songs dedicated to the "love" category, are the songs dedicated to the notion of "inner feeling(s)".

•   Category II. INNER FEELING(S). Main themes: thankfulness to life (exultation), feeling of unity with nature, spiritualism. For instance:

Refrain (Lys Assia, Switzerland, 1956); *Net Als Toen* (Corry Brokken, Netherlands, 1957); *Dors, mon amour* (André Claveau, France, 1958); *Een Beetje* (Teddy Scholten, Netherlands, 1959); *Tom Pillibi* (Jacqueline Boyer, France, 1960); *Nous les amoureux* (Jean-Claude Pascal, Luxembourg, 1961); *Un premier amour* (Isabelle Aubret, France, 1962); *Dansevise* (Grethe and Jørgen Ingmann, Denmark, 1963); *Non ho l'età (per amarti)* (Gigliola Cinquetti, Italy, 1964); *Merci, Chérie* (Udo Jürgens, Austria, 1966); *Puppet on a String* (Sandie Shaw, UK, 1967); *Vivo cantando* (Salomé, Spain, 1969); *Boom Bang-a-Bang* (Lulu, UK, 1969); *All Kinds of Everything* (Dana, Ireland, 1970); *Après toi* (Vicky Leandros, Luxembourg, 1972); *Tu te reconnaîtras* (Anne-Marie David, Luxembourg, 1973); *Waterloo* (Abba, Sweden, 1974); *Save Your Kisses for Me* (Brotherhood of Man, UK, 1976); *A-Ba-Ni-Bi* (Izhar Cohen & Alphabeta, Israel, 1978); *What's Another Year* (Johnny Logan, Ireland, 1980); *Si la vie est cadeau* (Corinne Hermès, Luxembourg, 1983); *Hold Me Now* (Johnny Logan, Ireland, 1987); *Ne partez pas sans moi* (Celine Dion, Switzerland, 1988); *Fångad av en stormvind* (Carola Häggkvist, Sweden, 1991); *Why Me?* (Linda Martin, Ireland, 1992); *In Your Eyes* (Niamh Kavanagh, Ireland, 1993); *Love Shine a Light* (Katrina and the Waves, UK, 1997); *Take Me to Your Heaven* (Charlotte Nilsson, Sweden, 1999); *Fly on the Wings of Love* (Olsen Brothers, Denmark, 2000); *I Wanna* (Marie N, Latvia, 2002); *Every Way That I Can* (Sertab Erener, Turkey, 2003); *My Number One* (Elena Paparizou, Greece, 2005); *Molitva* (Marija Šerifović, Serbia, 2007); *Fairytale* (Alexander Rybak, Norway, 2009); *Satellite* (Lena, Germany, 2010); *Running Scared* (Ell & Nikki, Azerbaijan, 2011); *Only Teardrops* (Emmelie de Forest, Denmark, 2013); *Amar pelos dois* (Salvador Sobral, Portugal, 2017); *Arcade* (Duncan Laurence, Netherlands, 2019).

Figure 9.1 Category I: Love songs (including love-related emotions and attitudes).

L'oiseau et l'enfant (Marie Myriam, France, 1977), *Hallelujah* (Milk and Honey, Israel, 1979); *Nocturne* (Secret Garden, Norway, 1995).

• Category III. SELF. Songs that express feelings and emotions linked to the self (although not necessarily romantic), such as *Poupée de cire, poupée de son* (France Gall, Luxembourg, 1965); *La, La, La* (Massiel, Spain, 1968), *Ding-a-dong* (Teach-In, Netherlands, 1975); *Making Your Mind Up* (Bucks Fizz, UK, 1981); *Diggi-Loo Diggi-Ley* (Herrey's, Sweden, 1984); *The Voice* (Eimear Quinn, Ireland, 1996); *Believe* (Dima Bilan, Russia, 2008), *Zitti e buoni* (Måneskin, Italy, 2021).

- Category IV. ARCHETYPE. Sometimes the musical person identifies itself with an archetypal character, drawn from folklore, oral traditions, and history. For example, *De Troubadour* (Lenny Kuhr, Netherlands, 1969); *Un jour, un enfant* (Frida Boccara, France, 1969); *Diva* (Dana international, Israel, 1998); *Heroes* (Måns Zelmerlöw, Sweden, 2015).
- Category V. IDEALS. The musical person conveys a mixed message, at the same time existential and ethical, for example, emphasising positive ideals such as peace, love, and fraternity. For instance, *Ein bißchen Frieden* (Nicole, Germany, 1982), and *1944* (Jamala, Ukraine, 2016).
- Category VI. COLLECTIVE IDENTITY. The musical person champions the ideal of unity between different countries. *Insieme: 1992* (Toto Cutugno, Italy, 1990).

In summary, those contents that express an ideal model of existential values, such as emotions, feelings, intuitions, attitudes, intentions, and expectations, are represented by five main categories: love, inner feeling(s), self, archetype, ideals, and collective identity. These categories have one trait in common: all of them are desires expressed by the musical person. To the extent that these wishes are purely subjective, we cannot yet assume that they reflect an intersubjective agreement.

Step Two: positive and Negative Features

The number two class of concepts are composed of projected character traits (virtues and vices), and models of behavior (both positive and negative).

An essential point is that these values are not necessarily "positive". The richness of the scheme is that the musical person includes both positive values, that is, values that are good, nice, and right to feel, as well as negative values, or values that would be better not to feel, because they are harmful, dangerous, or just plain wrong. Negative values normally remain *tacit*, although in some cases they fulfil explicit roles within the functions of musical discourse. See Figure 9.2.

The musical person expresses both virtuous character traits, in the pure Aristotelian sense (e. g. loyalty, fidelity, self-restraint, softness, tenderness, self-esteem, inner vision, wisdom, autonomy), as opposed to some set of implicit vices (such as disloyalty, infidelity, immoderacy, roughness, low self-esteem, ignorance, bias, heteronomy). It also conveys certain ideal models of attitudes and conduct (e. g. loving life, self-affirmation, nostalgia and remembering, introspection, love-your-neighbour attitude, goodness, reciprocity), including certain political and ideological goals, such as the wish for the unity of the European countries (see Vuletic, 2018).

Within the semantic cluster of positive desires, the notion of self-control and the expression of good feelings and thoughts are recurring themes. The concepts of self-confidence and reciprocity are expressed precisely to counteract the emergence of negative character traits such as low self-esteem, selfishness, and mercilessness. Virtues and vices are represented at an equally subjective level, indicating a tension or contradiction between them. Each of these values, taken individually, serves to convey purely optional desires. However, some of these

MUSICAL PERSON'S TYPES OF VALUES	INTERPRETER OF THE MUSICAL PERSON.
Loyalty Fidelity	*Een Betje* (Netherlands, 1959).
Containment Self-restraint	*Refrain* (Switzerland, 1956).
Softness (tenderness) Goodness	*Net Als Toen* (Netherlands, 1957).
Willful ignorance Willful blindness (choosing to ignore) Bias	*Tom Pillibi* (France, 1960).
Love your neighbor Goodness	*Nous les amoureux* (Luxembourg, 1961).
Nostalgia and remembering	*Un premier amour* (France, 1962), *All Kinds of Everything* (Ireland, 1970), *Rock 'n' Roll Kids* (Ireland, 1994); *Fairytale* (Norway, 2009).
Now is not the right time Inadequacy	*Non ho l'età* (Italy, 1964).
Introspection	*Poupée de cire, poupée de son* (Luxembourg, 1965).
Thank you, but good-bye	*Merci, Chérie* (Austria, 1966).
Give-and-take Reciprocity	*Si La Vie Est Cadeau* (Luxembourg, 1983).
Feeling that one is used, manipulated Anger Indignation	*Puppet on a String* (Luxembourg, 1965).
Inner vision Wisdom Autonomy	*Making Your Mind Up* (UK, 1981), *The Voice* (Ireland, 1996).
Renouncing Giving up	*Waterloo* (Sweden, 1974).
Happiness Positive sensations Loving life Goodness	*La det swinge* (Norway, 1985); *J'aime la vie* (Belgium, 1986); *Rock Me* (Yugoslavia, 1989).
Sharing a positive feeling (definite or indefinite)	*Dansevise* (Denmark, 1963), *Boom Bang-a-Bang* (UK, 1969), *Un banc, un arbre, une rue* (Monaco, 1971), *Everybody* (Estonia, 2001); *Wild Dances* (Ukraine, 2004); *Euphoria* (Sweden, 2012).
A united Europe	*Insieme: 1992* (Italy, 1990).
Be careful, this person is dangerous Peril Risk	*Hard Rock Hallelujah* (Finland, 2006).
Reborn Renewal Change.	*Rise Like a Phoenix* (Austria, 2014). *Zitti e Buoni* (Italy, 2021).
Self-affirmation, Self-esteem.	*Toy* (Israel, 2018).

Figure 9.2 Types of core values expressed by the musical person in winning songs in the ESC.

values point to a connotation that is not optional, but rather mandatory, that is, they express moral duties.

Step Three: from the Musical Person to the Moral Person

The model of *persona* that emerges from the winning songs does not end in the configuration of a mere "musical" person. Certain songs make direct reference to the values and virtues that the moral person defends by conviction, for example, certain ethical-moral values such as peace, humanity, respect, dignity, and reciprocity.

For instance, the song "1944", performed by Jamala (2016), denounces the lack of scruples of the soulless invaders of Ukraine, but above all the absence of a mechanism that ensures moral and legal accountability for the atrocities committed. Even if the youth of the moral person has been snatched away, it is still possible to trust each other, for the sake of building a peaceful future. This can be done only by returning to the notions of the soul and the heart, since brute force rests on the absence of the soul, and the loss of the inner moral feelings. The attribute that allows us to connect with others is the notion of the heart: do we not all have a heart?

There is a very subtle point in this song that we must not overlook. It is about the notion of a "moral fourth person": the actor's role of the song it is neither the /*I, we, me,* and *us*/, nor is it the /*you*/, and it also transcends the /*she, he, they,* etc./. The moral person includes and exceeds the three traditional grammatical persons. Accordingly, we can classify her as a *fourth* person, for instance, in the expressions: "humanity cries", "everyone dies", "our souls", "people (are) free to live and love", and, finally, "humanity rise" (other winning songs, such as "Rise Like a Phoenix", could be interpreted along the same lines).

All these various concepts are linked to each other by the same finality: the purpose of understanding human nature from a non-exclusive point of view, thus rejecting any type of prejudice, discrimination, or cultural/ideological intolerance.

The Moral Fourth Person in the ESC

After studying the sixty-eight winning songs of ESC, I conclude that they can be divided into three large classes:

   I subjective, self-expressive songs: fifteen songs,
  II songs that describe the passionate or emotional relationship between two people: thirty-nine songs,
III songs that describe fraternal or solidarity relationships between *more* than two people (including exaltation of human society, life, nature, and spirituality): fifteen songs.

Point (III) is especially relevant insofar as it condenses two of the central features of the moral perspective, namely: the sense of goodness (expressed through notions such as solidarity, benevolence, love, empathy, having a heart or a soul) and the sense of universality (expressed through the fourth person). However, for a decision or an action to be truly moral, it is still necessary to include another dimension, which is the sphere of moral prescriptions. Ideals are completely moral when they refer to just actions. And justice is not simply an optional type of action, it is rather an unavoidable prescription.

The winning ESC's songs convey three different types of *ethical* values:

1   positive emotions such as care, respect, and consideration, as opposed to negative mental states and feelings such as heartlessness and cruelty,
2   fraternity: a future of peace and harmony between different peoples, as opposed to war, antipathy, or strife,
3   ethical rules: reciprocity, prohibition against harm, prohibition of lies, which are moral prescriptions contrary to a lack of solidarity, aggressiveness, or mendacity.

Only when reached the third level it is possible to speak of a truly "moral person", following the classical deontological principle espoused by Immanuel Kant, which remains valid: a person is moral to the extent that they act autonomously for the sake of fulfilling and enforcing the ideals of goodness, justice, and fairness.

Moreover, is there a winning song that summarises the message of a shared framework of values, both for affective values (love) and for ethical (moral) values? Is there an example in which we can verify the materialisation of the moral fourth person? There is more than one example, but for the sake of showing a specific case, let us mention "Si la vie est Cadeau", by Corinne Hermès (Luxembourg, 1983).

In this song, an accurate example of the moral person is reflected. It is not just about sharing certain values considered as virtuous (i. e. the act of loving), or about choosing them voluntarily and without coercion (i. e. autonomy). It is even beyond the mere notion of mutual help (i. e. cooperation). Rather, it includes the necessity of defending a fair type of relationship from the beginning: the musical person is appealing to the category of *reciprocity*.

"Prend l'amour comm' un cadeau, Cadeau donne, Cadeau repris, Cadeau vole". Reciprocity is the opposite of arbitrary distinction. It is also linked to the *queer* aspect of different types of musical performances in the ESC. Far from creating a barrier between the different members of the audience, the "queerness effect" deepens the attitude of transgressing the artificial limits established between people: "Queerness transgresses the boundaries separating the event from its fans, the show from its following, or the text from its receptions" (Lampropoulos 2013, 167).

The notion of reciprocity, far from binding ourselves to a unique model of being, places us in the position of reaching a fair and equitable agreement between different — and, in some cases, conflicting — visions about crucial issues such as the boundaries of the self, the personality, gender, moral agency, and the various social/cultural roles. The highest level of morality is precisely the autonomous capacity for "giving justice to those who can give justice in return" (Rawls 1999, 447).

Accordingly, in defining the moral fourth person, it is pertinent to consider not just the internal competence of each person to feel pleasure or pain, but also to highlight the universal capacity to entertain a conception of the good connected with the sense of justice, "expressed by a regulative desire to act upon certain principles of right" (Rawls 1999, 493).

A Comparative Perspective between the ESC and the OTI Song Festival

The same content-analysis approach used for the ESCn songs, focused on the transition from the musical person (whose values are optional) to the moral person (whose values are moral duties), is also applicable to the winning songs of the OTI Festival (Festival OTI de la Canción), the annual singing competition, held between 1972 and 2000, among member countries of the *Organización de Televisión Iberoamericana* (OTI) [Ibero-American Television Organization], with 28 winning songs.

In this comparison, there are strikingly similar results, but also marked differences. Among the points of similarity, the lyrics of OTI songs include certain categories that were already present in ESC, for example,

- I. Category of LOVE. For instance: *El amor ... cosa tan rara* (Denise de Kalafe, Brazil, 1978), *Cuenta conmigo* (Daniel Riolobos, Argentina, 1979), *Un bolero* (Carlos Cuevas, Mexico, 1990), *A dónde voy sin ti* (Francisco, Spain, 1992), *Enamorarse* (Ana Reverte, Spain, 1993).
- III. Category of the SELF. Feelings of the inner self. *Hoy canto por cantar* (Nydia Caro, Puerto Rico, 1974).
- IV. Category of ARCHETYPES. The musical person identifies with a specific cultural archetype. *Qué alegre va María* (Imelda Miller, Mexico, 1973), *Quincho Barrilete* (Guayo González, Nicaragua, 1977), *Latino* (Francisco, Spain, 1981); *Estrela de Papel* (Jessé, Brazil, 1983).
- V. Category of IDEALS. Existential-moral message. *Todos (All of us)* (Damaris, Miguel Ángel Guerra & Eduardo Fabiani, United States, 1986).
- VI. Category of COLLECTIVE IDENTITY. Latin-American unity: *Se diga lo que se diga* (Iridian, Mexico, 1997).

  Additionally, two new categories conveyed by the musical person appear in OTI *winning* songs:
- VII. Category of RECTIFICATION. Acknowledging mistakes and overcoming the past. *Contigo mujer* (Rafael José, Puerto Rico, 1980).
- VIII. Category of MUSICAL GENRE. Praise of a musical genre. *El fandango aquí* (Eugenia León, Mexico, 1985).

Regarding the typology of the core values expressed by the musical person, the OTI Festival winning songs shares the following core values with those of the ESC: (Figure 9.3)

MUSICAL PERSON'S TYPES OF VALUES	INTERPRETER OF THE MUSICAL PERSON.
Thank you, but good-bye	*Una cancion no es suficiente* (Analy, Mexico, 1989).
Give-and -take Reciprocity	*Todos* (Damaris et al, United States, 1986), *Mis manos* (Anabel Russ, Spain, 1996).
Feeling that one is used Manipulated	*Todavía eres mi mujer* (Guillermo Guido, Argentina, 1988).
Happiness Positive sensations Loving life Goodness	*Que alegre va María* (Imelda Miller, Mexico, 1973), *Agualuna* (Fernando Ubiergo, Chile, 1984), *La felicidad está en un rincón del corazón* (Alfredo Alejandro, Venezuela, 1987).
Sharing a positive feeling (definite or indefinite)	*Puedes contar conmigo* (Grupo Unicornio, Venezuela, 1982), *Adonde estás ahora* (Claudia Brant, Argentina, 1991).
A united America (s)	*Se diga lo que se diga* (Iridian, Mexico, 1997).
Be careful, this person is dangerous Peril Risk	*Hierba mala* (Chirino Sisters, Cuban group representing the United States, 2000).
Reborn Renewal Change	*Eres mi debilidad* (Marcos Llunas, Spain, 1995), *Fin de siglo* (Florcita Motuda, Chile, 1998).
Self-affirmation Self-esteem	*Canción Despareja* (Claudia Carenzio, Argentina, 1994).

Figure 9.3 Types of core values expressed by the musical person: the OTI Festival.

Additionally, in the winning songs of the OTI Festival, other types of feelings are reflected that were not *explicitly* marked in the winning songs of the ESC. For example, the feeling of /hopelessness/, expressed through two specific songs: *Hoy canto por cantar* (Nydia Caro, Puerto Rico, 1974) and *La Felicidad* (Gualberto Castro, Mexico, 1975).

As a counterpart, and together with the love-songs, the sentiment most present in OTI's songs is that of /hope/: *Canta, cigarra* (María Ostiz, Spain, 1976); *Cuenta conmigo* (Daniel Riolobos, Argentina, 1979), *Puedes contar conmigo* (Grupo Unicornio, Venezuela, 1982). Here the interesting detail is that the American notion of "hope" expressed in these songs is based on the notion of *solidarity*, understood as a concrete manifestation of the attitude of *reciprocity* that is, curiously, the central feature of the ESC's moral person.

Both the values of sharing a positive feeling (e.g., *Puedes contar conmigo*, 1982; *Adonde estás ahora*, Claudia Brant, Argentina, 1991), and of solidarity and hope (e.g., *Cuenta conmigo*, 1979, *Puedes contar conmigo*, 1982), are linked in the songs of OTI by the same moral fourth person. Accordingly, optional feelings are transformed into moral virtues through the application of certain fundamental premises, such as goodness, reciprocity, and fairness.

The role that Corinne Hermès's "Si la vie est Cadeau" plays in the ESC is played in the OTI Festival by the song *Todos* (1986), interpreted by Damaris, Miguel Ángel Guerra, and Eduardo Fabiani, representing the United States.

Comparing the lyrics of the ESC's songs with those of the OTI Festival, the transition from the "musical person", a vehicle for non-mandatory positive and negative values and emotions, to the "moral fourth person", based on mandatory ethical principles, is carried out through the affirmation of specific categories such as gratitude, loving life, positive feelings, self-esteem, care, respect, consideration, autonomy, solidarity, reciprocity, and goodness. The last three values are probably the most important ones, because they are genuinely moral concepts.

Conclusion

Now it is possible to answer the initial questions, namely:

a What are those ideal aspects (sentiments, beliefs, values, virtues) of the musical person that emerges from the lyrics of the songs in the Eurovision Song Contest (ESC), also in comparison with the OTI Festival?

The ideal aspects of the "musical person" are reflected in the contrast between desired and rejected values, expressed via emotions, feelings, attitudes, sentiments, and thoughts. The musical person is constructed through the tension between *positive* factors (which summarise what is preferred and best to feel and do), and *negative* factors (typically depicted as all those feelings and conducts that it is better to avoid). This opposition between good/correct and bad/incorrect characters and actions can be treated in many possible ways, but in the case of ESC, and of the OTI Festival's, winning songs, it is addressed by appealing to a fourth person who reflects the universal point of view.

b   Do those ideal values point toward one specific direction, that is, are they part of an intersubjective and interpersonal *ideal* model of the human person?

The answer to point (b) is affirmative. Indeed, once the musical person manages to express her commitment to upholding higher values such as the principles of human dignity and fairness, the *musical person* gradually becomes the *moral fourth person*. The transition from the musical person (ethnomusicology) to the moral person (ethics) occurs through the expression of three fundamental categories, namely: solidarity, reciprocity, and goodness.

The content of the songs studied here, both in the ESC and in the OTI Festival, is structured in a dynamic process of construction of a moral fourth person, which is committed to the core ethical principles that apply to all human beings regardless of conventional boundaries, but without denying their right to have distinct individual feelings, goals, and wishes. In short, it is possible to agree on the essentials, while preserving the differences.

The most significant contribution of the study of the musical person in the case of the lyrics of the songs of ESC and OTI Festival consists in the transit it describes between subjective desires and intersubjective principles and duties. This transit is one of the main objects of study of various academic disciplines such as critical theory of discourse, literary theory, sociology of the mass spectacle, semiotic theory, semantic theory, pragmatics, sociolinguistics, ethnomusicology, cultural anthropology, moral philosophy, and the neuroscience of moral cognition, among others.

In every one of these branches of knowledge, the recurring question is: What makes us human? There are no definitive answers, but the songs studied here point to two central questions: human values are often in conflict, and the moral point of view is an effective way of dealing with those conflicts between desire and obligation, and between opposing obligations.

Eurovision enters the academy not only because it is a legitimate object of cultural study, but because, fundamentally, it is a space for producing and understanding human society with all its edges and its potential and actual meanings.

References

Auslander, P. (2006). Musical Personae. *The Drama Review*, *50*(1) (T 189), Spring, 100–119.

Carston, R. (2002). *Thoughts and utterances: The pragmatics of explicit communication*. Blackwell.

Du Bois, J.W. (2003). Discourse and grammar. In M. Tomasello, ed., *The new psychology of language: Cognitive and functional approaches to language structure* (vol. 2, pp. 47–87). Lawrence Erlbaum Associates.

Givón, T. (2002). *Bio-linguistics: The Santa Barbara lectures.* John Benjamins.

Graver, D. (2003). The Actor's Bodies. In P. Auslander (Ed.), *Critical Concepts: Performance* (pp. 157–174). Routledge.

Hopper, P.J. & Thompson, S. A. (1984). The discourse basis for lexical categories in universal grammar. *Language, 60,* 703–752.

Kirkegaard, A. (2013). The Nordic Brotherhoods Eurovision as a Platform for Partnership and Competition. In: D. Tragaki (Ed.). *Empire of song: Europe and nation in the Eurovision Song Contest* (pp. 79–107). The Scarecrow Press.

Lampropoulos, A. (2013). Delimiting the Eurobody: Historicity, Politicization, Queerness. In: D. Tragaki (Ed.). *Empire of song: Europe and nation in the Eurovision Song Contest* (pp. 151–172). The Scarecrow Press.

Levinson, S. (2000). *Presumptive meanings: The theory of generalized conversational implicature.* MIT Press.

MacDonald, R., Hargreaves, D. J., & Miell, D. (Eds.). (2017). *Handbook of musical identities.* Oxford University Press.

Nahajec, L. (2019). Song lyrics and the disruption of pragmatic processing: An analysis of linguistic negation in 10CC's 'I'm Not in Love'. *Language and Literature 2019, 28*(1), 23–40.

Obregón García, A. (2019). *El Festival de Eurovisión: Un fenómeno necesario.* Universidad Pontificia Comillas. http://hdl.handle.net/11531/36874

Rawls, J. (1999). *A theory of justice.* The Belkanp Press.

Van Hoey, T. 2016. *Love love peace peace': a corpus study of the Eurovision Song Contest.* Graduate institute of Linguistics. National Taiwan University.

Vuletic, D. (2018). *Postwar Europe and the Eurovision Song Contest.* Bloomsbury.

10 Eurovision in the Boardroom: What Does Voting Order Tell Us about Decision-Making?

Jose Luis Arroyo-Barrigüete,
Lourdes Fernández, and Antonio Obregón

Introduction

This chapter seeks to explore how the order of participation in the Eurovision Song Contest (ESC) influences final voting results. Through a quantitative research methodology, it postulates the possibility of transferring the conclusions to other scientific fields, in which decision-making can be influenced by the order of the elements considered. In Yair's recent literature review (2019: 1013), the author points out that research on the ESC can be grouped into four main areas: "(1) studies of imagining a unified Europe [...]; (2) studies focusing on gender and what is often referenced as gay or 'camp' features in the Eurovision Song Contest; (3) studies of Euro-Divisions which focus on political bloc voting and cultural alliances [...]; and (4) studies making use of Eurovision data as a cultural seismograph for explaining external phenomenon[...]".

It is in the third of these groups that much of the literature analysing voting bias is concentrated. Starting with the papers of Yair (1995) and Yair and Maman (1996), which proved the existence of a bloc voting structure, numerous papers have delved into this issue (Schweiger & Brosius, 2003; Gatherer, 2006; Dekker, 2007; Saavedra et al., 2007; Clerides & Stengos, 2012; Mantzaris et al., 2017). While geographic proximity is not the only factor that explains the composition of these blocs (Fenn et al., 2006), several researchers have explored the biases induced by additional cultural, social, religious or political factors (Spierdijk & Vellekoop, 2009; Budzinski & Pannicke, 2017; Ginsburgh & Noury, 2008; D'Angelo et al., 2019). In particular, cultural distance seems to be an important factor (García & Tanase, 2013; Blangiardo & Baio, 2014). However, some authors minimise the existence and true influence of such voting blocs since their identification varies within the literature. In any case, the results are dynamic with the passing of time (Millner et al., 2015). Other researchers have analysed additional effects, such as the use of votes as a route towards increasing a country's score rank (Mantzaris et al., 2018), or the fact that the biases induced by bloc voting are less pronounced in countries with a greater degree of impartiality in their institutions (Charron, 2013). Also, other factors stand out that influence voting behavior, such as the language of the song and the gender of the performing artist (Dogru, 2012). Likewise, it is worth mentioning the attempts to

DOI: 10.4324/9781003188933-12

predict the results of the popular vote through the use of a variety of analytical methods (Ochoa et al., 2009; Kumpulainen et al., 2020). Furthermore, particularly relevant is the fact that the incidence of factors of voting bias, principally of a cultural nature, help in the explanation of economic phenomena (Felbermayr, & Toubal, 2010; Kokko & Tingball, 2012; Siganos & Tabner, 2020). Certainly, the voting dynamics and biases are extremely complex since, as Stockemer et al. (2018) point out, 36 per cent of participants would vote for a song that is neither their preference, the likely winner, nor a rational choice.

In addition to the aforementioned factors, several studies have proven the importance of exposure effects in the ESC, that is, the public's preference for stimuli to which they have already been exposed (Abakoumkin, 2011; Verrier, 2012; Abakoumkin, 2018). Finally, and turning to the focus of the present study, some studies have centered on the effect of the order of appearance, which are summarized in Table 10.1. In all cases, the conclusion was that participants in later places had, on average, a certain advantage over those in earlier ones. Haan et al. (2005) additionally reported that professional juries were less influenced than the general public by factors other than musical quality, such as order of appearance. The conclusions of these analyses could be useful in other scientific fields in which, for a long time now, the order effect has been a specific subject of investigation. Accordingly, as stated previously, in addition to the field of economics, this approach could be applied to psychology (Hogarth & Einhorn, 1992; Highhouse & Gallo, 1997; Huber et al., 2011), business (Butt & Campbell, 1989; Biswas et al., 2009), politics, principally in the electoral sphere (Meredith & Salant, 2013; Blom-Hansen et al., 2016; Grant, 2020), or especially in the legal area (Walker et al., 1972; Eisenberg & Barry, 1988; Kerstthold & Jackson, 1999).

The bias due to order of appearance has been reported in other music competitions such as The Queen Elisabeth Musical Competition (Flôres & Ginsburgh, 1996; Glejser & Heyndels, 2001; Ginsburgh et al., 2003) and the Pop Idol series (Page & Page, 2010), although not in the case of the Bundesvision Song Contest (BSC) (Budzinski & Pannicke, 2017). This has also been observed in other competitions involving juries, such as men's gymnastics (Plessner, 1999), women's gymnastics (Ansorge et al., 1978) or figure skating (Bruine de Bruin, 2005; 2006)[1].

The aim of this paper is to analyse the above-named order effect in the ESC, with a special focus on the period from 2014 to 2019. This temporal focus is due to the

Table 10.1 Main papers in order effects in the ESC

Authors	Period analysed
Bruine de Bruin (2005)	1957–2003
Haan et al. (2005)	1957–1997
Abakoumkin (2011)	1957–2008
Clerides & Stengos (2012)	1981–2005
Antipov & Pokryshevskaya (2017)	2009–2012

fact that the volume of information available on the ESC is significantly greater than that in previous periods, whilst disaggregated information is available at a much higher level of detail than in previous editions. On the one hand, there is the comprehensive ranking assigned by the jury and televoting, and not only concerning the scores, which are limited to the participants located in the best positions. On the other hand, disaggregated information is available at the level of each individual jury. As a result, while the aforementioned studies have worked with samples ranging in size from hundreds to thousands of data, this present study uses 37,290 records, of which 37,024 correspond to the period from 2014 to 2019. Additionally, other periods have also been considered for comparative purposes.

Two research hypotheses are proposed:

H1 The ESC shows an order effect in that participants who perform at the end of the event obtain better results than those who perform at the beginning of the event.

H2 This order effect is more pronounced for the televote (non-professional, public jury) than for the professional jury.

To verify these hypotheses, this study is structured as follows: first, the methodological issues are detailed, including both a description of the sample and the statistical instruments used in the analysis. Next, the results obtained are described, which are interpreted and compared with those achieved in previous research. Finally, the limitations of the research and its implications are analysed.

Subject Matter and Methodology

This study adopts a quantitative research methodology, developed in four successive phases: (i) identification of the time periods with similar characteristics according to the ESC's rules and regulations; (ii) data collection; (iii) exploratory analysis of the data; and (iv) statistical analysis. All of the analysis has been developed in R (language and environment for statistical computing and graphics, http://www.r-project.org), using three additional packages: *reshape* (Wickham, 2007), *DescTools* (Signorell et al., 2019) and *plyr* (Wickham, 2011).

Data

All the data have been obtained from the official ESC website (www.eurovision.tv). For some years, the website itself has allowed the direct downloading of files with all the information, while in others it has been necessary to collect them manually. In all the time periods analysed, which are discussed in detail below, data has been obtained on the order of appearance and ranking. When disaggregated information has been available between the televoting and jury results, an individual analysis has been carried out for each of them. Finally, it should be noted that, while the number of participants has varied in some years, the transformation proposed by Haan et al. (2005: 65) has been used for both ranking and order: "the contestant that performs as number i has a value for APPEARANCE that equals $(i - 1)/(n - 1)$. Hence the first contestant gets a value of zero, and the last contestant a value of one. [...] same normalization for the variable RANK, [...] therefore that a lower value of RANK implies a better performance".

Procedure

In order to determine the existence of order effects, the Spearman correlation coefficient is used in all cases, since we are using ordinal data. While researchers often collect ordinal data and treat them as metrical, using Pearson's correlation coefficient, research has illustrated the problems resulting from this approach (for a detailed analysis, see Choi et al, 2010). It is true that the final effect on the result is minimal, but methodologically it is more appropriate to use Spearman's correlation coefficient, as carried out in the present study, or the Kendall's Rank Correlation (Kendall's tau-b). The confidence intervals are calculated at a confidence level of 95 per cent, using the R *DescTools* package, which computes them using Fisher z transformation, and, in all cases, bilateral contrasts have been used.

In addition, there are two details to clarify regarding the treatment of the information. Firstly, in those cases in which two participants are equal in points, the criteria of Antipov and Pokryshevskaya (2017) have been chosen when defining the ranking, that is, using the average value. For example, two participants with the same points and placed by the European Broadcasting Union (EBU) and the host broadcaster, in positions ten and eleven will be assigned the position 10.5. Secondly, in all cases and in addition to the overall correlation, the correlations have been calculated in two steps, i.e., the first half and second half of the contest. The criterion for assigning participants is the transformed order, assigning to the first half those with values less than or equal to 0.5 and to the second half those with values greater than 0.5. The reason is that in 2015, with twenty-seven participants, Austria, which acted in fourteenth position (standardised ranking of 0.5), was assigned to the first half. This analysis only makes sense in the period from 2014 to 2019, for reasons detailed below, but the exercise has been replicated in the period from 1998 to 2008 for comparative purposes.

The Period from 1998 to 2008

In 1997 there occurred, according to Gauja (2019: 205), "perhaps the most important change to the nature of voting in the contest", as the EBU allowed viewers to cast a vote by calling a phone number at the end of the sequence (upon the finishing of all the performances) on a pilot basis; however, only five countries made use of this mechanism, and it is in fact in 1998 when the tele-voting system becomes widespread. For this reason, the analysis of the present study begins in that year. In this period, the order of participation was random, decided by drawing lots. Most of the voting was done by televote, although in 2001 and 2002, some countries also used a jury, determining the scores either with a 50 per cent jury and 50 per cent televote system, or with 100 per cent jury. Although this system was mainly employed during the years identified, the jury was also used to a lesser extent before and after, due principally to the difficulties related to the telephonic infrastructure of the country or other technical reasons.

Ideally, we should treat the televote, jury and mixed systems (50 per cent jury and 50 per cent televote) differently. The problem we encountered is that, in this period, the EBU did not provide voting details. In other words, individual voting for each country in the order of first to last place is not available; only the first places, i.e., those that get points, are available. It would be possible to reconstruct the ranking by eliminating the countries that used the jury-only system or the mixed jury/television system, but in the end it was decided not to do so for several reasons. First, the use of these systems, except in 2002, is very much in the minority, and in fact the academic literature analysing this period generally treats the information without including these nuances (Abakoumkin, 2011; Clerides & Stengos, 2012). Second, since it is not possible to access the details of those countries that used a mixed fifty-fifty jury, eliminating these would imply a loss of relevant information regarding televoting. Finally, the juries used in this period were not strictly professional, unlike those used in later years, so it does not seem completely justified to differentiate them from the televoting, which is undertaken by non-professionals. Therefore, and assuming these nuances, the correlation in this period has been calculated, which should really be defined as "mainly televoting".

The Period from 2009 to 2012

This period was analysed by Antipov and Pokryshevskaya (2017) because the running order of contestants was determined randomly, and split jury and televoting results were available. Nevertheless, the voting system in 2010 and 2011 was different from that of the 2009 and 2012 shows. During these editions, it was possible to vote throughout the duration of the broadcast, and not only at the end. This is not a step-by-step procedure, which asks judges to evaluate each performance as it ends, since there is the possibility of giving the decision at any time. Nor is it an end-of-sequence procedure that asks for all judgments after all performances have been seen, a system used in all other years. It is true that Bruine de Bruin and Keren (2003) and Bruine de Bruin (2005) reported similar serial position effects with end-of-sequence and step-by-step procedures, but the underlying problem is that in this case none of these systems were used. The mixed dynamic, end-of-sequence procedure in 2009 and 2012 and continuous voting in 2010 and 2011 do not allow a homogeneous comparison with the other two periods, and that is the reason why we have excluded this period from the analysis.

The Period from 2014 to 2019

The year 2013 is peculiar, given that the EBU, instead of publishing the breakdown of televoting and jury points, released the average of each country's rankings, without going into further detail. For this reason, 2013 is a year that has been excluded from the analysis, with the third period therefore commencing in 2014. Certainly, this last period is by far the richest in information, given that the EBU provided the data disaggregated not only between jury and televoting, but for each of the jury members, also indicating the complete ranking in all cases. Therefore, a year by year individual analysis has been carried out, in addition to calculating the aggregate correlation for the entire period. However, during these years, the dynamics of the contest was somewhat different to previous editions, while the assignment of the order was only partially random. A draw was done to determine who would perform in the first half and in the second half, but it was the producer of the event (the host broadcaster under the EBU's supervision) itself that subsequently decided the specific order of participation in each of these parts, except in the case of the host country, whose position was assigned randomly. The implications of this system will be dealt with in detail in the discussion section.

We must also explain some details about the data:

- in 2014, Albania and San Marino did not use the televote, so we only have information about their jury votes, due to an insufficient number of votes cast during the televote period.
- in 2015, the votes of the juries of F.Y.R. Macedonia and Montenegro were annulled by the EBU, apparently for breach of the established rules, meaning that in the case of these countries only the results of the televotes were used; in the case of San Marino only the jury votes were used;
- in 2019, all data, jury and televotes, have been eliminated for Belarus. The reason is that, due to an error with the voting, the EBU decided to recalculate the points allocated by this country based on an algorithm that took into account the votes of nearby countries.

In the case of televoting, the voting system was end-of-sequence, as calls were only initiated after all the performances had been completed. As far as the jury is concerned, we can assume a similar system, since the final result was a complete ranking of all participants.

Results

In the period from 1998 to 2008, for which we have 266 records, all of them corresponding to televotes, a negative and statistically significant correlation is observed, with a very low p-value (Table 10.2). The detail by half points for a negative and significant correlation in the second part, as shown in Table 10.3.

Table 10.2 Spearman correlation for the period 1998–2008

Year		n	Rho	P-value	CI_{lower}	CI_{upper}
1998 to 2008	Televote	266	−0.24	7.5E-05	−0.35	−0.12

Table 10.3 Spearman Correlation for the period 1998–2008, distinguishing between the first and second halves of the competition

Year		First part				Second part			
		Rho	P-value	CI_{lower}	CI_{upper}	Rho	P-value	CI_{lower}	CI_{upper}
1998 to 2008	Televote	-0.14	1.0E-01	-0.30	0.03	-0.19	2.8E-02	-0.35	-0.02

Table 10.4 Spearman correlation coefficient and confident intervals (CI) for individual years in the period 2014–2019

Year		n	Rho	P-value	CI_{lower}	CI_{upper}
2014	Televote	885	0.02	6.5E-01	−0.05	0.08
	Jury	4,680	−0.02	2.7E-01	−0.04	0.01
2015	Televote	1,026	−0.15	1.4E-06	−0.21	−0.09
	Jury	5,000	−0.03	5.9E-02	−0.05	0.00
2016	Televote	1,066	−0.08	1.0E-02	−0.14	−0.02
	Jury	5,330	0.01	7.1E-01	−0.02	0.03
2017	Televote	1,066	−0.18	2.3E-09	−0.24	−0.12
	Jury	5,330	−0.02	2.1E-01	−0.04	0.01
2018	Televote	1,092	−0.29	< 2.2E-16	−0.34	−0.23
	Jury	**5,460**	**−0.06**	**2.5E-05**	**−0.08**	**−0.03**
2019	Televote	1,015	−0.24	3.0E-15	−0.30	−0.19
	Jury	5,074	0.00	8.7E-01	−0.03	0.03

Table 10.5 Spearman correlation coefficient and confident intervals (CI) for the period 2014–2019

Year		n	Rho	P-value	CI_{lower}	CI_{upper}
2014 to 2019	Televote	6,150	−0.16	< 2.2E-16	−0.18	−0.13
	Jury	30,874	−0.02	7.2E-04	−0.03	−0.01

For the period from 2014 to 2019, by carrying out an individual analysis of each year (Table 10.4), a negative and statistically significant correlation appeared at 5 per cent in five out of the six years (televote) and in one of them for the jury.

Analysing the period as a whole (Table 10.5), negative and significant correlations appear both for the jury and for the televote, although in the case of the first group, it is very close to zero. Finally, distinguishing between the first and second half of the competition (Table 10.6), negative and significant correlations also appear both for the jury and for the televote, although for the televote it is more than double that for the jury. It should be noted that, even for a significance level of 0.005^2, the global correlations remain significant.

Discussion

With regards to the first hypothesis, it appears confirmed that there is an order effect that benefits the participants performing in the later positions, a result that coincides with that of previous research (Bruine de Bruin, 2005; Haan et al.,

Table 10.6 Spearman correlation coefficient and confident intervals (CI) for the period 2014–2019, distinguishing between first and second half of the competition

Year		First part				Second part			
		Rho	$P\text{-}value$	CI_{lower}	CI_{upper}	Rho	$P\text{-}value$	CI_{lower}	CI_{upper}
2014 to 2019	Televote	-0.23	< 2.2E-16	-0.26	-0.19	-0.25	< 2.2E-16	-0.28	-0.21
	Jury	-0.12	< 2.2E-16	-0.13	-0.10	-0.12	< 2.2E-16	-0.14	-.11

2005; Abakoumkin, 2011; Clerides & Stengos, 2012; Millner et al., 2015; Antipov & Pokryshevskaya, 2017). On the one hand, the results of the period from 1998 to 2008, in which the order of participation was random, show a significant negative correlation of –0.24, which also appears mainly in the second half of the contest. On the other hand, the analysis of the period 2014 to 2019 also points to the same conclusion. In this second period, the order of performance is only partially randomly assigned: by means of a draw determining who will perform in the first half and in the second halves, but it is the broadcaster that, subsequently, decided the specific order of appearance in each of these parts. However, if we consider only the global correlation, and not that for each of the halves, there is a clear order effect manifested in five of the six years for the televote and in one year for the jury. Along the same lines, considering the aggregate of the whole period, both televoting and jury voting show a negative and significant correlation. In the case of televoting, we find a correlation of –0.16, evidencing the order effect. However, as far as the jury is concerned, the correlation is –0.02. Regardless of whether it is statistically significant, this can be considered to be a mere mathematical detail, since the coefficient is so close to zero that, in practice, we cannot speak of an order effect. Our interpretation is, therefore, that no relevant order effect is observed in the professional jury.

This leads to the second hypothesis, which can be directly evaluated by analysing the correlations by halves in the period from 2014 to 2019. The results show negative and significant correlations in both halves, both by the jury and for the televote. This is an expected result in that, within each half, the order is not random, so it can be expected that the EBU and the host broadcaster, in order to enhance the show, organised an attractive order, with the best participants at the end of each half. The fact that the overall correlation for the jury is practically zero, and yet is –0.12 in each of the halves, seems to support this hypothesis. We would not therefore be facing an ordering effect for the jury, but rather this correlation is due to the order established by the host broadcaster under the EBU's supervision, reserving the best performances for the end of each part. What is interesting, however, is that the effect on the televoting is practically double, –0.23 and –0.25 for the first and second half respectively. This implies that, even discounting the effect of the non-random order we observed in the professional jury, there is still a remaining order effect that seems to be linked, to the order of participation. In other words, the pure order effect that does seem to affect the televoting and not the jury voting is enhanced by a non-random order that reserves the best participants for the end. These results appear to confirm the second research hypothesis, with the nuance that it is not that the effect on the televote is greater than on the jury, but that we simply do not observe an order effect on the jury voting in the ESC. This result is consistent with that of Haan et al. (2005), which additionally has been verified in other areas such as election outcomes, proving that "name-order effects were stronger in countries where voters were less knowledgeable about politics" (Miller & Krosnick, 1998: 291).

Similarly, Chen et al. (2014: 115) maintain that "a lack of information and ambivalence underlie candidate name order effects".

Concerning limitations of this research, the primary one is the use of information corresponds only to the ESC. It is true that we have to be aware of the fact that the ESC has a strong competitive element, up to the point that, as indicated by Stockemer et al. (2018: 428), the ESC is "probably the world's largest election for a non-political office"; or, as Vuletic points out, it is "Europe's biggest election" (Vuletic, 2018: 1), for which the high volume of data used provides robustness to the result. However, it would be necessary to extend the analysis to other areas. Likewise, and as a future line of research, a model could be developed that incorporates all the effects identified in the academic literature, from the order effect or voting blocs, to the exposure effects and the potential eclipse effect. In other words, the impact on the score obtained of performing immediately before or after one of the favorite participants. In fact, these effects can be expected to operate differently depending on whether the jury is professional or not. Beyond the order effect analysed in this study, in the specific case of the ESC, it is expected that, for example, the exposure effects are more pronounced in the jury voting because, unlike the televote, it is certain that they have heard at least ten songs before the final, since all of them have had to vote before in a semi-final. Another interesting line of research is to assess the extent to which making the judges aware of the bias due to order effects contributes to its reduction.

Finally, in end-of-sequence judgments, the presence of order effect has been confirmed when the judgment is carried out by non-professionals and is absent or has a very residual influence when the jury is professional. This result implies that, for the purposes of decision-making, when the alternatives are presented sequentially and judged after all of them have been presented, the bias derived from the order of presentation can be mitigated very significantly by the mere fact that the assessment is carried out by specialists in the area. Perhaps the most obvious business application of this finding is in personnel selection processes. This result points out that, regardless of the fact that the manager responsible for the area must participate in the process, this person should always be accompanied by a Human Resources professional, whose opinion mitigates the bias induced for the manager by the order of presentation of the candidates. However, this understanding can be applied generally to other areas of business decisions, such as the choice of a specific supplier of goods or business services. Additionally, and as anticipated, the conclusions drawn concerning the order effect could help in other fields, such as law, in which the order of elements considered in a legal decision acquires a certain relevance (Plonsky et al., 2020; Engel et al., 2020), and in which the intervention of legal players with different levels of specialised training, such as professional judges or lay juries, produce different assessments of proof brought before legal processes (Benton et al., 2006).

Notes

1 Regarding the order effect, we have to mention the interesting work of Unkelbach et al. (2012), who conclude that judges tend to avoid extreme scores, positive or negative, at the beginning, being more likely to use them with the last participants.
2 Recently, 72 academics published in *Nature Human Behaviour* (Benjamin et al., 2018) a proposal "to change the default P-value threshold for statistical significance for claims of new discoveries from 0.05 to 0.005", in order to improve replicability in research.

References

Abakoumkin, G. (2011). Forming Choice Preferences the Easy Way: Order and Familiarity Effects in Elections 1. *Journal of Applied Social Psychology*, *41*(11), 2689–2707. 10.1111/j.1559-1816.2011.00845.x

Abakoumkin, G. (2018). Mere Exposure Effects in the Real World: Utilizing Natural Experiment Features from the Eurovision Song Contest. *Basic and Applied Social Psychology*, *40*(4), 236–247. 10.1080/01973533.2018.1474742

Ansorge, C. J., Scheer, J. K., Laub, J., & Howard, J. (1978). Bias in Judging Women's Gymnastics Induced by Expectations of Within-Team Order. Research Quarterly. American Alliance for Health. *Physical Education and Recreation*, *49*(4), 399–405. 10.1080/10671315.1978.10615552

Antipov, E. A., & Pokryshevskaya, E. B. (2017). Order Effects in the Results of Song Contests: Evidence from the Eurovision and the New Wave. *Judgment and Decision Making*, *12*(4), 415–419.

Benjamin, D. J., Berger, J. O., Johannesson, M., Nosek, B. A., Wagenmakers, E. J., Berk, R., ... & Cesarini, D. (2018). Redefine Statistical Significance. *Nature Human Behaviour*, *2*(1), 6–10. 10.1038/s41562-017-0189-z

Benton, T. R., Ross D. F., Bradshaw, E., Thomas, W. N., & Bradshaw, G. S. (2006). Eyewitness Memory is Still not Common Sense: Comparing Jurors, Judges and Law Enforcement to Eyewitness Experts. *Applied Cognitive Psychology*, *20*(1), 115–129. 10.1002/acp.1171

Biswas, D., Biswas, A., & Chatterjee, S. (2009). Making Judgments in a Two-secuence Cue Environment: The Effects of Differential Cue Strengths, Order Sequence, and Distraction. *Journal of Consumer Psychology*, *18*, 88–97.

Blangiardo, M. & Baio, G. (2014). Evidence of Bias in the Eurovision Song Contest: Modelling the Votes Using Bayesian Hierarchical Models. *Journal of Applied Statistics*, *41*(10), 2312–2322. 10.1080/02664763.2014.909792

Blom-Hansen J., Elklit, J., Serritzlew, S. & Villadsen, L. R. (2016). Ballot Position and Election Results: Evidence from a Natural Experiment. *Electoral Studies*, *44*, 172–183. 10.1016/j.electstud.2016.06.019

Bruine de Bruin, W. & Keren, G. (2003). Order Effects in Sequentially Judged Options Due to the Direction of Comparison. *Organizational Behavior and Human Decision Processes*, *92*(1-2), 91–101. 10.1016/S0749-5978(03)00080-3

Bruine de Bruin, W. (2005). Save the Last Dance for me: Unwanted Serial Position Effects in Jury Evaluations. *Acta Psychologica*, *118*(3), 245–260. 10.1016/j.actpsy.2004.08.005

Bruine de Bruin, W. (2006). Save the Last Dance II: Unwanted Serial Position Effects in Figure Skating Judgments. *Acta Psychologica, 123*(3), 299–311. 10.101 6/j.actpsy.2006.01.009

Budzinski, O., & Pannicke, J. (2017). Culturally Biased Voting in the Eurovision Song Contest: Do National Contests Differ? *Journal of Cultural Economics, 41*(4), 343–378. 10.1007/s10824-016-9277-6

Butt, J. L. & Campbell, T. L. (1989). The Effects of Information Order and Hypothesis-Testing Strategies on Auditors' Judgments. *Accounting, Organizations and Society, 14*(5/6), 471–479.

Charron, N. (2013). Impartiality, Friendship-networks and Voting Behavior: Evidence from Voting Patterns in the Eurovision Song Contest. *Social Networks, 35*(3), 484–497. 10.1016/j.socnet.2013.05.005

Chen, E., Simonovits, G., Krosnick, J. A., & Pasek, J. (2014). The Impact of Candidate Name Order on Election Outcomes in North Dakota. *Electoral Studies, 35*, 115–122.

Choi, J., Peters, M., & Mueller, R. O. (2010). Correlational Analysis of Ordinal Data: From Pearson's r to Bayesian Polychoric Correlation. *Asia Pacific Education Review, 11*(4), 459–466. 10.1007/s12564-010-9096-y

Clerides, S., & Stengos, T. (2012). Love thy Neighbour, Love thy Kin: Strategy and Bias in the Eurovision Song Contest. *Ekonomia, 15*(1), 22–44.

D'Angelo, S., Murphy, T. B., & Alfò, M. (2019). Latent Space Modelling of Multidimensional Networks with Application to the Exchange of Votes in Eurovision Song Contest. *The Annals of Applied Statistics, 13*(2), 900–930. 10.1214/18-AOAS1221

Dekker, A. (2007). The Eurovision Song Contest as a 'Friendship' Network. *Connections, 27*(3), 53–60.

Dogru, B. (2012). Modeling Voting Behavior in the Eurovision Song Contest. *Journal of Research in Economics and International Finance, 1*(6), 166–168.

Eisenberg, M. & Barry. C. (1988). Order Effects: A Study of the Possible Influence of Presentation Order on User Judgments of Document Relevance. *Journal of the American Society for Information Science, 39*(5), 293–300.

Engel, C., Timme, S., & Glöckner, A. (2020). Coherence-based Reasoning and Order Effects in Legal Judgments. *Psychology, Public Policy, and Law, 26*(3), 333–352. 10.1037/law0000257

Felbermayr, G. & Toubal, F. (2010). Cultural Proximity and Trade. *European Economic Review, 54*, 279–293. 10.1016/j.euroecorev.2009.06.009

Fenn, D., Suleman, O., Efstathiou, J., & Johnson, N. F. (2006). How Does Europe Make its Mind Up? Connections, Cliques, and Compatibility Between Countries in the Eurovision Song Contest. *Physica A: Statistical Mechanics and its Applications, 360*(2), 576–598. 10.1016/j.physa.2005.06.051

Flôres Jr, R. G., & Ginsburgh, V. A. (1996). The Queen Elisabeth Musical Competition: How Fair is the Final Ranking? *Journal of the Royal Statistical Society: Series D (The Statistician), 45*(1), 97–104. 10.2307/2348415

García, D., & Tanase, D. (2013). Measuring Cultural Dynamics Through the Eurovision Song Contest. *Advances in Complex Systems, 16*(8), 1350037. 10.1142/S0219525913500379

Gatherer, D. (2006). Comparison of Eurovision Song Contest Simulation with Actual Results Reveals Shifting Patterns of Collusive Voting Alliances. *Journal of Artificial Societies and Social Simulation, 9*(2).

Gauja A. (2019). Europe: Start Voting Now! Democracy, Participation and Diversity in the Eurovision Song Contest. In: J. Kalman, B. Wellings, & K. Jacotine (eds), *Eurovisions: Identity and the International Politics of the Eurovision Song Contest since 1956* (pp. 201–219). Singapore: PalgravMacmillan. 10.1007/978-981-13-9427-0_10

Ginsburgh, V. A., & Van Ours, J. C. (2003). Expert Opinion and Compensation: Evidence from a Musical Competition. *American Economic Review, 93*(1), 289–296. 10.1257/000282803321455296

Ginsburgh, V., & Noury, A. G. (2008). The Eurovision Song Contest. Is Voting Political or Cultural? *European Journal of Political Economy, 24*(1), 41–52. 10.101 6/j.ejpoleco.2007.05.004

Glejser, H., & Heyndels, B. (2001). Efficiency and Inefficiency in the Ranking in Competitions: The case of the Queen Elisabeth Music Contest. *Journal of Cultural Economics, 25*(2), 109–129. 10.1023/A:1007659804416

Grant, D. P., Testing for Bias in Order Assignment (September 22, 2020). Available at SSRN: https://ssrn.com/abstract=3697584 or 10.2139/ssrn.3697584

Haan, M. A., Dijkstra, S. G., & Dijkstra, P. T. (2005). Expert Judgment Versus Public Opinion–evidence from the Eurovision Song Contest. *Journal of Cultural Economics, 29*(1), 59–78. 10.1007/s10824-005-6830-0

Highhouse, S. & Gallo, A. (1997). Order Effects in Personnel Decision Making. *Human Performance, 10*(1), 31–46.

Hogarth, R. M. & Einhorn, H. J. (1992). Order Effects in Belief Updating: The Belief-adjustment Model. *Cognitive Psychology, 24*(1), 1–55.

Huber, M., Van Boven, L., McGraw, A. P., & Johnson-Graham, L. (2011). Whom to Help? Immediacy Bias in Judgments and Decisions About Humanitarian Aid. *Organizational Behavior and Human Decision Processes, 115*, 283–293.

Kerstthold, J. H. & Jackson, J. L. (1999). Judicial Decision Making: Order of Evidence Presentation and Availability of Background Information. *Applied Congnitive Psychology, 12*(5), 445–454. 10.1002/(SICI)1099-0720(199810)12 :5<445::AID-ACP518>3.0.CO;2-8

Kokko, A. & Tingvall, P. G. (2012). The Eurovision Song Contest, Preferences and European Trade. *Ratio Working Papers, 183*, 1–30.

Kumpulainen, I., Praks, E., Korhonen, T., Ni, A., Rissanen, V., & Vankka J. (2020). Predicting Eurovision Song Contest Results Using Sentiment Analysis. In: A. Filchenkov, J. Kauttonen, & L. Pivovarova (eds), *Artificial Intelligence and Natural Language. AINL 2020. Communications in Computer and Information Science* (pp. 1292). Cham: Springer. 10.1007/978-3-030-59082-6_7

Mantzaris, A. V., Rein, S. R., & Hopkins, A. D. (2017). Examining Collusion and Voting Biases between Countries During the Eurovision Song Contest Since 1957. The Journal of Artificial Societies and Social Simulation, 21*(1), 1. 10.18564/ jasss.3580.

Mantzaris, A. V., Rein, S. R., & Hopkins, A. D. (2018). Preference and Neglect Amongst Countries in the Eurovision Song Contest. *Journal of Computational Social Science, 1*(2), 377–390. 10.1007/s42001-018-0020-2

Meredith, M., & Salant, Y. (2013). On the Causes and Consequences of Ballot Order Effects. *Political Behaviour, 35*, 175–197. 10.1007/s11109-011-9189-2

Miller, J. M., & Krosnick, J. A. (1998). The Impact of Candidate Name Order on Election Outcomes. *Public Opinion Quarterly, 62*, 291–330

Millner, R., Stoetzer, M. W., Fritze, C., & Günther, S. (2015). Fair Oder Foul? Punktevergabe und Platzierung beim Eurovision Song Contest. *Jenaer Beiträge zur Wirtschaftsforschung, 2015/2*, Ernst-Abbe-Hochschule, Fachbereich Betriebswirtschaft, Jena.

Ochoa, A., Muñoz-Zavala, A., & Hernández-Aguirre, A. (2009). A Hybrid System Approach to dDetermine the Ranking of a Debutant Country in Eurovision. *Journal of Computers, 4*(8), 713–720.

Page, L., & Page, K. (2010). Last Shall be First: A Field Study of Biases in Sequential Performance Evaluation on the Idol Series. *Journal of Economic Behavior & Organization, 73*(2), 186–198. 10.1016/j.jebo.2009.08.012

Plessner, H. (1999). Expectation Biases in Gymnastics Judging. *Journal of Sport and Exercise Psychology, 21*(2), 131–144. 10.1123/jsep.21.2.131

Plonsky, O., Chen, D., Netzer, L., Steiner, T. & Feldman, Y. (2020). Best to Be Last: Serial Position Effects in Legal Decisions in the Field and in the Lab. SSRN Electronic Journal, June 2020, 10.2139/ssrn.3414155

Saavedra, S., Efstathiou, J., & Reed-Tsochas, F. (2007). Identifying the Underlying Structure and Dynamic Interactions in a Voting Network. *Physica A: Statistical Mechanics and its Applications, 377*(2), 672–688. 10.1016/j.physa.2006.11.038

Schweiger, W., & Brosius, H.-B. (2003). Eurovision Song Contest – Beeinflussen Nachrich-tenfaktoren die Punktvergabe durch das Publikum? *M&K Medien & Kommunikationswissenschaft, 51*(2), 271–294. 10.5771/1615-634x-2003-2-271

Siganos, A. & Tabner, I. T. (2020). Capturing the Role of Societal Affinity in Cross-border Mergers with the Eurovision Song Contest. *Journal of International Business Studies, 51*(2), 263–273, 10.1057/s41267-019-00271-3

Signorell, A. et al. (2019). DescTools: Tools for Descriptive Statistics. R package version 0.99.30. URL: https://cran.r-project.org/package=DescTools

Spierdijk, L., & Vellekoop, M. (2009). The Structure of Bias in Peer Voting Systems: Lessons from the Eurovision Song Contest. *Empirical Economics, 36*(2), 403–425. 10.1007/s00181-008-0202-5

Stockemer, D., Blais, A., Kostelka, F., & Chhim, C. (2018). Voting in the Eurovision Song Contest. *Politics, 38*(4), 428–442. 10.1177/0263395717737887

Unkelbach, C., Ostheimer, V., Fasold, F., & Memmert, D. (2012). A Calibration Explanation of Serial Position effects in Evaluative Judgments. *Organizational Behavior and Human Decision Processes, 119*(1), 103–113. 10.1016/j.obhdp.2012.06.004

Verrier, D. (2012). Evidence for the Influence of the Mere-exposure effect on Voting in the Eurovision Song Contest. *Judgement and Decision Making, 7*(5), 639–643.

Vuletic, D. (2018). *Postward Europe and the Eurovision Song Contest*. London, New York: Bloomsbury Academic.

Walker, L., Thibaut, J., & Andreoli, V. (1972). Order of Presentation at Trial. *The Yale Law Journal, 82*, 216–226.

Wickham, H. (2007). Reshaping Data with the Reshape Package. *Journal of statistical software, 21*(12), 1–20. 10.18637/jss.v021.i12

Wickham, H. (2011). The Split-apply-combine Strategy for Data Analysis. *Journal of Statistical Software*, *40*(1), 1–29. 10.18637/jss.v040.i01

Wolther, I. (2008). Mehr als Musik: die Sieben Dimensionen des "Eurovision Song Contests". In K.-S. Rehberg (Hrsg.), *Die Natur der Gesellschaft: Verhandlungen des 33. Kongresses der Deutschen Gesellschaft für Soziologie in Kassel 2006*. Teilbd. 1 u. 2 (S. 4896-4905). Frankfurt am Main: Campus Verl. https://nbn-resolving. org/urn:nbn:de:0168-ssoar-154477

Yair, G. (1995). Unite Unite Europe' The Political and Cultural Structures of Europe as Reflected in the Eurovision Song Contest. *Social Networks*, *17*(2), 147–161. 10.1016/0378-8733(95)00253-K

Yair, G., & Maman, D. (1996). The persistent Structure of Hegemony in the Eurovision Song Contest. *Acta Sociologica*, *39*(3), 309–325. 10.1177/00016993 9603900303

Yair, G. (2019). Douze point: Eurovisions and Euro-divisions in the Eurovision Song Contest–review of Two Decades of Research. *European Journal of Cultural Studies*, *22*(5-6), 1013–1029. 10.1177/1367549418776562

Part III

From Stage to Screen:
Film, Media, and Music

11 High, Low and Participatory: The Eurovision Song Contest and Cultural Studies

Jessica Carniel

Introduction

As the second longest running song contest in the world after the Sanremo Italian Song Festival, the Eurovision Song Contest (ESC) is useful for examining changing tastes and styles in popular music. The contest also highlights the impact of changing technologies on broadcasting and audience participation within the broader context of increased cultural globalisation and transnationalism. By examining important cultural shifts in practice through its history, shifts in cultural theory and method in scholarship can be explored. Various changes to the ESC over time illustrate historical tensions around notions of 'high' and 'low' cultural forms that the discipline of cultural studies specifically sought to address. These changes also highlight shifts in cultural studies scholarship that move from simply providing scholarly attention to popular cultural forms toward understanding the complex personal and cultural interactions between people and texts, such as the ESC, that manifest as participatory culture and global fandom. Arguably, some of the longevity of the ESC stems from its responsiveness to the changing nature of global culture and technologies.

The chapter begins with a comparison of the first ESC and the sixty-fourth edition in 2019 to illustrate the changing modes of production, consumption and aesthetics that have occurred over the decades that separate them. The comparison provides an overview of the transition from modest television production to facilitate the growth of a regionally-identified audience to multi-platform mega-event with a truly global reach. The evolution of the ESC and what we are able to know and experience of it necessitates changed theories and methods for understanding the event and its cultural impacts. Understanding the ESC is a project undertaken by a wide variety of disciplines, from history to musicology, from television and theatre studies to international relations. I am concerned here with how the ESC is studied and understood within the discipline of cultural studies. This chapter takes cultural studies' original provocation — a deepened understanding of everyday life and culture in contrast to scholarship focused on high cultural forms — alongside the ESC's own transformation into a transnational global spectacle that is at once popular, in various senses of the word, and an artistic celebration. To begin, I explore the origins of

DOI: 10.4324/9781003188933-14

the ESC as something driven by from above (the television industry as Todd Gitlin's (1979) cultural elites), contextualising this within the emergence of cultural studies as a field in the 1960s as a response to bifurcating ideas of culture that were collapsing readily with the rise of mass culture. This is contrasted with the greater emphasis placed on fans and audiences from the late 1990s, and the increased power and agency these groups can yield in the age of convergence and participatory cultures.

A Tale of Two Contests: a Contrast in Aesthetics and Audience

A comparison of the first ESC in 1956 with the sixty-fourth edition in 2019 provides an opening illustration of these various shifts. The first ESC was held in Lugano, Switzerland, in 1956. The venue was the Kursaal Theatre, a casino and theatre designed by Italian architect Achille Sfrondrini in the nineteenth century,[1] and sadly demolished in 2001, replaced by a large concrete edifice for the Lugano Casino. As no video footage beyond the winner's reprise survives the event, the only images available of the night are various stills. We might then use our imaginations and other contextual information to piece together the atmosphere. Though grand in style, the Kursaal Theatre was relatively small, seating perhaps a few hundred people at most in comparison to the thousands packed into the modern arenas that are the venues of the ESC today. The theatre in the contemporary casino has a capacity of 1200, but it is unlikely the original was any larger than this. Those attending the ESC in 1956 were dressed in evening attire and seated to enjoy an evening of musical entertainment. Marcus Pyka (2019, p. 453) describes the event as styled in an "idealised chanson-meets-grand-opera tradition, set up to promote European high-class culture." Pyka argues that the seriousness of the songs supports the idea of the first Eurovision as a respectable event. He suggesting that the songs — and the fact that they were sung only in the national languages of the participating countries — can also be interpreted as a defence against the incursion of American pop music styles, although Freddy Quinn's rock'n'roll-esque "*So geht das jede Nacht*" ("That's How It Is Every Night") offers counterevidence to Pyka's interpretation.

The event was broadcast on both television and radio, but only a single television camera was used (EurovisionWorld, n.d.). Representatives from ten television stations and twenty radio stations from around Europe were also present (Pyka, 2019, 453). The ratio seems to support the idea that the focus of the event was more on its radio audience than its television audience (EurovisionWorld, n.d.); television ownership was low then as television services in Europe were in their nascent phase. Furthermore, the radio broadcast was more readily able to be transmitted to European Broadcasting Union (EBU) members beyond the immediate European Broadcasting Area, including the Australian Broadcasting Corporation (ABC). The reach of the inaugural contest was therefore wide, but we do not have numbers for at-home listeners and viewers.

Seven countries competed in this first ESC: Belgium, France, Germany, Italy, Luxembourg, the Netherlands and Switzerland. Each artist performed two songs on a stage decorated with floral arrangements, and they were accompanied by a live orchestra. They were all solo performers; the rules were changed in the second contest to permit duos, but larger groups were not permitted at Eurovision until the 1970s. While all the songs of 1956 could be described as "popular in style", with again perhaps the exception of Quinn's song, most were not "pop music" per se, in that they did not reflect the new styles and tastes of youth music in the 1950s, to draw upon David Hatch and Stephen Millward's (1990) distinction between "pop" and "popular" music. Rather, most drew upon the chanson style, which was popular (and traditional) but not "pop". Indeed, pop music, while present throughout the early years of the ESC and successful with its audiences, struggled to gain a foothold with the juries (Pyka, 2019); France Gall's winning performance of the Serge Gainsbourg-penned "*Poupée de cire, poupée de son*" ("Doll of wax, doll of straw") in 1965 signals the breakthrough of pop music in the jury vote.

To decide the winner in 1956, each participating country sent two jury members to the contest. A secret voting system meant that there was no moderation of votes, enabling juries to vote for their own country's entries. Luxembourg was unable to send a jury, so the Swiss jury voted on their behalf. Some claim that it was this oversight in the voting system that led to the Swiss victory. The results have never been made public. The winning song in 1956, Lys Assia's "Refrain", was a sweet, traditional chanson lamenting the lost loves of youth.

Let us compare this to the sixty-fourth edition of the ESC held in Tel Aviv, Israel, in 2019. The venue was Expo Tel Aviv, a modern convention centre. Specifically, it was held in Pavilion Two, which was inaugurated in 2015, and boasts a capacity of up to 9000 attendees, which is in line with the EBU requirements of a minimum capacity of 7000. The arena is organised along the same lines as any music concert: tiered seating on its perimeters and a large general admission area where a crowd stands for the duration of the show. The dress code could be broadly defined as casual, although many attendees wear themed costumes and wave national or rainbow flags in the air: the atmosphere is one of carnival. Initially, KAN had indicated the contest would be held in Israel's capital, Jerusalem. The official reason provided for selecting Tel Aviv instead was its stronger infrastructure for hosting a mega-event (Granger, 2018b). The Deputy Mayor of Tel Aviv also claimed Tel Aviv to be "the city cultural centre of Israel" (Granger, 2018a). However, it must be acknowledged that hosting in Tel Aviv neatly eluded significant diplomatic implications and security concerns posed by Jerusalem (*Times of Israel*, 2018).

Forty-one countries participated in the 2019 ESC, submitting one song each. They performed on a glossy neon-lit stage to pre-recorded music. The logistics of quick stage changes that must occur within eighty seconds prevent the setup of playable instruments, and many of the diverse musical styles found at Eurovision have diverged from what could be easily and effectively played by an in-house orchestra, so only the vocals are performed live. Thirty-two of the entries included lyrics in English, although some songs included lyrics in multiple languages. One performer, the Australian representative Kate Miller-Heidke, sang a hybrid opera-electronic dance music song while swaying on the top of a five-metre pole. Nine group acts performed, and all performances adhered to the rule that no more than six people are permitted on stage at once. The event spanned across three nights, comprising two semi-finals and a grand final, but each of these involves two further non-broadcast performances that function both as live events performed to an audience and technical rehearsals. These are the 'jury show' that is streamed to the international juries in their home countries and the 'family show' held in the afternoon. This is preceded by a week of rehearsals, accessible only to the accredited press corps, where the delegations tweak performances and costumes as these must be finalised and remain consistent throughout the jury and televised shows that comprise the official competition.

An estimated 182 million people watched the 2019 event worldwide, either on broadcast television or streamed via the internet; however, some — including lifelong fans of the contest — boycotted the event in protest against Israel's treatment of the Palestinians. One performing group, the Icelandic BDSM punk band Hatari, controversially held up a scarf in Palestinian colours during voting. One of the backup dancers for the interval act, international (American) icon Madonna, also had a Palestinian flag pinned to the back of their costume. The voting was performed according to strict rules, aggregated by a third party, German telecommunications company Digame, and monitored by global accounting firm Ernst & Young. In 2019, there was an error in the jury voting, wherein three jurors from three different countries appeared to have submitted their votes backwards. The error was found by a fan independently analysing the results (Robertson, 2019). The scoreboard was amended after the event, changing some of the rankings, but not affecting the overall winner of the event. That was the Netherlands' Duncan Lawrence with "Arcade", a slow ballad performed at a piano, lamenting a doomed love.

A comparison of these two editions of the ESC illustrates the vast changes that have occurred socially, culturally and politically over the sixty-three years that separate the two events. The first is on a small scale in terms of a live event, but one with lofty ambitions of both attracting viewers to a new international broadcasting service while also providing its largely European audience with a shared cultural experience. The second is a large mega-event comprising both a sizeable live audience and a televisual audience, and that also shares the aim of providing a shared cultural experience for its viewers. However, those viewers – both those in the arena and those at home – are now integrated into a spectacle with a truly global reach that is experienced and shared on multiple platforms.

Eurovision, Television, and the Rise of Cultural Studies in the Post-War Era

The enduring myth of the ESC is that it was an event to unite Europe in the aftermath of the Second World War. The more prosaic reality of the Contest was that it was a means of attracting popular interest in the EBU's newly established Eurovision Network, from which the ESC takes its name. Nevertheless, the idea that the ESC was conceived of and acts to provide a form (albeit sometimes tenuous) of cultural unity is not entirely false, as it was a clear goal for the Eurovision Network to provide shared cultural experiences to its pan-European audiences via television and radio. However, the idea that this was in service of the ideology of a united Europe rather than the practicalities of a successful media network is likely the result of romanticised narratives around the ESC perpetuated by the EBU, media commentators, fans, and scholars. The origins of the ESC, the EBU, and its Eurovision Network reveal much about how television was perceived in its early days, particularly in its relation to the dissemination of ideology, and the cultivation of community that was reflected also in theoretical engagements with the new technology.

The ESC's parent organisation, the EBU, was established in 1950 as an agreement between twenty-three public broadcasters to replace the International Broadcasting Union (IBU) (Bourdon, 2007, 264). The EBU was formed with a variety of both technical and legal aims, such as the sharing of resources and the mediation of disputes, as well as facilitating an exchange of programming. Despite some initial successes with cultural programming in the experimental stages of the network, sport — a popular cultural form with its own class tensions (Horne et al., 1999) that, with few exceptions, is nevertheless positioned as a low form of cultural entertainment rather than an artistic form — emerged as the most popular programming in this period, foreshadowing its ongoing importance for the network today (Vuletic, 2018, 27). Jerome Bourdon suggests that the members of the EBU were "convinced that television was the medium that could forge a new collective conscience and help the new Europe supersede old nations" (2007, pp. 264–5). However, Dean Vuletic (2018, 30) points out that Marcel Bezençon, director of the EBU between 1954 and 1970, was "initially more concerned with how programme exchange could benefit the infant television services of states ... than the idea of an integrated Western Europe." Nevertheless, in the late 1950s and 1960s, he did speak of the ways in which the Eurovision Network exemplified ideas of European unity because it sought to be apolitical and was focused on the technical questions of media resources (Vuletic, 2018, p. 32–33). To promote ideas of European culture and identity, Bezençon envisioned a series of "Euro–events" to draw together the television audiences, several of which focused on elements of European high culture, such as classic plays and operas (Bourdon, 2007, p. 265).

We can see in this idea of cultural programming, albeit drawn from Bourdon's interpretation of Bezençon's intentions, the perceived division between high and low that categorises hierarchically artistic forms such as music (specifically opera and classical orchestral music), drama (specifically theatre), the visual arts, and literature in contrast to pop music, cinema and television, fashion and photography, and journalism and popular fiction (Hartley, 2002, 37). Although certain forms of popular culture have emerged as a product of technological advancements, the distinction between high and low forms of culture has a longer, albeit still relative recent history. In his overview of the distinction between high and low culture and its impact of cultural studies scholarship, Simon During (2004, 194–195) identifies a bifurcation of culture in the mid–eighteenth century into the elite and the vernacular. While both were commercialised and literate, they had vastly different social and moral connotations. Elite culture was centred on moral and aesthetic principles that positioned culture as timeless, a source of moral guidance, a form of self–fulfilment, and as being the production of (male) genius. By contrast, vernacular culture was organised around market principles and centred on ideas of pleasure and entertainment, which in turn connoted, for its critics, ideas of passivity and moral vacuousness. By the late nineteenth century, there was a movement toward thinking about higher forms of culture as a defence against the vagaries of modern life. High cultural institutions became useful for "disseminat[ing] hegemonic forms of civility" (195) and a means of increasing shared cultural capital within a society. Through this, the tie between the idea of high culture and middle–class respectability was consolidated.

This division between high and low culture and their moral and ideological implications is particularly interesting to note given one strategy for the Eurovision Network's shared content was to deliver 'high' culture, such as operas and plays, through the 'low' culture format of television for the purpose of encouraging a shared European culture and public sphere. The styling of the inaugural ESC — its black–tie dress code, floral stage decorations, and the live orchestra, as well as its "chanson–meets–grand–opera" style — indicates concerted efforts to position the event as a "positive, pan–European evening of culturally valuable entertainment" (Pyka, 2019, 453). As previously discussed, Pyka (2019, 453) suggests that, in the ESC at least, the emphasis on ideas of highbrow European culture was in part a defence against the threat of American popular culture, indicating other cultural hierarchies based upon national or regional culture beyond those of elite and vernacular. As such, while we can remain critical of over–romanticising the European unity project of the ESC, there is nevertheless the sense that even a pluralistic European culture should be distinguished from and even valued higher than cultures outside its imagined perimeters. In this way, the Eurovision media network project exemplifies some of the major tensions in mid–century cultural politics — the perceived struggle between high and low cultures, and various national and regional responses to the perceived threat of Americanisation. And it epitomised one of the solutions: holding high art and popular art together, to extrapolate from Hall and Whannel (cited in Hartley, 2002, 43).

Despite having earlier origins, television is largely a post–war cultural medium and phenomenon. A similar observation could be made of the development of cultural studies as a post–war discipline that sought to capture and understand a changing socio–cultural, political, and technological context. During (2005, 109) even goes as far as to state that cultural studies "has been formed around its encounter with TV". The work of critical theorist Theodor Adorno represents an early and important foray into critical engagement with television. Although Adorno was not a cultural studies scholar per se, his ideas have been influential in the field and continue to provide some provocation for the form and function of television in modern society. Writing in the very years of Eurovision's genesis, as the EBU was formulating and developing the broadcast strategies described above, Adorno was already expressing concern with television's "socio–psychological implications and mechanisms" (Adorno, 2002, 213). Such concerns were not isolated to academic analysis. For example, in Bezençon's native Switzerland, where he was Director–General of the Swiss Broadcasting Corporation, there was significant opposition to television on the basis of these perceived "social dangers" (Bezençon, cited in Vuletic, 2018, 30).

Although Adorno viewed mass culture as a toxic influence on social processes, the critique nevertheless highlights the utter seriousness with which he considered the mass media and culture industries (Witkin, 2003, 2). Television in particular was an emerging industry with the potential for considerable social and economic power. For this reason, Adorno spoke in terms of mass culture and the culture industry, rather than of popular culture. This was in order to better distinguish between texts or practices that were produced by the populace rather than those that were produced for their mass consumption and entertainment (Witkin, 2003, 2). Writing several decades later, Todd Gitlin (1979) framed the ideological processes of commercial culture and commercial society as emerging from both above (the elites or the industry) and below (the audiences). He highlighted that the culture industry "does not *manufacture* ideology; it *relays* and *reproduces* and *processes* and *packages* and *focuses* ideology" that is already in circulation within that society at both the elite and popular levels (Gitlin, 1979, 253). At their inception, the EBU's Eurovision Network and its ESC represent a clear case of the kind of social and cultural power of the emerging television industry that Adorno sought to critique and that Gitlin sought to explain. The Eurovision Network and its ESC did not manufacture the ideology of European unity, but did effectively relay, reproduce, package and focus these ideas for popular consumption and for the purpose of constructing a European audience.

The idea of the ESC as a celebration of unity persists today. However, as the EBU seeks further global expansion of the ESC's audience and format, this idea of unity is universalised and accompanied by other purported universal values, such as diversity and acceptance. While the EBU actively perpetuates this narrative, its genesis is arguably more vernacular, emerging from what the ESC came to represent for its fans and audiences rather than what its official history suggested. A core part of this is the significance of the ESC for LGBTQIA+ audiences, which in turn has been a significant part of the scholarship on Eurovision (see, for example, Baker, 2019b, 2015, 2017; Carniel, 2015; Cassiday, 2014; Halliwell, 2018; Lemish, 2004; Rehberg, 2013).

Beyond (the) Birmingham (School): the Rise of Eurovision as Participatory Mega–Event

Commentary on Eurovision often cites Dana International's victory at Birmingham as signalling its coming out as a queer event.[2] Birmingham is also significant in marking a shift toward an audience– and fan–centred event hosted in concert arenas rather than theatres (Baker, 2019a, 103). It was also the last year that the orchestra was part of the ESC. In many ways, it could be considered to signal the beginning of the ESC as we know it today — associated with diversity, the live event as a significant pilgrimage for fans, and focused on the event as television spectacle as much as the idea of the music itself. It is perhaps fitting that such shifts occurred in Birmingham. After all, this was home to the famous Centre for Contemporary Cultural Studies (CCCS), known also as the Birmingham School, that was from its inception in 1964 to its closure in 2002 "the key institution of the history of the field" (Turner, 2003, 62). Perhaps its most significant contribution to scholarship was a focus on the politics of media. When combined with its additional interest in everyday life and culture, this expanded beyond the textual analysis of popular cultural forms toward more ethnographic approaches to understanding audiences and subcultures. Such audiences included those attached to particular forms of music or television shows, leading also to the emergence of fan studies as a further area of specialisation in its own right. This turn from television as simply text to also an experience, a source of community, and an object of audience devotion, is mirrored in the evolution of the contemporary ESC.

The ESC had always sought to combine live entertainment with a television broadcast, but it is ultimately a television show. This in itself is perhaps unextraordinary as live variety shows are common in most television cultures, but the early days of such programming — the early years of the ESC included — exemplified Stuart Hall's (1971, 11) observation that "television only weakly imposes its own forms on the already–formed material" of the live events being televised. As the ESC evolved, its embrace of the "staged performance" —defined by Hall (1971, 11) as "a television production which has been specifically mounted for television ... where camera angles, *mise–en–scene*, acting or performance is shaped and guided throughout by the technical limits and opportunities of the medium" — became far more sophisticated. Interestingly, this sophisticated embrace of the possibilities of television as a medium coincides with the increased importance of the live audience. As Chris Hay and I have argued both together and separately, a core feature of the contemporary Eurovision production is the use of the audience as part of the *mise–en–scene* (Hay & Kanafani, 2017; Carniel & Hay 2019). The audience is often incorporated into the production design of performances, such as the use of mobile phone lights, or to provide colour and atmosphere through outlandish costumes and flag–waving. The irony of this is that, in many ways, the performance on the stage is *not for them*. That is, the staging and choreography of the performances are frequently designed for how it will appear on camera to the viewers at home rather than for the entertainment of those in the arena; the broadcast audience is thus privileged over the live audience (Hay & Kanafani, 2017). Although the in-arena experience of Eurovision holds its own pleasures, the live audience is in effect watching the live recording of a television show, albeit one that enjoys and leverages the effects of having a large and enthusiastic live audience. There is, however, much slippage between these ideas, particularly through the utilisation of the live audience as part of the production aesthetic that might fool the at–home audience into thinking or feeling as though they are the ones watching a live concert.

In a similar vein, fans are increasingly incorporated into the organisation of the ESC and afforded particular privileges in exchange for the emotional and — this is important to emphasise — actual labour they contribute to the contest. Each chapter of the global fan network *Organisation Générale des Amateurs de l'Eurovision* (OGAE; General Organisation of Eurovision Fans) is allocated a portion of tickets prior to the public sale that are distributed to its members via ballot. All OGAE members, regardless of how they obtained their tickets, are provided with access to the Euroclub afterparties. The Fan Café will often tier events and passes, distinguishing between members and the general public. Beyond OGAE, fans are afforded further privileges by the EBU as fan media organisations can apply for a special category of fan press accreditation. Importantly, many of these fan media organisations are voluntary and not–for–profit. This means that the individual member of the fan–press pays for their own accommodation and travel, receiving only their tickets in exchange for the labour they provide as passionate promoters and reporters for the ESC. Together with the Eurovision Village, an area set up in a public square to create a space for public viewings of the ESC and its auxiliary events, the Euro Fan Café and the high value of tickets to the event highlight how Eurovision has evolved from a simple television event into an important tourist attraction for the host city and nation (Carniel, 2019).

Fans also play a large role in the life of the ESC outside of its official duration in one week in May. The 'Eurovision New Year', as it is known to fans, commences on the first of September, which is the date from which songs released may be eligible for submission into the contest. Thus begins a cycle of speculation over the new songs of artists who have expressed interest in the contest or who are considered by fans to be ideal candidates. The national final season begins soon after, involving in–depth reportage and live–tweeting of each event as it happens. There is also commentary over the organisation of the event in the host city, such as its plans for and placement of the Eurovision Village. One fan, known on social media as Mr Gerbear (n.d.), creates a webpage for sorting each of the selected songs into an order of preference. Fan sites often gather their own 'professional juries' to create pseudo–jury votes as part of their projections. The week of the contest itself is undoubtedly the peak of fan activity, with reporting, live tweeting, and analysis of each final and its performances, and in–depth analysis of the final votes.

In the contemporary ESC, it is no longer possible to entirely separate the fans and audience from the production and culture of the contest itself. Despite the growth in scholarship on Eurovision in the past two decades and the proliferation of the EBU's own communications strategies (via the contest's website, press releases, and social media engagement), fan–produced sites are rich sources of information and analysis. While the EBU might still control the actual process and broadcast of the event, fans work to drive the broader discourse that surrounds it. Such practices and relations between the producers and consumers exemplify the notions of participatory culture and convergence culture that have dominated understandings of fan practices, particularly since the advent of Web 2.0 (Jenkins 2006; Banks & Deuze, 2009; Baym & Burnett 2009). Participatory culture describes the phenomenon of media producers and consumers interacting with each other in new ways, whereby the latter are also producers and contributors to media cultures. Meanwhile, convergence culture describes not only the technical processes of multimedia and cross–platforming, but also the "cultural shift as consumers are encouraged to seek out new information and make connections among dispersed media content" (Jenkins, 2006, 3).

This is perhaps best exemplified in fan and EBU–produced responses to the cancellation of the ESC due to Covid–19 in 2020, when the fans arguably led the way for producing content to maintain a connection to the ESC through such initiatives as #EurovisionAgain. This was a live online viewing party of historical contests developed by British journalist and fan Rob Holley, comprising not only the broadcast of the old contests, but also contextualisation by hosts and historian Catherine Baker, and a fan voting system wherein the results of the contest were often entirely revised. The EBU itself soon became involved in assisting the organisers in obtaining full versions of the show and hosting the livestream on their own YouTube channel. In addition to demonstrating this converged relationship between fans and producers, #EurovisionAgain "aims to recreate the celebratory liveness of Eurovision" (Waysdorf, 2020, 299). Furthermore, it illustrates how television fandoms are not, as Adorno feared, passively consuming projected ideologies, but demonstrating political agency in how the ESC is projected, understood, and remembered. Specifically, Abby Waysdorf (2020, 301) argues that #EurovisionAgain reinforces the "casual queerness of Eurovision and Eurofandom". She highlights how the events provided "an escape from the anxieties of everyday pandemic life" (Waysdorf, 2020,302). In these ways, #EurovisionAgain reminds us of some of the core concerns of cultural studies scholarship — understanding everyday life, marginalised cultures and identities, and the politics of media — through the slightly newer lenses of convergence and participatory cultures.

The audience of the ESC is no longer one of dignitaries in black tie seated for an evening of respectable entertainment. Its increased turn to the viewing public through the introduction of the popular televote to complement that of the professional juries, and the presence of fan audiences as both an aesthetic and a driving force in the show's production and consumption, has further altered the ESC's meaning and approach. Although its logistics and production is still driven "from above", the dynamics of participatory and convergence culture, as well as the democratisation of media offered by digital and social media technologies now affords fans and audiences greater power and agency to drive and shape the culture, text, and the very meaning of Eurovision.

Notes

1 The Wikipedia entry for the Teatro Kursaal states that it was designed in 1804, but this was before Sfrondrini was born. It appears that the casino was established in 1804, but that the building was commissioned later in the nineteenth century by the Lugano Theatre Society, which was established in 1885.
2 Other commentators cite Pall Oskar's performance in 1997 as Eurovision's true coming out, but Dana International holds great symbolic weight because it was not just queer presence but rather a queer victory.

References

Adorno, T.W. (2002). How to look at television. In *Hollywood Quarterly* (pp. 222–240). University of California Press.

Baker, C. (2015a). Gender and geopolitics in the Eurovision song contest. *Contemporary Southeastern Europe*, 2(1), 74–93.

Baker, C. (2015b). Introduction: Gender and Geopolitics in the Eurovision Song Contest. *Contemporary Southeastern Europe*, 2(1), 74–93.

Baker, C. (2017). The 'gay Olympics'? The Eurovision Song Contest and the politics of LGBT/European belonging. *European Journal of International Relations*, 23(1), 97–121. 10.1177/1354066116633278

Baker, C. (2019a). I am the voice of the past that will always be': The Eurovision Song Contest as historical fiction. *Journal of Historical Fictions*, 2(2), 102–125.

Baker, C. (2019b). If love was a crime, we would be criminals': The Eurovision Song Contest and the queer international politics of flags. In *Eurovisions: Identity and the international politics of the Eurovision Song Contest since 1956* (pp. 175–200). Springer.

Banks, J., & Deuze, M. (2009). Co-creative labour. *International Journal of Cultural Studies*, 12(5), 419–431.

Baym, N.K., & Burnett, R. (2009). Amateur experts: International fan labour in Swedish independent music. *International Journal of Cultural Studies*, 12(5), 433–449.

Bourdon, J. (2007). Unhappy engineers of the European soul: The EBU and the woes of pan–European television. *International Communication Gazette*, 69(3), 263–280.

Carniel, J. (2015). Skirting the issue: Finding queer and geopolitical belonging at the Eurovision Song Contest. *Contemporary Southeastern Europe*, 2(1), 136–154.

Carniel, J. (2019). Nation branding, cultural relations and cultural diplomacy at eurovision: between Australia and Europe. In *Eurovisions: Identity and the international politics of the Eurovision Song Contest since 1956* (pp. 151–173). Springer.

Carniel, J., & Hay, C. (2019). Conclusion – Australia Decides. *Eurovision and Australia*. Springer.

Cassiday, J.A. (2014). Post–Soviet pop goes gay: Russia's trajectory to Eurovision victory. *The Russian Review*, 73(1), 1–23.

During, S. (2004). *Cultural studies: A critical introduction*. Routledge.

Eurovision 1956 Results: Voting & points. (n.d.). Eurovisionworld. Retrieved 7 May 2021, from https://eurovisionworld.com/eurovision/1956

Gitlin, T. (1979). Prime Time Ideology: The Hegemonic Process in Television Entertainment. *Social Problems*, 26(3), 251–266.

Granger, A. (2018a, July 24). Eurovision'19: Jerusalem & Tel Aviv Confirm Details of Eurovision Hosting Bid. *Eurovoix*. https://eurovoix.com/2018/07/24/eurovision19–jerusalem–tel–aviv–confirm–details–of–eurovision–hosting–bid/

Granger, A. (2018b, July 28). Eurovision'19: Israeli Minister states Jerusalem does not have the resources to host Eurovision. *Eurovoix*. https://eurovoix.com/2018/07/28/eurovision19–israeli–minister–states–jerusalem–does–not–have–the–resources–to–host–eurovision/

Hall, S. (1971). Deviancy, politics and the media. Centre for Contemporary Cultural Studies, University of Birmingham.

Halliwell, J. (2018). 'All kinds of everything'? Queer visibility in online and offline Eurovision fandom. *Westminster Papers in Communication and Culture*, 13(2).

Hartley, J. (2002). *A short history of cultural studies*. Sage.

Hatch, D., & Willward, S. (1990). *From blues to rock: An analytical history of pop music*. New York: St. Martin's Press.

Hay, C., & Kanafani, B. (2017). Boos, tears, sweat, and toil: Experiencing the 2015 Eurovision Song Contest live. *Popular Entertainment Studies*, 8(1), 57–73.

Horne, J., Tomlinson, A., & Whannel, G. (1999). Understanding sport: An introduction to the sociological and cultural analysis of sport. Routledge.

Jenkins, H. (2006). *Convergence culture: Where old and new media collide*. New York University Press.

Lemish, D. (2004). 'My kind of campfire': The Eurovision Song Contest and Israeli gay men. *Popular Communication*, 2(1), 41–63.

Mr Gerbear. (n.d.). *Eurovision 2021 favorites sorter*. Retrieved 10 May 2021, from http://esc.gerbear.com/sorter2021.htm

Pyka, M. (2019). The power of violins and rose petals: The Eurovision Song Contest as an arena of European crisis. *Journal of European Studies*, 49(3–4), 448–469.

Rehberg, P. (2013). Taken by a stranger: How queerness haunts Germany at Eurovision. In K. Fricker & M. Gluhovic (Eds.), *Performing the 'New' Europe: Identities, feelings and politics in the Eurovision Song Contest* (pp. 178–193). Palgrave Macmillan.

Robertson, B. (2019, May 23). *Questions and answers about the voting at Eurovision 2019*. ESC Insight. https://escinsight.com/2019/05/23/eurovision–song–contest–2019–voting–problems–mistakes–belarus–poland–san–marino/

Times of Israel staff (2018, September 13). Tel Aviv confirmed to host 2019 Eurovision Song Contest. *Times of Israel*. https://www.timesofisrael.com/tel–aviv–confirmed–to–host–2019–eurovision–song–contest/

Turner, G. (2003). *British cultural studies: An introduction*. Psychology Press.

Vuletic, D. (2018). *Postwar Europe and the Eurovision Song Contest*. Bloomsbury Publishing.

Waysdorf, A.S. (2020). This is our night: Eurovision Again and liveness through archives. In Keidl, P.D., Melamed, L., Hediger, V., & Somaini, A. (Eds.), *Pandemic media: Preliminary notes toward an inventory*, 295–302. Meson Press.

Witkin, R.W. (2003). *Adorno on popular culture*. Routledge.

12 Queer Camp against Franco: Iván Zulueta's Eurovision Song Contest Parody *Un Dos Tres*

Robert Tobin

When *Eurovision Song Contest: The Story of Fire Saga*, directed by David Dobkin, started streaming on Netflix in June of 2020, the deliriously delightful confection provided much-needed escapist entertainment to a public confined by the COVID-19 pandemic. Reviewing the film, *The Hollywood Reporter* referred to the ESC's "campy gold," emphasizing "the astonishing display of so-bad-it's-brilliant musical kitsch" and the "weirdly earnest intensity" of the character, played by Will Farrell, who also produced the movie (Rooney, 2020). Finding the film "over the top," but "more tribute than parody," the *New York Times* admired "Dan Stevens's high-camp turn" as the Russian contestant, who denies his homosexuality as strenuously as he seems to exhibit it (Catsoulis, 2020). The film and its reviewers clearly mine a long tradition of viewing the competition as camp, as Sarah Fones's article in *CR Fashion Book*, "The Campiness of Eurovision," demonstrates (2019). Implicitly or explicitly, these articles rely on Susan Sontag's understanding of camp as an apolitical, loving send-up of conventional artistic standards or established gender structures, often with gay overtones.

Fifty years before *The Story of Fire Saga*, Iván Zulueta's 1969 film *Un dos tres... al escondite inglés* featured one of the first parodies of the ESC on record. The second part of the title refers to a children's game, frequently translated as "hide and seek," but more accurately rendered as "red light, green light." The plot is as simple as it is outrageous. The state-run television announces "Mentira, mentira" (Lie, lie) as its entry in an international song competition called *Mundocanal* (World Channel), obviously modelled on the ESC. Although she will not sing the song in the contest, the composer Marina de Obregón (played by an un-credited Clara Beneyas) introduces it to the public. The song is an immediate hit among the bourgeoisie, including three old ladies who cheer excitedly for it and who return periodically throughout the film as a kind of campy Greek chorus. On the other hand, "Mentira, mentira" horrifies a group of hipsters who congregate at an alternative record store called Ugh, which is devoted to "authentic popular music," like Aretha Franklin, the Beatles, the Rolling Stones and Jimmy Hendrix. In order to prevent the performance of the piece at the contest, the hipsters travel about Spain, violently eliminating all the bands who might be able to perform the piece. The movie itself consists primarily of performances by these bands, which

DOI: 10.4324/9781003188933-15

were actual successful Spanish groups from the 1960s, such as Los Ángeles, Ismael, Los Beta, Los Buenos, Fórmula V and Los Mitos. In the end, with no more bands available, one of the hipsters, Judy (played by Spanish pop star Judy Stephen), gets to perform the song. Once on stage, she sabotages the contest, screaming "Mentira, mentira," demolishing the set on the stage and bringing on "Los Pop Tops," who perform some "authentic popular music" in front of the seated, shocked and stodgy Mundocanal audience.

Ivan Raykoff's research on Eurovision parodies finds that only Benny Hill's 1969 "Ting-a-ling-aloo," along with Monty Python's "Europolice Song Contest" of 1970 are as old and neither one of those two short skits are nearly as extended as Zulueta's ninety-five-minute film (2021, p. 73). Nor do they have its ambitious political agenda. For all its lighthearted, nonjudgmental insouciance, *Un dos tres* focuses on a question that had real geopolitical significance at the time: the participation of Francisco Franco's fascist Spain in the European Broadcasting Union (EBU), the ESC, and by analogy in Western Europe at the height of the Cold War. Franco, born in 1892, assumed dictatorial control over Spain as caudillo in 1939, with the help of Adolf Hitler and Benito Mussolini; he remained in power until his death in 1975. Debuting in the ESC in 1961, Spain won in 1968 with the seemingly silly, but politically fraught, song "La, la, la." The young star Joan Manuel Serrat was supposed to sing the song. When he decided to sing it in Catalan, the Franco government replaced him with Massiel, who sang in Castilian Spanish and won the competition (Gutiérrez Lozano, 2012, pp. 14–15). In the 2008 television documentary, *1968: Yo viví el mayo español* (1968: I Lived the Spanish May), Montsé Fernandez Villa quoted José María Iñigo, who plays the television announcer in *Un dos tres*, claiming that Franco bought the votes that ensured Spain's victory that year. Subsequently Iñigo recanted and apologized to Massiel, explaining he was just repeating rumors that he had heard. Dean Vuletic points out that Iñigo's account implied that Bulgaria and Czechoslovakia participated in the ESC, which was not the case in that year. Vuletic concludes that Iñigo was likely conflating Spain's participation in Eurovision with its particiation in the Intervision Song Contest (2018, p. 227, n. 31). In any case, the victory was important for Spain. The first episode of the highly successful television series, *Cuéntame cómo pasó* (Remember When), which first aired in 2001, culminates in Massiel's 1968 victory as a marker of the transition to a new modern European Spain (Bernardeau & Ladrón de Guevara, 2001). Amusingly, the title of the series refers to the song 'Cuéntame' by the group Fórmula V, who are slated for elimination in Zulueta's film. As the victor, Spain hosted the ESC in 1969, allowing the totalitarian government to showcase a youthful, optimistic and cheerful popular culture alongside such leaders of the West as the United Kingdom and France. Progressives throughout Western Europe abhorred the symbolism. Austria stayed away rather than seem to support Franco's dictatorship in Spain.

Un dos tres references the events of 1968 quite explicitly. In the last ten minutes of the movie, the Federal Republic of Germany presents a song called "Sa, sa, sa"; if that allusion to "La, la, la" is not clear enough, the next performer wears a dress remarkably similar to the one that Massiel wore. As Brad Epps concludes, *Un dos tres* is not only "a deliciously perverse incursion into consumer culture," but also "conveys an irreverence toward Spain and the presumably enlightened and carefree Europe into which many Spaniards desired to lose themselves in order, supposedly, to find themselves again" (2012, p. 585). In this context, Zulueta's movie's campy portrayal of Spain's entry in Mundocanal takes on a harder edge. The hipsters' search for alternative music seems genuinely revolutionary. Zulueta's film, *Un dos tres*, suggests that a vibrant popular culture can play a role in fighting fascism, as can camp. It does so by using some of the ideas found in Sontag's famous "Notes on Camp," but refracts them with Walter Benjamin's hopes for the possibility of political redemption through the artwork in the age of its mechanical reproducibility. As it encourages its audience to embrace politically progressive campy art, Zulueta's film also admonishes its viewers to think more carefully about the meaning of camp in the ESC.

Biography

Born Juan Ricardo Miguel Zulueta Vergarajauregui in 1943, Zulueta grew up in San Sebastián, in the heart of the Basque Country (the city is known as Donostia in Basque). His parents were artistically inclined—his mother painted, and his father directed the city's renowned film festival from 1957 to 1960. Waiting for admission to the film school in Madrid, he took a merchant ship to New York City in 1963, where he was involved with the Art Students League and was exposed to Andy Warhol's world of pop art (Losada). Upon returning to Spain, he matriculated at the Escuela Oficial de Cine in October 1964, where he began working with his lifelong mentor and friend, José Luis Borau (1929–2012), who had begun teaching there just two years before.

In 1968, Borau and Zulueta co-produced a television variety show called *Ultima Grito* (Latest Trends). The show, with deliberately amateurish production values, featured José María Iñigo and Judy Stephen as anchors who introduced songs like Zager and Evans' hit, "In the Year 2525," with groovy visuals highlighting Spanish translations of the words. Borau and Zulueta used the same techniques and many of same actors, including Iñigo and Stephen, in *Un dos tres*, which Borau took on as the first project of his new production company, El Imán. In fact, Borau was listed as the director of *Un dos tres* because Zulueta did not have the credentials for a director's union card when he made the film. It was presumably Borau's connections that allowed the young filmmaker Zulueta to premier *Un dos tres*, his first feature-length film, at the Cannes Film Festival in 1969.

Borau sponsored, protected and promoted an atmosphere of sexual, social and political dissent in the twilight of the Franco regime. As Marsha Kinder notes, "both through his teaching and his producing the movies of other film-makers, Borau's personal impact on the New Spanish Cinema was able to go far beyond his own directorial efforts as an *auteur*" (1986–87, p. 38). Besides Zulueta, another of Borau's disciples whose work verged on the critically queer was Jaime

Chárivarri, who co-wrote the script of *Un dos tres* with Zulueta. Born in 1943, the same year as Zulueta, Chárivarri's 1977 film, *A un dios conocido* (*To an Unknown God*), focuses on an aging homosexual reminiscing about the outbreak of the Spanish Civil War and his youthful love of Federico Garcia Lorca. Admittedly, *A un dios conocido* appeared after Franco's death in 1975, but, even before Franco died, Borau produced in 1972 *Mi querida señorita* (My Dearest Señorita), directed by Jaime de Armiñan. Co-written by Armiñan and Borau, the film focuses on a person from a small town who, after years of living as a woman, discovers his masculine identity and moves to Madrid to explore his new life. The gender-bending film was nominated in the competition for Best Foreign Film at the 1973 Oscars, suggesting both Borau's ability to project Spanish film internationally and his openness to queer topics.

Following the release of *Un dos tres*, Zulueta screened the experimental short film, *Leo es pardo* (Leo is Dark), in 1976 at the Berlin Film Festival. In 1979, he directed one more feature-length film, *Arrebato* (Rapture), which has become a camp classic and a critical favorite, rereleased by the German company Bildstörung on DVD in 2010. "A drug-driven, metacinematic tale of vampirism in which a Super 8 camera armed with an interval timer plays the part of Dracula," as Epps describes it (2012, p. 582), the film revels in many of Zulueta's primary obsessions at the time, particularly heroin use and queer sexuality between men. As screenwriter and author Augusto M. Torres, who was also involved with the production of *Arrebato*, writes in his introduction to the published version of the script, "it is a story of homosexuality and drugs, but especially, an apology for drugs, suicide, and despair" (2002, p. 19). In Andrés Duque's 2004 documentary, *Iván Z*, Zulueta himself discusses his heroin use extensively, which peaked while he was making the film. Zulueta implicitly compares the hours that the spectator spends in the cinema, transported to another world, to the experience of using heroin. In 2011, the actress and journalist Cayetana Guillén Cuervo organized a colloquium on *Arrebato*, where Zulueta's colleagues Chávarri and Iñigo made the same case. Despite this artistic and intellectual justification for heroin, the drug took its toll on Zulueta, who returned home in an effort to distance himself from the drug scene and avoid overdosing.

If the filmmaker spoke quite openly about the connections between his drug use and his art, he was much more coy about the connections between his sexuality and his creations. This is not unusual for queer artists born in the 1940s and is all the more understandable for a filmmaker who came of age under Franco's Catholic dictatorship. Although the *Movida*, the exciting post-Franco scene in Madrid, was known for its celebration of sexual freedom, Alberto Mira argues in a footnote that the movement was nonetheless "largely closety about homosexuality" (2009, p. 168, n. 4). Mira suggests that in Zulueta's film in particular, "homosexuality is there, but never brought out into the open, and especially never 'labeled'" (2009, p. 159). Nonetheless, Mira aligns Zulueta with "a strand in homosexual culture which was explicitly misogynistic, vocationally marginal, hungry for darkness and surrounded by fantasies of suicide" (2009, p. 159). Epps prefers the term "queer" (2012, p. 592). Mira and Epps repeat

Torres's claim that the festivals in Cannes and Berlin both rejected *Arrebato* not only because of its celebration of heroin use but also because of its explicit homoeroticism (Torres, 2002, p. 19).

Duque's documentary shows the older Zulueta as a relaxed, cheerful, friendly and funny man, living in San Sebastián with his vivacious mother in a large comfortable house filled with artworks, overlooking their swimming pool and a breathtaking view of the ocean. When Zulueta died in 2009 at the age of sixty-six, Pedro Almodóvar, who had a small uncredited role in *Arrebato* and hired Zulueta in the 1980s to design posters for his movies, gave a moving eulogy, concluding, "Spanish cinema loses a unique individual, and José Luis Borau his best disciple. I remember those days in his flat in Plaza de España in Madrid so clearly. Everything was charged with life, and we used to laugh so much!" (Almodóvar, 2020).

Un dos tres and Camp

Reminiscent of Richard Lester's psychedelic musicals about the Beatles, *A Hard Day's Night* (1964) and *Help!* (1965), *Un dos tres* features multiple examples of camp, suggesting that the links between the ESC and camp have a long heritage. The concept of "camp" had been circulating widely since Sontag's famous essay, "Notes on Camp," appeared in 1964 in *Partisan Review*, just a year after Zulueta had spent time in New York City. Camp had been a recognized source of amusement and sustenance in the gay world for some time. The American author Gore Vidal uses the term in his 1948 novel about male homosexuality, *The City and the Pillar*, as does Christopher Isherwood in his 1954 novel, *The World in the Evening*. Sontag's 1964 essay, however, hurtled the term into the mainstream American and British press, which responded to Sontag's "discovery" with alacrity. According to Cleto, *The New York Times Magazine, Holiday*, the *New Statesman, The Village Voice, Harper's Magazine, The New Yorker, Saturday Night, The Herald Tribune, Life*, and *Art Forum* all published on the subject in 1965 (2019, p. 29).

Although it is not certain that Zulueta had direct contact with the essay "Notes on Camp," his film *Un dos tres* is shot through with characters and scenes who are campy in Sontag's sense. *Un dos tres* clearly has the "relish for ex-aggerations of sexual characteristics and personality mannerisms" that Sontag identifies as typically campy (Sontag, 1966, p. 279). This is true both of the hipsters and Marina de Obregón, who features "the corny flamboyant female-ness" that Sontag finds frequently in camp (1966, p. 279). Both she and the hipsters clearly embody camp's glorification of what Sontag calls "instant character": "Character is understood as a state of continual incandescence—a person being one, very intense thing" (1966, p. 286). Marina de Obregón's perfor-mance at the opening of the film exemplifies what Sontag calls "pure Camp": a powerful, incandescent character; an exaggerated representation of Spanish femininity; absolutely, unironically serious about her art.

The hipsters based at the record store Ugh are just as campy. With their dandyish costumes, their posturing and posing, their insistence on the superiority of their taste in music, they too have what Sontag calls "the proper mixture of the exaggerated, the fantastic, the passionate, and the naïve" (1966, p. 283). Elaborately dressed and coifed, applying slabs of raw beef to their eyes, the hipsters take on their challenge of eliminating all potential singers of "Mentira, mentira" with deadly seriousness. Judy declares: "If we aren't professionals, we'll quit. But if we are, we'll continue on." Her friend Juste (played by the singer and actress Mercedes Juste, who went on to perform in, among other films, Almodóvar's *Labyrinth of Desire*) has a breakdown, punctuated by a montage of shots in which she exclaims "I... I.... I.... I...," until she recites her commitment to leftwing politics: "*I* have burned newspapers in the Gran Vía. *I* have read the diary of Che. *I* have protested against the Vietnam War. *I* have renounced a comfortable economic lifestyle to have this business with you all. *I* am going to demonstrate to you what I'm capable of!"[1] However laudable these political acts might be, the film presents them as absurdly unselfconscious. As she speaks, the camera cuts to the three old ladies who had cheered so enthusiastically for Marina de Obregón, reinforcing the connection between the campy composer of "Mentira" and the pop culture enthusiasts who hate the song.

Arguably, one element of the film's campy aesthetic is its constant play with the boundaries of the real. Sontag mentions Mae West, Tallulah Bankhead and Bette Davis as examples of actresses who "camp"; although Sontag disapproves of these actors, she herself became something of a camp figure, with her diva-esque temper tantrums and trademark streak of white hair, à la Cruella de Vil. The reproduction of the absolutely serious performance of character allows the spectator to see and study the construction and the artifice that goes into the character. Zulueta's colleague from *Ultimo grito*, José María Iñigo (1942–2018), plays himself as the announcer responsible for finding the right band to perform at the actual competition. In a twist that continued to blur the lines between fact and fiction, Iñigo went on to a long-term association with the ESC, announcing the jury results for Spain in 1975 and 1976 and providing the commentary for Spanish Television's broadcast of the contest from 2011 to 2017. In this way, even the performances of the bands who must not be allowed to perform "Mentira, mentira" can verge on camp, with all of camp's ambivalences. While the hipsters are systematically eradicating the Spanish bands, the audience gets to hear their music. Thus, the movie is a showcase of local Spanish talent, even as it attempts to deconstruct the musical nationalist pride built into the ESC. As Matt Losada writes, "the film combines critique with complicity, subversion with promotion" (2010). This is a mirror image of the loving spoof that applies to Marina de Obregón and the hipsters.

In general, *Un dos tres* demonstrates the attitude of the "connoisseur of Camp," who "is continually amused, delighted" (Sontag, 1966, p. 289). This is especially clear in the case of "Mentira, mentira," for, even though the hip musicians from Ugh despise the song, the movie "relishes, rather than judges, the little triumphs and awkward intensities of 'character'" (Sontag, 1966,

p. 291). As Sontag argues, "[c]amp taste is, above all, a mode of enjoyment, of appreciation—not judgment ... Camp taste doesn't propose that it is in bad taste to be serious; it doesn't sneer at someone who succeeds in being seriously dramatic. What it does is find the success in certain passionate failures" (1966, p. 291). Nor does the film ridicule the efforts of the hipsters to challenge Mundocanal. Zulueta's *Un dos tres* is able to find the success in the passionate failure of both Marina de Obregón and the hipsters as they pursue and sabotage the nation's ESC plans.

Gender, Homosexuality and Politics

Sontag famously identifies "a peculiar affinity and overlap" between camp and homosexuality (1966, p. 290). At the same time, she infamously declares that camp is "disengaged, depoliticized—or at least apolitical" (1966, p. 277). For Sontag, the kind of privileged, distanced, critical, yet ultimately appreciative stance that camp embodies applies most smoothly to gender and its permutations. The camp aesthetic glorifies the androgyne and the epicene, according to Sontag. While it celebrates exaggerated femininity and masculinity, it also promotes "going against the grain of one's sex" (1966, p. 279). In the aesthetic of travesty, female impersonation and the drag queen, Sontag sees a humorous take-down of gender norms. It is not as though the drag queen detests the conventions of gender that she so assiduously masters. Although many have pilloried Sontag for her claim that camp is apolitical, she is not alone in this assessment. As Andrew Ross observes, "because of its zeal for artifice, theatricality, spectacle, and parody, camp has often been seen as prepolitical, even reactionary" (1993, p. 72).

In the course of her life, Sontag herself did not insist upon the apoliticism of camp with religious fervor. Benjamin Moser points out that the original version of the camp essay, drafted already in 1958, was called "Notes on Homosexuality." At that time, she saw homosexuality as "a criticism of society— a form of internal expatriation. Protest against bourgeois expectations" (Moser, 2019, p. 231). Ross notes that, in a 1975 interview, she argued that camp had connections to the feminist movement (1993, p. 72). Very early on, many people recognized the political potential of camp, particularly in terms of gender and sexuality. Working with drag queens in her groundbreaking 1972 study, *Mother Camp*, Esther Newman reported that her subjects understood drag's ability to expose the conventions of the modern gender system: "Gay people know that sex-typed behavior can be achieved, contrary to what is popularly believed" (1993, p. 45–46). In *Gender Trouble* (1990), Judith Butler would provide a revolutionary philosophical framework for the argument that camp was political, as David Bergman clarifies: "for Butler... the hyperbolic, parodic, anarchic, redundant style of camp is the very way to bring heterosexist attitudes of 'originality,' 'naturalism,' and 'normality' to their knees" (1993, p. 11). This Butlerian understanding of the subversive nature of camp fits in well with

Sontag's original thinking about the way that homosexuality can represent a social critique.

Those who see camp as political, however, often see it as political primarily in its critique of conventional gender roles and heteronormativity. While *Un dos tres* is full of ridiculously exaggerated performances of masculinity and femininity, starting with the singer/songwriter Marina de Obregón and the television announcer José María Iñigo and continuing through the hipsters, its attitude toward gender and sex roles does seem to be more along the line of the detached amusement that Sontag proposes in her camp essay. Perhaps as part of the general taboo regarding homosexuality in the late 1960s in Spain (and elsewhere), there is no direct take-down of traditional gender roles and heterosexuality in the film. Casting a skeptical eye on the idea that drag was always a subversive activity in the Butlerian sense, Bergman provides a useful counterexample of how camp could have helped queers and other gender nonconformists in Zulueta's world: "In a pre-Stonewall world, camp functioned as an argot that provided an oppressed group some measure of coherence, solidarity, and humor, and it allowed gay men and women to talk to one another within the hearing range of heterosexuals who might be hostile to them" (1993, p. 13). Given the number of people interested in queer themes in Zulueta's cinematic world, the campy elements of *Un dos tres* might have served the purpose of signaling to other like-minded individuals that there was a space of sexual freedom in the Madrid subculture, even in the 1960s, particularly in the world of the ESC.

For many LGBTQ+ activists, however, camp had—despite Sontag's claims—a political potential that went beyond gender and sexuality. In his influential 1977 essay, "Camp and the Gay Sensibility," gay activist and film critic Jack Babuscio insisted that "Camp can be subversive—a means of illustrating those cultural ambiguities and contradictions that oppress us all, gay and straight, and, in particular, women" (1993, p. 28). In the late 1980s, Andrew Ross argued that "the question of 'camp'.... becomes political all over again, not only because of its articulate engagement with the (commodity) world of popular taste, but also because camp contains an explicit commentary on feats of *survival* in a world dominated by the taste and interests of those whom it serves" (1993, p. 62). Zulueta's characters, struggling to come to terms with the politics of mass-produced popular culture, from the Beatles to the ESC, come into focus here. Scott Long's beautiful reflections in "The Loneliness of Camp" make the political power of camp even clearer, albeit within the context of political powerlessness: "Camp may only occupy something like a terrorist's status, conducting intermittent raids on the authoritative centers of ignorance and indifference, but marking only minor victories on a giant backdrop of defeat" (1993, p. 89–90). Camp in this sense flourished in the gay community in the days before gay rights, when homosexuals lived in overwhelmingly heteronormative and homophobic environments. To the outsider, their actions might seem apolitical, but in fact these campy interventions could be small strikes against the system. As Cleto concludes in his introduction to the catalog for the

2019 exhibition on camp and fashion at New York City's Metropolitan Museum of Art, "camp represented a survival strategy vis à vis stigma"; it "cemented solidarity among marginalized subjects coping with a hostile reality" (2019, p. 35). Although camp in this understanding flourished particularly in the gay male world, it could apply to many oppressed people who needed to fight against overwhelming odds.

Zulueta's *Un dos tres* clearly has a political edge. The hipsters from Ugh admire "authentic popular music" because it represents opposition to the repressive government, much as Eastern Europeans such as Václav Havel glorified Western rock music as an antidote to communism. Nonetheless, their resistance has a sly campy humor to it, rather than straight sincerity. Judy's destruction of the Mondocanal stage in front of the cruel, complacent, self-satisfied establishment, as grotesque in their tuxedos and evening gowns as any sketch of the Weimar Republic by George Grosz, is hilariously campy, because of its ridiculous, over-the-top obsession with the bad pop music of the ESC. It's one of those "minor victories," those "intermittent raids on the authoritative centers of ignorance and indifference," that Scott Long identifies as camp. Nor are the hipsters the only political force in the film. As noted before, Marina de Obregón's unkempt hair as she submerses herself in the emotions of her song is a camp fest. Yet, far from ignoring it as ridiculous, the moderator Iñigo halts her performance before she is able to finish her song. Zulueta shows that even an artist working within an understanding of camp very similar to Sontag's can find an avenue for campy political action.

Walter Benjamin and Mass Culture

To see how Zulueta produces a politics of camp out of Sontag's apolitical vision, it is worth remembering that one of her examples of campy naïve seriousness is "the public manner and rhetoric of de Gaulle" (1966, p. 284). Sontag is thus willing to see politics as camp. In *Un dos tres*, Zulueta does the same. If one thinks of "Mentira, mentira" as a state-sponsored message, then Marina de Obregón's outrageous production implies that the state's propaganda is camp. As the singer literally spits "Palabras, palabras" (words, words) at the camera, causing Iñigo to recoil in horror, the accusation that the government's propaganda is nothing but empty phrases is broadcast across the nation. The argument that the state has become nothing but lying words mean that it is becoming stylized, aesthetic, campy. The ESC, with its state-sponsored broadcasts of national popular music, obviously undesrscores this linkage of nationalism and camp.

The claim that the messaging of fascist governments verges on camp brings to mind critiques of Nazi aesthetics, including Sontag's own essay on Leni Riefenstahl, "Fascinating Fascism" (originally published in 1975 in the *New York Review of Books*, republished in *Under the Sign of Saturn*, 1980). Sontag sees Riefenstahl and the National Socialists as promoting an apolitical vision of "art as life, the cult of beauty," a world which is all style, no content, much like camp

(1980, p. 96). The "sensibility of camp," Sontag claims, allows people to admire fascist aesthetics, while also maintaining a certain distance. She adds that, nowadays, "for most people," art that invokes the fascist aesthetic is "probably no more than a variant of camp" (Sontag, 1980, p. 97). This is the familiar apolitical Sontagian camp that finds everything a hoot. The danger is that this "aesthetic view of life" can neutralize the political message of fascism (Sontag, 1980, p. 100).

Sontag's dual claims that "aestheticized camp" can both undergird fascism and undermine politics bring to mind Walter Benjamin's "Work of Art in the Age of Technological Reproducibility," which famously ends with the argument that, while fascism aestheticizes politics, "communism replies by politicizing art" (Benjamin, 2008, p. 42). Sontag was one of the earliest and most influential champions of Benjamin's work in the United States; indeed, the title essay of her collection *Under the Sign of Saturn* is a celebration of his thinking (Moser, 2019, p. 381). In "Notes on Camp," Sontag asserts that camp answers the question, "how to be a dandy in the age of mass culture," which echoes Benjamin's concerns about intellectual and artistic life in the age of mechanical reproduction (Sontag, 1966, p. 288). Given Benjamin's optimistic beliefs about the possibility of politically activist art emerging from mechanical reproducibility, Sontag seems to suggest that camp could have a role to play in combatting the conservative commercialization that Theodor Adorno worries about in pop culture. While the aestheticism of camp might predispose it to fascism, its reliance on mass culture might give reason for hope.

Sontag sees the mass production and mass culture as the important distinction between dandyism and camp: "Camp—Dandyism in the age of mass culture— makes no distinction between the unique object and the mass produced object. Camp taste transcends the nausea of the replica" (1966, p. 289). Cleto explains that camp takes on the ideology of the nineteenth-century dandy, but instead of fetishizing one-of-a-kind luxury objects, it adopts a "feignedly 'democratic' appreciation of vulgarity" (2019, p. 29), which goes hand in hand with the age of mass production. As Mira observes, the dandy was an important ideal for the filmmakers of the Movida (2009, p. 155–156). Zulueta's own bourgeois bohemian background gave him the detached privilege of the camp connoisseur. The hipsters of *Un dos tres*, with their carefully curated wardrobes and record collections, are all dandies par excellence.

At the same time, the documents of Zulueta's life show his fascination with reproduced images, including the posters with which he supported himself financially. His films constantly foreground the technology of making and reproducing images. *Un dos tres* is intensely aware of the role of technology in mediating and reproducing the work of art. The song "Mentira, mentira" is introduced on a bank of eight televisions in the show's production studio, emphasizing the highly mediated and technologically produced nature of the ESC. Through the mediation of television screens and cameras, the spectator gets the close-up of the performer's hands. Shots of the camera reveal Zulueta's fascination with the power of film. The hipsters hear the song through the medium of television too. The hipsters, of course, congregate in a shop that promotes technologically reproduced mass culture. On another level, the plot of the movie is based on the idea that the song is reproducible in the sense that the musical establishment is looking for another band to perform the song that Marina de Obregón premieres. In multiple ways, Zulueta underscores the connection to which Sontag alludes between camp and technological reproducibility. At the same time, the film implies that both the "authentic pop culture" favored by the hipsters and the subversive hysteria of Marina de Obregón's performance of her own song can have a politically positive effect. He thereby opens the way for the possibility that it might be possible, as Benjamin would say, to politicize aesthetics, rather than to aestheticize politics. Campy mechanically reproducible art, such as can be found in the ESC, can reveal its own constructedness in ways that allow for the deconstruction of ideology.

Zulueta's final feature film, *Arrebato*, with its constant close-up of cameras, timers and film, underscores his focus on technology. Citing Almodóvar, Mira underscores that Zulueta was "an experimental filmmaker concerned to the point of obsession by film language itself and by the physicality of lenses and celluloid" (2009, p. 160). Mira points out that "Zulueta ends his second feature film with two film-makers being devoured by a film camera" (2009, p. 167). Epps delves into the subject more theoretically, noting that "the emphasis on filmstrips, frames, and pauses in *Arrebato* is such that 'the invisible act of editing' is brought into view" (2012, p. 581). All of the interest in technological reproduction is already present in *Un dos tres* as it deconstructs the ESC.

Conclusion

Zulueta's struggles with heroin have made him into a kind of antihero, a brilliant genius unable to recover from Franco's dictatorship. Mira sees him as a *maudit*, a failed dandy (2009, p. 156). Other critics have interpreted particularlly *Arrebato* as a prediction of the death of cinema, as Epps notes. Yet, Zulueta's film *Un dos tres* is a much more joyous celebration of the possibility of a politically progressive popular culture. *Un dos tres* suggests the possibility of a pop culture not marked by fascism, holding out the hope that perhaps the very reproducibility of art could help defeat the fascism under which it was made. Within the framework of *Un dos tres*, this revolutionary reproducibility could happen on two levels. First, the hipsters could find political energy in the "authentic" pop culture streaming in from the United Kingdom and the United States in the form of artists like the Beatles, the Rolling Stones, and Aretha Franklin, showing up the state culture foregrounded by Mundocanal. Second, however, even artists working within the system, like Marina de Obregón and other ESC artists, can utilize their camp energy to subvert official politics.

Reading Susan Sontag through the lens of Walter Benjamin, it is possible to see camp as political, particularly in the Spanish context. By the time *Un dos tres* appeared, Franco was, along with António de Oliveira Salazar in Portugal, in fact the last remnant of the fascist wave that swept over Europe in the 1930s, the very wave against which Benjamin hoped that his essay, "The Work of Art in the Age of Technological Reproducibility," could intervene. Because of the exigencies of the Cold War, the West, which sponsored the ESC, found itself embracing Franco. In that context, Zulueta picks up on Benjamin's ideas on how to find a progressive politics in mass culture. Zulueta's *Un dos tres* shows how Benjamin can nudge Sontag's conception of camp back into the political arena.

At the same time, *Un dos tres* underscores the need for a more nuanced view of camp in the ESC. Fans and the mass media typically rely on a view of camp that harks back to Sontag's 1964 essay: light-hearted, apolitical, slightly homosexual. When people say that the ESC is campy, they usually mean that it is a glorious festival of mass-produced music, so bad that it is good, something that particularly its gay fans can appreciate. Zulueta's *Un dos tres*, however, is a reminder that camp can also serve as a biting attack against an oppressive heteronormative fascist world order—one that the ESC itself once represented. Zulueta's film provides an example of how queer and campy fandom can be a political response to the ESC and how the study of the ESC can contribute to a philosophy of activism.

Note

1 My thanks to my Clark University students Kira Houston and Pamela Klassen Gutierrez, who worked on the translation of this section for me.

References

Almodóvar, P. (April 20, 2020). Ivan: Pedro Almodóvar on Iván Zulueta (M. Diestro-Dópido, Trans.). *Sight and Sound: The International Film Magazine.* https://www2.bfi.org.uk/news-opinion/sight-sound-magazine/features/pedro-almodovar-on-ivan-zulueta

Babuscio, J. (1993). Camp and the gay sensibility. In D. Bergman (Ed.), *Camp Grounds: Style and homosexuality* (pp. 19–38). University of Massachusetts Press.

Benjamin, W. (2008). *The Work of Art in the Age of its Technological Reproducibility and Other Writings on Media.* M.W. Jennings, B. Doherty, & T.Y. Levin, Eds. Harvard University Press.

Bergman, D. (1993). Introduction. In D. Bergman (Ed), *Camp Grounds: Style and homosexuality* (pp. 1–18). University of Massachusetts Press.

Bernardeau, M.A., & Ladrón de Guevara, E., A. Macías [Writers]. (2001, Sep. 13). El retorno del fugitivo. In M.A. Bernardeau, *Cuéntame cómo pasó* [Executive Producer]. Television Española.

Catsoulis, J. (2020, June 26). Eurovision Song Contest Review: Over the top and around the bend. *New York Times*, p. C6. https://www.nytimes.com/2020/06/26/movies/eurovision-song-contest-the-story-of-fire-saga-review.html

Cleto, F. (2019). The spectacles of camp. In A. Bolton (Ed.), *Camp: Notes on fashion* (Vol. 1, pp. 9–59). Metropolitan Museum of Art.

Cuervo, C.G. (2011, October 4). Coloquio *Arrebato*. In *Version española*. Radio y Television Española. https://www.rtve.es/alacarta/videos/version-espanola/version-espanola-arrebato/1215035/

Dobkin, D. (2020). *Eurovision Song Contest: The story of Fire Saga* [Film]. European Broadcasting Union, Netflix, Gary Sanchez Productions, Gloria Sanchez Productions, Truenorth Productions.

Duque, A. (2004). *Ivan Z* [Film]. Available as additional material on the DVD of Ivan Zulueta (2010), *Arrebato*. Bildstörung.

Epps, B. (2012). The space of the vampire: materiality and disapperance in the films of Iván Zulueta. In J. Labanyi & T Pavlović (Eds), *A Companion to Spanish Cinema* (pp. 580–594). John Wiley and Sons.

Fones, S. (2019, April 25). The campiness of Eurovision. *CR Fashion Book*. https://www.crfashionbook.com/culture/a27241869/eurovision-history-camp/

Gutiérrez Lozano, J.F. (2012, Nov. 29). Spain was not living a celebration: TVE and the Eurovision Song Contest during the years of Franco's Dictatorship. *VIEW: Journal of European Television History and Culture*, *1*(2), 11–17.

Kinder, M. (1986–87, Winter). José Luis Borau *On the Line* of the national/international interface in post-Franco cinema. *Film Quarterly*, *40*(2), 35–48.

Long, S. (1993). The loneliness of camp. In D. Bergman (Ed.), *Camp Grounds: Style and Homosexuality* (pp. 78–91). University of Massachusetts Press.

Losada, M. (2010, October). Iván Zulueta's cinephilia of ecstacy and experiment. *Senses of Cinema*, *56*. https://www.sensesofcinema.com/2010/feature-articles/ivan-zulueta%E2%80%99s-cinephilia-of-ecstasy-and-experiment/

Mira, A. (2009). The dark heart of the movida: vampire fantasies in Iván Zulueta's *Arrebato*. *Arizona Journal of Hispanic Cultural Studies*, *13*, 155–169.

Moser, B. (2019). *Sontag: Her Life and Work*. HarperCollins.

Newman, E. (1993). Role models. In D. Bergman (Ed.), *Camp Grounds: Style and homosexuality* (pp. 39–53). University of Massachusetts Press.

Raykoff, I. (2021). *Another Song for Europe: Music, taste, and values in the Eurovision Song Contest*. Routledge.

Rooney, D. (2020, June 24). "Eurovision Song Contest: The Story of Fire Saga" film review. *The Hollywood Reporter*. https://www.hollywoodreporter.com/movies/movie-reviews/eurovision-song-contest-story-fire-saga-film-review-1299975/

Ross, A. (1993). Uses of camp. In D. Bergman (Ed.), *Camp Grounds: Style and homosexuality* (pp. 54–77). University of Massachusetts Press.

Sontag, S. (1966). *Against Interpretation and Other Essays*. Farrar, Straus and Giroux.

Sontag, S. (1980). *Under the Sign of Saturn*. Farrar, Straus and Giroux.

Torres, A.M. (2002). Mi personal *Arrebato*. In I. Zulueta, *Arrebato: Guión cinematografico* (pp. 7–21). Ocho y Medio.

Vuletic, D. (2018). *Postwar Europe and the Eurovision Song Contest*. Bloomsbury.

Zulueta, I. (2010). *Arrebato* [Film]. Bildstörung. Originally released 1979.

Zulueta, I. (2015). *Un dos tres ... al escondite* inglés [Film]. Mercury Films. Originally released in 1969.

13 The Eurovision Song Contest and European Television History: Continuity, Adaptation, Experimentation

Mari Pajala

The Eurovision Song Contest (ESC) is a television programme and a media event by definition. Unlike events such as the Olympic Games, the ESC would not exist without television. It was created for this medium when the European Broadcasting Union (EBU), an organisation of public service broadcasting companies, wanted to come up with a programme to symbolise its Eurovision Network for programme exchange in the mid-1950s. In light of this, perhaps surprisingly little research on the ESC has been done in the framework of media studies. Major anthologies on the ESC, for instance, have been more influenced by performance and popular music studies than by media studies (e.g., Raykoff & Tobin, 2007; Fricker & Gluhovic, 2013). Yet, the ESC has much to offer to media studies and vice versa. In this chapter, I will first discuss the most prominent theme in media studies research on the ESC, namely the contest's functioning as a media event. Then, I will consider how the ESC's history can contribute to our understanding of two aspects of contemporary media events, namely their televisual aesthetics and temporality. I will argue that the exceptional longevity of the ESC as a media event rests on continuity, adaptation as well as experimentation.

The ESC as a Media Event

Media scholars have used the ESC to explore how media events work and to interrogate some of the assumptions in the theory about media events. Media events have been theorised most influentially by Daniel Dayan and Elihu Katz (1992) in their book *Media Events: The Live Broadcasting of History*. Dayan and Katz define media events as broadcasts that break the mundane flow of media content. They are "must-watch" television that demands attention. In Dayan and Katz's typology, media events are divided into contests, conquests and coronations. The ESC obviously fits the first category, in which events focus on finding out who is the best in a competition that follows a specific set of rules. Dayan and Katz emphasise media events' relationship to power: arranged by public organisations and governments, media events celebrate a society's

DOI: 10.4324/9781003188933-16

hegemonic values. Media events connect viewers to the symbolic centre of the society and "celebrate not conflict but reconciliation" (ibid., p. 8).

Arguably, the central hegemonic values celebrated in the ESC have been nationhood and the idea of Europe as consisting of nation states (e.g., Bolin, 2006; Georgiou, 2008). However, as Abby S. Waysdorf (2020, p. 298) argues, within Eurovision fandom, the contest functions rather differently than Dayan and Katz's theory about media events as "top-down" creations suggests. Although the ESC is structured around the notion of nations, "[t]he ideal of Eurovision fandom is not that of opposing nations asserting their superiority, but of marginalised groups coming together to celebrate through music and spectacle," Waysdorf (2020, p. 298) writes, emphasising the contest's special relevance for LGBTIQ viewers.

Indeed, empirical research with Eurovision fans suggests that the fandom nurtures a cosmopolitan sensibility that departs from the celebration of nationhood in the contest itself. Myria Georgiou (2008) has compared attitudes towards the ESC on the British Broadcasting Corporation's (BBC) online forum and among fans in focus group discussions. On the forum, discussions were "nation-centric" (ibid., p. 145) and made use of national stereotypes, constructing a hierarchic East-West binary that denigrated East European participants. In contrast, the more committed fans in the focus groups showed an "emergent cosmopolitan imagination" which sees "Europe as a meeting point rather than as a conflict point" (ibid., p. 150). For these fans, the attraction of the ESC is in the "cosmopolitan exploration" of performances and languages, enabled by the quality of the ESC as a stand-alone media event outside the habitual flow of popular television programming (ibid., p. 150). Similarly, Maria Kyriakidou et al. (2018) use the ESC to question Dayan and Katz's theory about the "integrative potential" (ibid., p. 604) of media events. Kyriakidou et al. did fieldwork among fans who follow the ESC on site. They argue that the nationalism performed by fans—flag waving, dressing up—is playful, non-antagonistic and ironic by nature. On site, the ESC opens up a kind of "cosmopolitan space" where "'openness' towards cultural difference" is valued (ibid., p. 604). However, as traveling to the ESC requires time and disposable income, the event produces an "elite kind of cosmopolitanism" (ibid., p. 614), where participation relies on class structures. Research on Eurovision fans thus emphasises how media events' significance for audiences is not determined by the events' organisation and manifest meanings.

Moreover, the ESC shows how, even in the first decades of television, when programming addressed a family audience, a mainstream entertainment programme could have a distinct significance for marginalised groups. As one of the fans interviewed by Brian Singleton et al. (2007, p. 15) in their study of queer Eurovision fans in Ireland reminisces: "When I was growing up, Eurovision was a gay thing; it was like your private property. Even though your mother watched it, your father watched it, your grandmother watched it, maybe there was like a secret code." For older gay fans, Eurovision was like an "open secret" among gay viewers (Singleton et al., 2007, p. 16). The existence of these kinds of "secret" interpretative communities highlights the need to look beyond the most obvious meanings of major media events.

Dayan and Katz formulated their theory during the era of analogue broadcasting, and later scholarship has sought to understand how media events function in the contemporary online media environment. As media events spread across different platforms, they have become more complex and also more difficult to control for their organisers (Ytreberg, 2017; Couldry & Hepp, 2018). Indeed, it is increasingly hard to define what the ESC as a media event consists of. For many fans, for instance, the ESC does not consist merely of three nights' spectacle. Rather, the event begins perhaps when delegations arrive in the host city for rehearsals, which are reported about extensively on fan media as well as on EBU's official channels. This culmination of the ESC season is preceded by a series of smaller events, as fans follow national finals in different countries. The ESC event is created not only by the host organisation and the EBU but also by various other outlets, such as fan sites and performers' social media channels. As a result, the ESC is a completely different event for casual viewers who follow the final and for fans who follow a stream of constant updates for many weeks or even months. For scholars, the ESC's expansion as a media event makes it increasingly difficult to define, what the ESC as a research object consist of and which materials to use to study it. In the following sections, I will discuss two aspects of the ESC—televisual aesthetics and temporality—to highlight characteristics of contemporary media events and place them in the historical continuum of European television history.

The ESC and European Television History: Adaptation and Experimentation[1]

The ESC has been a part of the European television landscape continuously from the 1950s, when television was a new medium, to the present, when television programmes—or "content"—are increasingly accessed on platforms other than broadcast television. As a result, the contest offers a unique opportunity for studying and teaching European television and media history. However, few scholars in media studies have been interested in the ESC's history. The ESC itself encourages an emphasis on the new: each year brings a new contest, with new controversies and concerns. Media studies as a field also tends to focus on novelty, being more interested in new media than the past. Yet, studying the history of the ESC can also help us to see its present with new eyes by highlighting that that which now seems normal and self-evident was not always so.

In his influential periodisation, John Ellis (2000) divides the history of European television into three eras: scarcity, availability and plenty. Television's social role and relationship to its audience has been figured differently in each of these eras. The ESC was a creation of the *era of scarcity*, when public service broadcasters were the dominant—and in many countries the only—producers of television. Countries typically had one or two television channels and television addressed a large national audience, functioning as a "powerful instrument of social integration" (ibid., p. 45) that provided a kind of "private life" of the nation (ibid., p. 46). In this context, a Saturday night entertainment show like the ESC was almost guaranteed a large audience, and the choice of national entries could provoke intense media debate (see Pajala, 2006). In the course of the 1980s, European television entered the *era of availability*. New commercial channels and satellite and cable television made the media environment more competitive. Television moved to addressing viewers as members of distinct groups instead of as a mass audience (Ellis, 2000). In this environment, the ESC had much more competition than before. A traditional family-friendly song contest seemed old-fashioned in comparison to newer forms of television entertainment, such as music videos. In the *era of plenty*, the amount of available programming has grown and programmes can be accessed through new technologies. Television viewers are seen as consumers who select the content they want to watch from diverse sources (Ellis, 2000). As viewers increasingly choose what they watch and when, one could expect an old programme like the ESC to become lost in the competition. In fact, however, the ESC has adapted well to the current environment. Live competitions have become valuable for television companies, as they offer a way of attracting a large simultaneous audience. At the same time, social media has provided new ways of engaging with the ESC. As well as addressing a large undifferentiated audience, the ESC has started to address specific audiences, such as Eurovision fans and LGBTIQ people more explicitly than before.

It is quite remarkable that the ESC has survived through fundamental changes in the European media landscape, and a programme developed for the nascent medium of television in the 1950s is arguably thriving in the multiplatform media environment of the 2020s. Several factors have contributed to the contest's longevity. The EBU as an institution has provided a stable grounding, and the member companies have been motivated to uphold the ESC as the most visible product of the organisation. The ESC has maintained its relevance in the changing geopolitical landscape of Europe, and received a boost with the arrival of new participating broadcasters from the formerly Eastern Bloc countries eager to introduce themselves to an international audience. Also, the ESC has been able to create enthusiasm and commitment, which is reflected in the careers of some former Eurovision fans who have gone on to work in the production and develop the contest (such as Christer Björkman and Sietse Bakker). Moreover, the ESC works as entertainment: the basic format of the final—live performances followed by voting and the repeat performance of the winning song—has remained the same for decades. For the ESC as a television programme and media event, however, adaptation and experimentation have been essential to its survival.

As José Patricio Pérez-Rufí and Águeda María Valverde Mestre (2020, p. 28) argue, experimentation characterises the ESC as a television production. One of the aims of the EBU is to support public service broadcasting companies in keeping up with technological development (EBU, n.d.). Accordingly, the ESC has served as a stage for introducing the possibilities of new technologies. When the contest was created, a live international television broadcast was a novelty. Later on, the ESC was used, for instance, to develop the use of televoting in a large-scale, international context (Anon, 2013, p. 102). The fact that the responsibility for organising the ESC moves to a different broadcaster every year has contributed to the contest's development: people who have participated in the production have noted how each organiser attempts to outdo last year's programme (Anon, 2013, p. 103; Skey et al. 2016, p. 3388). While the ESC has often been branded as old-fashioned in terms of popular music, as a television production the contest has been forward-looking.

Although the basic format of the ESC final has remained recognisable for decades, the production has been continuously adapted to the changing media environment. This shows, for instance, in the contest's approach to television aesthetics. Like much early television entertainment, the ESC built on the tradition of stage entertainment (see Williams, 1990, pp. 64–66). The programme was basically a concert filmed by a few cameras and transmitted via television. As a live, international broadcast, the ESC showcased the novel possibilities offered by television, which enabled people in different countries to watch the same show at the same time. However, in other ways the ESC did not necessarily fulfil the contemporary criteria for good television. As a filmed stage show, the ESC did not seem to make sufficient use of the specific capacities of television. For instance, Nordic broadcasters discussed the ESC in the meetings of their Nordvision network in a very critical tone in the 1960s. Television professionals felt that the programme should be improved, but as the contest promoted the Eurovision Network, withdrawing entirely from the contest did not seem like an option either.[2]

The BBC's production of the 1963 ESC was an attempt to create a more televisual programme. Unlike the previous editions, the contest was not filmed in a concert hall but in television studios, with the host, orchestra, and performers placed in one studio and the audience and scoreboard in another. The studio location enabled the producers to use more varied stage props. In addition, new rules allowed the participating television companies to send a maximum of three assistants, such as instrumentalists or dancers, to accompany their singers. Relatively few countries, however, took advantage of this option. Instead, many performances relied on the power of the close-up shot to create a sense of intimacy, which was seen as a key characteristic of television as the medium that was able to bring performers to the audience's living rooms (Miettunen, 1966). As the most extreme example of this, Nana Mouskouri's part in "À force de prier" (By Persistently Praying) was filmed in a single close-up shot, with the singer looking directly at the camera. Director Yvonne Littlewood has reminisced that the use of close-ups was partly motivated by technical concerns, to keep microphones out of the frame (EuroSong News, 2003). At the same time, close-ups were seen as a form of expression that suited the small screen and differentiated televisual expression from the radio and cinema (Miettunen, 1966). Nevertheless, the 1963 experiment was a one-off and the following contests were again filmed in great halls in front of an audience.

The 1963 production points to an alternative development for the ESC as studio entertainment. Why did the studio version of the ESC not take off? Perhaps the sense of a live occasion, created by having the singers perform in front of an audience, was seen as more important than the more televisual aesthetic and the greater variety enabled by a studio setting. The ESC was, however, continuously adapted in more subtle ways. Technological developments and rule changes brought more visual variety to the performances: the BBC produced the first colour ESC in 1968, at a time when colour broadcasts were generally at an experimental stage in Europe. The use of more cameras brought varied camera angles and hand-held microphones enabled singers to move on stage. New rules allowed artists to use backing tracks and bring instrumentalists and dancers on stage. Whereas until the early 1970s the ESC focused on solo singers, by the early 1980s groups and choreography were prominent. Postcard films, first introduced in 1970, brought visual variety to the programme. Yet, the ESC remained largely what it had been from the start: televised stage entertainment.

As television entered the era of availability, the ESC faced more competition from commercial television. At the same time, Music Television and the rise of the music video changed the audiovisual aesthetics of popular music. The ESC needed to adapt in this new environment. The 1990 ESC in Zagreb exemplifies these developments. Although the contest was filmed in a concert hall, the televised performances were not as tied to the realist space of the concert hall as before. The stage was low, allowing cameras to move to and from the stage and circle among the performers. Numerous camera angles and moving cameras allowed television viewers to see the performers from angles that were not available for the audience on site. Two large video walls provided a second, simultaneous view of the performers. Although a live orchestra was still used, backing tracks were increasingly important, as became clear when the Spanish performance had to be restarted due to a problem with the backing track. In these ways the contest departed from the "realist" space of the contest hall to produce audiovisual performances that fit contemporary understandings of televisuality, making use of the possibilities of up-to date technology. The 1990 contest was an impressive production: the BBC's long-time commentator Terry Wogan admired the "spectacular" hall and video walls, saying: "It's been a very, very fine contest, very well staged."

Wogan's comments on the staging of the 1990 ESC highlight its spectacular quality. Due to its relatively small screen, television has not been associated with spectacle to the same extent as cinema. However, as Helen Wheatley (2016) argues, television has always attempted to create spectacular moments and programmes which are "designed to be stared at... contemplated and scrutinized" (ibid., p. 1). Spectacular productions can be found from all eras of television, but "spectacular television" has become an especially prominent aesthetic category in the 2000s, with the possibilities offered by digital production technology, larger television screens and greater image quality (Wheatley 2016). The ESC is well suited for producing spectacular television: EBU cooperation brings greater resources for producing the shows than most national broadcasters could afford alone. Production teams are eager to impress with their ability to create a technically slick show and introduce novel possibilities for visualising the acts. Moreover, entries compete to stand out from each other, and national delegations may spend significant sums on hiring a team of professionals to design their performance as well as on costumes, props, pyrotechnics, and special effects.

Spectacle is not new to the ESC—in the early decades of the contest, the large scale and expense of the international contest made it spectacular in itself. Nowadays, however, the scale of the technological apparatus—lighting, led walls, augmented reality technology—is enormous. While ESC producers created a distinct visual look for each performance already in the shows in the 1960s, today it is possible to create a whole different world to suit the story of a song, as in the case of the 2019 Australian performance, in which singer Kate Miller-Heidke and her backing dancers seemed to float in space. Accordingly, the ESC has become a platform for showcasing the skills not just of singers and songwriters, but also of stage directors (Robertson, 2021). In-demand directors, such as Fokas Evangelinos and Sacha Jean Baptiste, have been returning to the contest year after year and have each created several spectacular, innovative and successful performances. Thus, while the ESC maintains its original form as stage entertainment, it also incorporates the spectacular aesthetics of contemporary television.

The ESC and Mediated Temporality: Continuity and Change

With its long history, the ESC allows us to consider both continuity and change in the way television organises temporality. As Paddy Scannell (1996, p. 152) argues, "[b]roadcasting, whose medium is time, articulates our sense of time." In his phenomenological study of radio and television, Scannell describes how broadcasting created an annual calendar of events. As a major media event in television's era of scarcity, the ESC was one of the elements of this calendar. The annual cycle of the ESC has remained recognisable for decades, although the ESC now takes place later in the spring than it used to (until the early 1980s, the ESC was held in March or April). The contest's importance in structuring time for its fans can be seen in the meme where months of the year are listed as "January, February, March, April, Eurovision, June ..." Liveness has been central to the way the ESC organises time. When television was a new medium, liveness was seen as a key quality that separated it from the older audiovisual medium, cinema. Unlike the cinema, television could bring events to the audience's living rooms as they happened. A great part of the attraction of the ESC has been the feeling that you are watching a live event as it happens together with a large number of people in different countries—even if the experience is quite different in the majority of European countries where the contest takes place in prime time, in countries like Azerbaijan where it starts late at night or in Australia, where fans wake up to watch the ESC early on Sunday morning. The continuing attraction of liveness has been referenced in slogans such as "Share the moment" (ESC 2010) and "#JoinUs" (ESC 2014).

While the ESC continues to be a live event with a regular place in the annual calendar of media events, in other respects the programme reflects changes in mediated temporality. The development of the ESC underlines how time is no longer a scarce resource on television, as it was in the first decades of television when countries had few television channels and limited broadcasting time. In the current multi-platform television environment, the duration of ESC broadcasts has grown greatly. For instance, the 1980 ESC final lasted about two hours and seventeen minutes. In comparison, the 2021 final lasted almost four hours (not to mention the fact that it was preceded by two semifinals of about two hours each). The difference is caused partly by the number of participants—there were nineteen entries in the final in 1980 and twenty-six in 2021. However, a greater difference is made by the expansion of the interval acts and the voting.[3] Similarly, the Finnish national final of 1975 lasted an hour, including nine entries, a vote by regional juries and the repeat performance of the winning entry. The tone of the programme was brisk and efficient if compared to the 2021 national final *Uuden Musiikin Kilpailu* (UMK, Contest for New Music), which featured seven entries and lasted 105 minutes. In television's era of scarcity, even major events had to be relatively concise whereas now, the sense of an event seems to require a greater duration and more "extra" content in the form of interval acts.

While the duration of the ESC has expanded, the contest simultaneously highlights the importance of short-form content for contemporary television. Television entertainment is now more and more about creating "moments" that can be circulated on various platforms and incorporated with different content. Victoria Jay, the Head of Multiplatform Commissioning for Drama, Comedy and Entertainment at the BBC, describes the double value of moments for television:

> But television is to be celebrated and feels special because it is transient, it comes and goes, and we create a lot of hype about it being transient. All our marketing effort is about that. But simultaneously and independently, we are also saying there is an archival value to that transience. ...
>
> We create those moments, that's what the BBC does, moments. But now those moments are no longer just gone (Evans, 2011, pp. 116, 119).

Jay argues that, while transience is central to television, television is now equally invested in creating moments that can be archived and circulated. The ESC, with its focus on three-minute songs and visual spectacle, is well-suited for creating these kinds of moments, as Jay further describes:

> *Eurovision* this year blew the minds of the Television Audience Insight team ... this year it was an aggressive short-form strategy and it got 8.6 million views of the short-form around the event ... These moments are absolutely what people continue to want to share and talk about. It's

about sweating those assets, getting those moments out immediately to fuel social currency. In the entertainment space, where there's such talkability around the shows, it's absolutely essential to get short-form out immediately and for it to be the best moment.

(Evans 2011, pp. 117–118)

The contemporary ESC is thus not only a long live show, but also consists of clips that are archived and circulated. Clips of individual entries' performances are released immediately on the contest's official YouTube channel along with a wealth of other short-form material, such as rehearsal snippets and interviews.

The current media environment has also created new value for old archived ESCs, which for decades were only available for people with access to television companies' internal archives or fan networks in which video copies circulated. Now, YouTube houses an endless supply of old Eurovision shows and clips, uploaded in the first instance by fans and more recently also by the EBU, which is curating a kind of official version of ESC history. Eurovision archives gained new significance during the covid-19 pandemic, as Abby S. Waysdorf describes. After the 2020 ESC was cancelled, the fan project "Eurovision Again" offered a way of maintaining connection with the contest and other fans. On Saturday evenings, fans would watch an old ESC edition, tweet about it using the #EurovisionAgain hashtag and vote for their favourites. While #Eurovision Again was a fan in-itiative, the EBU joined in, streaming old contests on its official YouTube ac-count. As Waysdorf argues, "Eurovision Again" paradoxically turned archival material into a live event through the experience of shared viewing (Waysdorf, 2020). The appeal of "Eurovision Again" extended beyond the cancellation of ESC 2020, and the project returned in the summer of 2021.

To sum up, the ESC illustrates the variety of ways event television is experi-enced. First, the ESC is a part of the flow of television. In his foundational book *Television: Technology and Cultural Form*, Raymond Williams (1990, p. 95) identified flow as the "central television experience". Television programming consists of a planned flow of programmes and other elements—commercials, announcements—between programmes (ibid., pp. 86–118), and many people continue to watch the ESC as part of the flow of television, perhaps tuning in for only part of the program. Second, the ESC is a live media event that many viewers experience as celebratory viewing that breaks the mundane flow of television. Third, in the contemporary media environment, the ESC is also ex-perienced in the form of moments that circulate on various platforms and can be reframed and relived. Fourth, as archived ESC broadcasts have become available, old shows can also be watched as stand-alone works removed from their original broadcasting context. Thus, the ESC exemplifies how old and new forms of televisual temporality coexist in the contemporary media environment.

The Value of Media Studies for ESC Research

In this chapter I have explored how the ESC can contribute to our understanding of the development of contemporary media events in the context of European television history. I have highlighted both continuity and change in the ESC as television entertainment and pointed to the importance of adaptation and experimentation for maintaining the relevance of the ESC. By way of conclusion, I want to discuss some areas in which I think media studies could make more of a contribution to ESC studies as a field. Media studies looks at media as an assemblage encompassing technology and production, content and form, distribution and reception. Media studies research on the ESC has so far perhaps been most interested in audiences and reception (e.g., Kazakov & Hutchings, 2019; Miazhevich, 2017; Sandvoss, 2008). Less research has been done, for example, on the audiovisual aesthetics of the ESC, with the exception of José Patricio Pérez-Rufí and Águeda María Valverde Mestre's (2020) recent study about music video aesthetics in the contemporary ESC. Scholars from different fields have studied the articulation of nationality, gender and sexuality in Eurovision performances, analysing elements such as lyrics, costumes, choreography and gestures. However, less attention has been paid to the way these elements are mediated: how camera work and editing create dramaturgy, how close-ups are used for emphasis, and how the creation of Eurovision performances has changed with the development of technology and aesthetics. Yet, considering these kinds of questions would help to deepen even the analysis of the cultural meanings of ESC performances.

Another area in which media studies could make more of a contribution to ESC research is production. Within media studies, interest in production studies has grown over the past decade. Indrek Ibrus et al. (2019) exemplify this trend in their study of how the Estonian public service broadcaster Eesti Rahvusringhääling (Estonian Public Broadcasting) has developed the Estonian national final *Eesti Laul* (The Estonian Song) into a large-scale, cross-media event by entering into a partnership with private companies such as the Saku Suurhalli arena and the media company Eesti Meedia (Estonian Media). Earlier, several articles have addressed issues relating to the production of the ESC itself, such as the objectives of national broadcasters and other stakeholders (e.g., Bolin, 2006; Jordan, 2015; Skey et al., 2016). Yet, a more extensive study of the production of the ESC is missing. The ESC offers valuable material for studying the production culture of large, transnational media events. Moreover, at a time when the transnational production of television fiction is a major trend in European television industry, the ESC provides an example of the long tradition of transnational collaboration in public service television (see Pajala, 2021).

Finally, the field of ESC studies could perhaps benefit from media studies in considering its relationship to various research materials. The recent decades, as research on the ESC has grown, have witnessed a huge change in the availability and cultural status of Eurovision shows. To use a personal example, when I started doing research on Eurovision in the early 2000s, it was hard to access old ESC broadcasts. At the time, Finland, like many other countries, did not have a public television archive. The Finnish Broadcasting Company's (Yleisradio, YLE) programme archives were primarily meant for internal use, but I was able to gain access to them as a member of a research project on media history. I remember the first time I visited YLE to watch videos of 1970s Finnish national selections. The programmes looked alien and fascinating to me: the hosts addressed viewers in a tone that seemed formal and serious, not what I would have expected from an entertainment programme at all. Was this what television entertainment was like in the 1970s? What I experienced was a kind of a shock at the difference between past television and television as I knew it. Television scholar Charlotte Brunsdon (2004, p. 126) has described this experience of watching archived television as an encounter with the "*unheimlich* quality to pace and tone and relationships in these programmes which throws in to relief what we now take for granted". Now, of course, the availability of old ESCs has been transformed and the 1970s Finnish national finals can be viewed on YLE's public online archive. As Brunsdon (2009, p. 29) notes, for scholars this transformation "affects more than the availability of the study text". It is a different task to describe to readers media that they have not seen than media that is available to them (ibid.). As old ESC shows circulate on television, DVD and YouTube, they gain new contexts and meanings. The experience of watching an old ESC programme on YouTube, for instance, is very different from watching it on television—the image ratio may be altered, the YouTube algorithm surrounds the video with re-commendations of other content, comments and commercials provide new framings for the video, the viewer can easily stop and skip the video ... The specific qualities of different media therefore shape how Eurovision scholars interact with their research material. Being mindful of these qualities can help us to sharpen our analyses of the ESC as a cultural phenomenon.

Notes

1 Some material in this section is based on previous publications in Finnish in Pajala (2007) and Pajala (2021).
2 Central Archives for Finnish Business Records (ELKA), YLE collection, folder 3397:2359:"Referat av Nordvisionsmötet i Helsingfors 29/2-2/3 1964". Denmark's television did eventually leave the contest for the period from 1967 to 1977.
3 In 1980, the intermission between the last entry and the voting lasted about eight minutes and was filled by a single performance by a steel pan band; the voting took a little over half an hour. In 2021, the break between the last competing entry and the start of the voting had extended to about fifty-three minutes and the voting lasted close to an hour. The longer interval is explained partly by the need to make time for the public televote, including showing several recaps of the songs and verifying the votes. However, the break between the songs and the voting was shorter when televoting was first introduced.

References

Anon (2013). "The Eurovision Song Contest is a battlefield": Panel discussion with Eurovision Song Contest producers. In K. Fricker & M. Gluhovic (Eds.), *Performing the 'new' Europe: Identities, feelings, and politics in the Eurovision Song Contest* (pp. 94–107). Palgrave Macmillan.

Bolin, G. (2006). Visions of Europe: Cultural technologies of nation states. *International Journal of Cultural Studies*, *9*(2), 189–206.

Brunsdon, C. (2004). Taste and time on television. *Screen*, *45*(2), 115–129.

Brunsdon, C. (2009). Television criticism and the transformation of the archive. *Television & New Media*, *10*(1), 28–30.

Couldry, N., & Hepp, A. (2018). The continuing lure of the mediated centre in times of deep mediatization: *Media events* and its enduring legacy. *Media, Culture & Society*, *40*(1), 114–117.

Dayan, D., & Katz, E. (1992). *Media events: The live broadcasting of history*. Harvard University Press.

Ellis, J. (2000). *Seeing things: Television in the age of uncertainty*. I.B. Tauris.

EBU. (n.d.). *Your Guide to EBU Services*. https://www.ebu.ch/files/live/sites/ebu/files/Publications/EBU-Members-brochure_EN.pdf

EuroSong News. (2003). Interview Yvonne Littlewood. *EuroSong News*, *83*, 13–17.

Evans, E.J. (2011). The evolving media ecosystem: An interview with Victoria Jaye, BBC. In P. Grainge (Ed.), *Ephemeral media: Transitory screen culture from television to YouTube* (pp. 105–121). British Film Institute.

Fricker, K., & Gluhovic, M. (Eds.). (2013). *Performing the 'new' Europe: Identities, feelings, and politics in the Eurovision Song Contest*. Palgrave Macmillan.

Georgiou, M. (2008). "In the end, Germany will always resort to hot pants": Watching Europe singing, constructing the stereotype. *Popular Communication*, *6*(3), 141–154.

Ibrus, I., Rohn, U., & Allessandro Nanì, A. (2019). Searching for public value in innovation coordination: How the Eurovision Song Contest was used to innovate the public service media model in Estonia. *International Journal of Cultural Studies*, *22*(3), 367–382.

Jordan, P. (2015). From Ruslana to Gaitana: Performing "Ukrainianness" in the Eurovision Song Contest. *Contemporary Southeastern Europe*, *2*(1), 110–135. http://www.contemporarysee.org/en/jordan

Kazakov, V., & Hutchings, S. (2019). Challenging the 'information war' paradigm: Russophones and Russophobes in online Eurovision communities. In M. Wijermars & K. Lehtisaari (Eds.), *Freedom of expression in Russia's new mediasphere* (pp. 137–158). Routledge.

Kyriakidou, M., Skey, M., Uldam, J., & McCurdy, P. (2018). Media events and cosmopolitan fandom: "Playful nationalism" in the Eurovision Song Contest. *International Journal of Cultural Studies*, *21*(6), 603–618.

Miazhevich, G. (2017). Paradoxes of new media: Digital discourses on Eurovision 2014, media flows and post-Soviet nation building. *New Media & Society*, *19*(2), 199–216.

Miettunen, H. (1966). *Radio- ja TV-opin perusteet*. Weilin + Göös.

Pajala, M. (2006) *Erot järjestykseen! Eurovision laulukilpailu, kansallisuus ja televisiohistoria*. Nykykulttuuri.

Pajala, M. (2007). Epätelevisionomaista spektaakkelitelevisiota? Eurovision laulukilpailu 1960-luvun suomalaisessa televisioympäristössä. In J. Wiio (Ed.), *Television viisi vuosikymmentä: Suomalainen televisio ja sen ohjelmat 1950-luvulta digiaikaan* (pp. 292–308). Suomalaisen Kirjallisuuden Seura.

Pajala, M. (2021). Laulukilpailusta show-kilpailuksi? Televisiospektaakkelin ylirajaistuva tuotanto Eurovision laulukilpailussa. *Lähikuva, 34*(1), 9–32.

Pérez-Rufi, J.P., & Valverde Mestre, Á.M. (2020). The spatial-temporal fragmentation of live television video clips: Analysis of the television production of the Eurovision Song Contest. *Communication & Society, 33*(2), 17–31.

Raykoff, I., & Tobin, R.D. (Eds.). (2007). *A song for Europe: Popular music and politics in the Eurovision Song Contest.* Ashgate.

Robertson, B. (2021, March 11). Melodifestivalen, angry songwriters, and directors in the spotlight. *ESCInsight.* https://escinsight.com/2021/03/06/melodifestivalen-angry-songwriters-directors-spotlight/

Sandvoss, C. (2008). On the couch with Europe: The Eurovision Song Contest, the European Broadcast Union and belonging on the old continent. *Popular Communication, 6*(3), 190–207.

Scannell, P. (1996). *Radio, television and modern life: A phenomenological approach.* Blackwell.

Singleton, B., Fricker, K., & Moreo, E. (2007). Performing the queer network: Fans and families at the Eurovision Song Contest. *SQS, 2*, 12–24.

Skey, M., Kyriakidou, M., McCurdy, P., & Uldam, J. (2016). Staging and engaging media events: A study of the 2014 Eurovision Song Contest. *International Journal of Communication Studies, 10*, 3381–3399.

Waysdorf, A.S. (2020). This is our night: Eurovision again and liveness through archives. In P.D. Keidl, L. Melamed, V. Hediger, & A. Somaini (Eds.), *Pandemic media: Preliminary notes toward an inventory* (pp. 295–302). Meson Press.

Wheatley, H. (2016). *Spectacular television: Exploring televisual pleasure.* I.B. Tauris.

Williams, R. (1990). *Television: Technology and cultural form* (2nd ed.). Routledge.

Ytreberg, E. (2017). Towards a historical understanding of the media event. *Media, Culture & Society, 39*(3), 309–324.

14 From Trouble to Bubble? The Ambiguous Relationship between Professional Journalists and Fan Media in the Eurovision Song Contest

Irving Wolther

Since its creation in 1956, the Eurovision Song Contest (ESC) has become a media event comparable to major sporting events such as the World Cup or the Olympic Games. In their concept of media events, Daniel Dayan and Elihu Katz (Dayan & Katz, 1992) refer to live events that interrupt daily routines and schedules, are pre-planned and organized by a large public or other bodies, involve ceremonial elements that are presented with reverence, and electrify very large audiences. All these characteristics undoubtedly apply to the ESC. Other characteristics defined by Dayan and Katz do not fit the competition, for example that the original impulse for creating media events lies outside the media itself.

Media scholars Scherer and Schlütz (2003) therefore created the term 'media-staged (pseudo)media event'[1], further developing Daniel J. Boorstin's concept of 'pseudo-events', which, unlike real events, are planned and arranged for the sole purpose of triggering media coverage. The success of the pseudo-event is measured by the amount of coverage provided. Since the production of pseudo-events costs money, "somebody has an interest in disseminating, magnifying, advertising, and extolling them as events worth watching or worth believing" (Boorstin, 1962, p. 39). Scherer and Schlütz also conclude from the great effort involved in the organization of such pseudo-events that the organizers are pursuing precise objectives (Scherer & Schlütz, 2003, p. 17). In the case of the ESC, these relate first and foremost to showcasing the technical and organizational superiority of public television broadcasting over private competitors (Wolther, 2006, p. 64 ff.).

However, with the exception of Scherer and Schlütz's analysis of the German national final for the ESC in 2000 in Hanover, press work at the ESC has not yet been an area of scholarly focus. This is surprising for a media event primarily aiming at a large media coverage. This chapter tries to shed light on this particularly interesting field of research from a German perspective, describing how press work developed throughout the past decades, and how this knowledge serves for teaching journalism to students. It argues that alongside the building of the Eurovision brand, the European Broadcasting Union (EBU) has also

DOI: 10.4324/9781003188933-17

streamlined its communication practices to have the maximum control over the image of the contest conveyed in all sorts of media, and to facilitate press work for its member broadcasters. Guided interviews with professional journalists, fan journalists and press officers offer an important insight into the complex relationship between journalists, organizing bodies and fans.

A Music Show outside the Focus of Music Journalism

Until 2000, the perception of the ESC as a music competition was justified by paragraph two of its official rules: "The purpose of the Contest is to promote high-quality original songs in the field of popular music, by encouraging competition among songwriters and composers through the international comparison of their songs" (EBU, 1999, p. 2). The "World's Most Popular Song Contest" (Thielen, 2016) was considered, back then, to be a song writing competition, and music journalists reporting on the ESC still consider it as such (Grow, 2021) or are pointing to its origins (Bayer, 2020).

After the increasing commercialisation of the contest in the late 1990s (Vuletic, 2018, p. 177 ff.) and a subsequent branding initiative in 2004, when the ESC received a unique logo (EBU, 2017, p. 3), the EBU deleted the goal of promoting music from its official rules. Since then, the document only refers to the contest as a "state-of-the-art, world-class television production of a competition between musical acts representing countries of the Members of the European Broadcasting Union (EBU)" — in accordance with the EBU's self-conception as a provider of "world-class content from news to sports and music" (European Broadcasting Union, 2021) for its member broadcasters. A detailed production *bible* ensures "that there is consistency over time, and the competition retains a unique 'brand' within an increasingly competitive (and global) media landscape" (Skey, 2020, p. 10).

Even before the branding initiative, the music presented at the ESC was rarely in the focus of German media coverage. Dedicated music magazines like *Rolling Stone, Musikexpress* (Music Express) or *Musikmarkt* (Music Market) either did not mention the contest at all or criticized the lack of quality and commercial appeal, at least for the German entries (Der Musikmarkt, 1989, p. 36). However, they could not totally ignore a music show which — with or without satisfying results in terms of ranking or commercial success of the songs — continued to bring in large audiences (Koptuk, 2020). Therefore, to assure coverage without having to pay for travel and accommodation, they started to rely on freelance reporters who were already attending the ESC: that is, the fans. Yet, how did fans enter the ranks of the accredited press?

The First Fan Media Present at the ESC

The author attended his first ESC as an accredited member of the German delegation back in 1992. A few months after the reunification of Germany, the Mitteldeutscher Rundfunk (Central German Broadcasting, MDR) had taken over the role as broadcaster in charge for organizing the national final and picking the entry which was going to represent Germany in that year's ESC in Malmö[2]. After some disappointing results in the late 1980s, the Bayerischer Rundfunk (Bavarian Broadcasting, BR) had handed this task to the newly created regional broadcaster operating in the formerly East German federal states of Thuringia, Saxony, and Saxony-Anhalt. The press centre at the Stadthalle Magdeburg was freely accessible, and the press officers working for MDR urged people to apply for accreditation in Malmö to have MDR's first ESC efforts covered by as many German journalists as possible.

In 1989, two German fans, Martina Frambach and Peter Smeets, had attended the ESC in Lausanne as part of the German delegation for the first time: "Martina called the Bayerischer Rundfunk to ask for tickets, and they told her that a special department working only from January to May would care for the Eurovision Song Contest and connected her to the person in charge, Mrs Wieland" (Smeets, 2021). The lady invited them as guests of BR — with the possibility to attend rehearsals and press conferences. One year later, Smeets applied for regular accreditation with the help of his cousin who owned a local newspaper. "I was writing small articles, nothing big, but they were published", he adds proudly.

It is worthwhile to mention that coverage on the ESC by regular German media had become very limited at that time, and the big newspapers and magazines in several other countries had lost their interest in the competition, as well. Therefore, most national fan clubs emerging in the late 1980s were focussing on making up for this lack of information with their own newsletters, for example in Belgium (*Euroviziertjes* since 1986), the United Kingdom (*Eurovision Network News* since 1987), Spain (*Eurovisivos* since 1990), the Netherlands (*Eurovisions Artists* since 1992), and Germany (*Euro-Report* since 1990 and *OGi-Revue* since 1991). Additionally, from 1985, the international fan network OGAE (Organisation Générale des Amateurs de l'Eurovision) provided its members with its English language *OGAE News* on a quarterly basis (being edited by the national branches of OGAE in Finland, Israel, France, and finally by Irish-born Ivor Lyttle in Germany).

It is debatable whether or not these fanzines were delivering the media coverage the press officers from the national broadcasters involved in the ESC were looking for. The fact is that accreditation had been given to their editors since the late 1980s. As such, in 1992 the author was one of the few accredited German journalists in Malmö, along with Jan Feddersen, an ESC fan writing for the cooperative-owned daily newspaper *taz*, and Horst Senker, who worked as a radio journalist for Westdeutscher Rundfunk (West German Broadcasting, WDR).

From Fan to Journalist

Horst Senker's professional career is particularly interesting[3]. He watched his first ESC in 1969 and became a fan the year after, starting to collect all kinds of information about the competition. During his studies in media pedagogy, he

Figure 14.1 Evolution of the OGAE fan magazine's cover design between 1985 (*Eurovision News Bulletin*) and 2014 (*ESC-zine*).

began working for a number of radio and television stations, especially the WDR (Senker, n. d.). When he focused his journalistic work on music, his knowledge of the ESC that he had accumulated over the years made him a sought-after specialist for the contest (Senker, 2021). In 1982, he applied to be a member of the German jury for the ESC and was invited the next year to be part of the organizing committee for the 1983 ESC in Munich. The following year, Senker was again offered to be part of the organizing committee for the contest, then held in Luxembourg, intensifying his professional contacts with the radio journalist Günter Krenz who offered him the opportunity to start a career at the newly founded radio station WDR 4 (Senker, n. d.).

After a break in 1985, when he failed to become part of the organizing committee in Sweden due to the organizers requiring Swedish language skills, he turned back to the ESC as an accredited journalist in 1986 and worked until 1994 as an assistant to the German commentators. In 1995, he was offered the

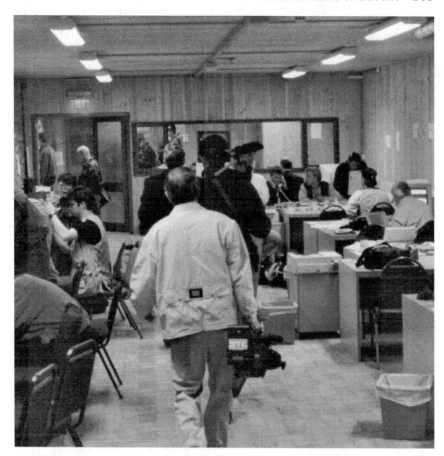

Figure 14.2 Press working area at the 1993 Eurovision Song Contest in Millstreet, Ireland. © Wolfgang Weber

opportunity to do the German commentary himself; however, his contract was not extended when Norddeutscher Rundfunk (Northern German Broadcasting, NDR) took over the organization of Germany's ESC entry from MDR in 1996. Since then, Senker has attended the ESC almost every year as a freelance radio journalist for the WDR and the German-language Belgian public broadcaster BRF.

For Senker, the ESC has become an integral part of his job: "The Song Contest, I have to stress it, has been the basis of my professional career. [...] I did not plan to start my career as a journalist through Eurovision, but then it happened, and I was more than happy about it", he states. Asked if he considers himself to be an ESC fan, however, he says: "Since I have earned a living from doing innumerable interviews and radio programs, I consider myself as a journalist specialized on the Contest. I am not the kind of fan who needs autographs from the artists; I just have a soft spot for Eurovision".

Senker's colleague, Thomas Mohr, has been working as a radio journalist for NDR since 1992, first as a freelancer, then as a permanent employee. He studied history, public law, and journalism in Hamburg and has been following the ESC since his early childhood (Domschky, 2021). However, like Senker, Mohr would rather not call himself a fan: "I have been covering the ESC as a journalist for many years and always referred to myself as a journalist to distance myself from Eurovision fans because in my opinion a certain distance to the subject is necessary to do proper journalistic work. [...] In private, I am a fan but professionally I am still a journalist" (Mohr, 2021). His argumentation reflects a famous quotation from a German reporter idol Hanns-Joachim Friedrichs, who, in his last interview, talked about what he learned when he worked for the British Broadcasting Corporation (BBC): "Keeping one's distance, not siding with a cause, not even a good one..." (Leinemann & Schnibben, 1995). Friedrichs was referring to professional behaviour in the face of tragedies, and this sentence has been often misinterpreted as an expectation for the total impartiality of journalists. However, it was and still is widely repeated in Germany as a guideline for good journalism.

"Meriting" Accreditation

After 1992, the number of accredited fans quickly increased[4] — and thus the potential for conflict with those who were gaining money with their journalistic work at the ESC. "It was a handicap because it became difficult to get hold of press kits. In the 1990s, colleagues started complaining a lot that there was a run on these press kits and that the fans were, so to say, better equipped than the journalists", Senker remembers. Before the beginning of the digital era, it was the biggest challenge for him as a radio journalist to get hold of audio recordings of the participating entries to present them in his morning show on the day of the final (Senker, 2021). Suddenly, he found himself competing with accredited fans looking for press kits as collector's items — since many of the songs were only released as promotional singles and were not available for regular purchase.

This situation led to sometimes violent scrambles for presumedly rare items, and several press officers had traumatic experiences of wild crowds rushing towards them, pressing them against a wall, snatching out of their hands the compact discs which were meant to be handed out individually, and sometimes even grabbing between their legs to fish the promotional materials out of their bags[5]. When, in 1999, a mob tumbled down an exhibition wall, carrying along a head of press, the delegations increasingly collected business cards from the media interested in press material to select which accredited people should get hold of the press kits and deposited them in their respective pigeonholes. This practice made it necessary for those covering the ESC to demonstrate more legitimate journalistic interest, possibly by working for a bigger media outlet or, even more promisingly, for a radio station[6].

In this context, Senker (and most other interviewees working professionally at the ESC) distinguishes between three groups: journalists, fans and fans working journalistically. This distinction was somehow internalized by the accredited fan community itself, with an increasing awareness that the privileges offered through accreditation needed to be "merited". This urge for "meriting" the accreditation came along with a continuous self-improvement of those fans who reported for small local newspapers and/or fanzines. Fan media became more and more professional, not least thanks to the increasing availability of consumer software making the processes of layout, photo and audio editing that had previously been reserved for professionals easily practicable for non-professionals (for the disruptive changes in the media ecosystem caused by convergence and digitization see e.g. Túñez-López et al., 2019). Publications that started as stapled leaflets consisting of glued newspaper cuttings and typescript text photocopied in black and white, progressively turned into four-colour magazines with an appealing layout and an editorial line.

Accreditation as a Bottleneck

However, this development created a new sort of fan hierarchy, privileging fans who "merited" their accreditation through journalistic work. This was especially the case for Germany, which, from the 1990s, saw the number of people wishing to be accredited growing continuously. When NDR took over the responsibility for Germany's entry, many fans who used to be accredited were rejected. This increased the pressure on those accepted to improve their reach — and caused increasing ill will against those who were accredited, despite "meriting" their privileges through journalistic work.

Yet, the increase in accredited fans started creating problems for the host broadcasters to plan for working spaces and other facilities in the press centre. For the national delegations, this development posed problems in terms of planning the amount of promotional material to prepare and how to organize their individual receptions in a way that would not see their buffets plundered by a hungry pack without having the slightest promotional impact. However, the introduction of F-accreditations in 2006[7], aimed at fans who seemingly do not need to get access to the working areas, did not lower the number of accredited people[8]. On the contrary, even scholars who wanted to conduct fieldwork at the ESC started offering journalistic services to local newspapers in order to do so (Bohlman & Polychronakis, 2013, p. 75).

The decision of who would get what kind of accreditation lay, and still lies, in the hands of the national broadcasters. Iris Bents has been working for the NDR since 1996. The graduate theologian started working as a freelancer at the *Hamburger Abendblatt* and broadened her journalistic skills as an editor for various news magazines and programme guides before she joined the NDR (Anonymous, 2016). As the head of press (HoP) in the German delegation for the ESC, she is one of the responsibles for deciding who is being accredited for Germany (with one exception 2021). "We are bound to the number of accreditations the EBU is offering us, so I need to select. In order to do so, I need to know how big a media outlet actually is, and in the end, I'd rather accept someone working for stern.de or the FAZ or faz.net instead of someone doing coverage for a very small fan club" (Bents, 2021).

Assessment and Abuse

However, the German head of press considers fan media to be "extremely important". To assure a fair accreditation process, she has, over the years, compiled a list with national and international online and offline fan media, their respective reach, and their representatives. "In the run-up to the accreditation process, I am contacting many of them to send me some of their material published, or they have to give me the name of a supervisor who can tell me about their activities. I am quite busy doing that", Bents explains and stresses that she does not know any other television format for which the NDR demonstrates so much care towards fans and fan media as it does with the ESC (Bents, 2021).

Applicants who have their accreditation refused by their national broadcaster occasionally contact delegation members they know from previous ESCs to try to get themselves accredited by countries they had never been to, or as the fan blog *EuroVisionary* puts it: "In the past years it has been known that fans from countries with a big fan scare went through smaller countries in order to get accreditation" (Jensen, 2009). Though this practice was stopped in 2009 when the EBU required people to have their primary residence in the country to which they applied for accreditation, applicants are still trying to figure out ways to sneak themselves in with the help of delegation members they have become friends with — sometimes offering to do voluntary work in exchange for the accreditation.

This practice raises questions in terms of journalistic independence and freedom of the press, when the accreditation is no longer just a means to gain access to the press centre to do one's journalistic work but becomes a kind of remuneration for this work. And it extends far beyond fans being accredited by media outlets in exchange for coverage without being paid: some national delegations seem to have entrusted fans with functions that originally were fulfilled by employees of the respective national broadcaster in order to save money. The author was even informed of one case, when employees of a national broadcaster were asked to use their annual leave for working at the ESC — and were replaced by fan volunteers after they refused.

Fan Careers

The fact that even the EBU's official ESC website eurovision.tv was for a long time relying on a voluntary workforce was addressed in an article by the official German ESC website eurovision.de:

> *Unlike the volunteers at major events such as the Olympic Games, who look pro bono after guests and artists, helping their home country to put on a great event on a one-off basis, the same authors have largely been working for WOW!works for years — as volunteers. They create content that is marketed and managed by the eurovision.tv website for free. WOW!works has been commissioned by the EBU to manage this website and receives money for doing so.*
> (Feddersen & Werwinski, 2015)

Figure 14.3 Press working area at the 2009 Eurovision Song Contest in Moscow, Russia. © Stefan Engel

Until 2019, the EBU had outsourced its communication and social media for the ESC, first to the Dutch company WOW!works created by Sietse Bakker, the editor-in-chief of esctoday.com, a fan website he started in October 2000 as an eighteen-year-old to impress his girlfriend, a devoted ESC fan. He was hired as Manager for New Media in 2006 to improve the EBU's own ESC website and subsequently rose within the organization, becoming event supervisor for the Junior Eurovision Song Contest in 2012 and executive producer for the 2021 ESC in Rotterdam (Ooms, 2019).

Even though Bakker's position as a service provider earning money with the voluntary work of other fans was and still is controversial (Anonymous, 2019; Feddersen, 2015; Rau, 2013), he is more admired than criticized by the fan media (Ooms, 2019; Peters, 2019). His career is a striking example of a former fan's success story at the ESC. However, he is not the only one. There are numerous fans

Figure 14.4 Press working area at the 2012 Eurovision Song Contest in Baku, Azerbaijan. © Stefan Engel

who used their accreditations for establishing contacts with artists and taking over their management: Ivor Lyttle, former editor of *EuroSongNews*, the fanzine of the international fan club OGAE, is now responsible for the commentators' briefing; and the current communications lead for the ESC, Dave Goodman, is a journalist and long-time ESC fan, who first began working for the EBU in 2013.

The Position of an EBU Representative

Unlike Senker and Mohr, Goodman openly acknowledges his love for the ESC: "It was always an ambition of mine to work professionally on Eurovision, but that is because I love the contest. [...] I mean, I work on Eurovision and I use my professional skills on the event now but I wouldn't want to have this job if I wasn't a fan of the event" (Goodman, 2021). He was first asked to cover the contest in

Figure 14.5 Press working area at the 2015 Eurovision Song Contest in Vienna, Austria. © Irving Benoît Wolther

2006 for BBC Radio Manchester, when the Mancunian Daz Sampson represented the United Kingdom in Athens. When Goodman left the BBC to work for Radio Netherlands Worldwide in 2009, he pitched to his new editor that, as a European news show, they should cover the ESC. Since then, he has attended the ESC every year, covering the contest for various employers, until, in 2013, he finally had the chance to work in the radio news department of the EBU:

> *I moved from that department into the communications department because obviously journalism and communications are sort of two sides of the same coin. [...] My ambition was always to work on Eurovision for the EBU, if possible, and it never seemed practical when I was a journalist because that was the career I pursued. But when I found myself working in radio in Geneva, and I was closer to the EBU, and I knew more about what the EBU did in other areas*

it became much more of something that was achievable. [...] So, when I got into the EBU that was my aim, to try and get over to the communications department and work with the Eurovision Song Contest team, but that came later. It wasn't immediate because at the time that was all handled externally by WOW!works".

(Goodman, 2021)

The ambition came true in 2019, when the EBU decided to take back control over its event communication activities, following the internalization of the event supervisor role in 2011: "There was a feeling within the EBU that a lot of the knowledge around the Song Contest was external, and it needed to be internalized because it needed to sit within the organization to be passed on to other people", Goodman explains. The journalistic approach of the new communications lead became evident when he introduced new, more transparent accreditation categories, reflecting the reach and target groups of the respective media: P1 (fan community media), P2 (regional and local media), P3 (national media), P4 (international media) and P5 (online press centre access only). The last category was introduced due to the Covid-19 pandemic, and but it will possibly continue into the future in order to downsize the on-site press centre (European Broadcasting Union, 2021a).

Even though Goodman underscores the importance of staying connected with the fan community media because they report on the event throughout the year, he leaves no doubt about his function: "My main objective is to encourage mainstream media to attend to see the event for itself because you can cover Eurovision from abroad, you can cover the event watching the television, but to see it in person, to see the whole circus, if you will, as it plays out and the machine of Eurovision and how much goes into it and the number of people that work on it and the resources that go into it, you have to be at the event to see. [...] So, we've always encouraged the big media to come and latterly media from the music press" (Goodman, 2021).

Changing Media Landscapes

The admission of a growing number of fans into the ranks of accredited journalists since the early 1990s might be interpreted as a promotional strategy by the EBU, as Bohlman and Polychronakis (2013) do: "The expansion of the contest since 2000 entailed a growing number of accredited journalists covering Eurovision. Fans that actually were journalists or managed to get a last-minute professional affiliation with a local newspaper or radio station rushed to take advantage of the many press passes on offer. The EBU needed all these fan journalists to promote the contest, ideally in a way that would comply with its carefully constructed profile as prime time 'pure' entertainment" (Bohlman & Polychronakis, 2013, p. 68). However, this perspective neither reflects the complexity of relations between "real journalists" and "fan journalists", nor does it take into account the recent and somehow disruptive changes in the media sector.

Figure 14.6 Press working area at the 2021 Eurovision Song Contest in Rotterdam, the Netherlands. © Irving Benoît Wolther

In fact, the growing number of fans reporting on the ESC seems to be a corollary of the developments and changes associated with Web 2.0 and the development of a blogosphere that does not differentiate between voluntary and remunerated journalism. While the communication scientist Olaf Hoffjann concluded that journalists "look rather disparagingly on bloggers", he defines them in a study as "underrated journalists" (Hoffjann & Haidukiewicz, 2018; Klöckner, 2018). Media convergence might have offered people the tools to publish whatever they choose, but these tools can only be used in an effective and truly journalistic way by people with a corresponding know-how and knowledge[9]. Consequently, the journalist Johannes Fischer states: "Classic journalism and weblogs in Germany are becoming more and more similar. Many bloggers work in journalism, and blogging is also becoming more and more natural for journalists and news portals" (Fischer, 2014).

Still, journalists talk negatively about bloggers in general, and even research (at least in Germany) is characterized by a rather condescending attitude when speaking of "amateur journalists" (Hans-Bredow-Institut, 2012, p. 52). The aforementioned study, however, confirmed that basic journalistic standards and goals are the same between journalists and bloggers, regardless of journalistic training and editorial background (Hoffjann & Haidukiewicz, 2018, p. 6). For the blogger Kathryn Lauren Filling (2015), the main difference between journalists and bloggers lies in journalism being "just facts, while blogs contain the opinion of the writer. [...] Without traditional journalism, bloggers would be left without information to blog about". A look at the ESC blogosphere proves her right.

Conflict Potentials

Indeed, most fan blogs report information from the mainstream media, especially eurovision.tv. However, since the information given on eurovision.tv had previously been coming from fans volunteering as journalists, the perceived reliability of information did not seem to be connected to whether or not the person writing an article has a journalistic background. On the other hand, one will hardly find articles in fan media referring to other fan media ("as the fan site xy reports ..."), maybe except for esctoday.com which is known to have close connections to the EBU due to its specific history. This is remarkable, since most fan media put a lot of effort into producing exclusive content. Their access to first-hand information in the domain of the ESC seems to trigger a journalistic race like the one in the mainstream media.

Meanwhile, the mainstream media does not perceive fans and their activities as a handicap to their own work — on the contrary, journalists take advantage of their knowledge, as Horst Senker affirms: "I have already made a lot of features about fans who have a lot to say. They are just so dedicated and have all the information of all the decades at hand, which I used to know as a fan myself and which I have lost over the years" (Senker, 2021). His colleague Thomas Mohr even goes one step further: "In 2021, scandalous things happened in North Macedonia or Belarus, for example[10]. Thanks to the social media and the fan reporters, who also have their own positions on this, we were updated very quickly on what happened. I wonder if I would have learned about that so easily fifteen years ago" (Mohr, 2021). However, both admit that it was easier to get interviews with the artists when there was less fan media hunting for exclusive footage.

Conflict potentials between the accredited journalists in the ESC may also be found in the clashing interests of media professionals. Hans Hoff, who attended Eurovision between 2010 and 2013 for the *Süddeutsche Zeitung*, holds strong opinions on the recent developments in journalism — "Journalism does not exist anymore" (Hoff, 2015) or "the term 'journalist' is beyond repair" (Hoff, 2020) — especially regarding journalistic standards. For him, the biggest obstacle in his work at the ESC are the photographers: "They form a wall between the artist and the other journalists, through which you can rarely penetrate, and they are also rarely reprimanded in a way to say, 'okay, now you have your photos and now please get out and let the people talk'. That does not happen, because the artists and the organizers appreciate the power of pictures" (Hoff, 2021).

The photographer Rolf Klatt is working as a freelancer for eurovision.de. He complains about the increasing number of people taking pictures at the ESC: "If you work professionally [...] you don't want to go to the venue two or three hours in advance and queue up there, only to find yourself standing in front of a phalanx of amateurs who don't earn their money with photography, but for whom it's just an ambitious hobby" (Klatt, 2021). He feels that the working conditions for professional photographers have alarmingly deteriorated and warns of the consequences if they desist from the ESC: "It is not just about taking a picture but taking a picture on the right level. Exclusive pictures are a prerequisite for front pages. [...] If you only produce identical material the interest of the media decreases, because they might know that Eurovision is taking place, but can only choose from off-the-shelf images" (Klatt, 2021).

The EBU has reacted to the problems arising from their own practice to offer exclusive photo material on their website eurovision.tv, another problem that Klatt addressed in his interview. What was meant to help spread the news on the grandiosity of the ESC and make hundreds of fan blogs running (which would probably not survive without these pictures) turned out to suffocate the exclusivity required by the big media. When the author met Rolf Klatt at the ESC in Rotterdam, the EBU had offered him and his professional colleagues special places in the venue, enabling them to take concert pictures out of the common.

Conclusions

Looking back to the developments of media coverage of the ESC, it becomes obvious that the EBU does not follow a masterplan when it comes to organizing press work. The organization is taking on opportunities, reacting to new developments, tackling abuse, and learning from mistakes — like the ESC's set of rules, which have been continuously revised and extended throughout the past sixty-five editions of the contest. However, the EBU has always acted with the clear objective of increasing the media coverage of the contest, and this will be its focus in the future, too. New developments, like the pandemic-driven introduction of an online press centre, might be turned into powerful tools to provide journalists, fans, and fans working journalistically with information on the ESC machinery, even if they do not have the possibility to attend in person.

These developments will become even more important with the EBU exporting its Eurovision brand to the United States (European Broadcasting Union, 2021b) and possibly other parts of the world that journalists and fans cannot attend easily. However, being the umbrella organization of public broadcasters in Europe and the Mediterranean rim, the EBU bears a responsibility in terms of journalism — towards its audiences and towards the people who are working for and with it. In an increasingly challenging environment, credibility is essential to justify the existence of public broadcasting. This does not only apply to news programs but also to the ESC, which is much more than just entertainment.

If it is true that organizers, artists, media representatives, and fans have become part of a "Eurovision bubble" thereby dissolving boundaries between people of different professional backgr,ounds. This opens new opportunities, especially for career changers. The bubble, however, also bears the risk of neglecting the standards of professionalism, which is not a venial sin for public broadcasters under enemy fire. To tackle the complexity related to a multi-layered program like the ESC, the EBU needs to rely on journalists with a solid professional background. Their recent decisions in terms of event communication have proven that the organization is aware of that.

Notes

1 If not stated otherwise, all German terms and citations have been translated by the author.
2 The Arbeitsgemeinschaft der öffentlich-rechtlichen Rundfunkanstalten der Bundesrepublik Deutschland (Working group of public broadcasters of the Federal Republic of Germany, ARD) is a joint organisation of Germany's regional public-service broadcasters. The network consists of nine independent broadcasters running their own regional television and radio programs und contributing in different proportions to the common nation-wide ARD program.
3 If not stated otherwise, all information on the background of the interviewees have been taken from personal interview conducted between 31 March and 9 June 2021.
4 Interesting enough, the number of people attending the San Diego Comic-Con, a convention for creators of comic books and their fans, evolved in a similar way, as a chart on reddit (u/eyeoutthere, 2014) suggests.
5 There have been repeated complaints about people grabbing CDs to put them on sale on eBay a few minutes after, sometimes even using a working space in the press centre to do so. In 2010 a group of fans, father, mother and two children, were reported to have their accreditations withdrawn by the EBU for that reason.
6 At the end of the 1990s there was a growing number of radio shows dealing with the Eurovision Song Contest on community radio stations all over Europe, e. g. *Eurostars* in Karlsruhe, Germany (since 1996) and *Radio International* in Den Haag, Netherlands (since 1997). The online radio station ESC Radio started in 2007.
7 2006 was also the year, when the Euro Fan Café was established as a separate venue for fans outside the Euroclub, the traditional meeting point for delegations and press.
8 In the following years, the EBU experimented with several different accreditation types from P1/P2 and F1/F2, respectively, to a confusing P/PF system in an attempt to regulate access to the different spaces in the press centre, thus creating a feeling of superiority among those who received a "real" P-accreditation.
9 Another important factor is the desire to communicate. Ivor Lyttle had to reduce the frequency of publication of the popular *EuroSongNews* because the national fan clubs contributed less and less to the magazine.
10 The Belarusian public broadcaster BNT picked a song for the Eurovision Song Contest in Rotterdam that aimed at ridiculing the opposition movement in the country while the North Macedonian representative Vasyl was attacked by nationalists for presumedly being pro-Bulgarian and gay.

References

Anonymous. (2016). *Iris Bents – Head of Press Germany*, watchado.com. https://www.whatchado.com/de/stories/iris-bents

Anonymous. (2019). Can a potential bid of Sietse Bakker for EBU's job cause some countries to withdraw? https://oikotimes.co.uk/sietse-bakker-eurovision-ebu-job/

Bents, I. (2021, 27.05.2021). Telephone interview with Iris Bents [Interview].

Bohlman, A. F., & Polychronakis, I. (2013). Eurovision Everywhere: A Kaleidoscopic Vision of the Grand Prix. In D. Tragaki (Ed.), *Empire of Song: Europe and Nation in the Eurovision Song Contest*. Scarecrow Press. https://books.google.de/books?id=NiHHjmEZcGEC

Boorstin, D. J. (1962). *The Image: Or, What Happened to the American Dream*. Atheneum. https://books.google.nl/books?id=2_0qAAAAIAAJ

Dayan, D., & Katz, E. (1992). *Media Events*. Harvard University Press. https://books.google.nl/books?id=Z64eoZiik5wC

Der Musikmarkt (Ed.). (1989). *30 Jahre Single Hitparade*. Josef Keller Verlag.

Domschky, B. (2021). Thomas Mohr: ESC-Fan seit Kindertagen. *2021*(13.06.). Retrieved 25.03.2021, from https://www.eurovision.de/news/Thomas-Mohr-ESC-Fan-seit-Kindertagen,mohr165.html

European Broadcasting Union. (2021a). Accreditation. https://eurovision.tv/mediacentre/accreditation

European Broadcasting Union. (2021b). 'American Song Contest' on screens in 2022. Retrieved 16.06.2021, from https://eurovision.tv/story/american-song-contest-2022

Feddersen, J. (2015). Wer hat die Macht im ESC? Jonglieren für Europa. https://taz.de/Wer-hat-die-Macht-im-ESC/!5248087/

Feddersen, J., & Werwinski, J. (2015). Wer Spaß hat, braucht keinen Lohn? Retrieved 14.06.2021, from https://www.eurovision.de/news/Unbezahlte-Arbeit-fuer-ESC,ebu128.html

Filling, K. L. (2015, 15.06.). Difference between blogging and journalism. *Kathryn Filling CAS272*. https://sites.psu.edu/fillingcas272/2015/03/05/difference-between-blogging-and-journalism/

Fischer, J. (2014). Was Blogger von Journalisten unterscheidet. Retrieved 15.06.2021, from https://www.goethe.de/de/kul/med/20364508.html

Goodman, D. (2021, 09.06.2021). Telephone interview with Dave Goodman [Interview].

Hans-Bredow-Institut. (2012). *Tabellenband zur Journalistenbefragung Tagesschau* https://www.hans-bredow-institut.de/uploads/media/Publikationen/cms/media/30a00b5039de0a084f16c70068db4ad538f08b96.pdf

Hoff, H. (2015). Der Journalismus existiert nicht mehr. Retrieved 15.06.2021, from https://www.dwdl.de/hoffzumsonntag/50332/der_journalismus_existiert_nicht_mehr/?utm_source=&utm_medium=&utm_campaign=&utm_term=

Hoff, H. (2020). Der Begriff "Journalist" ist nicht mehr zu gebrauchen. Retrieved 15.06.2021, from https://www.dwdl.de/hoffzumsonntag/77757/der_begriff_journalist_ist_nicht_mehr_zu_gebrauchen/?utm_source=&utm_medium=&utm_campaign=&utm_term=#:~:text=Jeder%20kann%20sich%20Journalist%20nennen,l%C3%A4ngst%20unbrauchbar%2C%20meint%20Hans%20Hoff.

Hoff, H. (2021, 04.05.2021). Telephone interview with Hans Hoff [Interview].

Hoffjann, O., & Haidukiewicz, O. (2018). *Deutschlands Blogger – Die unterschätzten Journalisten* (OBS-Arbeitsheft, Issue 94). https://www.otto-brenner-stiftung.de/fileadmin/user_data/stiftung/02_Wissenschaftsportal/03_Publikationen/AH94_Blogger_Hoffjann.pdf

Jensen, C. (2009). Need accreditation and visa for Moscow – apply now! *EuroVisionary, 2021*(14.06.). Retrieved 16.02., from https://eurovisionary.com/eurovision-news/need-accreditation-and-visa-moscow-apply-now

Klatt, R. (2021, 30.04.2021). Telephone interview with Rolf Klatt [Interview].

Klöckner, M. (2018). "Blogger sind die unterschätzten Journalisten". Retrieved 15.06. 2021, from https://www.heise.de/tp/features/Blogger-sind-die-unterschaetzten-Journalisten-4123783.html

Koptuk, E. (2020). *Television reach of the Eurovision Song Contest in Germany from 1976 to 2019.* https://www.statista.com/statistics/418288/eurovision-song-contest-tv-reach-in-germany/

Leinemann, J., & Schnibben, C. (1995). »Cool bleiben, nicht kalt«. *SPIEGEL*(13). Retrieved 26.03., from https://www.spiegel.de/politik/cool-bleiben-nicht-kalt-a-73e327d0–0002-0001-0000-000009176410?context=issue

Mohr, T. (2021, 08.04.2021). Telephone interview with Thomas Mohr [Interview].

Ooms, G. (2019). Sietse Bakker: 'Final of Eurovision could be less long-winded. https://songfestival.be/en/interviews/sietse-bakker-finale-songfestival-kan-gerust-korter/

Peters, L. (2019). Vom Fan-Journalisten zum Executive Producer: Sietse Bakker wird Event-Verantwortlicher des ESC 2020. https://esc-kompakt.de/vom-fan-journalisten-zum-executive-producer-sietse-bakker-wird-event-verantwortlicher-des-esc-2020/

Rau, O. (2013, 14.06.). Sietse Bakker: der Sepp Blatter der Eurovision? https://www.aufrechtgehn.de/2015/10/sietse-bakker-der-sepp-blatter-der-eurovision/

Scherer, H., & Schlütz, D. (2003). *Das inszenierte Medienereignis: die verschiedenen Wirklichkeiten der Vorausscheidung zum Eurovision Song Contest in Hannover 2001.* Halem.

Senker, H. (2021, 31.03.2021). Telephone interview with Horst Senker [Interview].

Senker, H. (n. d.). *Horst Senker.* Westdeutscher Rundfunk. Retrieved 13.06. from https://www1.wdr.de/radio/wdr4/ueber-uns/team/moderatoren/horstsenker100.html

Smeets, P. (2021, 09.06.2021). Telephone interview with Peter Smeets [Interview].

Thielen, D. (2016). The world's most popular song contest – and you've never heard about it. HuffPost (18 February). https://www.huffpost.com/entry/the-worlds-most-popular-s_b_9252196

Túñez-López, M., Martínez-Fernández, V.-A., López-García, X., Rúas-Araújo, X., & Campos-Freire, F. (Eds.). (2019). *Communication: Innovation & Quality.* Springer International Publishing AG.

u/eyeoutthere. (2014). *Attendance at San Diego Comic-Con.* Retrieved 13.06. from https://www.reddit.com/r/dataisdata/comments/2jff2s/attendance_at_san_diego_comiccon/

Vuletic, D. (2018). *Postwar Europe and the Eurovision Song Contest.* Bloomsbury Academic.

Wolther, I. (2006). *'Kampf der Kulturen'. Der Eurovision Song Contest als Mittel national-kultureller Repräsentation.* Königshausen & Neumann.

15 Domesticity, Mass Media and Moving-Image Aesthetics: The Visual Identity of the Eurovision Song Contest as a Hospitable Platform

José Luis Panea

Introduction

Television, as a media device, enters millions of homes around the world every day. Its "symbolic capital", claims Pierre Bourdieu, lies in the generation of imaginaries that foster more or less subliminal messages which end up reverberating, on a daily basis, in our intersubjective ways of interpreting reality (1997: 11). Therefore, analyzing aesthetics today entails assessing how the mass media intervene in our most immediate collective experience by means of the power of the moving image (Blom et al., 2016).

In this regard, certain types of events broadcast by television (such as the Olympic Games and the World Expo) make visible (on account of their ritual, ceremonial nature) a certain notion of unity and transnational collaboration that, thanks to the medium of television, have been "domesticated" (i.e., brought to the domestic space of millions of viewers [Bolin, 2006]). As Maurice Roche (2000) explains, such events contrast with everyday TV programmes insofar as the former are sporadic albeit multitudinous—and often global, which makes them very especial occasions. Nowadays, social media enhance and amplify these events, all within an "affective culture" of appeal and approval in which the spectator, far from being a passive recipient, interacts with the content relayed (Pajala, 2013; Highfield et al., 2013).

The Eurovision Song Contest (ESC) is among the most peculiar cases, inasmuch as it promotes, similarly to sports events, a particular competitiveness, although through a neither objective nor measurable medium: music (Bohlman, 2013: 37). Even though the contest is no longer only about music (in fact, the music is often discredited [Coleman, 2008]), it uses the "song" concept as a vehicle for placing all the competing nations on an equal footing (since all songs are performed on the same stage) over a limited time frame (they have to be three minutes long [Bohlman, 2013: 42]). In consequence, the qualitative element (i.e., what parameters should we use to choose the best song?) keeps being one of the major questions of the show.

Although an example of international cooperation a priori, the ESC, created in the post-war era with the aim of reconstructing Europe through telecommunications

DOI: 10.4324/9781003188933-18

(Henrich-Franke, 2010; Coupe & Chaban, 2020), is ultimately a competition with a winner and an entire advertising machine behind it. These aspects both contribute to the spread not only of the work of the singers and producers but also of the images of the participating countries (Pajala, 2012). Furthermore, it shows the technical capabilities of each country through an expensive logistical display—and the consequent importance of the symbolic capital at stake (Bourdieu, 1997: 15). Indeed, some countries, such as the former Soviet and Yugoslav republics, which took part in the contest shortly after becoming independent in the 1990s, owe an improvement in their international image, along with the forging of an identity or narrative of their own, to their participation in this contest (Sandvoss, 2008: 197–198; Baker, 2019: 108).

The question here, then, is: how has each host venue designed, year after year, the stage set in order to support that image of cross-border friendly competitiveness. Has this image possibly been subverted? Is it still effective? The present study, rather than addressing identity aspects concerning specific participants, will focus on an element that is key to certain aesthetic and political questions related to the precise historical time in which each edition has taken place. That element is, all things considered, the main *support* of the visual identity of the contest: the stage.

State of the Question and Methodology

While a few articles appeared as far back as the 1990s, the take off of the scholarly bibliography on Eurovision dates back to 2007, with the publication of the collective volume *A Song for Europe: Popular Music and Politics in the Eurovision Song Contest*, edited by Raykoff and Tobin (2007). This compilation inspired the organisation of many conferences and encouraged the writing of numerous papers and books. For the most part, such publications have dealt with identity politics (in relation to culture, ethnicity and gender), as well as analyses of the voting systems (Yair, 2019: 1015–1016).

Nonetheless, Mari Pajala's article "Mapping Europe: Images of Europe in the Eurovision Song Contest" (2012) pioneered the analysis of the visual aspect of the event. Afterwards, Fatma Merve Fettahoğlu master's thesis, *The Impact of Technology and Traces of National Representation on Eurovision Stages* (2017) it provided a research survey of the stage design of the contest from a technical and statistical perspective, and includes interviews with the main scenographers. On this basis, after several conversations with her, I decided to further contribute to this topic. In my article "The Set Design of the Eurovision Song Contest: Aesthetics, Technology and Cultural Identity at the Dawn of European Reconstruction (1956–1993)" published in 2020 (in Spanish), I included a warning of the need for a critical analysis of the discursive aspects inherent to the stage sets of the ESC. Whereas Fettahoğlu's approach was more genealogical and technical, given her background in design, my approach was more theoretical, on account of my academic background in the field of aesthetics and art theory (in a vein closer to Pajala's work, from which her studies on "affective capitalism"

[2013] applied to the event are noteworthy). Recently, at the end of 2020 was published a very thorough study on the topic, the bachelor thesis of Manuel Jesús Pantión, *The Eurovision Song Contest: a Study of Florian Wieder Scenography* (2020), in Spanish as well.

Accordingly, this chapter should be understood as delving into two aspects of aesthetics that are especially appealing: the concepts of domesticity (inasmuch as the competition is brought into the homes of the viewers via television or the internet) and hospitality (in relation to its overwhelming reception and the gathering of many countries for a transnational event [Derrida & Dufourmantelle, 2006; Penchaszadeh, 2014]). However, the various stage sets for the event need to be particularised in order to coherently focus the inquiry on specific elements that would enable us to carry out a case-by-case study. Two different stage types are clearly identifiable throughout the ESC's history: first, those that use neutral themes, preferably based on geometrical shapes so as to allow each contestant's act a high degree of stage personalisation; and second, those that incorporate onstage symbols referring to the cultural and natural heritage and the local architecture of the host country (Fettahoğlu, 2017).

I will go in depth on the latter trend, with the aim of taking Pajala's, Fettahoğlu's and Pantión's research to a new discursive stage, contributing this way to academic fields with a study relating visual identity, politics and spectacle through the ESC. As for the time period of analysis, since my former article covered the period from the origins of the ESC to the 1990s (with the signing of the Maastricht Treaty), on this occasion I will delve into the stage designs from then until now. However, in order to make the thematic itinerary evident, intersections between different periods will also be traced.

The Visual Identity of the Eurovision Song Contest

Flowers for a Europe in its Prime

At the start of the ESC, the symbolism of the set designs was simple in order to make the event as neutral and diplomatic as possible (Vuletic, 2018: 24). Certain elements started appearing on stage with a view to subtly publicising the city and the country where the spectacle was held. In this respect, Hilversum proved to be a significant venue in 1958, since the tourist potential of the competition (a massive gathering of countries in a single city during a few days) was noticed as early as only three years after its inauguration (Henrich-Franke, 2010: 69). Consequently, it was decided (as a local visual nod) that about one thousand tulips, in pots and bouquets, would be arranged all over the stage, the grandstand and the orchestra, thus "branding the experience" through the "national flower" and immersing all the participating candidates (i.e., the countries) in a "Dutch" atmosphere (Fettahoğlu, 2017: 24). This served to emphasise both the (hospitable) welcoming willingness of the host country and the imposition of a particular (domestic) setting to all the performers, reminding them throughout where they were.

By contrast, the 1962 ESC in Luxembourg featured a set design by Jean-Paul Conzemius with a more household appearance, dominated by large lattice windows dressed with majestic curtains, as well as ceiling lamps and faux porcelain vases resting on several levels of the floor. Characteristic also was the presence of flower arrangements adorning the orchestra, which evoked a *horror vacui* feeling next to the limited space assigned for the main stage. A few years later, the 1969 Madrid edition saw fifteen thousand carnations being distributed all over the stage by the scenographer Bernardo Ballester. During the full-colour revolution of the 1970s, a greater deal of experimentation with space and geometric-futuristic designs was carried out (Panea, 2020: 31). Thenceforth, The Hague 1980 edition, with a set design created by Roland de Groot, featured plants (namely tulips) on stage (which was in the then-in-vogue geometric style). The last instance with flower centrepieces was in 1983 in Munich, on a stage designed by Hans Gailling and Marlies Frese. In this casee, the flowers occupied the wings behind the main stage and imitated the shapes and colours of the national flags of the participating countries.

Even though the first editions of the ESC originally took place in late March or April, since the 1980s they began to be held mostly in May, which has remained the case since 1994 (Vuletic, 2018: 39). This way, a certain spring atmosphere (what the above described aesthetics tried to evoke) could be achieved. Nevertheless, plant symbolism had a prominent role on only a few more occasions. The design for the 2005 ESC in Kyiv 2005, directed by Illya Lazorkin, drew its inspiration from the awakening metaphor ("Awakening" being the slogan of the event that year). It included organic shapes dotted about the stage representing sub-aquatic plants, lichens, ferns, unicellular beings and other "latent" organisms. This hinted at a "potential" life that emerges from the depths in the same way as Ukraine (here is the political nod) after that year's Orange Revolution (Jordan, 2014: 113). As the contest board stated:

> [...] The stage will be more than a place on which the artists perform their songs. It will become a Garden of Eden with mystical plants and animal life where growth, wealth, colours, beauty, creativity and light are in the order of the day. And a day that will be completely new, symbolizing the dawn of a new age for both the Song Contest and Ukraine itself.
>
> (Esctoday, 2005)

An electric blue colour along with bubbles (the leitmotiv of the animations shown) contributed to create an environment full of vitality. Furthermore, the use of the Eurostyle font on the scoreboard emphasised this European flavour. As can be noted, the political nature of a seemingly insignificant design was explicitly stated. The last two occasions on which the plant motif has been staged have been Stockholm in 2016 and Lisbon in 2018. Regarding the the former, the plant motif was evident in its slogan ("Come Together") and its dandelion logo rather than in the set created by Viktor Brattström and Frida Arvidsson (which belonged to the abstract or geometric group of designs [Jordan, 2016]). Both the visuals and the logo used flying dandelion flowers as an allusion to the unity

Figure 15.1 The stage of the 2005 ESC in Kyiv. © EBU/Zinteco.

in diversity that the contest advocates. As for Lisbon, subaquatic plants appeared again, albeit in a secondary fashion, with the core topic being the sea; as will be shown later, this stage set encompassed several of the thematic blocks presented in this chapter. (Figure 15.1)

The Importance of Skylines as Frames of Reference

As Penchaszadeh states, the harmonious distribution of spaces is key for boosting a certain feeling of hospitality (2011: 17). In this regard, harmony is a trope often related with nature, and that is why it is also so present in the ESC stage designs. Nature constitutes a surreptitious means to allude to the host country without too apparently imposing national symbols liable to make the ever increasing and diverse list of guest countries uncomfortable (Pajala, 2012: 6). In a groundbreaking bid, the undulating shapes of the stage set designed by Bo-Ruben Hedwall for the 1975 ESC in Stockholm, inspired by the Baltic Sea waves and the Scandinavian landscape, were a nod to the notion of a meeting place (Fettahoğlu, 2017: 37). Eleven years later, in Bergen in 1986, the Norwegian designers Per Fjeld, Ingolf Holme and Tore Brockstedt likewise drew their inspiration from the local landscape. In this case, it was glaciers, which provided such a specific frame for the contestants, who were surrounded by striking ice columns that limited the artists' individual creativity. The same trend was followed in Lausanne in 1989, when the stage manager, Gilbert Gessens, chose the silhouette of Mount Matterhorn for both the logo and the main stage. The latter, based on a neon-tube structure, had this time been made very versatile since its lighting gave much scope to create many different possible arrangements (47).

The venue for the 1994 ESC in Dublin was designed by a veteran team at the contest: Tom Nolan, Alan Pleass, Paula Farrell, and John Casey. The outline of the river Liffey had been drawn on the stage floor, and on the background a suggestive set simulated the skyline of the Irish capital, rounding off a picture capable of transporting the viewer to the host city (Blake Knox, 2015: 153). Years later, in adherence to a sort of "astral aesthetics" inspired by the new millenium, Aigars Ozoliņš designed for the edition in Riga in 2003 a stage set based on the geography of the Latvian capital after being metamorphosed into another planet within its own solar system. The message was reinforced by the use of a slogan, which was an emergent trend in those years. Following the example of Tallin in 2002 (with its "A Modern Fairytale"), Riga devised its own one, "Magical Rendezvous", which allude to the possibility of a free "reinvention" of the country, of its place in Europe, appealing to the fulfilment of a community dreamed of for so long (Jordan, 2014: 89; Yair, 2019: 1017). Later, in Belgrade in 2008, the main stage was arranged as the confluence of the two rivers that delimit the Serbian capital, thus also subscribing to the aquatic metaphor, which will be discussed further below. Finally, the 2012 ESC in Baku, organised by the Azerbaijani broadcasting corporation and stage-directed by Florian Wieder, shows that, despite the fact that many of the stage designs from the 2000s until now are not based on local culture anymore, they still contain allusions to the elements that characterise the host countries (Pantión, 2020: 99–100). In this way, the logo and the slogan "Light Your Fire" referred to Azerbaijan's adopted motto "The Land of Fire" (Baker, 2019: 105). (Figure 15.2)

Figure 15.2 The stage of the 2008 ESC in Belgrade. © EBU/Stage One.

The Aquatic Metaphor for an Emerging Europe

When Sweden and Norway again hosted the contest in 1992 and 1996 respectively, the scenographers opted for scenery and props making reference to these countries, but this time featuring, instead of landscapes, a Viking ship (Malmö 1992, by Goran Arfs) and an oil platform (Oslo 1996, by Bjarte Ulfstein and Sigrun Giil). The latter included water within the very stage—an element which is among the prevalent symbols in the ESC, as well as in its entries, as a metaphor to provide the contest with an atmosphere of ease, openness, serenity, and freedom. Following these marine aesthetics, the set for Birmingham in 1998 revolved around the fishing culture of the United Kingdom, with the stage in the shape of a whale. The spaciousness of the venue marked a turning point for the venues to come, which also took advantage of the removal of the orchestra pit to maximise the space devoted to the stage and to the stalls (Vuletic, 2018: 58).

On several occasions, the set design has combined natural and cultural elements, with Dublin 1994 serving as an example. In addition to the River Liffey being featured (as mentioned above), water was also present in the most-remembered interval act of the contest, the dance ensemble Riverdance (Baker, 2019: 112). Years later, the 2006 ESC in Athens subscribed to this same hybridity: although Ilias Ledakis designed a stage based on an architectural element (as will be shown further on), the logo and the visual identity of the edition made reference to the sea in order to highlight Mediterranean culture. This was also promoted, as is the case with most editions, through the postcards used as tourism advertising. Two years later, "Confluence of Sound" (Zaroulia, 2013: 39) was the slogan for the Belgrade edition, a venue outlined above whose visual identity, according to its designer Boris Miljković, dealt with the concept of "flow", with streams of paint in the colours of the Serbian flag merging together in the animations (Marković, 2008: 16). The stage design itself, directed by David Cushing, was inspired by the silhouettes of the Sava and Danube rivers, which run through the city, with the stage placed in the middle. As Bohlman and Polychronakis point out:

> […] the official Serbian organizers promoted a fresh image of the country at the "confluence" of Europe's rivers. The stage literally mapped the intersection of the Sava and the Danube, recalling the Balkans' history as a cultural crossroads, even suggesting that Serbia might constitute a "New" Central Europe (2013: 64).

The ocean kept being a source of inspiration in subsequent years. Florian Wieder, the designer of the most outstanding stages of the last decade, made reference to the armillary sphere and to Portuguese naval history in Lisbon in 2018 (Jordan, 2017). The set consisted of a circular platform with two bridges starting at both sides and leading to an elevated walkway. These structures hung above the stalls, so the audience sat just underneath—with the effect that the performances seemed as if they were emerging from among the crowd. Three structures in the shape of concentric rings, reminiscent of the armillary sphere, sheltered the whole set. As a backdrop, a colossal row of fifty-six upright, parallel, smoothly undulating bars towered above

Figure 15.3 The stage of the 2018 ESC in Lisbon. © EBU/Thomas Hanses.

the stage, with their interstices tracing subtle ripples that resembled sea waves, according to the scenographers Ola Melzig and Joan Lyman (M&M Production Management, 2018). (Figure 15.3)

Animals on Stage

Another aspect to analyse with regard to the presence of nature among the symbols of the contest is the use of animals as emblems, linked to a particular nation to a larger or lesser extent. As Roche states (2000: 128–132), animals can give to these kinds of international encounters (like the Olympics, too) a very friendly and even 'domestic' milieu, softening the rivalry of the competition. Although the 1974 ESC in Brighton set a precedent with its dove logo, the trend gained ground only in the early 1990s, parallel with the post-Cold War Europeanist mood, such as with the Maastricht Treaty process (McNamara, 2015). The success of international events such as the World Expo in Seville or the Barcelona 1992 Summer Olympics, also highlighted how the the concept of the mascot gained interest for its potential to create a friendly and even homey atmosphere. In this way, Eurocat was featured in Zagreb 1990, and a seagull showed up in the postcards for the 1992 ESC in Malmö. Notwithstanding these symbols being strongly linked to the culture of their respective countries, they were also used to celebrate unity in diversity—the triumph of "European culture" (Sandvoss, 2008: 193) through the innocence of these domesticated animals.

Nevertheless, animals would thereafter no longer been used as mascots, as the above-mentioned example of Birmingham 1998 shows. On that occasion, the topic of fishing was brought into a stage erected by the BBC, which had replaced the classic landscapes, buildings or objects representative of the host country for a whale, symbolising the old British Empire. The stage, dominated by undulating shapes, imitated the tail, fins and skeleton of this cetacean, according to its designer, Andrew Howe-Davies (BBC, 1999). Years later, in Athens in 2006, the jellyfish featured in the logo served to recall Greece's cultural connection with the sea; the logo for the Moscow edition in 2009 included the shape of a bird; while that for Malmö in 2013 (both the stage and the logo) that of a butterfly. All of these were symbols of the freedom that the contest champions, which has also been conveyed through the recurring trope of water. Commenting on her own design for Malmö, Frida Arvidsson states:

> [t]o create the stage, inspiration was drawn from motion studies of butterfly wings and long-exposure photographs of moths in flight and from architectural details in modern 3D printed haute couture. These lines, motions and movements were perfect to transform into the basic shapes of the set.
>
> (Arvidsson, 2013)

As a last example, the stage design for the 2018 ESC in Lisbon was inspired by the ocean metaphor pointing to a world open to communication, as well as to Portugal's history in global exploration and the hospitality of Portuguese society (Lee Adams, 2017). As a matter of fact, the slogan chosen was "All Aboard!", and the logo, designed by Nicolau Tudela, was dominated by a seashell which also alluded to the warm welcome and the aim to make all the contestants part of the same structure—of the same project. (Figure 15.4)

Figure 15.4 The stage of the 2013 ESC in Malmö. © EBU/Frida Arvidsson.

The Architectural Turn: bringing Local History to a Global Stage

The agreements on Western European integration reached during the Cold War culminated in the Maastricht Treaty in 1993. That year the number of participating countries in Eurovision reached a peak of twenty-five. Most of the newly independent states that had been a part of Yugoslavia made their debut in those years, and the contemporary wartime experiences of Bosnia and Herzegovina and Croatia, together with recent memories of the fall of the Berlin Wall, motivated pacifist songs. In contrast to the wars in the south-eastern part of Europe, the ESC became more of a multicultural event where regional and local elements started to be significantly highlighted (Zaroulia, 2013: 32–33; Yair, 2019: 1017). At the 1992 ESC in Malmö 1, behind its Viking ship was "a representation of the Øresund Bridge – which, within a few years, would link Sweden with Denmark" (Blake Knox, 2015: 126). This is a prime example on how the contest was used by its organizers to delve into topics on union and celebration through stage designs. Nonetheless, as early as the 1961 ESC in Cannes, the scenographer Gerard Dubois had put up a Versailles-inspired portico as a stage set, with painted gardens as a backdrop. The 1979 edition in Jerusalem saw Dov Ben David's design which, drawing inspiration from the local architecture, consisted of a rotating sculptural structure simulating the Dome of the Rock on the Temple Mount (Ben David, 2020)—and also bore a great similitude to the logo of the Israel Broadcasting Authority (IBA), which ran the show (Panea, 2018: 129). Both sceneries presented Israeli architecture as being local yet, at the same time, open to diversity. Another significant precedent was that of the 1991 ESC in Rome. Given the unplanned way in which this venue had been elected, with the edition originally due to take place in San Remo, the team of Sergio Attisani and Bruno Cecchetto used remains of sets from old films shot in the Cinecittà Studios, where the ESC was held (Panea, 2020: 35). These included ancient Roman and even Egyptian temples, which lent the stage an orientalist, pastiche-like air in a cosy venue.

At the beginning of the new millennium, the contest was held in venues capable of seating no fewer than 10,000–15,000 spectators, on account of the increase in the number of participating countries and the establishment of the semifinals in 2004—at the same time as the sixth and largest expansion of the European Union, which then became the Europe of twenty-five (Baker, 2015: 74). In that sense, Turkey's victory in 2003 posed a considerable organisational challenge in 2004, since the capacity of the previous venues, Estonia and Latvia (each seating an audience of some 6,400 people), was doubled in Istanbul, reaching 12,270 seats. Whereas the visual identity of the former two revolved around the topic of the homeland through the filter of fantasy ("A Modern Fairytale", "Magical Rendezvous"), the structure of the spacious stage in Istanbul, designed by Servet Işık, alluded to history, drawing inspiration from the Hagia Sophia Grand Mosque and incorporating the slogan "Under the Same Sky". The aim, again, was to

Figure 15.5 The stage of the 2006 ESC in Athens. © EBU/Stage One.

welcome all the guest countries, but this time within a quite different frame, with the presence of the host being much more noticeable (Jordan, 2014: 66). A very similar stage set, mentioned above, was that of the Athens edition in 2006, inspired by the theatres of classical Greece, with stepped structures resembling the terraces. The question wa thus raised as to the ownership of cultural (architectural in this case) icons (Vuletic, 2018: 136). In a context in which mass media through ex-tremely creative digital tools brings possibilities of re-writing identities, debates on "cultural memory" are at stake (Blom et al., 2016: 12) However, the tricky nature of this architectural turn caused its relative decline over the following decade. Above all, this happened because the stage could impose such a rigid frame that it could overwhelm the creativity of the entries. There was, though, still a political controversy in the 2009 ESC due to the postcard which showed an images of a structure in the disputed area between Armenia and Azerbaijan. This underlined how the contest could especially be political in the context of the conflicts between states that haverelatively recently become independent (136–137). (Figure 15.5)

Objects and Symbols from the Cultural Heritage of the Host Country

Another trend has been to use objects belonging to the cultural heritage of the host country. In this regard, Fettahoğlu expresses the importance of this topic: "a method to associate a product to a nation has been the adoption of cultural heritage objects, as would be expected from touristic souvenirs" (2017: 78). Accordingly, in 1969, it was decided that the ESC in Madrid could help to promote Spanish art by commissioning Salvador Dalí to design the poster and Amadeo Gabino to design the onstage sculpture made out of metal, resembling a rose (Panea, 2020: 31). In the 1971 ESC in Dublin, the scenographer Alpho O'Reilly opted for a nod to eighteenth century local glassware for the structures in the background of the stage (Fettahoğlu, 2017: 34). Also in Dublin, but in 1981, Alan Pleass, Michael Grogan and Don Farrell decorated the background with the silhouette of the Petrie Crown, an Iron Age bronze headdress discovered in Cork, used for formal events and certain rituals (Fettahoğlu, 2017: 41–42). The above mentioned Øresund Bridge depicted in the Malmö contest in 1992 and the oil platform from the 1996 ESC in Oslo were also references to local culture.

Even though the trend described has always had to compete with the futuristic or geometric tendencies especially since 2000 (not discussed in this chapter), there are some recent examples to note. Among them, the design for Helsinki 2007, carried out by the company Dog Design, is important to mention. Its visual identity and scenography were imbued with Scandinavian design shapes (Bohlman & Polychronakis, 2013: 57), haloed by the slogan "True Fantasy". The ground plan (designed by Kalle Ahonen, Samuli Laine, Kristian Schmidt and Jenni Viitanen) of the Hartwall Arena, built for the Ice Hockey World Championships in 1997, represented a traditional music instrument, the *kantele* (Jordan, 2014: 132). Anyway, music instruments had already appeared on some earlier occasions, as in Dublin in 1997—with a harp in its logo. Moving on to Copenhagen, whereas in 2001 the city had already become the venue with the biggest capacity up to that point (with the Parken Stadium seating 38,000 spectators), in its second hosting in 2014 the initial budget allocated for the B&W Hallerne (a former shipyard remodelled for the occasion) was tripled (Vuletic, 2018: 187). The most significant feature of the design signed by Claus Zier was its use of led light beams evoking the shapes of a Viking ship under construction (Fettahoğlu, 2017: 81), thus somehow interweaving projections with reality, skill with destruction.

Currently, given the huge audiovisual display involved, with very specific technical requirements, most stages tend towards standardisation, including similar equipment and often hiring, year after year, the same personnel, such as Florian Wieder (Pantión, 2020: 87). As described in Section 3.2, the design of the stage in Baku was inspired by "The Land of Fire" slogan. In addition, as it is by fire that glass is made, crystalline shapes formed a stage with several platforms which gave the feeling of strength and solidity. Local features persist more in the logos than in the stage designs, like the dandelion for Stockholm 2016 (mentioned at the Section 3.1). Similarly, in Kyiv in 2017, the motto "Celebrate Diversity" was illustrated by a logo based on the Ukrainian traditional necklaces called "Namysto" (Panea, 2018: 127). To cite a current example, the armillary sphere from the Lisbon edition in 2018 can also be read, as stated above, as an artefact relating to cultural heritage, so as to remind everyone where they were but without getting too entangled. Finally, the design for the edition that took place in Tel Aviv in 2019 is worth mentioning:

Figure 15.6 The stage of the 2007 ESC in Helsinki. © EBU/Stage One.

in addition to the slogan "Dare to Dream", it gave the triangle (an allusion to the star of David) prominence by making it present both in the ground plan and in the visuals. According to Wieder himself: (Figure 15.6)

> [a] host country has never given any regulations to me. But I know Israel very well […] so I had thought to emphasize triangles strongly in the artistic language of my design and 'play' with them. From triangles the Jewish Star of David is also formed. And then I had the idea to symbolize the twelve tribes of the Jewish people. Of course translated into an artistic language, not immediately obvious.
>
> (Zárate, 2019)

Conclusion

The ESC was rooted in the idea of transnational exchange and cooperation through telecommunications and experimentation with the audiovisual medium. Nonetheless, this initial intent has often revealed its ambivalence when problematising the terms "hospitality" and "domesticity" through the main trends in the design of the stages. Firstly, flower motifs were used in the early years, not only as a welcoming touch but also as a national emblem—and, more recently, as an allusion to the notions of youth and vitality some "new" nations are willing to promote. Later on, the concept of "natural" landscape emerged around the 1970s, then developing from the 1990s to the present to incorporate its "urban" side too. All these trends are sometimes intermingled with the "aquatic metaphor", an especially significant device inasmuch as it has been a symbol of unity, smoothness and freedom (especially since the creation of the European Union) on numerous stages. Allusions to animals as mascots, or turned into patriotic emblems, have also been analysed.

A further aspect considered has been the allusion to the architecture of the host country; despite its apparent suitability to become a widespread trend, this study shows that that avenue has scarcely been explored throughout the history of the contest, due to the excessive constraints that such a frame imposes. In contrast, native cultural emblems have been widely used, although with a marked imbalance between the two periods studied: 1956–1993 and 1994 until now. Designs for the early editions favoured natural elements over cultural artefacts, wrapping the performances in a seemingly neutral atmosphere (yet risking the legitimation of certain cultural traits). However, from the 1990s to the present, examples abound of the use of symbols belonging to the cultural heritage of the host country—occasionally linked to natural elements, insofar as "nature" and "culture" are terms with porous boundaries.

All in all, since the creation of the European Union, there has been an increasing use of identity symbols evoking the culture of the host venue, combined with the provision of a hospitable, domestic frame for every guest contender. After this analysis, all tendencies discussed can be read as significative elements to understand changes about the idea of representation in contemporary aesthetics, whose media images create a problematic contrast between hospitality and domesticity in an increasing globalized and multicultural world. (Table 15.1)

Table 15.1 Motifs in the set designs of the ESC

Before Maastricht		*After Maastricht*	
Plants			
Hilversum 1958	Tulips	Kyiv 2005	Garden of Eden-inspired shapes
Luxemburg 1962	Flowerpots & bouquets	Stockholm 2016	Dandelion (only in logo)
Madrid 1969	Roses & carnations	Lisbon 2018	Subaquatic plants (logo & visuals)
The Hague 1980	Tulip-shaped structures		
Munich 1983	Floral centrepieces (in the intervals)		
Landscapes			
Stockholm 1975	Scandinavian rural landscape	Dublin 1994	Dublin city
Bergen 1986	Norwegian glacier	Riga 2003	Riga skyline & celestial shapes
Lausanne 1989	The Matterhorn (also in logo)	Belgrade 2008	Belgrade landscape
		Baku	"Land of Fire" (slogan & postcards)

(Continued)

Table 15.1 (Continued)

Before Maastricht		After Maastricht	
Water			
Malmö 1992	Viking ship	Dublin 1994	Liffey River
		Oslo 1996	Water in oil platform
		Birmingham 1998	Whale-inspired shapes
		Kyiv 2005	Subaquatic plants (also in visuals)
		Athens 2006	Maritime culture (only in visuals)
		Belgrade 2008	Sava and Danube Rivers
		Lisbon 2018	Waves of the sea
Animals			
Brighton 1974	Bird (only in logo)	Birmingham 1998	Whale-inspired shapes
Zagreb 1990	"Eurocat" mascot (only in visuals)	Athens 2006	Jellyfish (logo & visuals)
		Helsinki 2007	Northern pike (inspiration for Kantele)
Malmö 1992	Seagull (only in visuals)	Moscow 2009	Bird (only in logo)
		Malmö 2013	Butterfly shapes (also in logo)
		Lisbon 2018	Seashell (only in logo)
Local architecture			
Cannes 1961	Versailles-inspired portico	Oslo 1996	Oil platform
Jerusalem 1979	Dome of the Rock structure	Istanbul 2004	Hagia Sophia Mosque structure
Rome 1991	Roman Empire ruins	Athens 2006	Classical theatre terraces
Malmö 1992	Øresund Bridge		
Cultural properties			
Madrid 1969	Spanish artists	Dublin 1994	Dublin City (& Irish castle in logo)
Dublin 1971	18th-century Irish glassware	Oslo 1996	Oil extraction
Dublin 1981	Petrie Crown (& Irish map in logo)	Dublin 1997	Irish harp (only in logo)
Malmö 1992	Viking ship & Øresund Bridge	Riga 2003	Riga skyline (also in visuals)
		Helsinki 2007	*Kantele*-shaped ground plan
		Baku 2012	Crystalline shapes
		Copenhagen 2014	Viking shipyard
		Kyiv 2017	*Namysto* necklaces (only in logo)
		Lisbon 2018	Armillary sphere
		Tel Aviv 2019	Star of David (also in logo)

Underlined: venues with several types of motifs.

References

Arvidsson, F. (2013). Stage Design, Eurovision Song Contest 2013, Malmö Arena, SVT. *Frida Arvidsson*. Retrieved March 17, 2021, from http://www.fridaarvidsson.com/eurovision-song-contest-2013

Baker, C. (2015). Gender and Geopolitics in the Eurovision Song Contest, *Contemporary Southeastern Europe*, 2(1), 74–93.

Baker, C. (2019). I am the Voice of the Past That Will Always Be': the Eurovision Song Contest as Historical Fiction", *Journal of Historical Fictions*, 2(2), 102–125.

Ben David, D. (2020). An Interview With Dov Ben David on the Preparations for the Eurovision in Jerusalem, *Dov Ben David*. Retrieved March 17, 2021, from https://www.dovbendavid.com/en/portfolio/13

BBC (1999). Eurovision Song Contest - Information. 2 May 1999. Retrieved March 17, 2021, from https://web.archive.org/web/19990502114528/http://www.bbc.co.uk/eurovision/info2.shtml

Blake Knox, D. (2015). *Ireland and the Eurovision*. New Island Books, Stillorgan.

Bohlman, P. V. (2013). Tempus Edax Rerum. Time and the Making of the Eurovision Song. In: D. Tragaki (Ed.), *Empire of song. Europe and Nation in the Eurovision Song Contest* (pp. 35–56). Plymouth: Scarecrow Press.

Bohlman, A. F. & Polychronakis, I. (2013). Eurovision Everywhere: A Kaleidoscopic Vision of the Grand Prix. In: D. Tragaki (Ed.), *Empire of song. Europe and Nation in the Eurovision Song Contest* (pp. 57–78). Plymouth: Scarecrow Press.

Blom, I.; Lundemo, T. & Røssaak, E. (Eds.) (2016). *Memory in Motion. Archives, Technology, and the Social*. Amsterdam: Amsterdam University Press. doi: 10.2307/j.ctt1jd94f0.4

Bolin, G. (2006). Visions of Europe: Cultural Technologies of Nation-states, *International Journal of Cultural Studies*, 9, 189–206.

Bourdieu, P. (1997). *Sobre la televisión*, Barcelona: Anagrama.

Coleman, S. (2008). Why is the Eurovision Song Contest Ridiculous? Exploring a Spectacle of Embarrassment, Irony and Identity, *Popular Communication*, 6, 127–140.

Coupe, T. & Chaban, N. (2020). Creating Europe Through Culture? The Impact of the European Song Contest on European Identity, *Empirica*, 47, 885–908.

Derrida, J. & Dufourmantelle, A. (2006). *La hospitalidad*, Buenos Aires: Ediciones de la Flor.

Esctoday (2005). Kiev 2005: Rough Pictures of Virtual Stage Design, *Esctoday*. Retrieved March 17, 2021, from http://esctoday.com/4012/kiev_2005_rough_pictures_of_virtual_stage_design/

Fettahoğlu, F. M. (2017). *The Impact of Technology and Traces of National Representation on Eurovision Stages*, Istanbul: Istambul Technical University. Retrieved March 17, 2021, from https://tez.yok.gov.tr/UlusalTezMerkezi/tezSorguSonucYeni.jsp

Highfield, T., Harrington, S. & Bruns, A. (2013). Twitter as a Technology for Audiencing and Fandom: the #Eurovision Phenomenon. *Information, Communication & Society*, 16(3), 315–339.

Henrich-Franke, C. (2010). Creating Transnationality Through an International Organization? The European Broadcasting Union's (EBU) Television Programme Activities, *Media History*, 16(1), 67–81.

Jordan, P. (2014). *The Modern Fairy Tale: Nation Branding, National Identity and the Eurovision Song Contest in Estonia*, Tartu: University of Tartu Press.

Jordan, P. (2016). Stage Design for 2016 Revealed!. *Eurovision.tv*, February 15. Retrieved March 17, 2021, from https://eurovision.tv/story/stage-design-for-2016-revealed

Jordan, P. (2017). Exclusive: The stage for Lisbon 2018 is Revealed!. *Eurovision.tv*, December 5. Retrieved March 17, 2021, from https://eurovision.tv/story/2018-stage-design-revealed

Lee Adams, W. (2017). Eurovision 2018 Stage Design Honours Portugal's Connection with the Sea. *Wiwibloggs*, December 5. Retrieved March 17, 2021, from https://wiwibloggs.com/2017/12/05/eurovision-2018-stage-design-honours-portugals-connection-sea/203411/

M&M Production Management (2018). *Eurovision Diary 2018*, April 15. Retrieved March 17, 2021, from https://m-m-pr.com/index.php/references/eurovision-diary-2018/340-april-15

Marković, D. (2008). Circus in Wonderland: Interview with Boris Miljković, *BelGuest: Belgrade Visitor's Magazine*, *8*, 15–17. Retrieved March 17, 2021, from https://issuu.com/milena_mihaljcic/docs/belguestprolece08screen

McNamara K. R. (2015). *The Politics of Everyday Europe: Constructing Authority in the European Union*, Oxford: Oxford University Press.

Pajala, M. (2012). Mapping Europe: Images of Europe in the Eurovision Song Contest, *View: Journal of European Television History and Culture*, *1*(2), 3–10.

Pajala, M. (2013). Europe, with Feeling. The Eurovision Song Contest as Entertainment. In: Fricker, K. & Gluhovic, M. (Eds.), *Performing the 'New' Europe: Identities, Feelings and Politics in the Eurovision Song Contest* (pp. 77–93). London: Palgrave Macmillan.

Panea, J. L. (2018). Identity, Spectacle and Representation: Israeli Entries at the Eurovision Song Contest. *Doxa Comunicación*, *27*(2), 125–126.

Panea, J. L. (2020). Las escenografías del Festival de Eurovisión: Estética, tecnología e identidad cultural al albor de la reconstrucción europea (1956–1993). *Ámbitos. Revista de estudios de Ciencias Sociales y Humanidades*, *44*, 23–40. Retrieved March 17, 2021, from https://helvia.uco.es/xmlui/handle/10396/21179

Pantión, M. J. (2020). *Festival de la canción de Eurovisión: estudio de la escenografía de Florian Wieder*, Seville: University of Seville. Retrieved March 17, 2021, from https://idus.us.es/handle/11441/104298

Penchaszadeh, A. P. (2014). *Política y hospitalidad. Disquisiciones urgentes sobre la figura del extranjero*, Buenos Aires: Eudeba.

Raykoff, I., & Tobin, R. D. (2007). *A song for Europe: popular music and politics in the Eurovision Song Contest*. Ashgate.

Roche, M. (2000). *Mega-Events and Modernity: Olympics and Expos in the Growth of Global Culture*, Routledge: London & New York.

Sandvoss, C. (2008). On the Couch with Europe: The Eurovision Song Contest, the European Broadcast Union and Belonging on the Old Continent. *Popular Communication*, *6*(3), 190–207.

Vuletic, D. (2018). *Postwar Europe and the Eurovision Song Contest*, London: Bloomsbury.

Yair, G. (2019). Douze point: Eurovisions and Euro-Divisions in the Eurovision Song Contest – Review of two decades of research. *European Journal of Cultural Studies, 22*(5–6), 1013–1029.

Zárate, V. (2019). Eurovisión: la simbología oculta en los escenarios futuristas de Florian Wieder, el diseñador del Festival. *El País*, March 21th. Retrieved March 17, 2021, from https://elpais.com/elpais/2019/05/19/icon_design/1558220898_375116.html

Zaroulia, M. (2013). 'Sharing the Moment': Europe, Affect, and Utopian Performativities in the Eurovision Song Contest. In: Fricker, K. & Gluhovic, M. (Eds.), *Performing the 'New' Europe: Identities, Feelings and Politics in the Eurovision Song Contest* (pp. 31–52). London: Palgrave Macmillan.

All images used with permission from their owners.
Translation by Víctor Turégano.

16 Armchair Researchers: Modes of Ethnographic Research for Understanding and Experiencing the Eurovision Song Contest

Chris Hay and Jessica Carniel

As Eurovision researchers, we have been privileged to travel to Vienna and Lisbon in pursuit of our research object, as well as closer to home to the Gold Coast in Queensland, Australia, where the Australian national selection, *Eurovision – Australia Decides*, is held. For the most part, however, being Eurovision researchers in Australia has meant that we have conducted much of our primary research early in the morning, before the sun has risen, usually while wearing pyjamas on the couch, and often messaging each other furiously. It has also meant that our object of research has been not only this ostensibly European event, but also how the experience of the contest differs according to time, space, and distance from the live event. We also have both come to Eurovision research from a place of personal fandom and are conscious of our roles as aca-fans (Jenkins, 2012, p. 4) – academics studying a fandom to which we belong. This has had a profound impact on the ways we engage with the ESC as a text and, importantly, the ways we engage with the communities that surround it, to which we also claim a sort of belonging.

Both together and separately, our research into the ESC has involved a wide range of methods and methodological approaches drawn from our diverse disciplinary backgrounds in theatre history, performance studies, cultural studies, and international studies. We have focused on textual analysis of performances (Hay & Kanafani, 2017; Carniel, 2017), on liveness (Hay & Kanafani, 2017; Carniel & Hay, 2019), on national identity (Carniel, 2018) and regional experience (Hay, 2019; Carniel, 2019). In this chapter, we reflect upon the various methodological and theoretical implications that have arisen in the course of our research experiences. We argue that our collaborative (auto)ethnographic approach to Eurovision research presents useful techniques for conducting research on a broadcast text in a digital age, and that our personal investment in the contest as fans and as members of the fan community necessarily informs the ethics of this approach. Beginning with a reflection on the problematics and pleasures of the aca-fan researcher subject position as both the foundations to our approach and as an important act of transparency, we then examine the places and spaces of Eurovision research to frame a deeper exploration of the various methodological approaches that we have necessarily deployed as part of our

DOI: 10.4324/9781003188933-19

inter- and multidisciplinary approach to studying the ESC. In all of these, the boundaries between public and private, between personal and professional, between lounge wear and party wear are blurred.

Aca-Fan Researchers: Positionality and Responsibility

We come to the study of Eurovision and its fans as fans ourselves. Prior to any engagement with Eurovision scholarship, we each held viewing parties with friends, followed the contest on social media, and listened to the songs outside the contest season. Accordingly, we were already familiar with some of the fan practices and experiences, although we learnt through the course of our research that our own fandom barely scratched the surface of what was possible. It was important from the outset to reflect upon how our position as fans impacted our research, and how our research impacted our fandom and our relationship with other fans, both in and out of the research context. The concept of the aca-fan has been useful for this. Credited to Henry Jenkins, it captured a widespread theoretical and methodological concern for the emerging field of fan studies, itself drawn from the discipline of cultural studies. Jenkins never actually used the term "aca-fan" in the first edition of *Textual Poachers* in 1992, but later defined an aca-fan as one who writes "both as an academic (who has access to certain theories of popular culture, certain bodies of critical and ethnographic literature) and as a fan (who has access to the particular knowledge and traditions of that community)" (Jenkins, 2012, p. 5). The term has found other iterations, such as "scholar-fan" (Doty, 2000) and "academic fan" (Burt, 1998), that have different implications, as explored by Matt Hills (2002). Jenkins (2012, p. xii) observes that these scholars tend to treat this tension between academic and fan in the abstract, adopting objective voices to analyse the problematic. In response to this, self-reflexive research emerges as an important tool in contemporary fan studies scholarship, whereby the aca-fan embraces — and even utilises — their positionality. This mode of self-reflection has been important for not only exploring the specific subjectivity of the aca-fan, but also for examining and challenging the sometimes-unequal power relations that can emerge between the researcher and the researched.

One anxiety of the aca-fan centres on the validity of taking one's own fannish object as a subject of serious scholarly research. Hills (2002) observes that the idea of the fan as passionate and committed to their fannish object is perceived to be at odds with the imagined subjectivity of academia as rational and empirical. His comparative summary of Jenkins' aca-fan, Alexander Doty's scholar-fan, and Richard Burt's academic fan, reveals the various tensions perceived within the academy and with relation to that imagined academic subject. Jenkins is a critic of the notion of academic distance in fan studies, arguing that studies of popular culture phenomena are best conducted from within. Academic distance, he suggests, can lead to a judgement of fans rather than a conversation with the fan community (Jenkins, 2012, p. 6). Where Jenkins appears more concerned with the impact of the research on the community, Doty and Burt focus more on the perceptions of the researcher within the academy. Doty, for example, is concerned with the scholar-fan's anxieties about how to include autobiographical reflections, such as fan enthusiasms, in teaching and research, "without losing the respect of the reader/student by coming off as embarrassingly egotistical or gee-whizz celebratory" (Doty, 2000, p. 12). Although Doty seems to suggest that autoethnography in popular culture studies is something worth doing, it is nevertheless something that he is uncomfortable with in his own practice (as in *Flaming Classics*) because of that uncertainty over how it will be received. To compensate for this, aca-fans may be tempted to over-theorise or over-politicise cultural phenomena and fandoms "in order to make them more palatable to a cultural elite that does not need any more encouragement to dismiss what we study as frivolous and meaningless" (Larsen & Zubernis, 2012, p. 45). Burt's characterisation of the academic fan as a "figure of perverse plenitude" (Hills, 2002, p. 12) indulging in a fantasy of having it all — that is, engaging in rigorous academic work while also pursuing a personal interest — seems to realise Doty's anxieties.

At times we share Doty's discomfort and fear that we are, as Burt might suggest, indulgent of our object of study. Being Eurovision fans means that we grapple with "fannish feelings" (Hansal & Gunderson, 2020, para.1.1). Fandom is by its very nature a process of emotional investment in and attachment to a particular object, person, or text. There are further anxieties around sites and methods of research. Our fieldwork has involved attending the ESC live — a deep desire for many fans — and watching it at home, an activity we were doing already. Much humanities scholarship can involve emotional investment and attachment, as well as pleasurable pursuits, such as reading a novel in one's pyjamas as part of one's research activity as a literary scholar. Aca-fan researchers are thus wise to remember Joli Jensen's (1992) famed challenge to the false distinction between scholars or afficionados and fans, which she argues is a residue of cultural elitism. Like fans, Jensen observes, scholars, critics, and cultural patrons "display interest, affection and attachment" for the figures, objects, and texts of their chosen field but are not deemed "fans" nor deviant for their expertise or interest. Jensen argues that the "characterisation of fandom as pathology is based in, supports and justifies elitist and disrespectful beliefs about our common life" (1994, pp. 9–10). More recently, Alexis Lothian applied fan studies theory and methodology to an analysis of digital humanities scholarship, in which she argued, "people feel fannish about digital humanities and that digital humanities' networks operate like a fandom" (2018, p. 372). This can be seen in established fields with perceived value and gravitas, such as military history or Jensen's example of James Joyce studies, as much as it can be seen in self-identified aca-fan research into fandoms and shared fannish objects. Viewed in this light, aca-fans are not doing anything out of the ordinary, but their focus on popular culture phenomena can still be viewed as frivolous because of lingering elitism around what constitutes a worthy object of study.

The charge of cultural elitism has particular implications for the study of Eurovision. The ESC is frequently an object of ridicule and derision that is framed — and dismissed — as a kitsch and camp text. Such a view underestimates the cultural depth and value of the kitsch and the camp. As Christopher Isherwood wrote in *The World in the Evening*, "you can't camp about something you don't take seriously" (1954, p. 125). This relationship between camp and the serious is reflected also in Allen Pero's statement: "[c]amp is an experience of the sublime, but seen from the perspective of the ridiculous" (2016, p. 31). Kitsch works alongside this as "an aesthetic mechanism for domesticating radical difference and avoiding transcultural and ethno-national conflict" (Allatson, 2007, p. 91). We ought not forget, too, the political dimension of camp, especially as reclaimed by Moe Meyer in the formulation of "Camp-as-critique" (1994, p. 9). To this end, "[c]amp can be reclaimed [...] as a signifying practice that not only processually constitutes the subject, but is actually the vehicle for an already existent — though obscured — cultural critique" (Meyer, 1994, p. 10). This is not to suggest that all Eurovision's excesses carry a political dimension; rather, we emphasise here camp and kitsch's *potential* as aesthetic strategies that transcend frivolity.

In studies of Eurovision, the kitsch and the camp inhabit serious critical and theoretical roles in understanding the ESC and its fans. While kitsch and camp play an important role in the history, aesthetics, and politics of Eurovision, popular assumptions about this often preclude any acknowledgement or understanding of the artistic excellence and affective value of the ESC to its artists, participant nations, and audiences. The academic sphere is now far more likely to accept Eurovision as a valuable object of study, but it can still be seen as an amusing novelty in public discourse. Carniel has encountered this in some of her media engagements, wherein she has been invited as an expert charged with the responsibility of convincing interviewers that the ESC is not stupid. These kinds of debates, while of obvious interest to programmers and editors, are of less interest to us; like Ethan Thompson and Jason Mittell, "we are all concerned more with thinking critically about television than with proclaiming its artistic or moral merits (or lack thereof)" (2020, p. 1). Some 180 million viewers watch the ESC every year, and its fandom is ever-expanding as new media practices enable a wider range of engagements — there are enough people who do take it seriously, or at the very least who do not think it is stupid, to warrant critical attention.

It is difficult to determine whether we combat these perceptions of Eurovision as 'frivolous' or 'stupid' because we are fans or because we are defensive about the validity of our research. Our position as researchers gives us responsibility over how our participants — fellow Eurovision fans — are represented in our research and in the ways that we speak about Eurovision and Eurovision fans in other public fora. As Evans and Stasi (2014) emphasise, research is a form of representation work: the researcher is responsible for how others are represented in that research. Similarly, Jenkins argues that a researcher of fans is accountable to those fans. This does not erase the unequal power relations between researcher and fans, particularly in the public sphere, where the views of an 'academic expert' might be given more weight and authority than those of a fan without specific academic expertise, in part because of that lingering perception of fans as overcome by their own enthusiasm and emotions. Aca-fandom functions as a particular aspect of how contemporary fandom problematises the relationship between production and consumption within the context of convergence and participatory cultures. According to John Fiske, fans are differentiated from 'normal' audience members by the way that they read into texts excessively, finding and filling gaps in meaning (2002, p. 46). Aca-fans are the ultimate excessive readers, layering their reading of the text with further theoretical analysis and methodologies. Furthermore, they contribute to the body of texts produced by fans around their object of fandom and can even come to influence the production of the text itself. Although we cannot (yet) make any claims to impacting Eurovision (unlike some of our fellow Euroscholars, including Paul Jordan and Dean Vuletic), our academic publications are read by fans and cited in fan reportage, contributing to and being subject to fan-produced Eurovision media.

The status of aca-fan also influences our methods of research. Having a strong social media presence, where we are followed and valued in fan communities for providing expert commentary, enables easy recruitment of participants. This opens up interesting ethical issues around dual relationships and conflicts of interest, and the importance of finding ways to establish and maintain particular boundaries. Nevertheless, sharing an object of fandom with our participants enables us to connect with them in interviews in a peer-to-peer manner that in turn encourages further openness within the interview itself. For example, in conducting research for *We Got Love* (Carniel, 2018), participants often inter-rupted the interview to tell Carniel how pleased they were to have the oppor-tunity to discuss Eurovision in a context that takes it — and their love of it — seriously.

Emerging from these various issues is an ethics of aca-fandom to encourage greater responsibility and accountability for researchers. To address this, aca-fan scholarship encourages self-reflexivity. This, Evans and Stasi (2014) argue, helps not only to highlight power between the researched and the researcher, but also to be transparent about the ways in which these are often the same thing, or often share a particular subject position, such as that of fan. Inhabiting the aca-fan subject position, they suggest, lends itself almost immediately to self-reflexive autoethnography as a method, enabling an understanding of fandom as an embodied lived experience rather than simply a discursive practice. This can, however, privilege individual feelings. Evans and Stasi acknowledge this, sug-gesting integration with other methods, such as traditional ethnography and digital ethnography, to situate those individual reflections within a broader structural and political understanding of fandom as a networked phenomenon. Sophie Hansal and Marianne Gunderson advocate a "fannish methodology" that embraces the dual position of researcher and fan but also reflects critically upon it, with a particular questioning of the "dichotomous and oppositional con-ceptualisation of emotion and rationality, and its hegemony in academic thought" (2020, para. 8.2). Importantly, Hansal and Gunderson view re-searchers' fannish feelings as a resource rather than an impediment. Feelings, they argue, are not just a form of motivation or basis for analysis, but as a "starting point for critique of social and academic norms and values" (Hansal & Gunderson, 2020, para. 1.4). Fannish feelings have certainly provided a strong motivation for our research — and such motivation is much needed when getting up at 5am to watch the Contest live. That temporal difference in Australian Eurovision fandom — that we watch early in the morning while Europeans watch into the night — focusses our attention on the embodied, emplaced aspects of our research.

The Places and Spaces of Eurovision Research

As an event that involves both a live, in-house audience and at-home viewers, the sites of Eurovision research are multiple. For the majority of its audience, the ESC is something experienced in their own living rooms. Although many might wish to attend the live contest at some stage, this is a reality for a much smaller subset of the audience. The global viewership of the ESC is approximately 180 million, while the live audience in the show's arena is between 7000 and 12000. These two sites are further complicated by the use of social media, which in many ways becomes its own field site, and one that is not bounded temporally or physically in the same way that the live event of the contest (whether viewed in the arena or at home) is. Our own initial primary encounters with the ESC as fans was in the living room. Hay's début as a Eurovision researcher centred upon his experience at the 2015 ESC (Hay & Kanafani, 2017). Meanwhile, Carniel's début centred upon the abstracted televised text of the contest within its socio-political contexts (Carniel, 2015) and, later, the experience of the contest for Australians in Australia contrasted with her experience of the contest on-site (Carniel, 2018).

Understanding these multiple sites necessitates multiple methods and methodologies of data collection and theorisation, many of which require constant reflection and negotiation of the aca-fan duality. The focus of study can also shift quite significantly, depending on the location of the researcher. For example, the living room researcher might focus on the idea of social television watching with a group of assembled viewers. Alternatively, watching it alone, they might instead focus on the televisual text of the contest itself. Both of these might simultaneously involve attention to contemporaneous online engagements via social media, or be disengaged with this entirely. By contrast, the researcher on-site at the live event might focus on the production of the event as a nexus between live musical performance and produced televisual text, or on the embodied experience of being a fan engaging directly with their object of study. Although the disciplinary promiscuity of Eurovision studies has resulted in the employment of a wide range of framings and methodologies across existing scholarship, remarkably little research focusses on the embodied experience of the on-site ESC. Future research directions might take up this challenge, including examinations of embodied experiences and tourism.

Each of these scenarios have informed elements of our own research. Furthermore, our collaborative research has enabled a contemporaneous interplay between these sites and methods. For example, our data collection for *Eurovision – Australia Decides* in 2020 involved a mobile text-based dialogue between Carniel on-site at the Gold Coast event and Hay viewing the broadcast by the Special Broadcasting Service (SBS) at home. This approach enabled us to discuss and compare the two different live viewing experiences, and to consider the production of the event from two different perspectives. In this way, we are developing a new methodology best suited to our object of study, the live experience of which is split across at least two places. Efram Sera-Shriar describes this iterative quality to ethnographic research as a process of "learn[ing] to describe, analyse and represent the natural world according to the guiding principles of the research field's methodologies" that leads practitioners to not only "perceive their object of study in a specialised way," but "also refine their analytical and writing practices" (2014, p. 35).

Our approach hybridised the traditional idea of ethnographic research and participant observation as occurring on-site with new forms of ethnographic research that engage with digital, online, or broadcast experiences. By doing so, it highlights how the idea of 'on-site' in Eurovision research is multitudinous and necessitates a rethinking of how research sites are embodied.

The embodied experience of place has been an historically contentious requirement for 'authentic' ethnography, manifested especially in the binary between the 'armchair anthropology' of nineteenth-century gentleman ethnographers and the emergent fieldwork paradigm of the twentieth century. This derision for the armchair persists, as Robert Kenny notes:

> '[a] certain contempt surrounds our view of the practice of armchair theorists, sitting back, experiencing little more than their libraries, not going out to see for themselves, not going out to test things on the ground, not experiencing the context of *place* (2016, p. 226).

Like the binary of aca-fan before it, the embrace of fieldwork and the dismissal of the armchair masks a more nuanced understanding of the armchair scholar's contribution to the field. While "the quintessential armchair scholar from the 19th century did not engage in a practical study of humans per se, because [they] relied on the observations of untrained informants" (Sera-Shriar, 2014, p. 29), they nonetheless interpreted and arranged those observations in meaningful ways — as informed by whatever fieldwork they had previously conducted (or would indeed go on to conduct). When we refer to ourselves here as armchair researchers, it is to this expanded conception of the armchair "as the seat, so to speak, of sagacity" (Kenny, 2016, p. 226) that we invoke.

Unlike these nineteenth-century progenitors, our armchair is in the living room, crucially understood as both a communal and potentially liminal space. Unlike the library, with its associations of seclusion and quiet, individual contemplation, the living room is more boisterous, multi-screen, and in-between. The image of the armchair is also useful to us when it comes to digital ethnography; our characterisation of the living room accords with Tim Highfield, Stephen Harrington and Axel Bruns's description of the operation of online social media fandom on Twitter, in which

> distributed public conversations accompanying live broadcasts come to act as a kind of 'virtual loungeroom': a communal space where audience members can come together to discuss and debate, in real-time, their responses to what they are watching on the television screen (2013, p. 317).

The instantiation of a 'virtual loungeroom' "is the case especially for live television", such as the ESC, as it heightens the sense of watching the show together. Harrington et al (2013, pp. 405-6) describe Twitter as a "metaphorical 'watercooler' in the cloud" that enables instantaneous conversations and facilitates a more communal sense of watching television in the moment. Thus, from our dual living room, both physical and virtual, we both observe and participate in the performances practices we seek to understand.

This mode of research has become particularly critical to engagement with Eurovision during the ongoing effects of the Covid-19 global pandemic, when many researchers could not travel to the site of their fieldwork. Indeed, *Eurovision – Australia Decides* 2020, was one of the last public events in which we participated on-site before the advent of restrictions and eventual lockdowns. During this time, the 'virtual loungeroom' became the primary venue for Eurovision fandom. This facilitated the kind of blurred creator/consumer identity that Ryan Cassella identifies: "social media's interactive nature and technological flexibility will continue to blur the line between maker and consumer as both parties adapt to produce a more collaborative and interactive television experience" (2015, p. 2). Not only was it the primary venue for the fandom, it was also co-opted by official Eurovision online events, specifically the *Eurovision Home Concerts* YouTube series, so that the 'stage' for Eurovision and its performers became multi-sited, and often domesticated. In this series, Eurovision artists past and present invited fans into their homes as they recorded two songs — their own Eurovision entry and a cover version of another artist's song. Even in this, fans were accorded some collaborative power as they voted for the cover songs to be performed. Through concerted social media campaigns, they also influenced the selection of artists invited to perform in the series in "an attempt to realise opportunities to 'game' the systems of the media industries to generate conditions which support and favour the object of the fans' interests" (Highfield et al., 2013, p. 336). As normal transmission resumes, or a 'new normal' develops in its place, this mirage of control may well dissipate. After all, "sharing control of content is not the same thing as relinquishing control" (Cassella, 2015, p. 11). However, the lesson here for our work is that, moving forward, the 'virtual loungeroom' and the physical one are equally important research sites.

Beside those immediate spaces of Eurovision viewing and fandom, the national and international space also plays a significant role in our approach. Being

Australian researchers of an ostensibly European text was perhaps eased or legitimised by the coincidence of our initial research forays with Australia joining the ESC as a participating country in 2015, even as that development was — and remains — contested. Australia's entry into Eurovision again opened up new sites for research. Although an Australian fan presence at the ESC was long signified by Australian flags dotted throughout the "sea of flags" (to doff our cap to Jessica Mauboy's 2014 semi-final interval performance of the same name) for many years before Australia's official entry into the ESC, the significance of this presence was altered. Despite the much-touted Eurovision ethos of unity, it is ultimately a contest of nations. Fans are placed into a nationalistic space that can play out in both the in-person and mediated sites of research. From 2015 onwards, Australian fans are read as having a stake in, and capacity to affect, the contest's outcome. Those fans travelling to the ESC could now even be considered an informal subsidiary to the official Australian delegation. The newfound agency of Australian fans as full participants in the Eurovision process, especially since the advent of the national selection event from 2019 onwards, has in turn altered their online engagement.

The advent of social media and the specific forms of engagement with the ESC that it facilitates and accommodates has created a kind of third site, which transcends some of the binaries we have established above — living room/arena, private space/public space, domestic/national, and so on. It does so through a "reformation of the 'live' viewing audience" (Highfield et al., 2013, p. 317): already bifurcated between those live on-site and those watching live on television, the live audience now includes those engaging live in real time online via social media. (Indeed, in some countries, including the United States and New Zealand, this third space is the *only* means of live engagement with the ESC). Michael Skey et al. observe that "those with a longer-term interest in Eurovision, whether as organizers or followers, view it (or at least portray it) as a liminal space" (2016, p. 3396); our research methodologies thus need to take on a similar betwixt-and-between quality. To do so, we have expanded "the researchers' observational arsenal" (Sera-Shriar, 2014, p. 35) to apprehend the live experience of Eurovision across these multiple sites. In so doing, we are contributing to the development of a model of ethnographical fieldwork fit for the digital age — one in which the new potential of the armchair jostles with its historical limitations.

Conclusion

As an already multimodal event, with multiple live audiences across multiple sites, any analysis of the ESC demands an interdisciplinary approach. Such an approach, though, like the one we have outlined here, starts with understanding the ESC as a piece of television. Even then, this requires more than just watching, as Thompson and Mittell remind us, "[t]o understand TV, you need to watch TV" but also "some types of television require particular viewing practices to really understand them" (2020, p. 7). Our challenge is therefore to capture the "particular viewing practices" that the ESC demands — practices that can be, as we have argued elsewhere, geographically and temporally distinct (Carniel, 2018; Hay, 2019). As Australian aca-fans seeking to apprehend Eurovision, our experience of the ESC has always been "particular", whether through its pre-2015 time-delay, its live broadcast in the early morning rather than the evening, or our geographical distance from the live event. This distance, and difference, attuned us to the range of factors that informed our "contextualised viewing" of the ESC, even when that viewing took place as more or less traditional television consumption.

The web of signification in which that viewing is suspended has also developed and morphed across the period that we have been writing about the ESC, most notably through the development and deployment of the online fandom. While the extent to which the online fandom plays a role greater than just additional *mise en scène* for the ESC is debatable — it might be best understood as analogous to the happy, flag-waving fans in the auditorium who populate the margins of the live broadcast — it nonetheless represents additional context for viewing and understanding Eurovision. In our own collaborative research, then, in addition to examining both the auditorium and the broadcast as sites of live performance, we look to the online space as a third site, one curated and manipulated by *both* the global fandom *and* the ESC itself. This necessitates methodological shifts in how we examine Eurovision. In our research, this expands our view of 'fieldwork' to include a digital dimension and our conception of the 'live audience' to include those engaging in real-time online. For others, different adjustments may be required. This expanded view of the sites of Eurovision research places the study of the ESC in conversation with that of other spectacular global events whose audience is split across similar sites, including research that has inspired our own, such as that focussed on the National Football League's Super Bowl (Paterson & Stevens, 2013) and the Olympic Games (MacAloon, 2006).

Our various methods of research into the ESC have been driven not just by research questions but also by the necessities of our time and space. Being geographically distanced from the ostensible object of our study necessitated from the outset a different engagement with the space of the ESC, its fans, and its national and global audiences. In the time of Covid-19, this distance feels less unique to an Australian or broadly non-European experience of the ESC, and more of a key characteristic of so many social relations in this era. Despite the challenges of Zoom fatigue and social disconnection, movement into the online space has prompted researchers and event organisers to open up conferences to online audiences and participants, and to consider ways that research can be streamed and stored digitally for even greater accessibility. It has also seen the proliferation of both fan and artist productions shared and experienced online, as seen in the example of the *Eurovision Home Concerts*. Although we look optimistically toward a time when elements of our fieldwork might resume their pre-Covid-19 methods of on-site fieldwork, the challenges of this time have prompted greater creativity in how fieldwork is practiced in a variety of fields and, indeed, what constitutes a field of study. Not only does this broaden what and how we conduct research, it also broadens opportunities for who can conduct this research. Future aca-fan researchers might still hold fieldwork on-site at the contest itself as a personal and professional pinnacle, but by embracing the networked, multi-sited, and interconnected nature of the contemporary ESC and global society, we are no longer held by the tyranny of distance. Rather, we inhabit diverse sites of study that can contribute to a deeper understanding of the ESC and its meanings for global and local audiences around the world.

In studying this live audience, we are nevertheless part of it. We share the highs of the *douze points* and the lows of the *nul points* with a global audience of some 180 million people. Then there are more localised experiences as we section the globe into temporal and geographical commonalities. Some in Europe and the Americas might gather in living rooms with friends and families, or venture out to a public party. Those in the southern hemisphere might tuck a blanket around their knees against the late autumn chill as they watch the crowd enjoying their spring evening in the north. And then there are those in similar time zones to Australia, such as China and New Zealand, substituting a warm bed for a cosy living room and a cup of morning coffee, clad, like us, in our favourite pyjamas.

References

Allatson, P. (2007). Antes Cursi Que Sencilla": Eurovision Song Contests and the Kitsch-Drive to Euro-Unity. *Culture, Theory & Critique, 48*(1), 87–98.

Burt, R. (1998). *Unspeakable ShaXXXspeares: Queer Theory and American Kiddie Culture* (Revised ed.). Palgrave Macmillan.

Carniel, J. (2015). Skirting the Issue: Finding Queer and Geopolitical Belonging at the Eurovision Song Contest. *Contemporary Southeastern Europe, 2*(1), 136–154.

Carniel, J. (2017). Welcome to Eurostralia: The Strategic Diversity of Australia at the Eurovision Song Contest. *Continuum, 31*(1), 13–23.

Carniel, J. (2018). *Understanding the Eurovision Song Contest in Multicultural Australia: We Got Love.* Springer.

Carniel, J. (2019). It Really Makes You Feel Part of the World": Transnational Connection for Australian Eurovision Audiences. In C. Hay & J. Carniel (Eds.), *Eurovision and Australia: Interdisciplinary Perspectives from Down Under* (pp. 213–237). Springer.

Carniel, J., & Hay, C. (2019). Conclusion—Eurovision—Australia Decides. In C. Hay & J. Carniel (Eds.), *Eurovision and Australia: Interdisciplinary Perspectives from Down Under* (pp. 259–279). Springer.

Cassella, R. (2015). The New Network: How Social Media is Changing — and Saving — Television. In A.F. Slade, A.J. Narro, & D. Givens-Carroll (Eds.), *Television, Social Media, and Fan Culture* (pp. 1–22). Lexington Books.

Doty, J. (2000). *Flaming Classics: Queering the Film Canon.* Routledge.

Evans, A., & Stasi, M. (2014). Desperately Seeking Methods: New Directions in Fan Studies Research. *Participations, 11*(2), 4–23.

Fiske, J. (2002). The Cultural Economy of Fandom. In L.A. Lewis (Ed.), *The Adoring Audience: Fan Culture and Popular Media* (pp. 30–49). Routledge.

Hansal, S., & Gunderson, M. (2020). Toward a Fannish Methodology: Affect as an Asset. *Transformative Works and Cultures, 33.* 10.3983/twc.2020.1747.

Harrington, S., Highfield, T., & Bruns, A. (2013). More than a backchannel: Twitter and television. *Participations, 10*(1), 405–409.

Hay, C. (2019). Pyjama Fandom: Watching Eurovision Down Under. In C. Hay & J. Carniel (Eds.), *Eurovision and Australia: Interdisciplinary Perspectives from Down Under* (pp. 239–258). Springer.

Hay, C., & Carniel, J. (Eds.). (2019). *Eurovision and Australia: Interdisciplinary Perspectives from Down Under.* Springer.

Hay, C., & Kanafani, B. (2017). Boos, Tears, Sweat, and Toil: Experiencing the 2015 Eurovision Song Contest Live. *Popular Entertainment Studies, 8*(1), 57–73.

Highfield, T., Harrington, S., & Bruns, A. (2013). Twitter as a Technology for Audiencing and Fandom: the #Eurovision phenomenon. *Information, Communication & Society, 16*(3), 315–339.

Hills, M. (2002). *Fan Cultures.* Routledge.

Isherwood, C. (1954). *The World in the Evening.* Methuen.

Jenkins, H. (2012). *Textual Poachers: Television Fans and Participatory Culture* (Anniversary ed.). Routledge.

Jensen, J. (1992). Fandom as Pathology. In L.A. Lewis (Ed.), *The Adoring Audience: Fan Culture and Popular Media* (pp. 9–29). Routledge.

Kenny, R. (2016). Why the Armchair in the First Place? Then Why Get up from It? (And Why Did Some Remain Seated?). *Oceania, 86*(3), 225–243.

Larsen, K., & Zubernis, L.S. (2012). *Fan Culture: Theory/Practice.* Cambridge Scholars Publishing.

Lothian, A. (2018). From Transformative Works to #transformDH: Digital Humanities as (Critical) Fandom. *American Quarterly, 70*(3), 371–393. 10.1353/aq.2018.0027.

MacAloon, J. (2006). The Theory of Spectacle: Reviewing Olympic Ethnography. In A. Tomlinson & C. Young (Eds.), *National Identity and Global Sports Events: Culture, Politics, and Spectacle in the Olympics and the Football World Cup* (pp. 15–39). State University of New York Press.

Meyer, M. (1994). Introduction: Reclaiming the Discourse of Camp. In M. Meyer (Ed.), *The Politics and Poetics of Camp* (pp. 1–19). Routledge.

Paterson, E., & Stevens, L. (2013). From Shakespeare to the Super Bowl: Theatre and Global Liveness. *Australasian Drama Studies, 62,* 147–162.

Pero, A. (2016). A Fugue on Camp. *Modernism/modernity, 23*(1), 28–36.

Sera-Shriar, E. (2014). What is armchair anthropology? Observational practices in 19th-century British human sciences. *History of the Human Sciences, 27*(2), 26–40.

Skey, M., Kyriakidou, M., McCurdy, P., & Uldam, J. (2016). Staging and Engaging with Media Events: A Study of the 2014 Eurovision Song Contest. *International Journal of Communication, 10,* 3381–3399.

17 Between Concepts and Behaviours: The Eurovision Song Contest and Ethnomusicology

*Sofia Vieira Lopes and
João Soeiro de Carvalho*

The Eurovision Song Contest (ESC) celebrated its sixty-fifth anniversary in 2021. During its long history, the ESC has been a display for national representations through music – more precisely, for what national public service broadcasting organisations perceived as the music that could be representative of their countries. Despite being conceived as a contest for new songs, in 2015 the EBU declared that "[t]he Eurovision Song Contest is about much more than just music" (European Broadcasting Union, 2015). Nearly hidden in an enormous technological apparatus – and frequently in the shadow of political and diplomatic issues, commercial interests and media affairs – is the music, which continues to be at the heart of the ESC. In fact, the representativeness of the countries through music is a complex subject, and musical sound is just a small part of the transmedia narratives conveyed by the ESC's entries. In a contest like the ESC, televised music encompasses a myriad of dimensions beyond sound, such as: visual and behavioural dimensions, corporealised in performances; textual dimensions in the lyrics; and the media discourses created around it. In that sense, the complex media network that surrounds the ESC has been vital to mediate and reify discourses about music and its meanings and relationship with society. As a highly mediatised show, the ESC is one of the best examples through which we can analyse the relationship between music and media, as well as the relationship between music and society. Ethnomusicologists play an essential role in unveiling, analysing and understanding the processes related to music making, music mediation and music reception, and in proposing the meanings behind these processes.

For over six decades, the ESC has been a stage for the political and social challenges that Europe has been experiencing. ESC music has been a way of bringing societal issues to the public realm, such as national and European identities, differences and similarities, social struggles and reconciliation. This beckons an important question: how has ESC music conveyed social values? Music is not limited to composition, stage performances, commercial recording and broadcasting. In the twenty-first century, music goes far beyond musical scores. In the ESC, musical meaning is accomplished by a set of sounds,

DOI: 10.4324/9781003188933-20

behaviours and concepts that the public experiences through song. In this chapter, we look to this complex set of phenomena in order to consider the ability of music to convey underlying values. In that sense, and to put it differently, how can we embrace and analyse this complex set of meanings? This chapter demonstrates how the ESC can be a privileged field for ethnomusicology, as it allows us to analyse the three dimensions of music – sound, behaviour and concepts – as proposed by Alan Merriam (1964). Exploring the fundamentals of this field, we analyse how the ESC encompasses ethnomusicological postulates. This chapter focuses on one example: the Portuguese participation and first ever victory in the ESC in 2017. Our aim is to demonstrate how musical meanings and values are assembled with, and conveyed by, the different sounds, behaviours and concepts related to them. Our goal is to shed light on the importance of the ESC as a privileged field for understanding how music encompasses and carries different narratives and values about society. At the same time, we believe that it is important to understand how these processes are part of social contexts. In that sense, we also look at the particular case of music reception related to the first Portuguese ESC victory.

To corroborate our argument, and following the proposed methodology of ethnomusicology, we employed a diverse set of methods, such as music and performance analysis, archival research on official documents and press reports, analysis of media content, ethnographic interviews, and field observation. In order to illustrate how ethnomusicology integrates the subjectivity of different agents, such as the experiences of the researcher, we have included some field-notes in the italicised sections.

Ethnomusicology and the ESC: the state of the art

Ethnomusicology has been an established field of academia since the 1960s. However, the study of the ESC as a popular music[1] event, is quite recent. The first ethnomusicological study of the ESC was the book *World Music: A Very Short Introduction*, published in 2002, by the ethnomusicologist Philip V. Bohlman. A chapter in the book is dedicated to the role of the ESC in fostering European unity, looking into the complex relationship between world music, the modern nation-state, and nationalism. By the same token, two years later, in his book titled *The Music of European Nationalism: Cultural Identity and Modern History*[2], Bohlman traces music's role in "the rise of the nation-state from the Enlightenment to the present-day of the European Union" (2004, back cover) and proposes that the ESC is a privileged field to understand the phenomena of modern nationalism expressed through music. Amongst other cases, the ESC is analysed as an example of the construction of "new Europeanness" using music. In Bohlman's words, "[t]o witness the ESC is to be swept into one of the most ecstatic experiences of music and nationalism, riveted by the transnational imaginary of global music-making" (ibid.:3). Bohlman's seminal contribution on music and nationalism in the ESC laid the ground for future research. However, we consider that such a field as rich as the ESC deserves a closer approach, along the lines of traditional ethnographies, immersing oneself into the fieldwork, according to the postulates of Geertz (1973).

It was not until 2013 that the first volume conceived under ethnomusicological postulates and entirely devoted to the ESC was published. Edited by Dafni Tragaki, *Empire of Song: Europe and Nation in the Eurovision Song Contest* is a multidisciplinary book and includes twelve contributions, combining approaches from ethnomusicology, music studies, history, social anthropology, feminist theory, linguistics, media ethnography, postcolonial theory, comparative literature and philosophy (2013:13). This work emerged from the first academic conference dedicated to the ESC, which was held in Volos in Greece in 2008. Since then, no major works on the ESC based on ethnomusicology's theories have been publised, despite the ESC being a fruitful field in which musical meanings are channeled to a broad section of society.

Bohlman's and Tragaki's works prove the importance of the ESC for the study of popular music, as well as an ethnomusicological capability to combine several ontologies, thereby encompassing the ESC's complexity.

It is important to clarify that music is a social behaviour: it is impossible to analyse it without being aware of social dynamics. So, why is the ESC a worthwhile subject for ethnomusicology? There are several answers:

1   In the ESC we can analyse:

  1.1   songs (sound, structure, melody, harmony, orchestration/arrangement, text) and performances;
  1.2   behaviours related to music, such as musical change processes, changes in technology, music industry dynamics and musical categorisation;
  1.3   the network of discourses created around music, such as direct speech and media narratives;

2   Through the ESC we can verify how music can be a vehicle for symbolic construction for different meanings and for values about music and society;
3   In the ESC we can observe political tensions within Europe and the geographical area covered by the membership of the EBU, as well as changing social dynamics;
4   The ESC allows us to understand how music can be used for cultural diplomacy, to construct narratives about identities, or how reception dynamics are constructed around a mega-event, such as the fandom phenomenon.

Is the ESC then just about music? Or is it a music event that is woven in a much more complex web and flow of realities and concepts? Among ethnomusicologists, the assumption that music has to be seen as culture is obvious. However, for those who are unfamiliar with this ontology, it may not be so simple. When Alan Merriam wrote his seminal work, *The Anthropology of Music*, in 1964, he certainly was not thinking about music and television. When Merriam explained that musical meaning lies in the understanding of a conceptualisation about music, the analysis of music's sounds, and the behaviour in relation to it, he was not thinking about the ESC. What Merriam knew was that ethnomusicology was constructing its own theories and methods based on the assumption that music is not a universal language, understood by all. Merriam argued that the differences we can find in music in different contexts are not consequences of evolutionary determinants. He deconstructed the idea that there was music that is less evolved than others. He stated that music is not only a manifestation of culture, but it is culture itself. In that sense, he proposed that an ethnomusicological point of view is not determined by the specific field that we study. Rather, it is the result of the specific way we look into the complex of behaviours and values that surround the production of sound. This assumption allows ethnomusicologists to study a distinct variety of fields and expressive behaviours: from an almost extinct tribe to night clubs; from music practices in an inaccessible village to music industries. The particularity of the ethnomusicological approach is the way in which subjects are studied, comprising a set of methods to encompass music making processes and the social dynamics linked to them. The results are obtained through direct contact with those who are involved in the music making processes, including in their mediation and reception. In the early 1960s, Merriam launched the basis to understand "music as culture" and used the concept of ethnomusicology as an adverb, defining ethnomusicology not as the study of the music of non-western cultures, but as the study of the relationship which music bears to society in all cultures. Moving the study of music apart from the musical sound, this shift in musical studies allowed us to look at music as a human behaviour that reveals the complex and fluid construct that culture is.

Combining anthropological methods with the specific tools of music analysis, ethnomusicologists are able to access the different dimensions of the musical experience: the production, mediation, and reception processes. They are the best ways to immerse the ethnomusicological researcher into cultures and practices, and the best manner to directly connect with the ethics that shape musical practices. Merriam proposed fieldwork as a main method of ethnomusicology, challenging the accuracy of the analyses produced by the "armchair musicologists", who performed their work in a controlled environment, without direct contact with those who were involved with music making. In ethnomusicology, the knowledge is a result of a dialogue with those who make music happen, giving place to broader interpretations, responding to "why" and "how", more so than describing events (Merriam, 1960).

The "how" question leads us to the other important topic for ethnomusicologists. Similar to culture, music is always changing. Two decades after Merriam postulated it, the ethnomusicologist John Blacking (1986) tried to understand the undercurrents that lead to changes in music. Blacking advocated that music change is a result of decision, both of musicians and agents involved in decision-making processes. In that sense, not only is contact with musicians important, but also contact with those who are involved in the processes of change: the actions of different stakeholders who intervene in decisions related to music.

Let us return to Merriam's arguments:

> [m]usic sound cannot be produced except by people for other people, and although we can separate the two aspects conceptually, one is not really complete without the other. Human behaviour produces music, but the process is one of continuity; the behavior itself is shaped to produce music sound, and thus the study of one flows into the other.
>
> (Merriam 1964:6)

In short, we could look at the ESC just as a music "catalog" with different musical styles in different times. However, ethnomusicological postulates allow us to access several dimensions of the event: not only the sound product, but also the consequences of stakeholders' social, physical and verbal behaviours. In this sense, musicians, audiences and decision-makers are creators and gatekeepers of different meanings that could be attached to the ESC.

Nowadays, this conceptual legacy is not a novelty. However, it is important to remember that the ESC's complexity must be encompassed by a wider analysis, considering that music is a human experience engrained in social contexts. Of course, the ESC deserves a multidisciplinary approach to grasp its complexity and the different dimensions that comprise it. Considering ethnomusicology's wide scope, we could argue that it might be one of the best ways to understand the many layers and complexity of meanings conveyed by the ESC's music. However, we cannot yet explain why ethnomusicologists did not look at the ESC as a subject before Bohlman's contribution.

Sound, concepts and behaviour in "Amar pelos dois" a paragraph Lisbon, 13/05/2017

I was dining at a friends' house. No one there was an ESC fan, and some of them told me that they don't like the ESC at all. However, I forced them to watch the ESC 2017 final because I wanted to see the Portuguese performance. During the voting part, we forgot all about the food and we were glued to the TV screen. One of my friends was screaming and cursing each country that didn't give twelve points to Portugal. My astonishment grew as the Portuguese points were inrcreasing. Until the end, I didn't believe in a Portuguese victory, because I had spent my entire life watching Portugal's low results. At the end, both the researcher and the non-fan friends all screamed for joy when the commentators announced Portugal as the winner.

After the announcement of Portugal's victory, and the visible bewilderment of the Portuguese delegation – a kind of symbolic reaction for all Portuguese people – Salvador Sobral went to the stage to receive the trophy. All viewers, both in the Kyiv arena and at home, were expecting his victory speech. Maybe we were waiting for a speech with excitement and a lot of "Thank you all! It's an honor! I wasn't expecting it ...". Surprisingly, Sobral went to the stage and started: "I want to say that we live in a world of disposable music, fast-food music without any content, and I think this could be a victory for music and people that make music that actually means something. Music is not fireworks. Music is feeling. So, let's try to change this and bring music back, which is really what matters". That same night, during the press conference, while observing the negative reactions of some ESC fans and journalists to his statement, Sobral explained: *"I wish I could bring a change. That would be my biggest joy. If I could bring some sort of change to these things and to music in general. A music with content ... This is a beautiful song. It has some emotional content and a lyrical message, a beautiful lyrical message, harmony ... Things that people are not used to listening to these days, because people are just listening to the radio, songs that are thrown to you, and say: 'you have to like it' because we will play it sixteen times a day".*

The basics of ethnomusicology can be observed in this episode: the understanding of music as a complex of three components- sound, behaviours and concepts. The Portuguese entry in the 2017 ESC is certainly a good example to test Meriam's theory, and can be considered a full statement of it. (Photo 17.1)

Let us begin with music sound.

As per the ESC's rules, Sobral's winning entry, "Amar pelos dois" (For The Both Of Us) is a three-minute song. Composed by Luísa Sobral to be sung by her brother, Salvador, it lays on a *cantabile* melody with a wide extension which demands some vocal flexibility and fits in his vocal range. It is written in the F major key, using the major bebop scale. Its harmonic path is very similar to jazz standards, since chords of submediant, subtonic and leading tone were used to

Photo 17.1 Salvador Sobral and Luísa Sobral, the winners on the stage.
Source: EBU / Andres Putting.

contour the normal I—IV—V—I path of most pop songs. The lyrics, written entirely in Portuguese, are an expression of a selfless love. The arrangement tried to convey the lyrics' message. The idea of a so-called "simplicity" in music is in line with the poem's intimate nature, as well as with the idea of loneliness and abandonment. Luís Figueiredo – a composer, arranger, pianist, teacher and PhD in ethnomusicology linked to the jazz world – made the song's arrangement. Figueiredo shared the same musical references with the Sobrals, and he had worked with Luísa in a previous recording (2014).

The song's structure is different from that of most ESC songs or mainstream pop songs:

	intro	verse 1	verse 2	chorus	instrumental	chorus	bridge	coda
		A	A	B		B	C	
Voice								
Strings								
Piano								

climax

Here we can visualise the structure of the song and how the instrumental lines interact with each other. We see the three timbre layers: solo voice (in light grey), strings (in grey) and piano (in dark grey). The song has eight parts: an introduction, the first melodic theme – A (with text verses 1 and 2), two sections of chorus with the same melody – B, an instrumental interlude in the middle of these two sections, a bridge with a different melody – C – and a different text, and an instrumental coda. The climax of the song is achieved almost in the end, during the bridge, in the last part where all lines play together. It begins with an instrumental introduction of twenty seconds, the longest such introduction in the history of the ESC, which is also very different from other pop songs, since they usually have an introduction that takes between two and three seconds. Figueiredo (2017) explained that, due to the character of the song, he felt that it was necessary to have a longer introduction before the voice started. Luísa sent him some ideas for the arrangement, and he suggested to her an instrumental part in the middle, to replace the usual buildup of pop songs. For the final part, they had five different options: in his opinion, the song should have stopped when the voice stopped, because "it is a festival. No one will listen after the voice ends". Luísa, however, wanted a small coda. The result is a song that is quite different in its structure from other competing songs. In Figueiredo's words, this song shows that "it is possible to do music with a different structure" (Figueiredo 2017).

The piano starts when the voice starts. If we listen carefully, we realise that the piano is present almost during the entire song, with two exceptions: at the beginning and also just before the end. "The piano gives the beat", Figueiredo explained (Figueiredo 2017). The piano's rhythmic pattern provides the music's movement: chords keeping changing, but the rhythm is always the same, played in a kind of *arpeggio*. The piano's line gives freedom to the string instruments to provide "color"

Photo 17.2 Salvador Sobral's performance in the ESC 2017 Grand Final.
Source: EBU / Andres Putting.

to the song, and to the voice to explore rhythmic and melodic inflections, based on improvisation. In accordance with Salvador's jazz background, his performances are always very different from each other. (Photo 17.2)

When Salvador sings "se o teu coração/não quiser ceder" ("If your heart/ won't be willing to give in"), the strings make a kind of punctuation – an accentuation – in the second beat of the three-time division. In this part, the low strings play *pizzicato*, while the treble strings play long notes, creating an effect of suspension. The song's climax is achieved by the strings' line. In the bridge, the voice seems to be alone, since the piano stops, and its rhythmic pattern moves to the strings. Just before the ascending path to the climax, we can find a short pause, a *fermata*, that creates a silence, a breathing, just before the section in which text and melody create a sense of *accelerando*. In the same interview, Figueiredo (2017) stated that nowadays music does not have silences, so "if you never get silence, how can you appreciate the music." At the end, in the final strings' suspension, if we listen carefully the studio version, we can find a final chord *arpeggiato*, played by the piano.

This analysis leads us to the conceptualisation of music. Accordingly, Figueiredo (2017) argued about the "simplicity" appointed to the song: "sometimes, simplicity is apparent". It is a complex song if you are attentive to the harmony and the several layers of music created by the arrangement, but it could seem "simple" if you think about a *cantabile* melody in a slow tempo, which is not too complex for the listener due to its fluidity and comprehensibility.

The idea of using strings came from Luísa Sobral, based on references to Billy Holiday, Chet Baker and some Brazilian musicians. With no electronics, no sampled music, no drums, no bass, no guitars – "no electricity", as Figueiredo (2017) puts it – Figueiredo based his arrangement on a solo voice with no back vocals, a piano and a five-part string orchestration. This is a formula that was commonly used in the 1940s and 1950s in songs which were hugely popular. At the same time, it is a reference to the songs in the ESC's first editions. In Figueiredo's (2017) opinion, this is what gives music a "retro feel", with listeners linking "Amar pelos dois" to those popular music references, as well as to "classical music". Some commentators published criticisms which questioned the musical references used by Luísa Sobral and linked them to movies soundtracks, using the concept of "Disney music", whatever that means. Such criticisms highlighted the several concepts and values that can be related to the song. If the structure and the performance, as well as the melodic and harmonic features, give us some ideas about the intention of the composer, the interpretation of the listeners and journalists – the "gatekeepers" – give us information about its reception. The processes of mediation and reception have the capacity to produce new meanings about music, shaped by individual and collective values, just as the music's sound is. This leads us to one of the core Merriam's proposition: "[w]ithout an understanding of concepts, there is no real understanding of music" (1964:84).

As discussed before, Salvador Sobral used his victory speech to make a statement on his assumptions about music. The mentioned concepts reveal the values on which he bases his musical production and his career. When he jumped on the stage and asserted that "music is feeling", he was proclaiming his concerns about the value of music creation, criticising its industrial production, with which he is competing. Referring to "disposable music", "fast food music without any content", Sobral revealed his opinion about the ESC and the mediatic ecosystem upon which it is based. If we think about his music education, Sobral studied and developed his career based on jazz, and therefore a set of assumptions about music that are certainly very different from the ESC's context. In several interviews, he explained that his sister's invitation to perform in the Portuguese national selection reminded him of his unpleasant past experience in talent shows. Setting himself apart from the ESC world, he mentioned that he did not follow the contest at all, and barely knew what it was. We are certain that he has a strong opinion about the ESC, despite Sobral never agreeing to give us an interview about this. Still, his statements about the ESC are still debated today in the interviews that he does give.

Several adjectives have been used to categorise and describe "Amar pelos dois": as mentioned above, "Disney music", which refers to popular music of the 1940s or to the songs that were performed in the ESC during the 1950s and the early 1960s; "simplicity"; and "difference". For an ethnomusicologist, music categorisation is a major issue. Categories can be created by musicians to describe their own music, but are more often created by the media and the music industry. More than being used to describe music features or technical specificities, they are an effort to direct "music products" to specific market targets. Since its beginning, the ESC has been linked to some particular categories, such as "light music", "pop music", or even "schlager".

In Portugal, the media, musicians, and popular discourses often use the concept of "música festivaleira" (festival music), with no objective definition, but being an attempt to describe a "proper" song to compete in and win the ESC. Those who offer a definition underline some idealised characteristics, such as the music being up tempo, having a strong beat and powerful bass, or being sung in English. It is, in fact, an adjective related to "low brow", mediated and industrialised music. At the same time, beyond these commercial assumptions, other commentators support entries with "traditional flavors" that represent "Portuguese culture", again with no objective definition, but referring to issues of national identity. "Amar pelos dois" challenged these assumptions about music, categorisation, and the ESC, since it used several references from different fields apart from popular music. Yet, at the same time, it was performed in a highly mediatised context.

National and international media reproduced several discourses about the "authenticity", "simplicity" and "difference" of "Amar pelos dois". Sobral's character, a kid of antihero, imbued with mystery about his illness[3], contributed to enkindle media discourses. His opinion about the ESC was revealed by his *blasé* behaviour, improvisation during the rehearsals, and some subversive and political – or "humanitarian", in his words – episodes, such as a sweater with the slogan "SOS Refugees" which he wore in a press conference (Photo 17.3). At the same time, the message of the lyrics was enhanced in performances by Sobral's apparent restrained attitude, which was very different when compared to the overproduced performances of other entries. The choice of Portuguese-language lyrics – all of the other

Photo 17.3 Salvador Sobral in the draw for the placement in the Grand Final.
Source: EBU / Andres Putting.

songs in the first semifinal that Sobral performed in were otherwise in English – was also viewed as a statement for difference. These options amplified the ideas about the "simplicity" and "authenticity" of "Amor pelos dois".

As Figueiredo explained, the initial plan was to make "a good song". In his opinion, "Amar pelos dois" had no possibility of winning the Portuguese national selection, let alone the ESC. It was "a good phenomenon" that made people think about "what music means, what it means going to a stage, what it means being a musician. Things that people are not used to discussing anymore". However, Sobral's winning "is not a result of a change, it is a phenomenon like others" (ibidem). The ESC is a contest for phenomena, and Salvador was one phenomenon more on this international stage (Figueiredo 2018).

Lisbon, 13/05/2017

May 13th is a kind of emblematic day for many Portuguese people, since it is linked to a Catholic miracle[4]. On the same day that Salvador won the ESC, Pope Francis was visiting Portugal, and one of the leading football teams was celebrating its victory in the national championship. Music, football and religion had a special day on that May 13th, 2017. While we were celebrating Sobral's win, Portuguese television channels showed the party of a thousand football fans in a square in Lisbon. Surprisingly, in the middle of the noisy celebration, the excited crowd suddenly fell silent to listen the initial chords of the first Portuguese winning song in Eurovision, and when Salvador's voice was heard, the crowd sang along. On that occasion, people were certainly not concerned about music and its value or role in society. They were just enjoying the celebration of a "national victory".

Just after the Portuguese victory in the ESC, the Portuguese national broadcaster, Rádio e Televisão de Portugal (RTP, Radio and Television of Portugal) promoted a debate about the future of Portuguese music both in Portugal and the ESC, asking: could this song be a milestone for musical changes in the ESC or was it just ani-solated phenomenon?"(Ferreira, 2017). This debate brings us to the issue of musical change (Blacking, 1986). In this sense, it is also important to talk about the role of decision-makers in Sobral's participation in the ESC in 2017. The Portuguese national selection- the Festival RTP da Canção (RTP Song Festival) went through a reforming process. In 2016, RTP decided to take a one-year break from the ESC to redesign its strategy for Portuguese participation. A change in the production and creative teams was a part of this transformation, bringing together people who were experienced in the Portuguese ESC delegation, people from the RTP's innovation center, and an external ESC expert, among others. The main goal was to link the competition to the contemporary Portuguese music industry. To do so, the strategy was to invite composers who were developing their careers outside of the ESC event bubble and apart from the television industry. In a joint venture with the national radio channel Antena 3, RTP mainly invited musicians from the emic category of "new Portuguese music". This strategy intended to engage a younger audience and assure the survival of the television format of the national selection. The idea was to again make music the main focus of the RTP song contest. As a result, Luísa Sobral – an unexpected presence in this kind of contest – participated and won. In the words of the creative director of the Portuguese national selection, "Salvador's winning was a legitimation for the change, showing which way RTP wants to go" (Madaíl, 2018[5]). It confirms what Merriam proposed: "[m]usic is a product of man and has structure, but its structure cannot have an existence of its own divorced from the behaviour which produces it" (1964:7). The choice of Salvador Sobral as the Portuguese representative in the ESC 2017 – a result of the expert jury vote which awarded him its highest score, and the public televote, which gave him its second-highest points – reflects precisely the role of different decision-makers in what can be considered "musical change".

As mentioned above, televised music also emphasises visual performance. In this context, performance is not only about the vocal part, but also the corporality, the staging, and the stage set. Analysing the stage production of Sobral's performance, we see very simple LED wall features, which were very different from the other entries which used more elaborate visual effects, such as fire or complex LED projections. During Sobral's performance, the blue lights of the stage combined with lights from the people in the audience and simulated a sky with stars. Carla Bugalho (2019), the head of the Portuguese delegation, explained that the option to perform on the small stage amongst the audience was a way to contour the low-key production of the stage performance. At the same time, it was a plan to convey the loneliness expressed by the lyrics, as well as the idea of "simplicity" that the Portuguese entry wanted to assert. For Figueiredo (2017), "Amar pelos dois" "forced" everyone to stop and listen, alluding to a possible capacity to transform – albeit momentarily – the audience's behaviour. On the same occasion, when he compared Luísa's song to pop songs, he stated: "[musicians] are selling not just music, but a whole way of life".

Music has the capacity to engage people. Behaviours and discourses about music are shared by people who have never met each other, creating an imagined community, in the same way that Anderson (1983) conceptualised it. Even in a song with no outward social or political content, values are conveyed and can be shared by a large community, thereby influencing behaviours. As a highly mediatised television show, the ESC enhances this intrinsic capability of music. Sobral's song challenged conceptions about the ESC's music as well as about Portuguese entries. It is not a pop song with several European idioms, as was the Portuguese entry in 1980. It is not based on "traditional music" and an imagination of the multicultural Portuguese identity, like the 1996 Portuguese entry, "O meu coração não tem cor" (My Heart Has No Colour) (Lopes, 2015). It is not about Portuguese history in a nationalistic sense, as was the 1989 entry, "Conquistador" (Conquistador) (Lopes, 2016). And it does not describe the "imagined" Portuguese psychological character, as the 1991 entry "-Lusitana paixão" ("Lusitanian Passion") – did (Lopes, 2017).

Lisbon, 14/05/2017

I didn't travel to Kyiv, but I went to the airport to attend to the Portuguese delegation's reception. As I expected, there were many people. Mostly, those I already knew as fans of

Eurovision. Those who went to the airport every year to welcome the Portuguese singer. They were talking about the qualities of the Portuguese entry, highlighting its difference from other ESC entries over the years. Within a short period of time, the airport was crowded with people waving Portuguese flags, wearing green and red scarves – normally used in football matches – and holding bouquets of flowers and posters. A few were wearing t-shirts with Salvador's and Luísa's faces. I could read "Thank you, Salvador" everywhere. The airport was getting small for so many people. People were singing the national anthem and "Amar pelos dois". While hugging, people were shouting "Salvador", as if they were waiting for a true Messiah, the Savior[6]. They had some reasons to do so: fifty-three years after its first participation in the Eurovision, Portugal had won. TV channels, radios and newspapers sent their reporters to cover this unexpected event. All TV news channels were doing live broadcasts from there, interviewing those who spent their Sunday afternoon to support the winner of the ESC. TV

Photo 17.4 Diogo Lobato, a Portuguese fan, at the airport in Lisbon awaiting Salvador Sobral after his ESC win.

Author: Sofia Vieira Lopes.

reports included commentaries by musicians and "figures from Portuguese culture" who explained the reasons for the "difference" and "authenticity" of Salvador and Luísa' song. (Photos 17.4 and 17.5)

As Merriam proposed, 'music sound is the result of human behavioural processes that are shaped by the values, attitudes, and beliefs of the people who comprise a particular culture' (1964:6). For ethnomusicology, the study of musical reception in a mediatised context like the ESC could be very challenging. Unlike the study of a small community, contact with audiences and understanding what music means for them is almost impossible. The study of fandom in the ESC can be a way to circumscribe this heterogenous group of viewers into smaller communities. Despite these groups being very interesting subjects – since they are not only receivers but also producers, mediators and gatekeepers of media contents and meanings – such a study produces a fractional analysis of complex dynamics. Several reactions to the Portuguese victory were broadcast and many tried to explain its reasons: for Simone de Oliveira (2017), the singer of the Portuguese ESC entries in 1965 and 1969, it has 'a melody and the lyrics' and to win 'it is necessary to sing well'; for Paulo de Carvalho (2017), the Portuguese singer in the 1974 ESC, it was 'serious music, well composed and made with love'. Both attributed to the technical features of the song the same

Photo 17.5 The enthusiastic welcome to the Portuguese ESC delegation at the airport in Lisbon after Salvador Sobral's ESC win.

Author: Sofia Vieira Lopes.

level of importance as to emotional factors. These mediated opinions from those who are recognised as experts could also have been shared by audiences. Former participants were summoned as gatekeepers, and their opinions contribute to audiences' construction of assumptions about 'Amar pelos dois', its composer and singer, as well as about the ESC.

A final reflection

Merriam emphasised the human facet of music:

> [m]usic is a uniquely human phenomenon which exists only in terms of social interaction; it is made by people for other people, and it is learned behavior. It does not and cannot exist by, of, and for itself; there must always be human beings doing something to produce it. In short, music cannot be defined as a phenomenon of sound alone, for it involves the behavior of individuals and groups of individuals, and its particular organization demands the social concurrence of people who decide what it can and cannot be (1964:27).

We share Merriam's view when he proposed, fifty-seven years ago, that 'music is a means of understanding peoples and behaviour and as such is a valuable tool in the analysis of culture and society' (1964:13). As one of the most popular television shows in the world, the ESC is based on music, but also on a performative and mediatic apparatus, conceived to convey an idea of a Europe united by music. Even in a mainstream pop song, with no ostensible message, the contest conveys a set of values and assumptions about what composers, decision-makers, gatekeepers, singers and audiences believe. As with all kinds of expressive behaviour, ESC entries and the show itself are open to a multiplicity of interpretations and thus change their meaning according to time, context and observer. Throughout its long history, the ESC has provided a critical view about people's relationship with music, and that should be acknowledged as a foremost feature of its extraordinary social and cultural role.

Notes

1 As Middleton and Manuel stated, the word popular music is 'used widely in everyday discourse, generally to refer to types of music that are considered to be of lower value and complexity than art music, and to be readily accessible to large numbers of musically uneducated listeners rather than to an élite. It is, however, one of the most difficult terms to define precisely' (2001: n.p.). The authors note other factors to distinguish popular music, such as the link with popularity and with a large scale of activity, such as a large audience and/or large consumption. They also have linked the 'popularity with means of dissemination', related particularly with the 'development and role of mass media', connected to the 'technologies of mass distribution' (ibidem.).
2 This book has two other editions (2010 and 2011) with a different title: *Focus: Music, Nationalism, and the Making of the New Europe.*

3 When Salvador Sobral won the ESC 2017 he was suffering from a longstanding heart condition. He received a heart transplant in December 2017. Due to his health condition, his sister replaced him in the first week of the rehearsals for the ESC in Kyiv. Since his victory in the Portuguese national selection, his illness, first kept secret, has sparked much speculation in the media and social media.

4 On 13 May 1917, three children, shepherds, had a vision of the Virgin Mary in the Portuguese town of Fátima. Since then, this religious phenomenon has been followed by millions of believers. In the place where the miracle took place, a Catholic sanctuary was built that receives millions of pilgrims annually and has been visited several times by popes. The last papal visit was on 13 May 2017, celebrating the centenary of the apparitions of Fátima, with Pope Francis then canonising two of the three shepherds.

5 Gonçalo Madaíl is the creative director of the Portuguese national selection since 2016. He was also the creative director of the 2018 ESC. This interview was conducted as part of Sofia's PhD research.

6 In Portuguese, 'salvador' means 'savior'.

References

Anderson, B. (1983) (2006). *Imagined communities: Reflections on the origin and spread of nationalism*. Verso.

Blacking, J. (1986). Identifying processes of musical change. *The World of Music*, *28*(1), 3–15.

Bohlman, P.V. (2002). *World music: A very short introduction*. Oxford University Press.

Bohlman, P.V. (2004). *The music of European Nationalism. Cultural identity and modern history*. ABC-CLIO.

Bugalho, C. (2019, December 11). Personal interview.

De Carvalho, P. (2017). Interview for the TV channel SIC Notícias. Retrieved June 2021 from https://sicnoticias.pt/especiais/portugal-vence-eurovisao/2017-05-14-Paulo-de-Carvalho-diz-que-ganhou-a-musica-seria-e-feita-com-amor

De Oliveira, S. (2017). Interview for the TV channel TVI24. Retrieved June 2021 from https://tvi24.iol.pt/salvador-sobral-eurovisao/eurovisao/salvador-sobral-diz-que-foi-uma-vitoria-da-musica-que-significa-alguma-coisa

European Broadcasting Union (2015). 60th Anniversary Press Pack. Retrieved April 2021, from https://www.ebu.ch/files/live/sites/ebu/files/Events/Communication/Press%20kit%2060th%20anniversary%20ESC.pdf

Ferreira, F. C. (2017, May 29).Prós e Contras [Television broadcast]. Lisbon, RTP: Portuguese Public Broadcasting Service. https://www.rtp.pt/play/p3033/e290929/pros-e-contras/578232

Figueiredo, L. (2017). Interview for the YouTube channel HelloLillyTV. Retrieved May 2021 from https://www.youtube.com/watch?v=GSp3Rdp7Tq0&t=263s

Figueiredo, L. (2018). Interview for the TV channel Canal Q. Retrieved May 2021 from https://www.youtube.com/watch?v=YVojJWj-oac

Geertz, C. (1973). *The interpretation of cultures*. Basic Books, Inc., Publishers.

Lopes, S.V. (2015). Portugal no Coração – música e performance no Festival RTP da Canção enquanto veículos de narrativas identitárias. Conference proceedings *Europa no mundo e o mundo na Europa: crise e identidade*, Universidade do Minho, Braga (Portugal).

Lopes, S.V. (2016). "'...E ergueram orgulhosas bandeiras...': Portugal e a Europa no Festival RTP da Canção". Conference proceedings *III Encuentro Iberoamericano de Jóvenes Musicólogos*, Universidad de Sevilla (Spain).

Lopes, S.V. (2017, May). *Lusitana Paixão: Forging identities and engendering memories through a Song Festival.* Paper presented at CHIME Conference, Music, Festivals, Heritage, Siena.

Madaíl, G. (2018, December 18). Personal interview.

Merriam, A. (1964). *The anthropology of music.* Northwestern University Press

Merriam, A. 1960. Ethnomusicology: A discussion and definition of the field. *Ethnomusicology,* 4(3), 107–114.

Middleton, R., & Manuel, P. (2001). Popular music. *The Grove Dictionary of Music and Musicians.* Macmillan and Co.

Tragaki, D. (2013). *Empire of Song: Europe and nation in the Eurovision Song Contest.* Lanham, Toronto and Plymouth.

Index

Note: Page numbers in *italic* indicate figure and in **bold** indicate table, and page numbers followed by 'n' refer to notes.